Digital Constitutionalism

Investigating the impact of digital technology on contemporary constitutionalism, this book offers an overview of the transformations that are currently occurring at constitutional level, highlighting their link with ongoing societal changes. It reconstructs the multiple ways in which constitutional law is reacting to these challenges and explores the role of one original response to this phenomenon: the emergence of Internet bills of rights.

Over the past few years, a significant number of Internet bills of rights have emerged around the world. These documents represent non-legally binding declarations promoted mostly by individuals and civil society groups that articulate rights and principles for the digital society. This book argues that these initiatives reflect a change in the constitutional ecosystem. The transformations prompted by the digital revolution in our society ferment under a vault of constitutional norms shaped for 'analogue' communities. Constitutional law struggles to address all the challenges of the digital environment. In this context, Internet bills of rights, by emerging outside traditional institutional processes, represent a unique response to suggest new constitutional solutions for the digital age.

Explaining how constitutional law is reacting to the advent of the digital revolution and analysing the constitutional function of Internet bills of rights in this context, this book offers a global comparative investigation of the latest transformations that digital technology is generating in the constitutional ecosystem and highlights the plural and multilevel process that is contributing to shape constitutional norms for the Internet age.

Edoardo Celeste is Assistant Professor of Law, Technology and Innovation at Dublin City University, Ireland. He is the Coordinator of the DCU Law and Tech Research Cluster and the Programme Director of the European Master in Law, Data and Artificial Intelligence.

Routledge Research in the Law of Emerging Technologies

Artificial Intelligence, Healthcare, and the Law
Regulating Automation in Personal Care
Eduard Fosch-Villaronga

Health Data Privacy under the GDPR
Big Data Challenges and Regulatory Responses
Edited by Maria Tzanou

Regulating Artificial Intelligence
Binary Ethics and the Law
Dominika Ewa Harasimiuk and Tomasz Braun

Cryptocurrencies and Regulatory Challenge
Allan C. Hutchinson

Regulating Artificial Intelligence in Industry
Edited by Damian M. Bielicki

The Law of Global Digitality
Edited by Matthias C. Kettemann, Alexander Peukert and Indra Spiecker gen. Döhmann

Internet of Things and the Law
Legal Strategies for Consumer-Centric Smart Technologies
Guido Noto La Diega

For more information about this series, please visit: https://www.routledge.com/Routledge-Research-in-the-Law-of-Emerging-Technologies/book-series/LAWTECHNOLOGY

Digital Constitutionalism

The Role of Internet Bills of Rights

Edoardo Celeste

Routledge
Taylor & Francis Group
LONDON AND NEW YORK

First published 2023
by Routledge
4 Park Square, Milton Park, Abingdon, Oxon OX14 4RN

and by Routledge
605 Third Avenue, New York, NY 10158

Routledge is an imprint of the Taylor & Francis Group, an informa business

British Library Cataloguing-in-Publication Data
A catalogue record for this book is available from the British Library

ISBN: 978-1-032-18905-5 (hbk)
ISBN: 978-1-032-18906-2 (pbk)
ISBN: 978-1-003-25690-8 (ebk)

DOI: 10.4324/9781003256908

Typeset in Times New Roman
by codeMantra

Contents

Illustrations

Figures

Tables

Acknowledgements

As the Irish saying goes: *an té a bhíónn siúlach, bíonn scéalach* – he who travels has stories to tell. The story of this book, too, would not have been as is, if I had not been *siúlach*, a wanderer. I first had the idea of this work in 2014 in London. I wrote down a first draft of the proposal in the Italian Alps. Dublin has been my home for most of my research, but I developed many arguments on digital constitutionalism while I was in Berlin in 2018. Also, I cannot forget to mention two short, yet very productive, visits to picturesque Turin and Zurich, the summer weeks in my natal city, Rome, as well as many other places in beautiful Ireland, and all over Europe, where I have been for conferences or simply to take a break from city life and my laptop. Their amenities certainly inspired some of the ideas that I have tried to develop in this book. Nevertheless, these travels would not have been as stimulating without all the people who have accompanied me. To my travel companions, whose wisdom has guided my path, whose friendship has encouraged and comforted me, whose love has nourished my dreams and given me a reason to persevere, goes my deepest gratitude for making my journey so special.

Dublin
December 2021

1 Introduction

The most profound technologies are those that disappear. They weave themselves into the fabric of everyday life until they are indistinguishable from it.
– Mark Weiser, 1991

With these words, Mark Weiser, the American computer scientist who coined the term 'ubiquitous computing', opened a short article in the magazine *Scientific American*, published in 1991.[1] He compared digital technology with writing, interestingly defining the latter as 'perhaps the first information technology'.[2] Today, the technique of translating language into written signs permeates the modern world. One does not think of employing a 'technology' when writing or reading. Writing, intended as a technology, has 'disappeared' in our world. It is now such an integral part of our existence that one can hardly conceive human life without the possibility of expressing messages in a written form. In 1991, Weiser heralded the advent of an age where computers would have really become 'personal', and where digital technology would have been omnipresent, pervading every aspect of our existence. He spoke about a transition towards an 'embodied virtuality': hundreds of computers in one room, ubiquitous computing at our service.[3]

Thirty years later, one is surprised by the level of foresight of Weiser's statements. Without the need to evoke futuristic 'metaverses',[4] today, the so-called Internet of Things is a concrete reality: it could in fact be claimed that our society went even beyond Weiser's expectations. Virtuality is not

1 Mark Weiser, 'The Computer for the 21st Century', *Scientific American* (September 1991) 94.
2 Weiser (n 1) 94.
3 Weiser (n 1) 98.
4 'Connect 2021: Our Vision for the Metaverse' (*Facebook Technology*, 28 October 2021) <https://tech.fb.com/connect-2021-our-vision-for-the-metaverse/> accessed 15 November 2021; Facebook, 'The Facebook Company Is Now Meta' (*Meta*, 28 October 2021) <https://about.fb.com/news/2021/10/facebook-company-is-now-meta/> accessed 15 November 2021; see also Micaela Mantegna, 'The Metaverse: A Brave, New (Virtual) World' (*Berkman Klein Center Collection*, 16 June 2021) <https://medium.com/berkman-klein-center/the-metaverse-a-brave-new-virtual-world-2f040cbae7d4> accessed 15 November 2021.

DOI: 10.4324/9781003256908-1

only progressively embodied in our physical world and in the objects that surround us but has also become an integral part of our life. The recent Covid-19 pandemic has demonstrated that most individuals are able to work entirely online. Those who were separated by the mobility restrictions that many governments imposed around the world know that through digital technologies we can express our love. Many have unfortunately lost their jobs and are now using the Internet to protest, claim welfare rights, or try to find an alternative profession. These few examples, which this unprecedented health emergency has created, show us clearly that nowadays we also *live* in the digital ecosystem[5]; one can no longer merely speak of a 'virtual reality'.[6] Today our physical and digital existence are bound in a way that can no longer be neatly distinguished. Our real and virtual selves compose a unique persona.

The digital revolution is producing a series of transformations creating extensive impact within contemporary society, including on our legal systems and, in particular, on our constitutional norms. Existing constitutions were shaped for an 'analogue' world and currently struggle to address the challenges of the digital revolution. Our constitutional charters enshrine principles on how to protect our physical body, however, offer no explicit guidance on how to afford guarantees to our digital self. Digital technology may help rebalance asymmetries of powers among constitutional actors; yet no recognition of these new opportunities is made in 'analogue' constitutional texts. A unique response to this scenario has been the emergence of what this work calls 'Internet bills of rights'. These documents represent non-legally binding declarations advocating constitutional principles for the digital society. They generally surface outside traditional political processes. They are promoted by a variety of actors, including civil society organisations and single individuals. A systematic legal analysis of this phenomenon is lacking. Do they represent isolated efforts? Why after centuries are we witnessing a new wave of declarations of rights? Why do these texts adopt a constitutional language? Why are the promoters of these initiatives not resorting to traditional constitutional processes? What is the message of these bills of rights? To what extent do they contribute to shape rights for the Internet age?

The present book aims to address these questions, investigating the phenomenon of the emergence of Internet bills of rights and focusing in particular on the role of these initiatives from a constitutional perspective. The first part of this work explains that the emergence of Internet bills of rights does not represent an isolated phenomenon, but that they are an integral component of a broader constitutional moment (Chapter 2). The advent of

5 See Gilles Dowek, *Vivre, aimer, voter en ligne et autres chroniques numériques* (Le Pommier 2017).

6 See Weiser (n 1) 94.

the digital revolution is putting under strain existing constitutional norms, originally shaped for an analogue world, in this way potentially engendering situations of disequilibrium in the constitutional ecosystem. As a reaction, a series of norms attempting to adapt the legal order to the mutated conditions of the digital society are emerging. These 'constitutional counteractions' are a consequence of the living nature of constitutional law, which has not been created to remain immutable, but historically has gradually evolved following the emerging needs of society (Chapter 3). The constitutional ecosystem is reacting to face the challenges of the digital society through different normative instruments, including, however not limited to, Internet bills of rights (Chapter 4). In light of the global and transnational character of the issues generated by the digital revolution, constitutional counteractions also emerge beyond the state dimension, for example, in the internal rules of powerful multinational technology companies. The constitutional discourse is no longer unitary but inevitably plural. However, these constitutional fragments can be interpreted as matching tesserae of a multilevel process of constitutionalisation, which aims to define a series of principles to guarantee the protection of fundamental rights and a balancing of powers in the digital ecosystem (Chapter 5). It is contended that these complementary normative responses share the goal of substantiating a form of digital constitutionalism, which is a new ideology aiming to translate the core values of contemporary constitutionalism in light of the mutated characteristics of the digital society (Chapter 6).

One of the most original instances of digital constitutionalism is the idea of crafting a 'constitution' for the Internet, which over the past few decades has progressively gained momentum and led to the publication of numerous 'Internet bills of rights' (Chapter 7). Adopting a functional perspective, the book claims that Internet bills of rights play a significant role from a constitutional point of view (Chapter 8). By using the lingua franca of constitutions, these declarations aim to be part of the conversation on how to shape our constitutional principles for the digital age. Crucially, their informal and non-binding character enables the participation of a broad number of actors and enhances their capability of advancing innovative ideas. It is therefore argued that Internet bills of rights compensate and, at the same time, stimulate the ongoing process of constitutionalisation of the digital society. They do not aim to establish cosmopolitan constitutions for the Internet but to nourish the current constitutional moment. Starting from this assumption on the constitutional role of Internet bills of rights, the book presents the analysis of their scope of application and substantive content as a litmus test of the health of our constitutional systems (Chapter 9). By analysing the innovative message that individuals and groups convey through Internet bills of rights, one can highlight areas of existing law affected by what this book calls 'constitutional anaemia', a significant mismatch between constitutional norms and social reality that requires an urgent update. The universal reach of these declarations as well as their inclusive methods of deliberation will be interpreted as a strong appeal to the constitutional ecosystem to overtake the binary state-citizens relation and to start generating, with the participation of all stakeholders, normative answers to the digital revolution that take into account individuals at a global level and the emergence of new dominant actors (Chapter 10). Lastly, the examination of the substantive content of Internet bills of rights will offer a comprehensive vision of the constitutional message of these declarations, investigating both the core values of contemporary constitutionalism that are simply reiterated or translated in the context of the digital society (Chapter 11) and the new principles proposed by these documents (Chapter 12).

The book will conclude with a reflection on the role that Internet bills of rights play to forestall the risk of constitutional anaemia during the current digital revolution, and with an outline of future pathways of research, highlighting their potential value in addressing the current challenges of digital constitutionalism (Chapter 13).

2 A new constitutional moment

Constitutional equilibrium

The hill of Posillipo, a couple of kilometres north-west from Naples, offers one of the best views of the Italian city and its bay. In the distance is the rocky isle of Capri and the lush peninsula of Sorrento. On the left is the imposing profile of the Mount Vesuvius and the variegated colours of the city of Naples, which plunge into the blue of the sea. One has the impression that this beautiful painting has been carefully ideated and accurately realised. One cannot suspect that this image of perfect equilibrium is in reality only apparent.

The whole area of Naples is surrounded by an arc of volcanoes and lies over an ancient underground magmatic cauldron.[1] In 79 A.D., the most famous eruption of Mount Vesuvius marked the end of the Roman cities of Pompeii and Herculaneum.[2] In several occasions, the ashes ejected by the volcano even reached the city of Constantinople, today's Istanbul.[3] Over the centuries, this whole area has been constantly transformed. Sudden eruptions and earthquakes have gradually changed its landscape.

The sense of beauty and equilibrium that this panorama gives us is in reality ephemeral and intrinsically fragile. There is a stark contrast between the incessant underground magmatic activity and the apparent immutability of the scenario over ground. A characteristic of this place is also that eruptions are not continuous, but occur at a relative distance of time; and this circumstance even reinforces in us the idea of a delicate equilibrium, which can be subject to unexpected changes.

1 Benedetto De Vivo, *Volcanism in the Campania Plain: Vesuvius, Campi Flegrei and Ignimbrites* (Elsevier 2006).

2 Haraldur Sigurdsson, Stanford Cashdollar and Stephen RJ Sparks, 'The Eruption of Vesuvius in A. D. 79: Reconstruction from Historical and Volcanological Evidence' (1982) 86 American Journal of Archaeology 39.

3 See Sara E Pratt, 'Benchmarks: March 17, 1944: The Most Recent Eruption of Mount Vesuvius' (2016) *EARTH Magazine* <https://www.earthmagazine.org/article/benchmarks-march-17-1944-most-recent-eruption-mount-vesuvius> accessed 20 September 2018.

DOI: 10.4324/9781003256908-2

This image, these two different faces of the beautiful Bay of Naples, can help us visualise a series of phenomena which are currently occurring in the constitutional landscape.

Constitutional law derives its name from the notion of constitution. Interestingly, this concept has never received a univocal definition.[4] For the sake of simplification, one could say that constitution has two essential meanings: one prescriptive and one descriptive.[5] In a prescriptive or normative sense, constitution is the body of norms that aims to establish the form of organisation of a community. These norms are sometimes collected in a single document, generally called 'constitution'.[6] In a descriptive or empirical sense, instead, constitution is the effective form of organisation of a given community, its actual way of existing. The present work will use the notion of constitutional law to intend the constitution in the prescriptive sense *lato sensu*, as the set of norms organising the polity, and not restricted to those enshrined in texts called constitutions.[7]

4 See Herbert John Spiro, 'Constitution', *Encyclopedia Britannica* (2018) <https://www.britannica.com/topic/constitution-politics-and-law> accessed 23 October 2018; Roger A Shiner, 'Constitutions' in Enrico Pattaro (ed), *A Treatise of Legal Philosophy and General Jurisprudence*, vols 3 'Legal Institutions and Sources of Law' (Springer 2005); Dieter Grimm, *Constitutionalism: Past, Present, and Future* (Oxford University Press 2016), in particular ch 1 'The Origins and Transformation of the Concept of the Constitution'; cf. Giovanni Sartori, 'Constitutionalism: A Preliminary Discussion' (1962) 56 The American Political Science Review 853. For an analysis of the historical meanings of 'constitution', see András Sajó and Renáta Uitz, *The Constitution of Freedom: An Introduction to Legal Constitutionalism* (Oxford University Press 2017); Olivier Beaud, 'L'histoire Du Concept de Constitution En France. De La Constitution Politique à La Constitution Comme Statut Juridique de l'Etat' (2009) Jus Politicum <http://juspoliticum.com/article/L-histoire-du-concept-de-constitution-en-France-De-la-constitution-politique-a-la-constitution-comme-statut-juridique-de-l-Etat-140.html> accessed 23 October 2018; Heinz Mohnhaupt and Dieter Grimm, *Verfassung.* (2nd ed., Duncker & Humblot 2002).

5 Grimm (n 4); see also Carl Schmitt, *Constitutional Theory* (Jeffrey Seitzer ed, (originally published in 1928), Duke University Press 2008), who first theorised this distinction; cf. Franco Modugno, *Lineamenti Di Teoria Del Diritto Oggettivo* (Giappichelli 2009).

6 This is the traditional meaning in the US context, see John H Merrill (ed), 'Constitutional Law', *American and English Encyclopaedia of Law* (Edward Thompson 1887) 670.

7 Matthew F Shugart and others, 'Constitutional Law', *Encyclopedia Britannica* (2016) <https://www.britannica.com/topic/constitutional-law> accessed 20 September 2018. Cf. the meaning of 'constitutional law' in other languages, such as Italian, more in the sense of 'constitutional law studies': 'Diritto costituzionale', *Enciclopedia Treccani* <http://www.treccani.it//enciclopedia/diritto-costituzionale> accessed 20 September 2018.

The basic way in which constitutional law organises a community is by constituting and regulating the exercise of power.[8] Power, in a general sense, is the ability of an actor to 'direct [...] the behaviour' of another actor.[9] Constitutional law regulates power by limiting such ability.[10] Historically, the power to be regulated was that of the actors who exercised a governmental function in the community, such as the king, the nobility, or the clergy.[11] As we can see from these examples, at these times, limitation of power also served to strike a balance between the prerogatives of different social classes.[12] From the seventeenth century, this conception gradually changed. The notion of limitation started to encompass the idea that powers should also be limited in respect to the single individual, not necessarily intended as a member of a social class.[13] The concept of 'individual rights' progressively emerged. Philosophers such as Locke argued that a series of 'inalienable rights' of the individuals existed by virtue of natural law.[14] The idea that individuals have rights, notwithstanding their formal recognition

8 See Nicholas W Barber, *The Principles of Constitutionalism* (Oxford University Press 2018), who distinguishes between a positive and negative form of constitutionalism; Christoph B Graber, 'Bottom-up Constitutionalism: The Case of Net Neutrality' (2016) 7 Transnational Legal Theory 524, 528.

9 Oxford English Dictionary Online, 'Power, n.1' <http://www.oed.com/view/Entry/149167> accessed 5 November 2018.

10 See András Sajó, *Limiting Government: An Introduction to Constitutionalism* (Central European University Press 1999); Shugart and others (n 7).

11 See Charles Howard McIlwain, *Constitutionalism: Ancient and Modern* (Amagi, originally published by Cornell University Press, 1947, 2007); Shugart and others (n 7).

12 See McIlwain (n 11); Steven G Calabresi, Mark E Berghausen and Skylar Albertson, 'The Rise and Fall of the Separation of Powers' (2012) 106 Northwestern University Law Review 527.

13 See Shugart and others (n 7). Another important transformation, which will occur only at a later stage, concerns the topic of the legitimacy of power. From the nineteenth century, we can observe a transition from a conception where the king derives its power directly from God to the idea of popular sovereignty. See Terence Ball and others, 'Liberalism', *Encyclopedia Britannica* (2018) <https://www.britannica.com/topic/liberalism> accessed 5 November 2018.

14 On Locke's theory of natural rights, see Alex Tuckness, 'Locke's Political Philosophy' in Edward N Zalta (ed), *The Stanford Encyclopedia of Philosophy* (Summer 2018, Metaphysics Research Lab, Stanford University 2018) <https://plato.stanford.edu/archives/sum2018/entries/locke-political/> accessed 8 November 2018; C Fred Alford, 'International Human Rights, Natural Law, and Locke' in C Fred Alford (ed), *Narrative, Nature, and the Natural Law: From Aquinas to International Human Rights* (Palgrave Macmillan US 2010); S Adam Seagrave, *The Foundations of Natural Morality: On the Compatibility of Natural Rights and the Natural Law* (University of Chicago Press 2014), especially ch I 'Locke on Natural Rights and the Natural Law'. More generally on natural law theories, see Encyclopaedia Britannica, 'Natural Law' <https://www.britannica.com/topic/natural-law> accessed 8 November 2018; John Finnis, 'Natural Law Theories' in Edward N Zalta (ed), *The Stanford Encyclopedia of Philosophy* (Winter 2016, Metaphysics Research Lab, Stanford University 2016) <https://plato.stanford.edu/archives/win2016/entries/natural-law-theories/> accessed 8 November 2018; John Finnis, *Natural Law and Natural Rights* (Oxford University Press 2011).

by the ruling actors, became a central claim of the Enlightenment.[15] Progressively, from the end of the seventeenth century, constitutional texts not only focused on the limitation of power in a horizontal sense, i.e., the idea of balance between dominant powers, but also included a vertical conception of limitation, in the sense of protection of individual rights against those powers.[16]

The Declaration of the Rights of the Man and of the Citizens, approved in 1789 by the French National Constituent Assembly, and still having constitutional value according to the Preamble of the Constitution of the French Fifth Republic, is exemplary of this conceptual evolution.[17] Its Article 16 provides that:

> Any society in which no provision is made for guaranteeing rights or for the separation of powers, has no Constitution.

The influence of the doctrine of natural rights is apparent. Rights are regarded as belonging to all men, and in other parts of the document are

15 Encyclopaedia Britannica (n 14); Ulrich Im Hof, *The Enlightenment* (Blackwell 1994), especially ch 24 'Natural Law, the Path to Human Rights'. At a later stage, from the nineteenth century, the idea that individuals possess rights by natural law progressively faded. However, this did not lead to a twilight of individual rights. Subsequent schools of thought, under the influence of Hegel, saw the individual and, more broadly, the whole civil society as an integral part of the State. The whole conception of individual rights was consequently overturned. Rights were no longer seen as natural and innate, but are merely 'reflex rights', or the result of the self-limitation of state power. For these accounts, see respectively Carl Friedrich von Gerber, *Über öffentliche Rechte* (H Laupp 1852); Carl Friedrich von Gerber, *Grundzüge des deutschen staatsrechts* (B Tauchnitz 1865); and Georg Jellinek, *System der subjektiven öffentlichen Rechte* (Mohr 1892); for a comprehensive analysis on these authors in English, see Michael Stolleis, *Public Law in Germany, 1800-1914* (Berghahn Books 2001); on the Italian interpretation of these theories, see Mario Caravale, 'La lettura italiana della teoria dei diritti riflessi' (2016) Rivista italiana per le scienze giuridiche 215.

16 Examples of these constitutional texts are the English Bill of Right of 1689, the Constitution of the United States of 1787, and the United States Bill of Rights of 1789. One could argue that the idea of individual rights emerged well before the seventeenth century and that documents like the Magna Carta would be evidence of this claim. However, it is important to highlight that, before the seventeenth century, these alleged rights were in reality 'privileges' accorded to specific social classes, generally, the dominant ones, like the barons, and were not conceived as universal rights of all individuals. See Michel Villey, *Le droit et les droits de l'homme* (Edition Quadrige 2014, Presses Universitaires de France 1983); cf. Gerhard Oestreich, *Geschichte der Menschenrechte und Grundfreiheiten im Umriss* (2nd ed., Duncker & Humblot 1978), who traces elements of the modern concepts of constitutional theory in the Greco-Roman and early-Christian philosophy.

17 An English translation of the Declaration is available on the website of the French Constitutional Council: <https://www.conseil-constitutionnel.fr/sites/default/files/as/root/bank_mm/anglais/cst2.pdf> accessed 20 November 2018.

described as 'natural', 'inalienable', 'sacred',[18] and 'imprescriptible'.[19] Moreover, it is recognised that the protection of individual rights plays a significant role that is as relevant as the 'separation of powers', i.e., what has been previously called the 'horizontal' limitation of power.[20]

The notion of power limitation, which, as we have seen, historically evolved from an original horizontal conception to also include a vertical dimension, has always been associated with the idea of equilibrium. Limitation of power has never meant annihilation of power, but rather referred to an action of balancing. Polybius and Cicero praised the Roman Republic for its 'mixed constitution' combining elements of the monarchical, oligarchical and democratic model, and therefore ensuring a balance between the different institutional actors and, consequently, the social classes involved.[21] The Magna Carta granted by King John of England in 1215 is another apparent example of balancing prerogatives between dominant powers: in that specific case, between the king and its barons.[22] Montesquieu is internationally known as the founding father of the idea of 'separation of powers', which, although one could be tempted to interpret it in a restrictive way as a 'delimitation' or 'demarcation' of powers, should be rather conceived in terms of 'balancing' and 're-distribution' of powers.[23] The Constitution of the United States of 1787 was heavily influenced by this doctrine, which further developed in the so-called 'checks and balances' model.[24]

Furthermore, the idea of equilibrium is also connatural with the conception of protection of individual rights. The Declaration of the Rights of the Man and of the Citizen of 1789 shows that, since its early developments, the doctrine of natural rights acknowledged the fact that individual liberties are

18 See the Preamble of the Declaration.

19 See Article 2 of the Declaration.

20 For an overview on the evolution of the concept of separation of powers from the eighteenth century, see MJC Vile, *Constitutionalism and the Separation of Powers* (2nd ed., Liberty Fund 1967); for an analysis of the meanings of the concept of separation of powers, see Mauro Barberis, 'Le futur passé de la séparation des pouvoirs' (2012) 143 Pouvoirs 5.

21 See Evgeny Morozov, 'The Case for Publicly Enforced Online Rights' (*Financial Times*, 27 September 2018) <https://www.ft.com/content/5e62186c-c1a5-11e8-84cd-9e601db069b8> accessed 2ay 2019, who argues that digital rights would not be expressed in our constitutions, but would rather be expressed as 'a bundle of permissions granted by technology platforms'; cf. Carl Friedrich von Gerber, *Über öffentliche Rechte* (H Laupp 1852) and; Georg Jellinek, *System der subjektiven öffentlichen Rechte* (Mohr 1892), who respectively intended individual rights as 'reflex rights' or as the result of self-limitation of state power.

22 See James Clarke Holt, *Magna Carta* (2nd ed., Cambridge University Press 1992); see also McIlwain (n 11). In particular, in Part IV, McIlwain analyses the thought of the English jurist Henri de Bracton (c. 1210–1268) reconstructing his distinction between *gubernaculum* and *iurisdictio*, i.e. between the sphere where the king detained an absolute power and the area of competence where he was subject to the limits of the common law.

23 See Vile (n 20); Armel Le Divellec, 'L'articulation des pouvoirs dans les démocraties parlementaires européennes : fusion et mitigation' (2012) 143 Pouvoirs 123.

24 See William B Gwyn, *The Meaning of the Separation of Powers: An Analysis of the Doctrine from Its Origin to the Adoption of the United States Constitution* (Tulane University 1965).

not absolute, but that living in a society requires a continuous balancing.[25] In more recent times, the case-law of the European Court of Human Rights, the jurisdiction created in 1948 in the context of the Council of Europe that enforces the European Convention of Human Rights, is exemplary of this action of balancing conflicting rights and interests. The text of the European Convention of Human Rights itself establishes for each right or freedom the grounds and the extent to which a state can limit them.[26]

All these examples show that the idea of equilibrium is pivotal in the economy of constitutional systems. Constitutional law strives to equalise dominant powers within a community and to balance competing rights, legitimate interests, and obligations. Recalling the distinction presented at the beginning of this section between prescriptive and descriptive constitution, one could distinguish two states of constitutional equilibrium. On the one hand, the *ideal* condition of equilibrium formally depicted by the body of constitutional norms. And, on the other hand, the *factual* condition produced by the application of constitutional norms within a community in normal conditions.

From a pragmatic point of view, constitutional law aims at guaranteeing a stable and long-lasting factual equilibrium. The relative rigidity of constitutional norms can be mentioned as one of the techniques generally used to generate this effect.[27] Nevertheless, it is obvious that the factual state of constitutional equilibrium is not absolute, but intrinsically relative. This condition of constitutional equilibrium is very similar to the view of the Bay of Naples that one can enjoy from the hill of Posillipo: an image of harmony, stability, beauty, but only ephemeral. Societal developments constantly shake and stir the magma underlying the constitutional equilibrium, until the pressure becomes so high that, as with the superficial tuffaceous rocks, the condition of relative balance collapses, and the landscape unavoidably changes.

Digital revolution

A series of contemporary societal transformations are challenging existing constitutional law apparatuses. Interestingly, this time, too, the main catalyst of these changes is related to significant technological developments.

25 See Article 4 of the Declaration: 'Liberty consists in being able to do anything that does not harm others: thus, the exercise of the natural rights of every man has no bounds other than those that ensure to the other members of society the enjoyment of these same rights. These bounds may be determined only by Law'.

26 See Eva Brems and Janneke Gerards, *Shaping Rights in the ECHR: The Role of the European Court of Human Rights in Determining the Scope of Human Rights* (Cambridge University Press 2013), e.g., ch 13 and 15.

27 See Arend Lijphart, *Patterns of Democracy: Government Forms and Performance in Thirty-Six Countries* (2nd ed., Yale University Press 2012), especially ch 12.

The great constitutional upheaval that occurred at the end of the eighteenth century was the heir of two centuries of scientific revolution, which laid the foundations for the Enlightenment, and substantially spurred the transition from the man-subject to the man-citizen, holder of his own rights and freedoms.[28] The emergence of the so-called 'second generation' of rights from the twentieth century, which led to the recognition of the rights of the workers and other essential social rights, was the consequence of the disruptive impact of the industrial revolutions.[29] Women and men were no longer farmers, oppressed by the abuses of the nobility and the clergy, but became workers, subject to the dominance of unscrupulous private companies. Also in relation to the so-called 'third generation of rights' emerging in the second half of the twentieth century,[30] it is possible to observe an underlying decisive role of scientific developments. For example, the 'new' right to a healthy environment, which today is progressively conquering major support, is emerging because scientific studies have demonstrated that the human being is not using the Earth in a way that could be sustainable in the long term.[31]

Today, it is impossible to ignore the disruptive impact that the advent and the impetuous development of digital technology have been generating in the last 25 years. After the scientific and the industrial revolutions, the end of the twentieth century has marked the beginning of the digital revolution.[32] The transformations that contemporary society is experiencing are comparable to those which led to the previous major constitutional changes. The dawn of the new millennium is witnessing a transition from the *homo faber/oeconomicus/lundens* of the twentieth century to the *homo sapiens informaticus*.[33] Twenty-first-century women and men not only act in the physical world but also live in a virtual ecosystem. Physical bodies do not have

28 See Chris Thornhill, *A Sociology of Constitutions: Constitutions and State Legitimacy in Historical-Sociological Perspective* (Cambridge University Press 2011) 181 ff; Thomas S Kuhn, *The Structure of Scientific Revolutions* (4th ed., University of Chicago Press 2012).

29 See Karel Vasak, 'A 30-Year Struggle. The Sustained Efforts to Give Force of Law to the Universal Declaration of Human Rights' (1977) XXX *UNESCO Courier* 29 for the first formulation of the theory of the three generations of human rights; see Norberto Bobbio, *The Age of Rights* (Allan Cameron tr, Polity 1996); cf. the many critical accounts, among which, Patrick Macklem, *The Sovereignty of Human Rights* (Oxford University Press 2015), ch. 3; Daniel J Whelan, *Indivisible Human Rights: A History* (University of Pennsylvania Press 2010).

30 See Vasak (n 29); Philip Alston (ed), *Peoples' Rights* (Oxford University Press 2001); cf. Macklem (n 29); Whelan (n 29).

31 See, ex multis, Dinah Shelton, *Human Rights and the Environment* (Edward Elgar 2011).

32 See Luciano Floridi, *Philosophy and Computing: An Introduction* (Routledge 1999) ch 1; Christian Fuchs, *Internet and Society: Social Theory in the Information Age* (Routledge 2008); Manuel Castells, *The Rise of the Network Society* (2nd edn, Blackwell 2000) ch 1.

33 This expression is used in Gilles Dowek, *Vivre, aimer, voter en ligne et autres chroniques numériques* (Le Pommier 2017); cf. Floridi (n 32) 221 ff on the evolution of homo faber/sapiens/ludens in homo poieticus.

access to the digital environment, but human actions are translated into interactions of data. Collections of data, which are ultimately mere digits imputed and stored in information technology systems, represent our bodies, ideas, preferences, relationships in the virtual domain. We are no longer only flesh and blood, or body and soul – as someone may think: we are also our digital selves.[34]

The effects of these transformations can be read from multiple perspectives. They have a 360 degrees impact on contemporary society: including on its constitutional equilibrium. In order to understand this phenomenon, it is necessary to adopt a constitutionalist standpoint. An initial exercise is to look at the present scenario through the lenses of the two historical missions of constitutional law: the limitation of power and the protection of fundamental rights.

Power over digital lives

As seen in the previous section, constitutional law aims to strike a balance between the powers involved in a community. In this way, constitutional norms strive to reach a condition of relative equilibrium in which all societal actors can live according to shared and established values. Traditionally, the cornerstone of modern constitutional systems is the state.[35] This entity pursues different functions: it represents the framework in which the powers of different institutions necessary to the organisation of the community are articulated and balanced; it plays an intermediary role between social classes; it can be globally regarded as *the* dominant actor and ultimate holder of power over the individuals,[36] and consequently as the key guarantor of their fundamental rights.

In the digital age, the state reinforces its powers over the individuals through the use of sophisticated technologies that monitor our digital lives. At the same time, the global nature of the virtual space favours the emergence of new powerful actors besides the state. Today, multinational tech companies control digital technologies, and by doing so, unavoidably shape our digital selves.

34 See Daniel J Solove, *The Digital Person: Technology and Privacy in the Information Age* (New York University Press 2004); Julie E Cohen, *Configuring the Networked Self: Law, Code, and the Play of Everyday Practice* (Yale University Press 2012); John Perry Barlow, 'A Declaration of the Independence of Cyberspace' (1996) <https://www.eff.org/cyberspace-independence> accessed 11 December 2018; Stefano Rodotà, *Il Mondo Nella Rete: Quali i Diritti, Quali i Vincoli* (Laterza 2014); cf. also the rationale of the Latin-American writ of 'habeas data' in Andrés Guadamuz, 'Habeas Data: The Latin-American Response to Data Protection' (2000) 2 The Journal of Information, Law and Technology <https://warwick.ac.uk/fac/soc/law/elj/jilt/2000_2/guadamuz>.

35 For a comprehensive socio-historical analysis of the role of the state, see Thornhill (n 28).

36 Cf. Max Weber, 'Politics as a Vocation' in David S Owen and Tracy B Strong (eds), Rodney Livingstone (tr), *The Vocation Lectures* (Hackett 2004).

Orwellian nightmares

In 2013, Edward Snowden, at the time a computer specialist working for the US intelligence services, disclosed a considerable number of classified documents revealing the existence of a system of global mass surveillance operated by six states.[37] The leaked files confirmed that national security agencies systematically had access to data related to phone calls, text messages, emails, web activities of all citizens which had contact with foreign correspondents. The world realised that the dystopian scenarios predicted by Orwell in his best-selling novel *Nineteen Eighty-Four* became reality.[38]

State surveillance is certainly not a novelty of the digital age.[39] However, until not long ago, mass surveillance was *de facto* a myth. Intelligence services did not have the technological means to operate a system of control over all the types of communications of a significant group of people. Therefore, even in cases where the aim of intelligence services was to constantly monitor the entire population, only a limited surveillance of targeted individuals was in fact possible.[40] However, recent technological developments have allowed intelligence services to collect, store, and analyse unprecedented masses of communications, which come very close to the Orwellian model narrated in *Nineteen Eighty-Four.* It is possible to talk of a paradigm shift in the practice of intelligence services.[41] Historically, this transition from a model of targeted monitoring to a system of mass surveillance emerged in the aftermath of the 9/11 terrorist attacks in the United States. The dramatic episodes which occurred in 2001 revealed that even people apparently above suspicion could act as terrorists.[42] Hence, the claimed need to shift towards a system of pre-emptive surveillance, which could identify hidden threats regardless of any prior suspect link with dangerous groups or activities.[43]

The development of digital technology has been a key factor in this change.[44] In a sort of vicious circle, on the one hand, people have started

37 For a general overview on the Snowden revelations, see David Lyon, *Surveillance after Snowden* (Polity Press 2015).

38 George Orwell, *Nineteen Eighty-Four* (originally published in 1949, Penguin Books 2004).

39 See David Lyon, *The Electronic Eye: The Rise of Surveillance Society* (Polity Press 1994).

40 See Gary Bruce, *The Firm: The Inside Story of the Stasi* (Oxford University Press 2010).

41 Valsamis Mitsilegas, 'Transatlantic Counterterrorism Cooperation and European Values' in Deirdre Curtin and Elaine Fahey (eds), *A Transatlantic Community of Law: Legal Perspectives on the Relationship between the EU and US Legal Orders* (Cambridge University Press 2014).

42 See Lawrence Wright, *The Looming Tower: Al-Qaeda and the Road to 9/11* (Vintage Books 2007).

43 See, e.g., Marieke de Goede, *Speculative Security* (Minnesota University Press 2012).

44 See Christian Fuchs and others (eds), *Internet and Surveillance: The Challenges of Web 2. 0 and Social Media* (Routledge 2011); David Lyon (ed), *Theorizing Surveillance: The Panopticon and Beyond* (Willan 2006).

to use digital technology instruments to transmit a considerable amount of their communications. Today, sending an email is far cheaper than posting a letter or dispatching a telegram. At the same time, on the other hand, intelligence services can now use more sophisticated systems that automatically collect and analyse an unprecedented number of communications. In other words, contemporary surveillance is relatively easier – or more accurately, more effective – than the inspection of correspondence or the wiretapping of some decades ago.[45]

The possibility of the state to monitor the behaviour of its citizens has always been a central issue in the constitutional equilibrium. The presence of provisions on the secrecy of correspondence in many national constitutions is exemplary.[46] Covert surveillance epitomises the power of state over the individuals. It clearly represents a restriction of individual rights, such as the right to freedom of expression and the right to private life. Its justification lies in a series of values, such as national security and public order, which are considered to be fundamental to guarantee a democratic life. The big conundrum of state surveillance is therefore represented by its limits. The main questions are to what extent a restriction of individual rights is tolerated in order to protect other collective values and which minimal guarantees should be ensured. This is the difficult task in which constitutional law has always been called to provide at least general guidelines. Today, it is apparent that recent advancements in the digital technology field have enhanced the asymmetry of power between states and individuals, by reinforcing the capability of the former of monitoring the lives of latter. The new scale and extent of state surveillance represent a paradigmatic shift, which unavoidably puts pressure on existing safeguards of individual rights, and consequently affects the overall constitutional equilibrium.

New rulers

In 2017, Denmark, first, followed by France, appointed a 'tech ambassador'.[47] One of the main duties of these governmental officers is to liaise with the technology industry. The rise of what has been defined as 'techplomacy',

45 In reality, today's surveillance is more complex than opening a letter, but it is more effective in terms of scale and final effects. See Bruce Schneier, *Data and Goliath: The Hidden Battles to Collect Your Data and Control Your World* (W W Norton & Company 2015).

46 See, e.g., Article 29 of the Belgian Constitution, Article 15 of the Italian Constitution, Article 19 of the Greek Constitution.

47 Office of Denmark's Tech Ambassador, 'TechPlomacy' (*Office of Denmark's Tech Ambassador*) <http://techamb.um.dk/en/techplomacy/> accessed 2 January 2019; Ministère de l'Europe et des Affaires étrangères, 'Digital Affairs – Appointment of an Ambassador (22.11.17)' (*France Diplomatie : Ministry for Europe and Foreign Affairs*) <https://www.diplomatie.gouv.fr/en/french-foreign-policy/digital-diplomacy/events/article/digital-affairs-appointment-of-an-ambassador-22-11-17> accessed 2 January 2019.

and not simply of a governmental department or office specialised in digital technology, recognises that today states have to deal with technology companies as between peers.[48] Not only because of the massive income that these multinationals generate in some countries but also because today technology companies can influence the life of individuals at a global scale in a manner very similar to states.

In contemporary society, big private corporations producing, selling, and managing digital technology products and services worldwide detain the power to regulate the use of digital technology instruments by individuals.[49] Nowadays, these instruments could be the only, or the most effective, way to exercise fundamental rights, such as accessing information, communicating, searching a job, organising a protest, or manifesting one's own faith.[50] Those private corporations, by determining how individuals can use these digital technology instruments, unavoidably interfere with the exercise of their fundamental rights.

The digital revolution has introduced new actors, besides nation-states, which play a dominant role in the constitutional ecosystem, and this circumstance subverts the existing constitutional equilibrium.[51] As we have seen, historically, the state became the main dominant actor within the polity and, consequently, modern constitutional law established ways to limit its power in order to guarantee individual fundamental rights (vertical dimension).[52] As a consequence, the legal obligation to respect individual rights only binds the state. Private entities are not directly subject to

48 Office of Denmark's Tech Ambassador (n 47).

49 See Edoardo Celeste, Amélie Heldt and Clara Iglesias Keller (eds), *Constitutionalising Social Media* (Hart 2022); Hans-W Micklitz and others (eds), *Constitutional Challenges in the Algorithmic Society* (Cambridge University Press 2022) ch 1; Nicolas Suzor, *Lawless. The Secret Rules That Govern Our Digital Lives* (Cambridge University Press 2019); Rikke Frank Jørgensen (ed), *Human Rights in the Age of Platforms* (The MIT Press 2019); Paul Nemitz, 'Constitutional Democracy and Technology in the Age of Artificial Intelligence' (2018) 376 Philosophical Transactions of the Royal Society A; Rikke Frank Jørgensen and Anja Møller Pedersen, 'Online Service Providers as Human Rights Arbiters' in Mariarosaria Taddeo and Luciano Floridi (eds), *The Responsibilities of Online Service Providers* (Springer 2017).

50 See Dowek (n 33); Edoardo Celeste, 'Digital Punishment: Social Media Exclusion and the Constitutionalising Role of National Courts' [2021] International Review of Law, Computers & Technology 1.

51 The emergence of these new actors more precisely affected what has been called before the vertical conception of limitation of power. See Gunther Teubner, 'Societal Constitutionalism; Alternatives to State-Centred Constitutional Theory?' in Christian Joerges, Inger-Johanne Sand and Gunther Teubner (eds), *Transnational Governance and Constitutionalism. International Studies in the Theory of Private Law* (Hart 2004); Shoshana Zuboff, *The Age of Surveillance Capitalism: The Fight for a Human Future at the New Frontier of Power* (PublicAffairs 2019); Christoph Graber, 'Freedom and Affordances of the Net' (2018) 10 Washington University Jurisprudence Review 221; Stefano Rodotà, 'Una Costituzione per Internet?' (2010) Politica del diritto 337.

52 See McIlwain (n 11).

these standards. It is a duty of the state to ensure that such entities respect these rights.[53] However, in the digital society, technology corporations, too, detain a form of power. They act as 'online gatekeepers'.[54] They have the power to regulate the access and use of individuals to digital technology instruments and, consequently, they can affect the way in which individuals exercise their rights through these instruments.

Certainly, violations of fundamental rights perpetrated by private actors are not a novelty produced by the advent of digital technology.[55] At national level, a series of mechanisms have been developed to ensure that the state compels private actors to respect individual rights.[56] At the international level, one can observe long-standing debates on how to make private actors accountable for their behaviour.[57] However, today, the massive diffusion of digital technology instruments among individuals, combined with the dominant role that these private corporations play in this sector, increases the likelihood of rights violations perpetrated by non-state actors. Technology companies control a substantial component of the everyday life of an unprecedented number of people.[58] The possibility that these non-state actors interfere with our fundamental rights becomes more likely and intense, and, at the same time, this circumstance is not adequately addressed by existing mechanisms of power balancing, which rather focus on the relationship between individuals and nation-states.

Digital rights

For many centuries, the notion of constitution and, consequently its study, was only related to the form of organisation of the society and, more specifically, to the relationship between the actors who held power within the community.[59] However, as we have seen, starting from the end of the eighteenth century, the idea that individuals enjoy a series of natural rights emerged and, consequently, besides the traditional notion of horizontal limitation of power, constitutional law embraced a new conception of limitation, this time a vertical one, aiming to restrict the power that dominant societal

53 Jørgensen and Pedersen (n 49).

54 Emily B Laidlaw, 'Private Power, Public Interest: An Examination of Search Engine Accountability' (2008) 17 International Journal of Law and Information Technology 113; see also Emily B Laidlaw, *Regulating Speech in Cyberspace: Gatekeepers, Human Rights and Corporate Responsibility* (Cambridge University Press 2015).

55 See, ex multis, Andrew Clapham, *Human Rights Obligations of Non-State Actors* (Oxford University Press 2006).

56 See, e.g., Eric Engle, 'Third Party Effect of Fundamental Rights (Drittwirkung)' (2009) 5 Hanse Law Review 165.

57 See Surya Deva and David Bilchitz (eds), *Human Rights Obligations of Business: Beyond the Corporate Responsibility to Respect?* (Cambridge University Press 2013).

58 See, e.g., Schneier (n 45).

59 See McIlwain (n 11); Thornhill (n 28).

actors could exercise on individuals. Today, the protection of fundamental rights can deservedly be regarded as one of the two quintessential missions of constitutional law besides the limitation of power, intended in a horizontal sense. The safeguard of individual rights is a necessary element to reach a condition of constitutional equilibrium within a society. It is a dimension which inherently pertains to the individuals and, consequently, is directly exposed to the action of societal developments.

When looking at the impact that digital technology has on the constitutional equilibrium through the lens of the protection of fundamental rights, one can observe a paradoxical scenario. Technological advancements show a Janus-faced attitude in relation to fundamental rights. On the one hand, digital technology enhances, or even concretises, the possibility to exercise a broad range of fundamental rights related to the exchange of information. Today, the use of digital technology seems so indispensable to exercising these rights that this situation even raises the question of the existence of new rights, ancillary to the previous ones, and intrinsically related to the digital age: in brief, *digital* rights, one could say. On the other hand, the development of digital technologies increases the risks of fundamental rights infringements. This is nothing but the other side of the coin that has been analysed in the previous section. The limitation of power and the protection of fundamental rights are *de facto* intertwined. The rising power of the state and new dominant actors, if regarded through the lens of the protection of fundamental rights, can be read as an increased risk of rights infringements from the perspective of the individuals. Even if the ultimate fundamental right to be protected is still the personal freedom of the individual, the specific principles that articulate this canon in the digital society have not been yet fully elaborated or recognised.

Enhanced freedoms

The development and the massive spreading of digital technology in the world have manifestly amplified the possibilities of individuals to exercise their fundamental rights. One of the most mentioned examples is the series of events now generally known as the Arab Spring.[60] In 2010, groups of Tunisian citizens started protesting against the authoritarianism of the government's power.[61] These events eventually led to the Tunisian dictator fleeing into exile and to the instauration of a democratic government

60 See Toby Manhire (ed), *The Arab Spring: Rebellion, Revolution and a New World Order* (Random House 2012); Antoni Abat i Ninet and Mark Tushnet, *The Arab Spring. An Essay on Revolution and Constitutionalism* (Edward Elgar 2015); Hamid Dabashi, *The Arab Spring: The End of Postcolonialism* (Zed Books 2012); cf. Gadi Wolfsfeld, Elad Segev and Tamir Sheafer, 'Social Media and the Arab Spring: Politics Comes First' (2013) 18 The International Journal of Press/Politics 115.

61 Manhire (n 60).

based on a new constitution in 2014. The effects of the Tunisian uprising blew a wind of protest in several countries in North Africa and the Middle East. Social media were heavily used by protestors to spread their revolutionary ideas.[62] Some authoritarian governments consequently shut down social networking websites and, in some cases, even obscured the entire web.[63] The relevance of social media as a catalyst of these changes in the Arab world was such that some of these events were subsequently denominated 'Twitter revolutions'.[64] In conclusion, the Arab Spring is exemplary of the power of digital technology to facilitate, or even to concretise, the exercise of fundamental rights, such as the freedom of expression and of assembly. However, it is not necessary to recur to major events, such as those of the Arab Spring, to understand how digital technology enhances our possibility to exercise fundamental rights. It suffices to think of the way in which today we communicate and seek information. These are only some of the many common examples of how nowadays digital technology has become extremely useful – not to say, indispensable – to exercise basic fundamental rights.

Generally speaking, digital technology expands the possibility to transmit information. From a constitutional point of view, this circumstance implies that all fundamental rights based on the exchange of information, such as freedom of expression, religious freedom, freedom of assembly or freedom to conduct a business, are enhanced. At first sight, one could think that this is essentially a positive transformation, and that, therefore, it cannot generate any problems in terms of constitutional equilibrium. However, a similar perspective risks neglecting part of the broader picture.

A transformation occurring at societal level, although positive, is nevertheless a transformation. This means that constitutional norms face a new societal landscape, a context that could not have been taken into account at the time of their original elaboration. Therefore, on the one hand, there could be circumstances in which stretching constitutional norms through a broad or evolutionary interpretation can still ensure the protection of certain values.[65] Let us take the example of the right to freedom of expression: one can easily imagine to protect the possibility of an individual to communicate through the Internet by applying a norm enshrining freedom of expression, even if that specific provision does not mention this new instrument because it has been elaborated in a pre-digital era. However, on the

62 See Sarah Joseph, 'Social Media, Political Change, and Human Rights' (2012) 35 Boston College International and Comparative Law Review 145.

63 Manhire (n 60).

64 Anne-Claire Jamart, 'Internet Freedom and the Constitutionalization of Internet Governance' in Roxana Radu, Jean-Marie Chenou and Rolf H Weber (eds), *The Evolution of Global Internet Governance* (Springer Berlin Heidelberg 2014).

65 See Giovanna De Minico, 'Towards an Internet Bill of Rights' (2015) 37 Loyola of Los Angeles International and Comparative Law Review 1.

other hand, the mutated conditions of the social scenario could also generate a series of gaps in the constitutional system. For example, today, it could seem impossible to exercise some of our fundamental rights without the help of digital technology. In some circumstances, material, economical, or legal obstacles to the use of these technologies have become an issue for the factual enjoyment of specific rights. Should therefore the access to the Internet be considered as a fundamental right? Is exercising our fundamental rights in an 'analogue' way still a valid option to be considered?[66] This seems to be a central dilemma that the massive diffusion and the increasing indispensability of digital technology instruments are generating at constitutional level. Today, the use of digital technology is so crucial to exercising these rights, that this situation raises the question of the existence of new rights, ancillary to the previous ones.

In conclusion, while, on the one hand, we can affirm that digital technology has amplified, or even concretised in some cases, the possibility to exercise many fundamental rights based on the exchange of communication; on the other hand, this transformation has eventually affected the constitutional equilibrium by generating a new set of quandaries to which existing constitutional norms could not be able to provide explicit solutions.

Higher risks

It is easier to realise that digital technology is affecting the constitutional equilibrium when one calls to mind the series of new threats it generates.[67] Paradoxically, there seems to be a connection between the enhancement of freedoms, analysed in the previous paragraph, and the increasing risks to our fundamental rights. The same amplified possibility to exchange information enabling the exercise of many fundamental rights can also become a source of threat. For instance, defamation, hate speech, disinformation, cyberbullying, and child pornography are some of the most common examples of how freedom of expression can be illegally used through digital instruments. In these cases, the constitutional equilibrium is directly affected because these forms of wrongdoings have an impact on other fundamental rights, such as human dignity, equality, non-discrimination, or the protection of the child.

It is apparent that we are not facing new kinds of threats: all these forms of wrongdoing can be perpetrated without recurring to modern technologies, and, in the majority of cases, emerged well before the advent of the digital revolution. What has changed is certainly the scale of this phenomenon

66 Cf. Tero Karppi, *Disconnect* (University of Minnesota Press 2018).

67 See Ingolf Pernice, 'Risk management in the digital constellation - a constitutional perspective (part I)' [2018] IDP Revista de Internet Derecho y Política 83; Ingolf Pernice, 'Risk management in the digital constellation – a constitutional perspective (part II)' (2018) IDP Revista de Internet Derecho y Política 79.

and the consequences of these offences.[68] The capillarity with which digital technology instruments are spread among the population, their extensive use in the everyday life and the, often, public nature of the exchanges of information which occur online unavoidably increase the likelihood of these wrongdoings being perpetrated. Furthermore, as previously said, the consequences of these illegal acts could be far more serious than in the traditional 'analogue' conditions. It is evident that in the digital context, the size of the 'audience' that we potentially target by spreading our thoughts on the Internet is hardly comparable with the reach that we could attain through analogue means. As Justice Stevens of the US Supreme Court more romantically put it in *Reno v. American Civil Liberties Union*:

> [t]hrough the use of chat rooms, any person with a phone line can become a town crier with a voice that resonates farther than it could from any soapbox.[69]

Moreover, digital technology not only enhances the possibility to transmit information but also allows:

i blocking or limiting such a transmission,
ii monitoring the content of the transmitted information, and
iii registering other information related to the individuals involved in the transmission.

In the first case, a limitation of the transmission of data could violate all the rights that are based on that exchange of information, such as freedom of expression, freedom of information, or freedom of association.[70] In the second case, monitoring transmitted information could involve confidential communications and include personal data. Therefore, an unauthorised access to such contents could violate all the rights aiming to protect the personal sphere of the individual, such as the right to privacy, right to respect of private life, secrecy of correspondence, and right to data protection, as differently articulated in the various legal systems.[71] In the third case, collecting other information concerning the transmission of information essentially means registering the when, who, where, and how of a

68 See Pernice, 'Risk management in the digital constellation - a constitutional perspective (part I)' (n 67).

69 *Reno v American Civil Liberties Union* (1997) US Supreme Court 521 U.S. 844, 870.

70 See, e.g., *Packingham v North Carolina* [2017] US Supreme Court 582 U.S. ____; Edoardo Celeste, 'Packingham v North Carolina: A Constitutional Right to Social Media?' (2018) 17 Cork Online Law Review 116.

71 See, e.g., the case-law of the ECtHR on interception of communications. A list of the main cases is available in European Court of Human Rights – Press Unit, 'Factsheet - Mass Surveillance' <https://www.echr.coe.int/Documents/FS_Mass_surveillance_ENG.pdf>.

communications exchange. These data, generally called traffic-, communications-, or meta-data, are not only personal data but could also reveal information about the individuals concerned as sensitive as in the case of interception of the content of information.[72] Therefore, also in this case, the series of rights aiming to protect the privacy, the private life, and the correspondence of individuals could be potentially infringed.

What has been just described, the increased risks generated by the development of digital technology, are nothing but the other side of the coin of the enhanced power of the state and of the emergence of private companies as new dominant actors. The rising power of dominant actors, if not balanced, unavoidably leads to an increased risk of rights infringements from the perspective of the individuals. One could claim that an increase of risks does not alter the ultimate fundamental right to be protected, which is still the personal freedom of the individual. According to this line of interpretation, constitutional systems could still be able to face the changes generated by the development of digital technology. However, even if the ultimate aim of constitutional law remains the same, this does not automatically imply that the specific principles that articulate this canon in the digital society have been already fully elaborated or recognised. This circumstance clearly shows the consequences of the impact of the digital revolution on the protection of fundamental rights: constitutional systems could still have to adapt their principles, develop new guidelines, and acknowledge the peculiarities of the new digital society.

Constitutional change

The factual constitutional equilibrium is not a permanent condition. Constitutional law strives to set a body of norms aiming to ensure a condition of long-lasting balance on the basis of a snapshot of present and past conditions of a community. However, societal developments constantly change the landscape in which constitutional law operates, and these transformations could have a variety of outcomes.

On the one hand, constitutional law could be able to protect its original values in the context of mutated social conditions. This option includes both the case where the constitutional norm is wide enough to 'encompass', as it is, new societal circumstances, and the situation in which a 'stretching' of the constitutional norm is necessary to allow it to successfully operate in the mutated reality. On the other hand, constitutional law, although stretched, could be unable to deal with a societal scenario which is no longer that depicted at the time of the initial elaboration of its norms. A constitutional

72 See, e.g., the case-law of the Court of Justice of the EU on bulk retention of meta-data; an overview of the main cases is provided by Edoardo Celeste, 'The Court of Justice and the Ban on Bulk Data Retention: Expansive Potential and Future Scenarios' (2019) 15 European Constitutional Law Review 134.

vacuum emerges because constitutional law does not articulate its general values and principles in the new societal context. Constitutional law is no longer able to point out the direction to be followed by societal actors. In other words, this means that the ultimate values and principles protected by constitutional law are violated in the new societal context. In these circumstances, the factual constitutional equilibrium is put in danger. Within the community, unbalanced outcomes could progressively arise due to a body of norms which do not match the societal reality anymore.

A peculiarity of constitutional systems – or, one could argue, of law in general – is that, in such a scenario, they do not remain motionless. As we said, constitutional law aims to achieve a condition of equilibrium. The necessary corollary of this intrinsic mission of constitutional law is that, when facing a situation of disequilibrium, the system should be rebalanced. This is a normative imperative.[73] Constitutional law is the product of historical moments but has the duty to keep pace with societal changes. The constitutional ecosystem is homeostatic.[74] When the constitutional equilibrium is affected by societal changes, the system starts to produce a series of counteractions in order to restore a condition of balance. In practice, in order to re-establish a constitutional equilibrium, constitutional law needs to be amended or integrated. This is why, notwithstanding its generally high degree of – at least factual – rigidity, modern constitutional law always provides a way to be modified.

This phenomenon is easily comparable with Newton's Third Law of Motion.[75] A societal reaction to the constitutional ecosystem is – or better, has to be – followed by a constitutional counteraction. One could even think of an analogy with Polanyi's 'double movement'.[76] The digital revolution is not dissimilar from the 'great' economic transformation described by Polanyi. Both these societal changes determine the emergence of a normative 'countermovement'.

73 See Zaccaria Giacometti, 'Festrede des Rektors Zaccaria Giacometti, Gehalten an der 122. Stiftungsfeier der Universität Zürich am 29. April 1955: Die Freiheitsrechtskataloge als Kodifikation der Freiheit', *Jahresbericht 1954/55* (Art Institut Orell Füssli AG 1955) 16 ff <http://bit.ly/2pXBwhn>; for a reformulation of Giacometti's thoughts in English, see Graber (n 8) 532 ff.

74 Cf. Stefano Rodotà, *Il diritto di avere diritti* (Laterza 2012) 191.

75 I used this metaphor for the first time in Edoardo Celeste, 'Terms of Service and Bills of Rights: New Mechanisms of Constitutionalisation in the Social Media Environment?' (2019) 33 International Review of Law, Computers & Technology 122.

76 Karl Polanyi, *The Great Transformation: The Political and Economic Origins of Our Time* (originally published in 1944, Beacon Press 2001); see Fred Block, 'Karl Polanyi and the Writing of The Great Transformation' (2003) 32 Theory and Society 275; see also Gunther Teubner, *Constitutional Fragments: Societal Constitutionalism and Globalization* (Oxford University Press 2012) 78 ff.

This cyclical alternation of conditions of relative equilibrium and moments of change is connatural with the history of constitutional law.[77] The theoretical approach which identifies a progressive emergence of 'generations' of rights is exemplary of this process.[78] As we have already seen, at the end of the eighteenth century, ordinary people were oppressed by the abuses of power of privileged social classes, like the nobility and the clergy. This led to the emergence of constitutional norms protecting the rights of individuals, notwithstanding their social status. They represented, what has been called, the 'first generation' of rights, including many 'civil rights', like freedom of thought, press, or religion, and 'political rights', such as the right to vote. From the twentieth century, the societal transformations which started during the industrial revolutions witnessed the transition from the farmer-artisan to the new figure of the modern worker and determined the affirmation of a 'second generation' of rights, mainly 'social rights', such as the right to work, to strike, trade union freedom, the right to education, and to public health-care. Lastly, in the second half of the twentieth century, a 'third generation' of rights started to emerge.[79] This category is variegated and includes the so-called 'new rights' reflecting the major issues that the world is experiencing in recent times, like the right to a healthy environment.[80]

From these examples, it is possible to understand that specific societal dynamics play a central role in relation to constitutional transformations. There is an evident link between societal and constitutional change.[81] Constitutional law naturally aims to provide a long-lasting societal equilibrium, but society is in constant evolution. As the magma fermenting under the crust of the earth, continuous societal developments can reach a condition of saturation which ineludibly requires a constitutional change. Nowadays, the constitutional landscape is experiencing this phenomenon again.

77 Polybius talked of 'anacyclosis'. See Stephan Podes, 'Polybius and His Theory of "Anacyclosis". Problems of Not Just Ancient Political Theory' (1991) 12 History of Political Thought 577.

78 See Bobbio (n 29); Thomas Humphrey Marshall, *Class, Citizenship, and Social Development* (Doubleday 1964); cf. Macklem (n 29) ch 3; Whelan (n 29); cf. Graber (n 51) 244 ff, who reconstructs Luhmann's theory of rights as 'institutions' emerging to protect society against its self-destructive impulses.

79 See Bobbio (n 29); cf. Philip Alston, 'A Third Generation of Solidarity Rights: Progressive Development or Obfuscation of International Human Rights Law?' (1982) 29 Netherlands International Law Review 307; Carl Wellman, 'Solidarity, the Individual and Human Rights' (2000) 22 Human Rights Quarterly 639.

80 See Shelton (n 31).

81 See, e.g., Ingolf Pernice, 'Die Verfassung der Internetgesellschaft: Zur Rolle von Staat und Verfassung im Zuge der digitalen Revolution' in Alexander Blankenagel (ed), *Den Verfassungsstaat nachdenken. Eine Geburtstagsgabe* (Duncker & Humblot 2014) <https://papers.ssrn.com/abstract=2964926> accessed 28 August 2018, who explains how the very concept of constitution is changed by the processes of globalisation, Europeanisation, and digitalisation.

A series of ongoing transformations in contemporary society are challenging existing constitutional law apparatuses. The transformations prompted by the digital revolution in relation to ourselves, our relationships with other individuals, and, ultimately, in the society at large ferment under a vault of constitutional norms shaped for 'analogue' communities. However, the constitutional ecosystem is not inert. We can observe the emergence of a series of constitutional counteractions. It is the case to say that we are witnessing a new constitutional moment.[82]

82 The notion of constitutional moment was originally coined by Bruce Ackerman in the context of American constitutional history to define phases of 'higher law-making' characterised by a greater involvement of citizens in constitutional matters: see Bruce A Ackerman, *We the People: Foundations* (Harvard University Press 1991). On the concept of constitutional moment in international law, see Anne-Marie Slaughter and William Burke-White, 'An International Constitutional Moment Focus: September 11, 2001--Legal Response to Terror' (2002) 43 Harvard International Law Journal 1; Andreas Fischer-Lescano, 'Redefining Sovereignty via International Constitutional Moments? The Case of Afghanistan' in Michael Bothe, Mary Hellen O'Connel and Natalino Ronzitti (eds), *Redefining Sovereignty: The Use of Force after the Cold War* (Brill-Nijhoff 2005); Christian Walter, 'Progress in International Organization: A Constitutionalist Reading' in Russell Miller and Rebecca Bratspies (eds), *Progress in International Law* (Brill Nijhoff 2008) 134 ff; in the digital context, see Rodotà, 'Una Costituzione per Internet?' (n 51); Viktor Mayer-Schönberger and John Crowley, 'Napster's Second Life?: The Regulatory Challenges of Virtual World' (2006) 100 Northwestern University Law Review 1775; Woodrow Hartzog and Neil Richards, 'Privacy's Constitutional Moment and the Limits of Data Protection' (2020) 61 Boston College Law Review 1687.

3 Constitutional counteractions

Targeted transformations

The constitutional ecosystem is not immune to the development of digital technology. The digital revolution impacts on the constitutional equilibrium and generates four kinds of effects. Digital technology: (1) reinforces the power of states to control our digital lives; (2) promotes powerful tech multinationals to the level of dominant actors by allowing them to shape our digital selves; (3) enhances a broad range of fundamental rights based on the exchange of information; and (4) at the same time, increases the risk of violations of several individual rights. Vis-à-vis these changes, the constitutional ecosystem, at its turn, reacts in order to restore a state of equilibrium in which powers are balanced and individual rights protected.[1]

The existing constitutional settings, created for an 'analogue' society, are being modified or integrated in a way that better addresses the challenges of the digital age. A global insight on this phenomenon does not reveal that a revolution of the constitutional system is ongoing. This constitutional moment does not equate to a constitutional upheaval.[2] We rather witness a series of targeted transformations. The following paragraphs will offer some illustrative examples that show how constitutional counteractions are emerging to address the four kinds of effects generated by the development of digital technology.

Four examples

Right to digital information

In modern representative democracies, one could think that the role of the ordinary citizens is limited to casting a vote from time to time in major

1 Cf. Christoph Graber, 'Freedom and Affordances of the Net' (2018) 10 Washington University Jurisprudence Review 221, who, building on Luhmann, reconstructs a theory of digital fundamental rights as a response to technological developments.

2 See, *infra*, Chapter 6.

DOI: 10.4324/9781003256908-3

occasions, such as general elections. We could talk of an 'intermittent' participation in the democratic life of a country. However, at the same time, one cannot deny that politicians and, more in general, all public actors are under the continuous scrutiny of ordinary people. Their behaviour cannot completely disregard the expectations and the judgment of their citizens. Therefore, in reality, ordinary people permanently play an important role in the democratic life of a society. They personify, what Rosanvallon calls, the 'contre-démocratie': they have the power to monitor, prevent, and judge their representatives.[3] This power, however, presupposes that citizens have an idea of what is going on in their country. Without any information about what politicians discuss and decide or public bodies do, for example, ordinary citizens cannot have the possibility to react and show their position. Transparency is therefore a fundamental requirement to citizens' counter-power against the potential arbitrariness of the state, and this is why people's right to obtain information from their government, commonly known as freedom of information, has a long-standing tradition in some democratic countries.[4]

Although this right dates back to the eighteenth century, one could claim that it is with the development of information communication technologies from the end of the last century that the freedom of information has been really substantiated. Digital technology has offered for the first time the technical possibility to provide all citizens with an Internet connection instantaneous and free access to an unprecedented amount of governmental information. It is thanks to these instruments that today we can theoretically conceive, what Bobbio called, a 'democracy in public'.[5] Digital technology allows us to monitor public institutions as through a glasshouse, and, consequently, to react, to express our disagreement, and to compel the elected

3 Pierre Rosanvallon, *La Contre-Démocratie. La politique à l'âge de la défiance* (Le Seuil 2006); also available in English: Pierre Rosanvallon, *Counter-Democracy: Politics in an Age of Distrust* (Cambridge University Press 2008); see also John Keane, *Global Civil Society?* (Cambridge University Press 2003), who analyses the role of civil society in contemporary democracies; cf. the similar concept of 'monitory democracy' in John Keane, *The Life and Death of Democracy* (W W Norton & Company 2009), and John Keane, *Power and Humility: The Future of Monitory Democracy* (Cambridge University Press 2018).

4 The first law on freedom of information was the 'Gracious Ordinance Regarding the Freedom of Writing and of the Press' enacted in 1766 by the Swedish King Adolphus Frederick, while the U.S. Freedom of Information Act 1966 is the first modern example of statute allowing access to governmental documents. See, respectively, Juha Mustonen (ed), 'The World's First Freedom of Information Act – Andres Chydenius' Legacy Today' <http://www.chydenius.net/pdf/worlds_first_foia.pdf>; Herbert N Foerstel, *Freedom of Information and the Right to Know – The Origins and Applications of the Freedom of Information Act* (Greenwood Press 1999).

5 Norberto Bobbio, *The Future of Democracy* (Richard Bellamy ed, Roger Griffin tr, University of Minnesota Press 1991).

democracy to be accountable to the electing democracy: in conclusion, to be really a counter-democracy.[6]

However, this account would be too simplistic, if one did not consider the role that legal norms and principles have to play to make transparency and people's counter-power possible. Digital technology cannot alone reveal the arcana of politics as a magic wand. This explains why, recently, a series of norms has been introduced in different jurisdictions in order to compel governmental actors to publish all their relevant information, proactively or on request, through digital devices.[7] In this way, the law recognises the fundamental role that digital technology plays in fostering transparency of public institutions and ultimately enhancing people's counter-power. The emergence of norms establishing citizens' right to digital information shows that the legal system has acknowledged the importance of digital technology as an instrument of power balancing.[8] Through the use of these technologies, the people have the possibility to act as watchdog of their public institutions and ultimately to perform an important role in their democracy.

In this sense, one can argue that such norms emerge to address the increasing power of states to control our digital lives. Of course, legal rules on transparency of public bodies do not limit the power of these entities directly. They cannot regulate the possibilities of the state to acquire, retain, and analyse an unprecedented number of data about our lives, for example. Nevertheless, one cannot deny that they provide ordinary citizens with the possibility to monitor what the state does. In a context where the digital revolution paradoxically makes the power of the state opaquer, and the life of individuals more transparent, these rules substantiate the idea of counter-democracy, creating a last-resort barrier to the arbitrariness of the state.[9] These norms entrust a limited counter-power to the people. One could argue that, in this way, they provide a partially new answer to the Platonic dilemma of who should control the guardians. The ruled, through the use of digital technology, becomes the safety net against potential anti-democratic deviance of the rulers. At the same time, the digital revolution seems to be exacerbating the old problem of state surveillance, and providing a new solution to it, by concretely substantiating people's possibility to control the conduct of public bodies and, if need be, to react against it.

6 See Rosanvallon, *La Contre-Démocratie. La politique à l'âge de la défiance* (n 3).

7 See, e.g., Article L311-1 of the Code des relations entre le public et l'administration, as modified by Article 3 of the Loi n° 2016-1321 du 7 octobre 2016 pour une République numérique (France); Article 2 of the Legislative Decree no. 33/2013 (Italy); Article 6, 10, 11, and 12 of Regulation (EC) 1049/2011 (EU).

8 On this point, see Pasquale Costanzo, 'Il fattore tecnologico e le sue conseguenze', *Costituzionalismo e globalizzazione* (2012) <http://www.associazionedeicostituzionalisti.it/convegno-annuale-aic-costituzionalismo-e-globalizzazione-salerno-23-24-novembre-2012-relazioni.html>.

9 See Stefano Rodotà, *Il diritto di avere diritti* (Laterza 2012) 337.

Due process online

In the digital society, states are not the only dominant actors whose power can directly affect individual rights. Private companies creating, managing, and selling digital technology products and service are the new Leviathan of the digital era. Laidlaw, specifically talking about Internet Service Providers, and in particular about search engines, rightly defines these actors as 'online gatekeepers'.[10] In the case of search engines, their power to control the access to information is apparent. Removing, or simply down-ranking a search result equates to being condemned to a digital inexistence, consequently restricting the right of individuals to access publicly available information.[11] However, more generally, Laidlaw's descriptor matches well the entire category of technology companies. By controlling the access to digital technology, they can shape the manner in which individuals use these instruments. In this way, they can potentially affect the exercise of our fundamental rights, not very differently from how nation-states do.[12]

In this context, a debate is emerging on whether, to what extent, and how to apply existing constitutional standards regulating the exercise of state power to these actors.[13] As seen in the previous chapter, constitutional systems emerged to limit the power of dominant actors and to safeguard the protection of fundamental rights of individuals. Their historical mission, however, aimed to address the power of the state. Existing constitutional norms do not articulate principles to delimit the power of the private entities. Yet, considering the similarity between the way states and private companies can affect individual rights, one is intellectually tempted to apply those principles to the private sector too.

From a legal point of view, private actors are not formally bound by international human rights.[14] It is the state's obligation to ensure that those

10 Emily B Laidlaw, 'Private Power, Public Interest: An Examination of Search Engine Accountability' (2008) 17 International Journal of Law and Information Technology 113; see also Emily B Laidlaw, *Regulating Speech in Cyberspace: Gatekeepers, Human Rights and Corporate Responsibility* (Cambridge University Press 2015).

11 Introna and Nissenbaum argue that 'to exist is to be indexed by a search engine' in Lucas D. Introna, Helen Nissenbaum, 'Shaping the Web: Why the Politics of Search Engines Matters' (2000) 16 The Information Society 169 at 171.

12 Chapter 2 has already illustrated the way in which these private companies can affect the exercise of individual rights. See Rikke Frank Jørgensen and Anja Møller Pedersen, 'Online Service Providers as Human Rights Arbiters' in Mariarosaria Taddeo and Luciano Floridi (eds), *The Responsibilities of Online Service Providers* (Springer 2017); Nicolas Suzor, *Lawless. The Secret Rules That Govern Our Digital Lives* (Cambridge University Press 2019).

13 See, ex multis, Suzor (n 12); Meryem Marzouki, 'The "Guarantee-Rights" for Realizing the Rule of Law' in Rikke Frank Jørgensen (ed), *Human Rights in the Global Information Society* (MIT Press 2006) 209 ff; Hans-W Micklitz and others (eds), *Constitutional Challenges in the Algorithmic Society* (Cambridge University Press 2022); Edoardo Celeste, Amélie Heldt and Clara Iglesias Keller (eds), *Constitutionalising Social Media* (Hart 2022).

14 See Jørgensen and Pedersen (n 12).

rights are also safeguarded by private entities. In 2008, the UN Special Representative John Ruggie issued a document establishing guiding principles on business and human rights, the so-called 'Ruggie principles'.[15] This text not only reiterates states' obligation to prevent human rights infringements perpetrated by private actors but also vigorously affirms private entities' responsibility to safeguard human rights. Although this document is not legally binding and therefore only imposes a moral duty on private actors, it witnesses the start of a legal reaction against the power of private entities.

In 2018, the UN Special Rapporteur on Freedom of Expression David Kaye issued a report on online content moderation, the activity of monitoring and managing user-generated content performed by online platforms.[16] This text reflects the bipartite structure of the Ruggie principles, which articulate norms for both states and private actors. On the one hand, Kaye highlights the major concerns of states' regulation of online content moderation. On the other hand, he affirms a series of principles for private companies. Interestingly, the standards that Kaye argues private companies should apply are all foundational principles of constitutional law rotating around the notion of due process, subsequently 'translated' – one could say – in the context of private actors.[17] The Special Rapporteur, for example, encourages private companies to ensure the 'legality' of their decisions, in other words, requiring that these actors define *a priori* their principles of content moderation and avoid arbitrary choices.[18] He also stresses the need to provide the possibility to appeal decisions, proposing the idea of

15 United Nations, 'Guiding Principles on Business and Human Rights' <https://www.ohchr.org/Documents/Publications/GuidingPrinciplesBusinessHR_EN.pdf>. This document elaborates a framework on business and human rights proposed by UN Special Representative Ruggie in 2008 and subsequently endorsed by the UN Human Rights Council.

16 David Kaye, 'Report of the Special Rapporteur on the Promotion and Protection of the Right to Freedom of Opinion and Expression - A/HRC/38/35' <https://documents-dds-ny.un.org/doc/UNDOC/GEN/G18/096/72/PDF/G1809672.pdf?OpenElement>.

17 For a historical analysis of due process rights, see Ronald Pennock and John W Chapman (eds), *Due Process* (New York University Press 1977); for a contextualised investigation of due process rights in contemporary society, see James Nickel, *Making Sense of Human Rights* (2nd edition, Wiley-Blackwell 2007) ch 7; Larry May, *Global Justice and Due Process* (Cambridge University Press 2011); Federico Fabbrini, *Fundamental Rights in Europe* (Oxford University Press 2014) ch 2; Giacinto della Cananea, *Due Process of Law Beyond the State: Requirements of Administrative Procedure* (Oxford University Press 2016). The field of automated decision-making offers another example of application of the notion of due process to private actors. See, Danielle Citron, 'Technological Due Process' (2008) 85 Washington University Law Review 1249; Danielle Keats Citron and Frank Pasquale, 'The Scored Society: Due Process for Automated Predictions' (2014) 89 Washington Law Review 1; Frank Pasquale, *The Black Box Society: The Secret Algorithms That Control Money and Information* (Harvard University Press 2015); Andrea Simoncini and Erik Longo, 'Fundamental Rights and the Rule of Law in the Algorithmic Society' in Hans-W Micklitz and others (eds), *Constitutional Challenges in the Algorithmic Society* (Cambridge University Press 2021).

18 Kaye (n 16), para. 46.

instituting an independent 'social media council'.[19] These two examples clearly show how these principles echo traditional constitutional standards developed to limit the power of the state, such as the rule of law, the right to appeal, and the separation of powers. Kaye's Report witnesses the ongoing trend to elaborate norms which translate existing constitutional principles in the context of online platforms.[20] This attempt to sensitise, what Kaye calls, 'platform law'[21] to foundational constitutional principles proves that the constitutional ecosystem is not inert. Conversely, this example shows how the latter has started reacting against the new challenges that the power of technology companies creates to the protection of individual rights.

Right to Internet access

Several times throughout human history, a new technology has become essential for the life of individuals. Today we could not imagine living without fridges, cars, or toothbrushes. These instruments allow us to eat, move, and clean ourselves, respectively. More generally, one could claim that they contribute to substantiating some of our fundamental rights, such as the right to life or to personal liberty. Yet, to date, there has been no debate to elaborate a right to a toothbrush. Conversely, there are ongoing discussions on a right to Internet access.[22] What is then the difference between the Internet and a toothbrush?

The digital technologies which allow us to access the Internet have significantly increased the possibility for individuals to exercise a broad range of fundamental rights which are based on the exchange of information. Today the Internet offers us an unprecedented possibility to communicate, to access information, to seek a job, to profess our faith, to organise a meeting or

19 Kaye (n 16), para. 58. Jørgensen and Pedersen (n 12) highlight the double role of tech companies as legislators and, at the same time, arbiters of their own platforms. See also Kate Klonick and Thomas Kadri, 'How to Make Facebook's "Supreme Court" Work' *The New York Times* (18 November 2018) <https://www.nytimes.com/2018/11/17/opinion/facebook-supreme-court-speech.html> accessed 20 November 2018 on the idea of creating a Facebook's 'Supreme Court'; 'Santa Clara Principles on Transparency and Accountability in Content Moderation' <https://santaclaraprinciples.org/images/scp-og.png> accessed 23 November 2018.

20 Cf. Suzor (n 12) who normatively stresses the need to translate existing constitutional principles in the context of online platforms.

21 Kaye (n 16), para. 1.

22 For a comprehensive account of the issues related to the right to Internet access, see Stephen Tully, 'A Human Right to Access the Internet? Problems and Prospects' (2014) 14 Human Rights Law Review 175; Paul De Hert and Dariusz Kloza, 'Internet (Access) as a New Fundamental Right. Inflating the Current Rights Framework?' (2012) 3 European Journal of Law and Technology; Tommaso Edoardo Frosini, 'The Internet Access as a Fundamental Right' (2013) 25 Federalismi.it; Matthias C Kettemann, *The Normative Order of the Internet: A Theory of Rule and Regulation Online* (Oxford University Press 2020) 287 ff.

a protest, to educate ourselves, etc. In contrast to other epochal inventions of the past, including other mass media invented in the last century, such as the radio or the television, digital technology plays a wide-ranging ancillary role in relation to fundamental rights. The television, the radio, the telephone all generated significant improvements in relation to our rights and in particular to freedom of expression. The television, for instance, amplified the possibility of ordinary people to receive information. The telephone allowed the mass to communicate simultaneously. However, the breadth of these changes has not attained the level of those produced by the advent of digital technology.

Metaphorically speaking, one could argue that the Internet has expanded the field of human action by creating a new space where individuals can act. Human interaction in the virtual dimension does not involve our physical bodies, but occurs through the exchange of data. We and our actions are expressed in transmitted and received digits. All our fundamental rights that involve a transmission of information are enhanced because digital technologies allow this exchange to occur with an unprecedented speed, easiness, and at a minimal cost. In other words, this implies that a higher number of individuals have the possibility to exercise some of their fundamental rights in an easier, more efficient, and cheaper way. Such effectiveness raises the standard at which we are used to exercising our fundamental rights. Seeking a job or accessing governmental information without the use of digital technology seem to be impossible, and this is true at least if one pretends the speed, costs, and efficiency analogous to those that the Internet would offer.

The Internet is now considered the *sine qua non* of the exercise of a range of fundamental rights. Its role has been normatively recognised even at constitutional level. Greece, amending its constitution in 2001, added a right 'to participate in the Information Society', entailing an obligation of the State to facilitate the access, production, exchange, and diffusion of electronically transmitted information.[23] The new Ecuadorian constitution of 2008 at Article 16.2 enshrined a right to 'universal access to information and communication technologies'.[24] The French *Conseil constitutionnel* and the Costa Rican *Sala Constitucional* recognised a right to connect to the Internet as springing from their respective constitutional frameworks.[25]

23 Article 5A of the Greek Constitution <http://www.hellenicparliament.gr/UserFiles/f3c70a23-7696-49db-9148-f24dce6a27c8/001-156%20aggliko.pdf> accessed 8 November 2018.

24 <http://pdba.georgetown.edu/Constitutions/Ecuador/english08.html> accessed 8 November 2018.

25 See, respectively, Conseil constitutionnel, decision n° 2009-580 DC du 10 juin 2009 <http://www.conseil-constitutionnel.fr/conseil-constitutionnel/root/bank/download/cc-2009580dc.pdf> accessed 8 November 2018; Sala Constitucional de la Corte Suprema de Justicia, sentencia n° 12790 de 30 de Julio de 2010 <https://www.poder-judicial.go.cr/salaconstitucional/index.php/servicios-publicos/759-10-012790> accessed 8 November 2018; cf. the more cautious approach adopted by the US Supreme Court in *Reno v. American*

According to more critical accounts, Internet access would not be an autonomous fundamental right. The Internet would merely play an instrumental role in relation to other existing rights and would not represent a right per se.[26] Moreover, existing formulations of fundamental rights in normative texts would be framed in such a general way that their exercise through digital technology instruments would not be excluded.[27] Yet, the previously mentioned examples of recognition of a right to Internet access and the ongoing debates demonstrate that even the higher level of accessibility and effectiveness of existing fundamental rights generated by the advent of digital technology affects the constitutional equilibrium and requires a series of adjustments. Demanding the recognition of a right to Internet access also means invoking a social right to obtain the necessary network infrastructure and an affordable access from the state;[28] a right to not be discriminated on the Internet, what is known under the name of net neutrality;[29] and, last, but not least, a right to media literacy.[30] These facets of the right to Internet access show that the enhancement of existing fundamental rights creates a series of other issues to be contemporaneously addressed. A positive alteration of the constitutional ecosystem is always an alteration, which requires targeted counteractions, such as the recognition of a series of rights related to Internet access, to be put in place.

Data protection

The first use of the word 'database' as a structured collection of data processed by a computer dates back to the 1960s.[31] Those years witnessed the rapid development of a new system for managing records: the automated

---

Civil Liberties Union, 521 U.S. 844 (1997) and *Packingham v. North Carolina*, 582 U.S. ___ (2017), No. 15-1194.

26 Vinton G Cerf, 'Internet Access Is Not a Human Right' *The New York Times* (4 January 2012) <https://www.nytimes.com/2012/01/05/opinion/internet-access-is-not-a-human-right.html> accessed 3 December 2018.

27 Hert and Kloza (n 22); see also Tully (n 22).

28 See Frosini (n 22).

29 See Luca Belli and Primavera De Filippi (eds), *Net Neutrality Compendium: Human Rights, Free Competition and the Future of the Internet* (Springer International Publishing 2016), ch. 2; Christopher T Marsden, *Net Neutrality: Towards a Co-Regulatory Solution* (Bloomsbury 2010); Milton Mueller and others, 'Net Neutrality as Global Principle for Internet Governance' (Social Science Research Network 2007) SSRN Scholarly Paper ID 2798314 <https://papers.ssrn.com/abstract=2798314> accessed 3 December 2018; cf. Christoph B Graber, 'Bottom-up Constitutionalism: The Case of Net Neutrality' (2016) 7 Transnational Legal Theory 524, who examines the possibility to consider net neutrality as an emerging fundamental right.

30 Council of Europe, 'Guide to human rights for Internet users', Recommendation CM/Rec(2014)6, <https://rm.coe.int/16804d5b31> accessed 8 November 2018.

31 Oxford English Dictionary Online, 'Database' <http://www.oed.com/view/Entry/47411> accessed 4 December 2018.

databank.[32] The advent of computing technologies allowed for the storage and retrieval of an unprecedented number of data at lower costs. Electronic communications networks increased the speed of transferring large amounts of information. The functioning of data management systems both in the public and in the private sector was significantly improved.

However, at the same time, a series of new risks related to the automated processing of data emerged.[33] Electronic databases could process data related to the private life of individuals, such as records on medical status, income, and social security or creditworthiness. Personal data, one would say today, are the digital projection of one person's physical life. Individuals could ignore the existence of these data, could be subject to decisions having significant effects on their life, and yet they could have no control on them.

National legislation addressing these issues emerged in Europe from the 1970s.[34] In 1973 and 1974, the Council of Europe adopted two resolutions 'on the protection of the privacy of individuals vis-à-vis electronic data banks', respectively, in relation to the private and the public sector.[35] From the 1980s, the issue of the compatibility of national legislation in a perspective of transnational transfer of data emerged. The OECD's Guidelines governing the protection of privacy and transborder flows of personal data of 1980 and the Council of Europe's Convention no. 108/1981 kicked-off a Europe-wide discussion on this issue that eventually led, in the mid-1990s, to the adoption of a European directive on data protection.[36] Remarkably, in 2000, the Charter of Nice, now renamed Charter of Fundamental Rights of the EU, established for the first time a right to data protection (Article 8) in a distinct provision from that enshrining the right to respect for private and family life (Article 7).[37]

This succinct and partial outline of European history of data protection law is an example of how, in less than half a century, the constitutional ecosystem reacted against novel challenges prompted by the development of digital technology.[38] Automated databanks generated new threats to the

32 See Hector Garcia-Molina, Jeffrey D Ullman and Jennifer Widom, *Database Systems: The Complete Book* (2 ed., Pearson 2008).

33 See Council of Europe, *Convention no. 108/1981 - Explanatory Report* <https://rm.coe.int/CoERMPublicCommonSearchServices/DisplayDCTMContent?documentId=09000016800ca434> accessed 4 December 2018.

34 See David H Flaherty, *Protecting Privacy in Surveillance Societies. The Federal Republic of Germany, Sweden, France, Canada, And the United States* (The University of North Carolina Press 1989).

35 Respectively Resolution (73) 22 and (74) 29. See Lee A Bygrave, *Data Privacy Law: An International Perspective* (Oxford University Press 2014).

36 See Bygrave (n 35).

37 Orla Lynskey, 'Deconstructing Data Protection: The "Added-Value" of a Right to Data Protection in the EU Legal Order' (2014) 63 International and Comparative Law Quarterly 569.

38 For a more exhaustive account, see Bygrave (n 35).

individual right to private life and to personal liberty in a multiplicity of ways, ranging from increased likelihood of intrusion into facts related to private life, to the possibility to be subject to automated decisions based on those information, to a lack of control on data concerning the individual. Automated databanks challenged pre-existing fundamental rights, but in a novel way. The response produced at constitutional level was the theorisation of a new right, which could be capable of addressing these issues.

The right to data protection, which conceptually derived from the right to privacy, is emerging as a distinct principle.[39] In particular, its ramifications are constantly developing. It is a right with multiple facets, which aims to prevent abuse of power by the data controllers and, at the same time, to empower the individual to control his personal data. As the recent adoption in Europe of the General Data Protection Regulation shows, there is still an ongoing process of elaboration of principles vis-à-vis the development of digital technology.[40] Contemporary society constantly changes and, consequently, so too does the set of norms which are supposed to preserve its foundational values.

Uneven elaboration

These four examples certainly represent a partial account of the normative counteractions currently emerging to face the challenges of digital technology. Nevertheless, they allow us to draw a series of conclusions.

Firstly, one can understand that the constitutional ecosystem has started reacting against all the alterations generated by the advent of digital technology in society. The affirmation of a right to access information related to state activities through digital devices can be read as a targeted response to the enhanced power of the state on individuals. The elaboration of norms applying basic principles of due process in the context of social media addresses the issue of the arbitrariness of power of private companies managing online platforms. The ongoing discussions on the opportunity to recognise a right to Internet access witness a willingness to recognise the essential role played by digital technology today as a necessary enabler of many fundamental rights. The conceptual emancipation of the right to data protection and the constant development of its multiple facets, finally, are an example of normative counteractions against the novel risks that digital technology has generated for our existing fundamental rights.

39 See Peter Blume, 'Data Protection and Privacy – Basic Concept in a Changing World' (2010) 56 Scandinavian Studies in Law 151; cf. from a US perspective David H Flaherty, 'On the Utility of Constitutional Rights to Privacy and Data Protection' (1991) 41 Case Western Reserve Law Review 831.

40 For a comprehensive commentary on the GDPR, see Denis Kelleher and Karen Murray, *EU Data Protection Law* (Bloomsbury Professional 2018).

Secondly, one can observe that the state of development of these normative counteractions, in terms of conceptual elaboration, is uneven. This circumstance can be related to two factors: firstly, the degree of normative 'emptiness' or 'fullness' of the context in which the alteration of the constitutional ecosystem occurs,[41] and, secondly, the novelty of the underlying issue.

In relation to the first factor, one can observe that there are contexts in which constitutional counteractions emerge to address an issue, which, to a certain extent, is already present in the 'analogue' society. In those circumstances, constitutional counteractions complement a pre-existing body of constitutional norms addressing a cognate issue. Therefore, since these contexts are normatively 'full', normative counteractions to digital technology issues may be more easily elaborated as an integral part of the legal system.

The emergence of norms establishing a right to access information about state activities *through digital technologies* is exemplary of this phenomenon. As we have seen, these norms aim to address the issue of the asymmetry of power between state and individuals. However, the relationship between state and individuals has been the central issue of constitutional law for centuries, and a normative apparatus aiming to achieve this aim already exists. This is a classic scenario of normative 'fullness', where the newly developed norm merely integrates an established block of rules by incorporating a technological element. States' obligation to publish information and allow individuals to access information *through digital devices* recognises the unparalleled role of digital technology in making state transparency effective. However, the existing set of constitutional norms have already laid down the rationale at the basis of the newly emerging counteraction. The new norm represents a digital renovation of an already established principle. Both these circumstances favour the conceptual definition of the new norm as an integral part of the legal system, as one can infer in our case from the fact that it was possible to find examples of legislation establishing a right to digital information.[42]

Conversely, the elaboration of norms articulating due process principles to be applied to online platforms occurs in a context of normative emptiness. Concepts such as due process, the rule of law and separation of powers have been conceived and formulated in relation to the power of the state.

41 This distinction has been inspired by an intervention by Professor Stefano Rodotà in the first meeting of the Italian Committee for the Internet's rights and duties. Rodotà distinguished the Italian legal context where he was asked to chair an ad hoc committee to draft a declaration of Internet rights and the Brazilian context where the Marco civil da Internet was adopted. The Italian legal system was considered normatively 'fuller' of norms regulating Internet related rights than the Brazilian one. The minute of the intervention, only in Italian language, is available at <http://www.camera.it/leg17/1175> accessed 6 December 2018.

42 See *supra* (n 7).

As we have seen, international human rights do not formally bind private actors. Therefore, when one, for instance, affirms that social media platforms should allow users to appeal decisions related to online content moderation, one is conceptually translating a facet of the principle of due process in a novel context, which is traditionally regulated by private contractual autonomy. This circumstance does not ease the elaboration of the new constitutional norm emerged to address an issue generated by the development of digital technology. In our case, for example, the contours of the constitutional counteraction which is seeking to apply due process principles in the context of online social platforms are not precisely defined. UN Special Rapporteur Kaye advanced suggestions and recommendations, which, especially in some cases, are not completely elaborated or are far from enjoying a universal consensus.[43]

A second factor that determines an uneven level of conceptual elaboration of the constitutional counteractions emerged so far is the novelty of the issue targeted by the norm. More novel issues generally show a lower level of definition of the normative counteraction. Looking at the examples presented above, this is apparent if one compares the degree of elaboration of the norms articulating the right to data protection and those concerning the right to Internet access. As previously seen, the socio-economic issues that led to the elaboration of rights protecting personal data date back to the 1960s. In the last 50 years, the value of data protection and the norms vested with the duty to defend its multiple articulations have progressively ripened. Conversely, the spreading of the Internet as an instrument of mass communication occurred only in the mid-1990s. The discussion about the key role of the Internet in exercising our fundamental rights consequently surfaced relatively not long ago. A consensus on the conceptual articulation of this right has not been reached yet, as the ongoing debates on the topic show.[44]

A third related observation concerns the overall status of the emergence of constitutional counteractions. Not only we can affirm that the conceptual elaboration of the constitutional counteractions emerged so far does not attain the same level of development, but also that it is generally unaccomplished. Even norms, such those related to the right to data protection, which show a high degree of conceptual elaboration, are subject to a constant discussion and are continually evolving.[45] The process of emergence of these constitutional counteractions does not terminate with their initial conceptual spring but is currently experiencing a phase of ripening, evolution, and adjustment.

43 See, e.g., *supra* in relation to the proposal of instituting an independent social media council.

44 See *supra* (n 22).

45 For instance, in Europe, the General Data Protection Regulation can be seen as the output of an ongoing phase of evolution of data protection norms. See Kelleher and Murray (n 39).

4 Norms beyond the state

A functional approach

When one talks about constitutional law in countries with a written constitution, it is instinctive to think of the solemn document, often called constitution, which receives a particular primary status in the legal system. The previous chapter has outlined four examples of normative counteractions emerging to address the challenges generated by digital technology. Namely, the development of a right to access information held by the state through digital means; the elaboration of norms ensuring due process principles when handling disputes concerning online content; the progressive affirmation of a right to Internet access, including a series of ancillary aspects that this principle implies; and, lastly, the evolution and consolidation of a right to data protection. Now, if one analyses more attentively these four examples, it is possible to notice that not all of these normative counteractions surfaced, at least from the outset, in constitutional instruments of primary rank, such as national constitutions. For instance, some of these normative counteractions emerged at the level of ordinary law, like those related to the right to data protection, and even in non-binding legal sources, like in the case of the recommendations on due process in online content moderation issued by the UN Special Rapporteur Kaye. However, although they are not formally enshrined in texts of constitutional rank, these norms have been included in the present analysis because they play a constitutional function. They aim to protect fundamental rights and to balance existing powers and are therefore part, *lato sensu*, of that body of norms that Chapter 2 called constitutional law.[1]

1 This functional-empirical approach is typical of the socio-legal approach to constitutionalism. For a brief, but clear overview of the main differences between a formal and a functional approach to constitutionalism, see Christoph B Graber, 'Bottom-up Constitutionalism: The Case of Net Neutrality' (2016) 7 Transnational Legal Theory 524. Similarly, a functional approach is also adopted in the field of regulatory governance: see, Colin Scott, 'Regulating Constitutions' in Christine Parker and others (eds), *Regulating Law* (Oxford University Press 2004). Even those who espouse a more formal approach have recognised the 'para-constitutional' value of these norms. See, e.g., Giorgio Resta, 'Il Diritto

DOI: 10.4324/9781003256908-4

This functional approach allows us to identify constitutional patterns beyond what is formally considered as 'constitutional'. One then realises that the constitutional panorama is much wider. Normative counteractions to digital technology issues not only emerge, within the legal system, at the level of norms of primary rank but also at a lower level.[2] Moreover, interestingly, if one fully embraces this functional perspective, one could go even further. It is possible to discover that, in relation to digital technology issues, constitutional counteractions also emerge in novel contexts, where legal rules are set by unconventional actors. The report on due process in online content moderation issued by the UN special rapporteur Kaye offers us a clue of this circumstance. As we have seen, Kaye not only addresses a series of recommendations to states but also to online platforms. In this way, he acknowledges the normative role that private companies play in today's digital society. If one values more the constitutional function played by legal rules, rather than their form, it is possible to understand that, in the digital society, constitutional norms are not only issued by the state but also by private actors.[3]

Traditionally, the production of constitutional norms is associated with the state dimension. The state is the dominant actor against which constitutional norms are created and, at the same time, the ultimate guarantor of the constitutional order. Constitutional law can be seen as an act of self-restraint of the state.[4] To visualise this process, different scholars evoked Jon Elster's metaphor of Ulysses binding himself to the mast to hear the songs of the Sirens.[5] However, in the digital society, private companies emerge besides the state as new dominant actors. Castell talks of

---

Alla Protezione Dei Dati Personali' in Francesco Cardarelli, Salvatore Sica and Vincenzo Zeno-Zencovich (eds), *Il codice dei dati personali. Temi e problemi* (Giuffrè 2004). Resta explains to what extent an ordinary law, such as the Italian code of data protection law, can play a constitutional role in establishing the fundamental right of every individual to protection of her personal data.

2 On the same point, see Peer Zumbansen, 'Comparative, Global and Transnational Constitutionalism: The Emergence of a Transnational Legal-Pluralist Order' (2012) 1 Global Constitutionalism 16, 50.

3 See Gunther Teubner, *Constitutional Fragments: Societal Constitutionalism and Globalization* (Oxford University Press 2012); Gunther Teubner, 'Societal Constitutionalism; Alternatives to State-Centred Constitutional Theory?' in Christian Joerges, Inger-Johanne Sand and Gunther Teubner (eds), *Transnational Governance and Constitutionalism. International Studies in the Theory of Private Law* (Hart 2004).

4 See Gunther Teubner and Anna Beckers, 'Expanding Constitutionalism' (2013) 20 Indiana Journal of Global Legal Studies 523; cf. András Sajó and Renáta Uitz, *The Constitution of Freedom: An Introduction to Legal Constitutionalism* (Oxford University Press 2017) 41 ff.

5 See Jon Elster, *Ulysses Unbound: Studies in Rationality, Precommitment, and Constraints* (Cambridge University Press 2000) ch 2; see also Teubner and Beckers (n 4); Sajó and Uitz (n 4).

an 'institutional neo-medievalism'.[6] The Westphalian vision based on the monopoly of the power of the state in its own territory is no longer the only existing paradigm. Today people also act in a virtual dimension, which is global, transnational, and parcelled out in private fiefs owned by multinational companies. The power of these private actors has to be limited; the rights of individuals have to be protected. The quintessential mission of constitutional law remains the same, but norms are unavoidably produced in, and for different contexts, also beyond the state dimension.[7]

By maintaining a constitutionalist perspective anchored to the role of nation-states, one would unavoidably neglect a significant part of this broader picture. Contemporary constitutional law becomes necessarily more 'hybrid'.[8] Constitutional norms addressing digital technology issues also surface in the private sphere. Civil society declarations emerge to reclaim new fundamental rights that are not yet enshrined in national constitutions. Multinational companies enact legislation for their virtual domains as legislators do in their own states. Private arbitrators develop autonomously from national courts their own case-law on issues affecting some of our fundamental rights. In essence, constitutional norms generated in the state dimension are matched by counteractions emerging beyond the state.

Without pretending to provide an exhaustive mapping of this phenomenon, the following sections will engage in the analysis of three main pairs of state-centric and non-state sources of constitutional counteractions.[9]

6 Manuel Castells, *The Rise of the Network Society* (2nd edn, Blackwell 2000); see Stefano Rodotà, *Il diritto di avere diritti* (Laterza 2012).

7 This phenomenon does not characterise exclusively the digital context, but affects more generally the contemporary globalised society. On the same point, see Colin Scott, Fabrizio Cafaggi, and Linda Senden, 'The Conceptual and Constitutional Challenge of Transnational Private Regulation' (2011) 38 Journal of Law and Society 1; Gunther Teubner, 'Global Private Regimes: Neo-Spontaneous Law and Dual Constitution of Autonomous Sectors?' in Karl-Heinz Ladeur (ed), *Public Governance in the Age of Globalization* (Routledge 2004).

8 See Andrea Simoncini and Erik Longo, 'Fundamental Rights and the Rule of Law in the Algorithmic Society' in Hans-W Micklitz and others (eds), *Constitutional Challenges in the Algorithmic Society* (Cambridge University Press 2021) 41; see also Matthias C Kettemann, *The Normative Order of the Internet: A Theory of Rule and Regulation Online* (Oxford University Press 2020), who analyses in detail the plurality of the Internet legal order.

9 I first provided a mapping of these sources of constitutional counteractions in Edoardo Celeste, 'Digital Constitutionalism: Mapping the Constitutional Response to Digital Technology's Challenges' (2018) HIIG Discussion Paper Series No 2018-02 <https://papers.ssrn.com/abstract=3219905> accessed 23 August 2018; for a further updated version, see Edoardo Celeste, 'Digital Constitutionalism: A New Systematic Theorisation' (2019) 33 International Review of Law, Computers & Technology 76.

Constitutions and declarations

Our first pair juxtaposes national and transnational constitutions with, what has been called, Internet bills of rights.

Constitutional charters

As seen in Chapter 2, the term 'constitution' can have multiple meanings. This section employs the term constitution in a formal sense, as the written document establishing the fundamental norms for the organisation of a polity. Traditionally, these texts are the constitutional instruments par excellence, and, in many legal systems, are considered as the natural 'riverbed' of constitutional norms. It is therefore not surprising to discover that constitutional counteractions to digital technology issues emerge in national constitutions.

The previous chapter has illustrated four examples of normative counteractions, respectively related to the right to digital information, due process online, the right to Internet access, and the right to data protection. We have seen how each of these counteractions addresses a kind of alteration of the constitutional equilibrium produced by the advent of digital technology.[10] The present section presents a series of cases that illustrate how these counteractions can at times emerge at the level of national constitutions. As we will see, they usually take the form of amendments or integrations to these texts.

Article 6(A)(V) of the Mexican Constitution, for instance, was amended in 2014 to introduce a new paragraph establishing a right to digital information, which reads:

> Government agencies (obligors) shall record and keep their documents in updated administrative files, and shall disclose, *through electronic media*, the complete and updated information about the use of public resources and their management indexes so that the information allows accountability procedures in regard to the fulfilment of their objectives and the results of their performance.[11]

In 2001, a constitutional reform added to the Greek Constitution of 1975 an Article 5A establishing a right to Internet access. It provides that:

> All persons have the right to participate in the Information Society. Facilitation of access to electronically transmitted information, as well as of the production, exchange and diffusion thereof, constitutes an

10 See *supra* Chapter 3.
11 Emphasis added. An English translation of the Mexican Constitution is available at <http://www.wipo.int/wipolex/en/text.jsp?file_id=454770> accessed 13 December 2018.

> obligation of the State, always in observance of the guarantees of articles 9, 9A and 19.[12]

Since its amendment in 1997, Article 35 of the Portuguese Constitution enshrines an autonomous right to protection of personal data processed through electronic means, precisely stipulating that:

> 1. Every citizen shall possess the right to access to all computerised data that concern him, to require that they be corrected and updated, and to be informed of the purpose for which they are intended, all as laid down by law. 2. The law shall define the concept of personal data, together with the terms and conditions applicable to its automatised treatment and its linkage, transmission and use, and shall guarantee its protection, particularly by means of an independent administrative body. 3. Computers shall not be used to treat data concerning philosophical or political convictions, party or trade union affiliations, religious beliefs, private life or ethnic origins, save with the express consent of the data subject, with authorisation provided for by law and with guarantees of non discrimination, or for the purpose of processing statistical data that cannot be individually identified. 4. Third-party access to personal data shall be prohibited, save in exceptional cases provided for by law. 5. The allocation of a single national number to any citizen shall be prohibited. 6. Everyone shall be guaranteed free access to public-use computer networks, and the law shall define both the rules that shall apply to cross-border data flows and the appropriate means for protecting personal data and such other data as may justifiably be safeguarded in the national interest. 7. Personal data contained in manual files shall enjoy the same protection as that provided for in the previous paragraphs, as laid down by law.[13]

So far, we have considered only texts of national constitutions as a vehicle of constitutional counteractions. However, targeted counteractions to digital technology challenges are also observable in *trans*-national constitutions. Today, it is apparent that national legal systems are integrated in different ways within supranational legal orders. As some scholars have observed, transnational constitutions to a certain extent work similarly to national constitutions by establishing standards of protection for individual rights

12 An English translation of the Greek Constitution is available at <http://www.hellenicparliament.gr/UserFiles/f3c70a23-7696-49db-9148-f24dce6a27c8/001-156%20aggliko.pdf> accessed 13 December 2018.

13 An English translation of the Portuguese Constitution is available at <http://www.en.parlamento.pt/Legislation/CRP/Constitution7th.pdf > accessed 13 December 2018.

and limiting the power of transnational institutions.[14] Certainly, the dynamics that these constitutional instruments address are more complex, due to the plurality of dominant actors interacting in multiple layers of the legal order. Nevertheless, the nation-state remains the basic unit of these entities, and the rationale underlying the norms that these texts establish is easily comparable to that of national constitutions.

As examples of constitutional counteractions emerging in transnational constitutions, following the illustrations of rights given at the beginning of this chapter, one can mention Article 5(3) of the Aarhus Convention of 1998, binding all EU member states, which establishes a right to digital information related to environmental matters[15]; Article 9 of the UN Convention on the Rights of Persons with Disabilities adopted in 2006, which stipulates a right of disabled persons to access information and communications technologies[16]; and Article 1 of Council of Europe Convention no. 108/1981, which recognises a right to protection of personal data processed by automated means.[17]

Limits of constitutions

After this second series of examples of normative counteractions, one would have noticed that we have not mentioned any provisions of national or transnational constitutions providing for due process rights in the online sphere. As seen before, the UN Special Rapporteur Kaye, in his report on online

14 See, e.g., Anne Peters, *Elemente einer Theorie der Verfassung Europas.* (Duncker & Humblot 2001); Deborah Z Cass, *The Constitutionalization of the World Trade Organization: Legitimacy, Democracy, and Community in the International Trading System* (Oxford University Press 2005); Ingolf Pernice, 'The Treaty of Lisbon: Multilevel Constitutionalism in Action' (2009) 15 Columbia Journal of European Law 349.

15 "Each Party shall ensure that environmental information progressively becomes available *in electronic databases* which are easily accessible to the public through *public telecommunications networks*." (emphasis added). Full text of the Convention is available at <https://www.unece.org/fileadmin/DAM/env/pp/documents/cep43e.pdf> accessed 13 December 2018.

16 "To enable persons with disabilities to live independently and participate fully in all aspects of life, States Parties shall take appropriate measures to ensure to persons with disabilities access, on an equal basis with others, to the physical environment, to transportation, to information and communications, including information and communications technologies and systems, and to other facilities and services open or provided to the public, both in urban and in rural areas. [...]". Full text of the Convention is available at <https://www.un.org/development/desa/disabilities/convention-on-the-rights-of-persons-with-disabilities/article-9-accessibility.html> accessed 13 December 2018.

17 "The purpose of this Convention is to secure in the territory of each Party for every individual, whatever his nationality or residence, respect for his rights and fundamental freedoms, and in particular his right to privacy, with regard to automatic processing of personal data relating to him ("data protection")." Full text of the Convention is available at <https://www.coe.int/en/web/conventions/full-list/-/conventions/rms/0900001680078b37> accessed 14 December 2018.

content moderation, directly addressed online platforms encouraging them to adopt rules in this regard. In fact, national or transnational constitutions are not set to provide mechanisms to affirm due process principles in the context of online content moderation. These instruments emerge in a dimension in which the nation-state is the dominant actor. They establish principles to limit the power of nation-states or other derived entities on individuals. They focus on a specific polity and only apply in a circumscribed territory. Their potential reach is therefore limited in comparison with the global and privately dominated digital environment.

Paul Berman recognised that, in the digital environment, private actors play a significant regulatory role.[18] They can, in fact, directly shape the architecture of the products and services they manage and sell by regulating the code of their software.[19] He argued that these actors should be subject to the values established by the constitution, which, in Berman's case, is that of the United States. In this way, national constitutional principles could represent new benchmarks to evaluate the behaviour of private actors. According to the American scholar, constitutional law is the legal source which is naturally inclined to establish general principles. He excluded that a similar role could be played at lower normative level, for example by ordinary legislation. According to Berman, this implies that the scope of application of constitutional law should be extended as to encompass the conduct of private actors. Therefore, in practice, he advocated in favour of overtaking the so-called 'state action doctrine', which, in the United States, limits the scope of application of the constitution to the conduct of public actors.

The normative nature of Berman's claims confirms that, in relation to digital technology issues, national and transnational constitutions can only provide a 'partial' answer.[20] Nicolas Suzor offered a more realistic account of the constitutional role of these instruments in a transnational and privately dominated context.[21] Firstly, he argued that national constitutional law can be used as a reference point to informally evaluate the conduct of

18 Paul Berman, 'Cyberspace and the State Action Debate: The Cultural Value of Applying Constitutional Norms to "Private" Regulation' (2000) 71 University of Colorado Law Review 1263; see also Celeste, 'Digital Constitutionalism' (n 9).

19 See Lawrence Lessig, *Code: And Other Laws of Cyberspace, Version 2.0* (Basic Books 2006); Joel Reidenberg, 'Lex Informatica: The Formulation of Information Policy Rules through Technology' (1998) 76 Texas Law Review 553.

20 Lars Viellechner, 'Constitutionalism as a Cipher: On the Convergence of Constitutionalist and Pluralist Approaches to the Globalization of Law' (2012) 4 Goettingen Journal of International Law 599; see also Anne Peters, 'The Globalization of State Constitutions' in Janne E Nijman and André Nollkaemper (eds), *New Perspectives on the Divide Between National and International Law* (Oxford University Press 2007).

21 Nicolas Suzor, 'The Role of the Rule of Law in Virtual Communities' (2010) 25 Berkeley Technology Law Journal 1817; see also Nicolas Suzor, 'Digital Constitutionalism and the Role of the Rule of Law in the Governance of Virtual Communities' (phd, Queensland University of Technology 2010) <https://eprints.qut.edu.au/37636/> accessed 30 August 2018.

private actors. Secondly, he claimed that constitutional values should inform states' ordinary law. As the next paragraph will show, Suzor contends that state law plays a crucial role in setting the boundaries of private autonomy. Therefore, constitutional law would only indirectly affect the power of private actors through state ordinary law.

Internet bills of rights

It is in this particular context, where national and transnational constitutions seem to lack power, or to give up pursuing their mission, that, interestingly, one can observe the emergence of a series of similar normative counteractions emerging beyond the state dimension. In relation to our example of due process online, one can mention, for instance, the publication in 2018 of 'The Santa Clara Principles on Transparency and Accountability in Content Moderation'.[22] This document articulates three minimal principles that private companies performing online content moderation should respect, and it represents the output of a series of conferences gathering NGOs and academics. This example is not isolated. More generally, one can observe that, over the last years, several kinds of civil society groups issued declarations to reclaim the respect of individual rights in the digital environment, especially by private actors such as online platforms.[23] These documents, which the present work has generally called 'Internet bills of rights', are neither legally binding nor enforceable; neither the product of democratic deliberation nor the output of institutionalised groups. Yet, there is evidence suggesting us to pair them with national and transnational constitutions.[24]

Firstly, the titles of these documents clearly evoke the constitutional dimension. One can mention the 'Charter of Fundamental Digital Rights of

22 'Santa Clara Principles on Transparency and Accountability in Content Moderation' <https://santaclaraprinciples.org/images/scp-og.png> accessed 23 November 2018.

23 The most comprehensive dataset of these documents is available online on the website of the Mapping Global Media Policy Project: <http://www.globalmediapolicy.net/node/15288> accessed 17 December 2018. For other comprehensive reviews of the texts, see Edoardo Celeste and others, 'Digital Constitutionalism: In Search of a Content Governance Standard' in Edoardo Celeste, Amélie Heldt and Clara Iglesias Keller (eds), *Constitutionalising Social Media* (Hart 2022); Rolf H Weber, *Principles for Governing the Internet: A Comparative Analysis* (UNESCO 2015) <https://unesdoc.unesco.org/ark:/48223/pf0000234435>; Lex Gill, Dennis Redeker and Urs Gasser, 'Towards Digital Constitutionalism? Mapping Attempts to Craft an Internet Bill of Rights' (2015) Berkman Center Research Publication No 2015-15 <https://papers.ssrn.com/abstract=2687120> accessed 30 August 2018; Sarah Oates, 'Towards an Online Bill of Rights' in Luciano Floridi (ed), *The Onlife Manifesto: Being Human in a Hyperconnected Era* (Springer 2015).

24 Gill, Redeker and Gasser (n 23) 22–23.

the EU',[25] the 'Magna Carta for the Digital Age',[26] or the 'Declaration of Internet Rights',[27] just to make some examples. Secondly, these texts employ the characteristic jargon of constitutions. For instance, one can see introductory paragraphs called 'preamble', sentences generally referred to 'everyone' or to 'all humans', and a widespread use of modal verbs such as 'must' or 'shall'.[28] Thirdly, beyond their 'constitutional tone',[29] one can observe that these documents also resemble constitutions with regard to their content. They articulate rights of individuals and establish obligations, as constitutions do. In these texts, one can find all the four categories of norms that we have mentioned before as examples of constitutional counteractions to digital technology issues. The APC Internet Rights Charter, for instance, provides a right to digital information at point 3.2, which reads:

> National and local government, and publicly-funded international organisations, must ensure transparency and accountability by placing publicly relevant information that they produce and manage in the public domain. They should ensure that this information is disseminated online using compatible and open formats and is accessible to people using older computers and slow internet connections.[30]

The Santa Clara Principles on Transparency and Accountability in Content Moderation offer an example of due process rights online, when establishing that "[c]ompanies should provide a meaningful opportunity for timely appeal of any content removal or account suspension".[31] Article 2 of the Declaration of Internet Rights presents an articulated provision on the right to Internet access:

1 Access to the Internet is a fundamental right of all persons and a condition for their individual and social development.
2 Every person shall have the same right to access the Internet on equal terms, using appropriate and up-to-date technologies that remove all economic and social barriers.

25 <https://digitalcharta.eu/wp-content/uploads/Digital_Charter_english_2018.pdf> accessed 17 December 2018.
26 <https://www.bl.uk/my-digital-rights/magna-carta-2015> accessed 17 December 2018.
27 'Declaration of Internet Rights' <http://www.camera.it/application/xmanager/projects/leg17/commissione_internet/testo_definitivo_inglese.pdf> accessed 17 December 2018.
28 See, e.g., 'Charter of Human Rights and Principles for the Internet' <http://internetrightsandprinciples.org/site/wp-content/uploads/2018/10/IRPC_english_5thedition.pdf> accessed 17 December 2018.
29 Edoardo Celeste, 'Terms of Service and Bills of Rights: New Mechanisms of Constitutionalisation in the Social Media Environment?' (2019) 33 International Review of Law, Computers & Technology 122.
30 'APC Internet Rights Charter' <https://www.apc.org/en/pubs/about-apc/apc-internet-rights-charter> accessed 17 December 2018.
31 'Santa Clara Principles on Transparency and Accountability in Content Moderation' (n 22).

3 The fundamental right to Internet access must be ensured with respect to its substantive prerequisites, not only as the mere possibility of connecting to the Internet.
4 Access shall include freedom of choice with regard to devices, operating systems, and applications, including distributed software.
5 Public institutions shall take the necessary measures to overcome all forms of digital divide, including those created by gender, economic condition, or a situation of personal vulnerability or disability.

Lastly, point no. 5 of the 10 Internet Rights and Principles recognises a right to protection of personal data specifically processed online, which says:

> Everyone has the right to privacy online. This includes freedom from surveillance, the right to use encryption, and the right to online anonymity. Everyone also has the right to data protection, including control over personal data collection, retention, processing, disposal and disclosure.[32]

As one can see, these documents manifestly present constitutional features. Even if they are not legally binding, one can consider them as constitutional counteractions because they are contributing to the normative discourse on which rights and obligations we should have, today, in the digital age. These texts are worth analysing besides national and transnational constitutions not because they are 'wannabe constitutions' themselves, one could say, but because, as Gill, Redeker, and Gasser argue, they are part of a 'proto-constitutional discourse'.[33] As we will explain in detail in Chapter 8, they show us which rules are missing from the existing constitutional ecosystem and nourish a debate on how fundamental rights and principles should be re-elaborated in light of the mutated digital society.

Public and private legislators

Our second pair examines in tandem two kinds of 'ordinary' law, showing that 'constitutional' counteractions to digital technology issues also emerge at this level. On the one hand, the laws adopted by 'public' legislators, be they based at national or transnational level, and, on the other hand, what can be called *lex digitalis*, the rules established by the 'private' legislators of the digital world, i.e. by technology companies.

32 'Charter of Human Rights and Principles for the Internet' (n 28) 7.
33 Gill, Redeker and Gasser (n 23) 2.

Advantages of ordinary law

With laws of public legislators, this work refers to what in the national context would be called ordinary law, i.e. acts normally passed by a parliament. In a transnational environment, the equivalent normative instruments are also adopted by a representative assembly and generally occupy an intermediary position in the hierarchy of legal sources between norms of primary rank, such as founding treaties, and implementing legislation, which is only applicable to specific addressees.

In principle, both these categories of legal instruments do not have a vocation to deal with constitutional issues. As already seen, they are regarded by part of the scholarship as a means to regulate daily-life issues, rather than to enshrine long-term foundational principles for the organisation of society.[34] Yet, ordinary law has been often used as a vehicle of constitutional values. For example, Jean Carbonnier, one of the most renowned French law professors of the twentieth century, defined the *Code civil* as the French "civil constitution", a text condensing, from a sociological point of view, the main constitutive ideas of French society.[35] Moreover, beyond its substantive content, ordinary law paradoxically presents several advantages in playing a constitutional function in comparison with constitutions themselves. Firstly, ordinary law is generally easier to adopt and to modify than constitutional texts. It can be passed by simple parliamentary majority and amended by subsequently adopting an act of the same legal value. Secondly, such easiness of adoption and flexibility allow national and transnational bodies to introduce and change ordinary law more quickly. Of course, timeliness is a quintessential element when regulation of fast-changing technologies is concerned. Thirdly, and lastly, contrary to constitutions, ordinary law has the vocation to apply to private actors. According to some scholars, this feature would make ordinary law a very suitable constitutional instrument for the context of the digital society.

In this regard, Brian Fitzgerald acknowledged that, in the digital age, the exercise of power is no longer exclusively in the hands of public actors.[36] Private actors, in fact, control the code of their own software, and, in this way, regulate the behaviour of all individuals using their digital technology products and services.[37] This peculiar setting would require, according

34 For example, for a negative account on the possibility that ordinary law could a constitutional function in the digital environment, see Berman (n 18).

35 Jean Carbonnier, 'Le Code civil' in Pierre Nora (ed), *Les lieux de mémoire*, vol 2 (Gallimard 1986); see also Pierre Mazeaud, 'Le code civil et la conscience collective française' (2004) 110 Pouvoirs 152.

36 Brian Fitzgerald, 'Software as Discourse? A Constitutionalism for Information Society' (1999) 24 Alternative Law Journal 144; Brian Fitzgerald, 'Software as Discourse? The Challenge for Information Law' (2000) 22 European Intellectual Property Review 47; see also Celeste, 'Digital Constitutionalism' (n 9).

37 See Lessig (n 19); Reidenberg (n 19). See also *infra* the section 'Code as a constitution'.

to Fitzgerald, a mixed governance structure.[38] Private actors' self-regulation should be subject to the oversight of public institutions, which still detain coercive power. Digital society would need that action of balancing, which is typical of the idea of constitutionalism. This time, however, not only involving public power, but mediating between public and private actors. Fitzgerald therefore talks of an 'informational constitutionalism', and, interestingly, he does not vest national constitutions with this function of regulating the relationship between public and private powers.[39] He considers that states' private law, such as intellectual property law, contract law, competition law, and privacy law, would be instead the most suitable 'constitutional' instrument to carry out this task.

Following Fitzgerald, Nicolas Suzor too considered contract law as the constitutional principles of virtual communities.[40] These entities would be governed by a set of unilaterally self-established contractual norms, which are simply accepted by their users. State's contract law, however, would intervene in regulating private autonomy to prevent virtual communities' rules from infringing core values of the state. As seen before, however, Suzor ultimately entrusts a role of guidance of state private law to constitutional principles. Ordinary law would not be autonomous in this constitutional task but would need to be complemented and informed by core values of national constitutions.

Some examples

Fitzgerald's and Suzor's positions manifestly speak to the ability of ordinary law to play a constitutional role vis-à-vis the power of private actors. This quality, combined with, as we have seen, a higher degree of adaptability and a faster process of adoption in comparison with national and transnational constitutions, paradoxically make ordinary law a very effective source of constitutional counteractions to face digital society issues, also with regard to state power and individual rights. At this level, one can identify examples of all the four types of counteractions that have been mentioned at the beginning of the chapter.

For instance, in 2016, the *Loi pour une République numérique* introduced in France the obligations for the public administration to publish online all information requested by single citizens as an exercise of their right to

38 Fitzgerald, 'Software as Discourse? A Constitutionalism for Information Society' (n 36); Fitzgerald, 'Software as Discourse? The Challenge for Information Law' (n 36).

39 Cf. Berman (n 18).

40 Suzor, 'The Role of the Rule of Law in Virtual Communities' (n 21); see also Suzor, 'Digital Constitutionalism and the Role of the Rule of Law in the Governance of Virtual Communities' (n 21).

information.[41] At transnational level, one can mention EU Regulation no. 1049/2001, regarding public access to European institutions' documents, which imposes electronic communications as the primary form of contact and exchange of information.[42]

The debated Act to Improve Law Enforcement on Social Networks (*Gesetz zur Verbesserung der Rechtsdurchsetzung in sozialen Netzwerken* or, shorter, *NetzDG*), adopted in 2017 in Germany to combat hate speech and fake news on social media, is a rare example of ordinary legislation requiring, among other things, social media platforms to enhance their transparency in relation to content removed and complaints received (Section 2) as well as to put in place and "an effective and transparent procedure for handling complaints about unlawful content" (Section 3), imposing in this way minimal due process rights in the social media context.[43]

Articles 4 and 7 of the Brazilian law known as 'Marco Civil da Internet',[44] adopted in 2014, recognise Internet access as an essential right.[45] While, at transnational level, one can cite the recent adoption of Directive (EU) 2016/2102 on the accessibility of the websites and mobile applications of public sector bodies.[46]

The EU General Data Protection Regulation, together with its national complementing legislation, is a perfect example of constitutional counteraction emerging at transnational and national level to face the potential increase of fundamental rights violations, in this case concerning the

41 Article L311-1 of the Code des relations entre le public et l'administration, as modified by article 3 of the Loi n° 2016-1321 du 7 octobre 2016 pour une République numérique, available at <https://www.legifrance.gouv.fr/> accessed 19 December 2018.

42 See articles 6, 10, 11, and 12 of Regulation (EC) 1049/2001, available at <http://eur-lex.europa.eu/legal-content/EN/TXT/HTML/?uri=CELEX:32001R1049&from=EN> accessed 19 December 2018.

43 An English translation of the law is available at <https://germanlawarchive.iuscomp.org/?p=1245> accessed 19 December 2019.

44 Lei n° 12.965/2014, <http://www.planalto.gov.br/> accessed 19 December 2019.

45 Article 4 reads: "The discipline of internet use in Brazil aims to promote: I – the right of all to access the internet; […]"; Article 7 reads: "The access to the internet is essential to the exercise of citizenship, and the following rights are guaranteed to the users: […]". An English translation of the act is available at <https://www.publicknowledge.org/assets/uploads/documents/APPROVED-MARCO-CIVIL-MAY-2014.pdf> accessed 19 December 2018

46 In particular, Article 1 of the Directive states: "In order to improve the functioning of the internal market, this Directive aims to approximate the laws, regulations and administrative provisions of the Member States relating to the accessibility requirements of the websites and mobile applications of public sector bodies, thereby enabling those websites and mobile applications to be more accessible to users, in particular to persons with disabilities". Text of the directive is available at <http://eur-lex.europa.eu/legal-content/EN/TXT/HTML/?uri=CELEX:32016L2102&from=EN> accessed 19 December 2018.

right to data protection, which are generated by the development of digital technology.[47]

Lex digitalis

As emerges from the reflections of Fitzgerald and Suzor, state law does not detain a monopoly in regulating the digital environment. Private actors, which manage and sell digital technology products and services, also play a significant role. Within their digital 'fiefs',[48] private companies concentrate in their hands an enormous power. They are at the same time legislators, executors, and, as we will better see in the next section, arbiters of their own rules.[49]

The law established by these private legislators, which one could generally call, *lex digitalis*[50] – or, in relation to specific actors, such as social media platforms, 'platform law'[51], or, even more specifically, '*lex Facebook*',[52] '*lex Google*', etc. – shapes the way in which people can behave in the digital environment. More and more individuals use digital technology instruments to exercise their fundamental rights, such as expressing their opinion, acquiring information, seeking a job, or professing their faith. The *lex digitalis* therefore unavoidably affects the way in which these fundamental rights can be exercised.

Interestingly, since the legal norms elaborated by these private legislators are a very effective and direct regulatory instrument of the digital dimension, they can also play a constitutional function better than other legal instruments. As previously seen, Berman hoped that national constitutional law would directly apply to private actors, but this was a normative claim, since in the United States, the state action doctrine inescapably prevents this possibility.[53] Both Fitzgerald and Suzor praised the constitutional role

47 Regulation (EU) 2016/679 on the protection of natural persons with regard to the processing of personal data and on the free movement of such data, and repealing Directive 95/46/EC, <http://eur-lex.europa.eu/legal-content/EN/TXT/HTML/?uri=CELEX:32016R0679> accessed 19 December 2018.

48 See Bruce Schneier, 'Power in the Age of the Feudal Internet' (2013) MIND 16.

49 See Nicolas Suzor, *Lawless. The Secret Rules That Govern Our Digital Lives* (Cambridge University Press 2019); Rikke Frank Jørgensen and Anja Møller Pedersen, 'Online Service Providers as Human Rights Arbiters' in Mariarosaria Taddeo and Luciano Floridi (eds), *The Responsibilities of Online Service Providers* (Springer 2017).

50 Cf. Gunther Teubner and Andreas Fischer-Lescano, 'Regime-Collisions: The Vain Search for Legal Unity in the Fragmentation of Global Law' (2004) 25 Michigan Journal of International Law 999; Reidenberg (n 19); Lee A Bygrave, 'Lex Facebook', *Internet Governance by Contract* (Oxford University Press 2015).

51 David Kaye, 'Report of the Special Rapporteur on the Promotion and Protection of the Right to Freedom of Opinion and Expression - A/HRC/38/35' <https://documents-dds-ny.un.org/doc/UNDOC/GEN/G18/096/72/PDF/G1809672.pdf?OpenElement>.

52 Bygrave (n 50).

53 Berman (n 18).

of state private law in setting the outer limits of private autonomy, but at the same time they admitted the necessity of a mixed governance system.[54] Suzor went even beyond, recognising that private self-regulation itself can also have a constitutional potential. He described the terms of service of social media as 'constitutional documents in that they are integral to the way our shared social spaces are constituted and governed'.[55] These constitutional instruments, according to Suzor, would not be perfect:

> Like constitutional documents, Terms of Service grant powers, but unlike constitutions, they rarely limit those powers or regulate the ways they are exercised.[56]

This circumstance is not surprising. The *lex digitalis* is unilaterally established; it is not the output of democratic concertation, a 'social contract' between rulers and ruled. Yet, one cannot deny that technology companies, by delimiting the scope of their own power, unavoidably restrict it, even if not in the manner one would wish. One could transpose in the context of these private actors Jon Elster's metaphor previously mentioned in relation to state power.[57] Technology companies replace the state in incarnating Ulysses tying himself to the mast. The *lex digitalis* represents an act of self-restraint of private companies' power.[58]

The ultimate challenge of this constitutional instrument, as Suzor advocates, is therefore to ensure that this self-allocation of power reflects the foundational values of constitutionalism. This can be achieved in different ways. Firstly, as Fitzgerald and Suzor argue, state law could directly impose its principles, whether or not under the influence of state constitutional law.[59] Here, an apparent example could be the adoption at EU level of the General Data Protection Regulation, which established a series of requirements for the processing of personal data operated by private actors. Secondly, as we will see in more detail in the next section, national or supranational judges could – in a 'maieutic' way, as Karavas put it – help private actors to translate constitutional values in their internal rules. Thirdly, as observed by Viktor Mayer-Schönberger and John Crowley, private actors could even

54 Fitzgerald, 'Software as Discourse? The Challenge for Information Law' (n 36); Suzor, 'The Role of the Rule of Law in Virtual Communities' (n 21).

55 Nicolas Suzor, 'Digital Constitutionalism: Using the Rule of Law to Evaluate the Legitimacy of Governance by Platforms' (2018) 4 Social Media + Society 1, 3.

56 Suzor, 'Digital Constitutionalism' (n 55) 6.

57 See Elster (n 5).

58 See Celeste, 'Terms of Service and Bills of Rights' (n 29); see also Viktor Mayer-Schönberger and John Crowley, 'Napster's Second Life?: The Regulatory Challenges of Virtual World' (2006) 100 Northwestern University Law Review 1775.

59 Fitzgerald, 'Software as Discourse? The Challenge for Information Law' (n 36); Suzor, 'The Role of the Rule of Law in Virtual Communities' (n 21).

voluntarily incorporate state constitutional values.[60] These two authors, in fact, regarded the spontaneous decision of the company managing a virtual community to recognise intellectual property rights on the creations made by users on its website as a 'constitutional' act of self-constraint.

Lex Facebook

What Bygrave called *Lex Facebook*, the terms of service of the social media giant Facebook, is a perfect example of how the internal rules of a private actor can be a vehicle of constitutional counteractions.[61] Until May 2018, Facebook's terms were named 'Statement of Rights and Responsibilities', a descriptor which explicitly echoes the content of constitutional texts.[62] The full entry into force of the European General Data Protection Regulation on 24 May 2018 pushed Facebook to revise its terms, and consequently this solemn name was also changed. The EU regulation, aiming to value transparency between companies and users, introduced a specific obligation for data controllers to provide all information "in a concise, transparent, intelligible and easily accessible form, using clear and plain language".[63] Facebook probably acknowledged that calling its terms 'statement of rights and responsibilities' could be misleading for the users, who are accustomed to less pretentious names used by other platforms.

Nevertheless, for the sake of our analysis, it is interesting to look at Facebook's pre-GDPR terms. What one could call Facebook's *lex abrogata*, in fact, personifies the constitutional intention – or aspiration – of this kind of private norms. The reasons that prompted Facebook to draft its terms of service in a constitutional style are debatable.[64] One could cynically argue that the social media platform adopted a constitutional tone as a mere marketing strategy, to build a sort of constitutional façade, a 'legal talisman', as Kendra Albert called it,[65] that distracts the user from the unfair terms unilaterally established by the company. Speculations apart, one cannot deny that Facebook's 'Statement of Rights and Responsibilities' was rather unique in the panorama of the terms of service of the major social networking websites.[66] At the outset of its now repealed terms, the company of Mark Zuckerberg declared that its norms conceptually derived from the

60 Mayer-Schönberger and Crowley (n 58).

61 Further on this point, see Edoardo Celeste, Amélie Heldt and Clara Iglesias Keller (eds), *Constitutionalising Social Media* (Hart 2022).

62 See Celeste, 'Terms of Service and Bills of Rights' (n 29).

63 Article 12 of the GDPR.

64 See Celeste, 'Terms of Service and Bills of Rights' (n 29).

65 Kendra Albert, 'Beyond Legal Talismans' (Berkman Klein Center for Internet & Society, Harvard University, 10 November 2016) <http://opentranscripts.org/transcript/beyond-legal-talismans/> accessed 21 December 2018.

66 See Celeste, 'Terms of Service and Bills of Rights' (n 29).

'Facebook Principles', a separate document listing the decalogue of Facebook's core values.[67]

Interestingly, the Principles include the majority of the examples of constitutional counteractions examined in the previous chapter. Principle 3, for instance, without directly mentioning the state, can be read as establishing a right to digital information:

> People should have the freedom to access all of the information made available to them by others. People should also have practical tools that make it easy, quick, and efficient to share and access this information.

Principle 9 addresses the issue of power imbalance between the platform and users by establishing that:

> Facebook should publicly make available information about its purpose, plans, policies, and operations. Facebook should have a process of notice and comment to provide transparency and encourage input on amendments to these Principles or to the Rights and Responsibilities.

In this provision, the element of self-constraint is apparent. Facebook imposes on itself the obligation to be transparent, and even (more) democratic, by involving users in the process of revision of the Principles and of its terms.[68]

Moreover, one can mention a series of principles that convey some of the pivotal ideas of the right to Internet access. Principle 1, which is entitled 'Freedom to Share and Connect', reads:

> People should have the freedom to share whatever information they want, in any medium and any format, and have the right to connect online with anyone – any person, organization or service – as long as they both consent to the connection.

Principle 4 enshrines the right to non-discrimination on the Internet:

> Every Person – whether individual, advertiser, developer, organization, or other entity - should have representation and access to distribution

67 The current terms no longer refer to these principles, but this document is still available on Facebook's website. See 'Facebook Principles' <https://www.facebook.com/principles.php> accessed 21 December 2018.

68 In 2009, Facebook even announced the opportunity for users to vote on any amendment to the terms. See Celeste, 'Terms of Service and Bills of Rights' (n 29); Jonathan Zittrain, 'A Bill of Rights for the Facebook Nation' (*The Chronicle of Higher Education*, 20 April 2009) <https://www.chronicle.com/blogs/wiredcampus/jonathan-zittrain-a-bill-of-rights-for-the-facebook-nation/4635> accessed 30 August 2018.

> and information within the Facebook Service, regardless of the Person's primary activity. There should be a single set of principles, rights, and responsibilities that should apply to all People using the Facebook Service.

Principle 10 advocates in favour of Facebook's accessibility from all over the world:

> The Facebook Service should transcend geographic and national boundaries and be available to everyone in the world.

Lastly, Principle 2 enshrines Facebook's philosophy in relation to every person's right to data protection:

> People should own their information. They should have the freedom to share it with anyone they want and take it with them anywhere they want, including removing it from the Facebook Service. People should have the freedom to decide with whom they will share their information, and to set privacy controls to protect those choices. Those controls, however, are not capable of limiting how those who have received information may use it, particularly outside the Facebook Service.

Code as a constitution

Finally, it is necessary at least to mention that, in contrast to public legislators, technology companies can also establish legal norms in a different way. These private actors have the ability to directly shape the code of their software, the architecture of the products and services that they sell and manage. In this way, they regulate people's conduct by determining how the latter can interact in the digital world. In their virtual domains, technology companies are not only legislators, as the state in its territory, but also architects and engineers of the virtual reality where individuals act. Joel Reidenberg called the output of this private rule-making through technical solutions *lex informatica*.[69] Lawrence Lessig concentrated this idea in the slogan 'code is law'.[70] In the digital world, private companies can regulate individual behaviour without enouncing norms that could potentially be infringed, but directly limiting people's possibility of action. The legal norm does not disappear.[71] It is implied in the way private company shape their architecture. One does not acknowledge the presence of a norm because it

69 Reidenberg (n 19).
70 Lessig (n 19).
71 Cf. Vaios Karavas, 'The Force of Code: Law's Transformation under Information Technological Conditions' (2009) 10 German Law Journal 463.

is not expressed with words. One necessarily discovers its presence by analysing the nature of code.

As said in relation to *lex digitalis*, the *lex informatica*, the code, being an effective regulatory tool, can also act as a vehicle of constitutional counteractions. Lessig extensively illustrated code's potential to integrate national constitutional values.[72] An example could be a social platform's sign-in procedure, which only requests or tracks a limited amount of personal data. In this way, the code's design would directly limit potential abuse by the private actor, which, for example, could have benefited from acquiring additional personal data in order to better target its advertisements.

In conclusion, the ropes that technology companies use to self-restrict their power are both their 'enounced' legal rules, their terms of service, and their 'applied' legal rules, i.e. their code.

Courts and arbitrators

This brief overview of the normative instruments in which one can observe the emergence of constitutional counteractions to the challenges of digital technology includes, of course, the case-law. The third and final pair analyses two kinds of case-law, arguing that both of these normative sources can be regarded as vehicles of constitutional counteractions. Firstly, we will examine decisions issued by national and supranational courts, judicial bodies *par excellence*, whose legitimacy is rooted within the state dimension. Secondly, we will focus on the rulings of 'private judges' emerging in the digital environment, drawing examples from the role of content moderation performed by online platforms and from the ICANN dispute resolution mechanism. In contrast to state courts, these private judges are not vested with any public function, but have *de facto* jurisdiction on a range of specific issues in which they apply their own internal rules, what has been previously called *lex digitalis*.

National and supranational courts

The decisions adopted by the institutions which are officially entrusted with the administration of justice, within a state or other state-centric organisation, play a significant normative role. Through judicial decisions, existing norms are articulated, interpreted, and adapted in order to be applied to particular situations, in this way ensuring a constant evolution of the legal system.

So far, this process of interpretation and adaptation carried out by national and supranational courts has been particularly relevant in the context

72 See Lessig (n 19); see also Simoncini and Longo (n 8).

of the digital revolution.[73] The continuous development of digital technology incessantly generates novel legal questions, to which existing law does not always provide an explicit answer. In some circumstances, those legal conundrums directly affect issues of constitutional nature, pertaining to the protection of fundamental rights or the balancing of powers. In such cases, judicial decisions can assume the character of constitutional counteractions.

A paradigmatic example is the role played by the courts of last instance of some countries in recognising the relevance of the Internet as a precondition for the exercise of a series of other fundamental rights. Back in 1997, the US Supreme Court, in the famous case *Reno v. American Civil Liberties Union*, considered the Internet as a necessary instrument to fully guarantee the principle of freedom of expression enshrined in the First Amendment to the US Constitution.[74] And more recently, in the case *Packingham v. North Carolina*, decided in 2017, the same court reiterated the importance of the Internet as a means of communication allowing an unprecedented number of people to interact. In this decision, the Supreme Court even affirmed, in absolute terms, that, today, the cyberspace and, in particular, social media, represent 'what for many are the principal sources for knowing current events' as well as 'the most powerful mechanisms available to a private citizen to make his or her voice heard'.[75]

In 2009, the *Conseil constitutionnel*, the court charged with constitutional questions in France, recognised the right to access the Internet, considering it as an essential instrument to participate in democratic life and to exercise one's own freedom of expression.[76] In 2010, referring to the decision of the

73 For a comprehensive mapping of the recent case-law on digital rights in Europe and the United States, see Oreste Pollicino, *Judicial Protection of Fundamental Rights on the Internet: A Road towards Digital Constitutionalism?* (Hart 2021); on the relevance of judicial activism in digital field in the European Union, see Giovanni De Gregorio, 'The Rise of Digital Constitutionalism in the European Union' (2021) 19 International Journal of Constitutional Law 41; in the context of social media, see Amélie Heldt, 'Content Moderation by Social Media Platforms: The Importance of Judicial Review' in Edoardo Celeste, Amélie Heldt and Clara Iglesias Keller (eds), *Constitutionalising Social Media* (Hart 2022); Edoardo Celeste, 'Digital Punishment: Social Media Exclusion and the Constitutionalising Role of National Courts' [2021] International Review of Law, Computers & Technology 1.

74 *Reno v. American Civil Liberties Union*, 521 U.S. 844 (1997), in particular 853, 870.

75 Packingham v. North Carolina, 582 US___ (2017), 8.

76 Conseil constitutionnel, decision n° 2009-580 DC du 10 juin 2009, in particular paragraph 12: "Considérant qu'aux termes de l'article 11 de la Déclaration des droits de l'homme et du citoyen de 1789 : « La libre communication des pensées et des opinions est un des droits les plus précieux de l'homme : tout citoyen peut donc parler, écrire, imprimer librement, sauf à répondre de l'abus de cette liberté dans les cas déterminés par la loi » ; qu'en l'état actuel des moyens de communication et eu égard au développement généralisé des services de communication au public en ligne ainsi qu'à l'importance prise par ces services pour la participation à la vie démocratique et l'expression des idées et des opinions, ce droit implique la liberté d'accéder à ces services", <http://www.conseil-constitutionnel.fr/conseil-constitutionnel/root/bank/download/cc-2009580dc.pdf> accessed 22 January 2019.

French *Conseil constitutionnel*, the *Sala constitucional*, the section of the Supreme Court of Costa Rica specialised in constitutional matters, explicitly declared that the access to digital technology and, in particular, to the Internet, is a fundamental right. According to this court, today, the use of these technologies represents

> a basic instrument to facilitate the exercise of fundamental rights, such as democratic participation (e-democracy) and citizens' control, education, freedom of expression and thought, access to information and to public services online, the right to contact public institutions through electronic means, and administrative transparency.[77]

More recently, as an example of a supranational judicial body, the European Court of Human Rights, too, acknowledged that

> the Internet has now become one of the principal means by which individuals exercise their right to freedom to receive and impart information and ideas, providing as it does essential tools for participation in activities and discussions concerning political issues and issues of general interest.[78]

These cases dealt with very different questions, ranging from the constitutionality of an act outlawing the transmission of indecent content on the Internet to the validity of a judicial order blocking specific websites, such as YouTube, for a considerable amount of time. However, all of these cases share some commonalities. Firstly, all these decisions consider the potential violation of some fundamental rights, in particular, freedom of expression. Secondly, in all circumstances, the Internet played a fundamental instrumental role in relation to these rights. Lastly, none of these courts could refer to an already existing norm explicitly acknowledging such a role. The novelty of these judgments lies in the recognition of the importance of the Internet and, more generally, of digital technology, as an essential instrument, today, to fully exercise a series of fundamental rights. These decisions became seminal cases in their respective jurisdictions because they articulated for the first time existing fundamental principles in the mutated context of the digital society. In this sense, one can consider these decisions as vehicles of constitutional counteractions to the challenges that digital technology generates in the constitutional ecosystem. These rulings contributed

77 Sala Constitucional de la Corte Suprema de Justicia, sentencia n° 12790 de 30 de Julio de 2010, <https://www.poder-judicial.go.cr/salaconstitucional/index.php/servicios-publicos/759-10-012790> accessed 22 January 2019, my translation.

78 ECtHR, *Cengiz and Others v. Turkey* [2015] (Applications nos. 48226/10 and 14027/11), para. 49.

to the process of evolution and adaptation of the legal order, re-elaborating existing norms in light of the peculiarities of the digital society.

Private arbiters

Chapter 2 explained that one of the alterations generated by the development of digital technology in the constitutional ecosystem is represented by the emergence of private actors as dominant players besides nation-states. In such a scenario, which some scholars have rightly compared to the institutional framework of the Middle Ages,[79] the administration of judicial power is no longer an exclusive monopoly of the state. Limited fields are progressively surfacing where the exercise of justice is in the hands of private actors. The case of content moderation performed by online platforms, as presented in Chapter 3, is a paradigmatic example. In this specific context, the first instance arbiter is the platform itself, a 'private judge' of sorts, who settles disputes according to its own rules.[80]

On the one hand, one could contend that the legitimacy of the judicial power held by these private entities is ultimately rooted in a more or less explicit act of delegation of the state. According to this vision, the *lex digitalis* that these private arbiters apply would in reality be subject to a series of prescriptions imposed by the state. There are circumstances in which, in effect, a relationship of delegation – or, one could even say, 'vassalage' – between the state and the private actor in relation to the administration of justice is more apparent.[81]

After the European Court of Justice's decision in the *Google Spain* case,[82] for example, search engines in Europe were officially entrusted with the duty to decide when to delist a research result in light of a person's right to be forgotten. In order to do so, search engines are required to carry out a real judicial activity, balancing a series of contrasting interests and rights, according to the criteria laid down by the European Court of Justice. Moreover, the previously mentioned German 'Act to Improve Law Enforcement on Social Networks',[83] imposing a series of obligations relating to the activity of content moderation performed by social media, is another example showing how the state can influence the judicial function of these private arbiters.

On the other hand, it is also possible to argue that these examples represent residual cases, and that, in principle, the judicial activity of private arbiters is independent from the state. Karavas espouses this vision, arguing

79 See Castells (n 6); Schneier (n 48); Rodotà (n 6).

80 See Jørgensen and Pedersen (n 49).

81 See Aleksandra Kuczerawy, *Intermediary Liability and Freedom of Expression in the EU: From Concepts to Safeguards* (Intersentia 2018), who talks of a 'delegated private enforcement'.

82 *Google Spain v APED* [2014] ECJ C-131/12, ECLI:EU:C:2014:317.

83 See *supra* (n 43).

that the state should interfere in these processes of private decision-making only in limited circumstances, and in a 'maieutic' way, providing general guidelines and allowing private actors' self-regulation to evolve.[84]

Although the state can, at times, exercise an influence on this private judicial activity, by shaping, more or less invasively, the *lex digitalis*, this does not nullify the ultimate ability of private arbiters to interpret, articulate, and apply general rules to specific cases: in other words, to develop their own case-law. By performing this activity in cases involving the protection of individual rights, the verdicts of these private arbiters, too, can become vehicles of constitutional counteractions. At least, theoretically, one could contend. In fact, on the one hand, one could criticise that, in these circumstances, private companies act both as legislators and judges – disregarding any basic application of the principle of separation of power, one would be inclined to say. According to this argument, one could therefore assert that private companies could hardly protect individual rights in a fair way, and ultimately generate a constitutional counteraction aiming to restore a state of equilibrium at constitutional level. On the other hand, it is materially difficult to provide empirical examples of constitutional counteractions emerging in this context. These private arbiters do not write judgments, or at least, they do not publish them, simply limiting themselves to apply their internal rules to specific cases.

ICANN's arbitrators

While constitutional counteractions are empirically difficult to detect in the judicial decision-making of private actors, such as social media platforms or search engines, there is another example that more clearly speaks to the production of constitutional counteractions by 'private judges': the ICANN dispute resolution mechanism.

The Internet Corporation for Assigned Names and Numbers (ICANN) is a non-profit company established under Californian law.[85] ICANN manages the systems of Internet domain names and numbers.[86] In order to solve disputes arising from the abusive registration of domain names,[87] ICANN established a set of rules, called Uniform Domain Name Dispute Resolution

84 Vagias Karavas, 'Governance of Virtual Worlds and the Quest for a Digital Constitution' in Christoph B Graber and Mira Burri-Nenova, *Governance of Digital Game Environments and Cultural Diversity: Transdisciplinary Enquiries* (Edward Elgar Publishing 2010); cf. Suzor, 'The Role of the Rule of Law in Virtual Communities' (n 21).

85 On ICANN's history, see Milton L Mueller, *Ruling the Root: Internet Governance and the Taming of Cyberspace* (MIT Press 2002).

86 For a comprehensive overview of ICANN's functions, see Lee A Bygrave, *Internet Governance by Contract* (Oxford University Press 2015) ch 4.

87 See Mairead Moore, 'Cybersquatting: Prevention Better than Cure?' (2009) 17 International Journal of Law and Information Technology 220.

Policy (often abbreviated as UDRP),[88] imposed a mandatory dispute resolution mechanism,[89] laid down its rules of procedure,[90] and identified a list of approved dispute resolution centres.[91] In other words, one could argue that ICANN created a sovereign and independent judicial system, with its own rules, its own arbitrators, and its own specific jurisdictional scope. Moreover, in contrast to the judicial decision-making of private actors, such as social media platforms or search engines, ICANN's panels of arbitrators often publish their decisions. This is an essential factor which allows subsequent panels to refer, follow, or overrule previous precedents, creating in this way, what could easily be compared with a proper case-law.[92]

At first sight, one may think that ICANN arbitrators are merely called to solve very technical issues. In reality, ICANN disputes can also involve fundamental rights aspects. Domain names, in fact, are one of the main attributes of online identity: regulating the use of these names affects the possibility of individuals to freely represent themselves on the Internet and, more broadly, to express themselves without constraints.[93]

The decision of the WIPO Arbitration and Mediation Center, one of ICANN's approved dispute resolution providers, in the case opposing the company Bridgestone Firestone and Mr Jack Myers offers a paradigmatic example.[94] Mr Myers, a former employee of Bridgestone Firestone, registered a website with the name 'bridgestone-firestone.net'. His aim was to complain about his former employer in relation to a series of issues related to his pension. The company, holder of the domain name 'bridgestone-firestone.com' lamented that Myers' website constituted abusive registration according to the ICANN Policy. The WIPO arbitrators eventually rejected the claim of the company. Myers' use of that domain name was not only non-profit but, since it aimed to criticise the company, it also represented a form

88 'Uniform Domain-Name Dispute-Resolution Policy - ICANN' <https://www.icann.org/resources/pages/help/dndr/udrp-en> accessed 23 January 2019; see Luke A Walker, 'ICANN's Uniform Domain Name Dispute Resolution Policy' (2000) 15 Berkeley Technology Law Journal 289; John G White, 'Icann's Uniform Domain Name Dispute Resolution Policy in Action' (2001) 16 Berkeley Technology Law Journal 229.

89 According to Paragraph 4(k) of the Policy, the parties can alternatively refer their case before a competent court.

90 'Rules for Uniform Domain Name Dispute Resolution Policy (the "Rules") - ICANN' <https://www.icann.org/resources/pages/udrp-rules-2015-03-11-en> accessed 23 January 2019.

91 'List of Approved Dispute Resolution Service Providers - ICANN' <https://www.icann.org/resources/pages/providers-6d-2012-02-25-en> accessed 23 January 2019.

92 Vagias Karavas and Gunther Teubner, 'Www.CompanyNameSucks.Com: The Horizontal Effect of Fundamental Rights on "Private Parties" within Autonomous Internet Law' (2005) 12 Constellations 262.

93 See Bygrave (n 86) 52 ff.

94 WIPO Arbitration and Mediation Center, 'Case No. D2000-0190, Bridgestone Firestone, Inc., Bridgestone/Firestone Research, Inc., and Bridgestone Corporation v. Jack Myers' <https://www.wipo.int/amc/en/domains/decisions/html/2000/d2000-0190.html> accessed 23 January 2019.

of exercising one's individual freedom of expression that needed to be protected. Interestingly, the WIPO panel observed:

> Although free speech is not listed as one of the Policy's examples of a right or legitimate interest in a domain name, the list is not exclusive, and the Panel concludes that the exercise of free speech for criticism and commentary also demonstrates a right or legitimate interest in the domain name under Paragraph 4 (c)(iii). The Internet is above all a framework for global communication, and the right to free speech should be one of the foundations of Internet law.[95]

In this way, the WIPO arbitrators incorporated the right to freedom of expression among the principles of the ICANN Policy that could justify a fair use of a domain name. As this quotation shows, the panel did not refer to any external source enshrining such right. The many references throughout the text to the US case-law may induce one to think that an allusion to the principle of free speech established in the First Amendment to the US Constitution is implicit. Nevertheless, as highlighted by Karavas and Teubner, the wording of the decision allows us to think that the WIPO arbitrators did craft their own norm protecting the freedom of expression in the context of domain names.[96] Certainly, one can argue that they were influenced by external sources, but yet one cannot deny their effort to translate and adapt a well-established principle, such as the freedom of expression, to a new specific context. In this sense, this case is an example showing the extent to which the 'case-law' of ICANN arbitrators can act as a vehicle of constitutional counteractions.

95 WIPO Arbitration and Mediation Center (n 94) para 6.

96 Karavas and Teubner (n 92); see also Lars Viellechner, *Transnationalisierung des Rechts* (Velbrück 2013).

5 The constitutionalisation of the digital society

Constitutional pluralism

The constitutional ecosystem does not remain inert vis-à-vis the challenges of the digital revolution. It progressively changes and evolves through a series of targeted transformations. These constitutional counteractions take the form of normative responses, seeking to protect fundamental rights and to balance the relationship between powerful and weak actors in the mutated contest of the digital society. The previous chapter has shown that, by adopting a functional approach, looking beyond the formal character of norms, one can also identify the emergence of constitutional counteractions beyond the state dimension. It is possible to understand that the reaction of the constitutional ecosystem does not only materialise in national constitutions, statutes, and judicial decisions. Civil society groups affirm their digital rights in non-binding declarations. Multinational technology corporations are pushed to introduce individual rights safeguards in their internal rules. Private companies' decision-making bodies progressively establish principles to protect users' rights in their own case-law.

The panorama of constitutional counteractions to the challenges of digital revolution therefore appears fragmented, plural, and polycentric. Constitutional patterns emerge both in legally binding and non-binding legal sources, through democratic and institutionalised processes, and through spontaneous deliberation of non-organised groups. Counteractions developing in the national dimension address the relationship between the state and individuals and apply within circumscribed territories, while transnational constitutional instruments focus on the power that private corporations exercise on their users on a global scale. The constitutional discourse is no longer uniform and unitary. Nor is it possible to refer to single legal orders. Each constitutional instrument is a 'fragment',[1] a 'partial constitution'.[2]

1 See Gunther Teubner, *Constitutional Fragments: Societal Constitutionalism and Globalization* (Oxford University Press 2012).

2 See Lars Viellechner, 'Constitutionalism as a Cipher: On the Convergence of Constitutionalist and Pluralist Approaches to the Globalization of Law' (2012) 4 Goettingen Journal of

DOI: 10.4324/9781003256908-5

We face a scenario of constitutional pluralism, a complex mosaic not only combining multiple sources but also intersecting different legal orders.[3]

The image of the medieval feudal system, where the power is layered and fragmented, where kings are such in one territory but subject in others, and the distinction between private and public blurs, once again comes to mind. However, it is not necessary to go back to the Middle Ages to retrace an analogous phenomenon.[4] Recent studies in the domain of international law explain that constitutional pluralism is a general phenomenon of our age, consequence of a specific contemporary trend: globalisation.

The age of globalisation

Interestingly, in international law, there is a long-standing tradition of scholars embracing a constitutionalist approach.[5] In fact, the roots of what has been called 'international constitutional law' date back to the first half of the past century.[6] In 1926, the Austrian legal scholar Alfred Verdross wrote a book entitled *The Constitution of the International Legal Community*, in which he argued that the norms regulating the sources, scope, and jurisdiction of international law represent its 'constitution'.[7]

International Law 599; Anne Peters, 'The Globalization of State Constitutions' in Janne E Nijman and André Nollkaemper (eds), *New Perspectives on the Divide Between National and International Law* (Oxford University Press 2007).

3 Viellechner (n 2); on the notion of 'constitutional pluralism', see Neil Walker, 'The Idea of Constitutional Pluralism' (2002) 65 The Modern Law Review 317; for a comprehensive analysis of the plurality of the Internet legal order, see Matthias C Kettemann, *The Normative Order of the Internet: A Theory of Rule and Regulation Online* (Oxford University Press 2020).

4 See Viellechner (n 2).

5 For a general overview, see Andrea Bianchi, *International Law Theories: An Inquiry into Different Ways of Thinking* (Oxford University Press 2016) ch 3; for an alternative systematisation of the constitutionalist schools of thought in international law, cf. Bardo Fassbender, *The United Nations Charter as the Constitution of the International Community* (Brill Nijhoff 2009) ch 2; for a critique on the use of a constitutionalist approach in international law, see Martti Koskenniemi, 'Constitutionalism as Mindset: Reflections on Kantian Themes About International Law and Globalization' (2006) 8 Theoretical Inquiries in Law 9; Alexander Somek, 'From the Rule of Law to the Constitutionalist Makeover: Changing European Conceptions of Public International Law' (2011) 18 Constellations 567.

6 This expression first appeared in Wolfgang Friedmann, *The Changing Structure of International Law* (Columbia University Press 1964).

7 Alfred Verdross, *Die Verfassung der Völkerrechtsgemeinschaft* (Springer 1926); see Bardo Fassbender, 'The Meaning of International Constitutional Law' in Ronald St John Macdonald and Douglas M Johnston (eds), *Towards world constitutionalism: issues in the legal ordering of the world community* (Nijhoff 2005); for an analysis of the 'precursors' of the constitutionalist approach in international law (Hans Kelsen, Hersch Lauterpacht, Alfred Verdross, and Georges Scelle), see also Thomas Kleinlein, *Konstitutionalisierung Im Völkerrecht: Konstruktion Und Elemente Einer Idealistischen Völkerrechtslehre* (Springer 2012) ch 3.

Starting from these premises, a stream of scholars went even further. They argued that core international values and principles would not be merely *analogically* constitutional, the fundamental rules of an autonomous legal order – that of interstate relationships – that is deemed to be distinct from domestic systems. These norms would really perform a constitutional function, *in conjunction with* domestic constitutional law.[8] The international legal order is no longer seen as an interstate, state-centric normative architecture. According to this vision, the weathercock of international law would have turned towards the individual dimension.[9] The entirety of constitutional law, both on an international and domestic plane, would share its primary aim. International constitutional norms too become inviolable principles seeking to protect individual rights, a series of norms which would be even superior to the will of the states.[10] States would still be the chief characters, but would act 'in a play written and directed by the international community'.[11]

Such a novel reading of the role of international law was explained in the context of the globalisation phenomenon. Globalisation is the process of progressive 'appearance of global, de-territorialised problems'.[12] Issues such as climate change, international terrorism, or mass migration cannot be addressed on the international plane by single nation-states, but would require the cooperation of a multiplicity of actors.[13] Such enhanced interdependence concretely manifests itself in a double, vertical shift of power. Part of nation-states' functions are, on the one hand, absorbed by higher level, supranational entities; on the other hand, entrusted to lower level, multinational non-state actors.[14] Dobner and Loughlin talk of an 'erosion

8 See, in particular, Christian Tomuschat, 'International Law: Ensuring the Survival of Mankind on the Eve of a New Century: General Course on Public International Law' (1999) 281 Collected Courses of The Hague Academy of International Law; further on Tomuschat's vision, see Armin von Bogdandy, 'Constitutionalism in International Law: Comment on a Proposal from Germany' (2006) 47 Harvard international law journal 223.

9 See Anne Peters, 'Humanity as the A and Ω of Sovereignty' (2009) 20 European Journal of International Law 513.

10 Christian Tomuschat, 'Obligations Arising for States without or against Their Will' (1993) 241 Collected Courses of The Hague Academy of International Law 195; cf. Fassbender (n 7).

11 Bogdandy (n 8) 228.

12 Anne Peters, 'Compensatory Constitutionalism: The Function and Potential of Fundamental International Norms and Structures' (2006) 19 Leiden Journal of International Law 579, 580.

13 See Jost Delbrück, 'Structural Changes in the International System and Its Legal Order: International Law in the Era of Globalization' (2001) 1 Swiss Review of International and European Law 1.

14 Peters, 'Compensatory Constitutionalism' (n 16); cf. Ingolf Pernice, 'The Treaty of Lisbon: Multilevel Constitutionalism in Action' (2009) 15 Columbia Journal of European Law 349, 375 ff, who argues that transferring powers to the EU level does not imply a loss of sovereignty for member states, since those functions, in any case, could no longer be successfully exercised by single nation-states.

of statehood'.[15] The nation-state is no longer the monopolist of power. A series of dominant actors emerge beyond the state dimension, creating new transnational contexts in which individual rights need to be protected, and the powers of the players involved balanced.

This novel circumstance generates a new constitutional question.[16] Domestic constitutions, only binding single nation-states, cannot address this issue alone. Global problems ultimately require constitutional pluralism.[17] The dispersion of power among various actors engenders the emergence of new constitutional mechanisms beyond the state: a phenomenon that has been called 'constitutionalisation'.[18]

Multilevel theory

Interestingly, in the study of phenomena of constitutionalisation, constitutional principles whose existence is identified or advocated at transnational level are not examined in isolation. The scholarship has also investigated the nature of the link between domestic and transnational constitutional ecosystems. These two constitutional levels would not amount to watertight legal orders, but could rather be seen as two communicating vessels. Working in tandem, when the domestic constitutional law vessel reaches its point of saturation due to the materialisation of global challenges beyond its reach, the inner fluid would start flowing in the international constitutional law container.

This relationship has been described by the scholarship in different ways. Christian Tomuschat analysed the role of international treaties in terms of 'völkerrechtliche Nebenverfassungen', literally translated as international law supplementary (or auxiliary) constitutions.[19] According to this vision,

15 Petra Dobner and Martin Loughlin (eds), *The Twilight of Constitutionalism?* (Oxford University Press 2010) pt 1.

16 See Gunther Teubner, 'Societal Constitutionalism; Alternatives to State-Centred Constitutional Theory?' in Christian Joerges, Inger-Johanne Sand and Gunther Teubner (eds), *Transnational Governance and Constitutionalism. International Studies in the Theory of Private Law* (Hart 2004).

17 Cf. Daniel Halberstam, 'Constitutional Heterarchy: The Centrality of Conflict in the European Union and the United States' in Jeffrey L Dunoff and Joel P Trachtman (eds), *Ruling the World?: Constitutionalism, International Law, and Global Governance* (Cambridge University Press 2009).

18 For a more detailed mapping of the existing scholarship on constitutionalisation, in particular in the context of the EU, see Edoardo Celeste, 'The Constitutionalisation of the Digital Ecosystem: Lessons from International Law' (2021) Max Planck Institute for Comparative Public Law and International Law (MPIL) Research Paper No. 2021-16 <https://papers.ssrn.com/abstract=3872818> accessed 1 July 2021; for a critical account, cf. Kettemann (n 3) 209.

19 Christian Tomuschat and Reiner Schmidt (eds), *Der Verfassungsstaat im Geflecht der internationalen Beziehungen. Gemeinden und Kreise vor den öffentlichen Aufgaben der Gegenwart: Berichte und Diskussionen auf der Tagung der Vereinigung der Deutschen*

international and domestic law would no longer have different aims, but would both share the goal of protecting individual rights.[20] International law's focus would be on human rights, rather than on interstate relations. Therefore, one can conceive one single integrated 'individual-oriented' system composed of multiple levels.[21] In this way, international law acquires a new constitutional function, supplementing domestic law vis-à-vis global challenges and even imposing a series of principles, superior to the will of the states.[22] In this way, Tomuschat eventually postulated a new hierarchy of legal sources, where international law acquires a foundational value for domestic constitutional law.[23]

Other scholars, although sharing similar premises, did not support the view of a hierarchical relationship between transnational and domestic constitutional law. In the context of the European Union, for example, EU law and member states' constitutions have rather been seen as complementary sources. According to Pernice, EU and national law would represent two 'formally autonomous systems', which, however, in contrast to what happens in federal states, would mutually affect each other without implying the existence of a hierarchy.[24] For Pernice, both these sources would aim to protect citizens' rights, and, as such, would form a *Verfassungsverbund*, a composed 'constitutional unit', though being 'in permanent interdependency'.[25] Pernice baptises this complex architecture 'multilevel constitutionalism', stressing that the presence of multiple layers does not necessarily imply the existence of a hierarchy.[26] Complementation between EU and national law would be a form of symbiotic interdependence.[27]

Staatsrechtslehrer in Basel vom 5. bis 8. Oktober 1977 (De Gruyter 2013) 51; see Bogdandy (n 8); see also Robert Uerpmann, 'Völkerrechtliche Nebenverfassungen' in Armin von Bogdandy (ed), *Europäisches Verfassungsrecht: Theoretische und dogmatische Grundzüge* (Springer Berlin Heidelberg 2003).

20 For a comprehensive outline of Tomuschat's position, see Bogdandy (n 8).

21 Tomuschat (n 8) 237.

22 See Tomuschat (n 10).

23 Tomuschat (n 8).

24 Pernice, 'The Treaty of Lisbon' (n 14) 383.

25 Pernice, 'The Treaty of Lisbon' (n 14) 352, 373, 379.

26 Pernice, 'The Treaty of Lisbon' (n 14); see also Ingolf Pernice, 'Multilevel Constitutionalism and the Treaty of Amsterdam: European Constitution-Making Revisited' (1999) 36 Common Market Law Review 703. Pernice will subsequently apply the theory of multilevel constitutionalism to the broader context of the contemporary society amidst the challenges of the digital revolution: see Ingolf Pernice, 'Global Constitutionalism and the Internet. Taking People Seriously.' in Stefan Kadelbach and Rainer Hofmann (eds), *Law Beyond the State: Pasts and Futures* (Campus Verlag 2016) <http://ssrn.com/abstract=2576697.>; Ingolf Pernice, 'Risk Management in the Digital Constellation – A Constitutional Perspective' (2017) HIIG Discussion Paper Series No 2017-07 <https://papers.ssrn.com/abstract=3051124> accessed 18 October 2018.

27 See JHH Weiler and Joel P Trachtman, 'European Constitutionalism and Its Discontents' (1996) 17 Northwestern Journal of International Law & Business 354.

Lastly, Anne Peters further characterises the relationship between transnational and domestic law in a different way. Globalisation would have put national constitutions under pressure.[28] Principles of national constitutional law appear 'dysfunctional' or 'empty' vis-à-vis phenomena which transcend the territory of the state.[29] A significant portion of state power is progressively transferred to transnational level. Both supranational organisations and multinational private actors emerge as new dominant players, but at the same time domestic constitutions are no longer 'total constitutions', capable of facing this mutated transnational scenario.[30] According to Peters, globalisation would not alter the assumption that the 'achievements of constitutionalism are to be preserved'.[31] She therefore affirms that this 'de-constitutionalisation' at domestic level normatively requires a 'compensatory constitutionalisation on the international plane'.[32] The final result, as in the previous case, is always a constitutional conglomerate composed of *both* domestic and transnational constitutional instruments. However, the rationale behind the symbiosis between these two sources of law changes: national constitutional law has lost its centrality, it is no longer effective, and consequently needs to be compensated by a series of normative instruments emerging at transnational level.

Double reflexivity

In the first act of Rossini's *The Barber of Seville*, Figaro, the hairdresser of the title, enters the stage on the notes of the famous aria 'Largo al factotum della città'.[33] Cesare Sterbini, the libretto's author, writes 'make the way for the factotum of the city' because effectively, in the eighteenth century, the barber was a man of all work: coiffeur, clock repairer, dentist, and even surgeon.[34] A role with a wide-ranging set of competences that today – luckily – are exercised by several other professionals.

The nation-state, before the advent of globalisation, somehow resembled Figaro: it was like the eighteenth century's barber, the factotum of

28 Anne Peters, 'Global Constitutionalism' in Michael T Gibbons (ed), *The Encyclopedia of Political Thought* (John Wiley & Sons 2014).

29 Jan Klabbers, Anne Peters and Geir Ulfstein, *The Constitutionalization of International Law* (Oxford University Press 2009) 347; see also Peters, 'The Globalization of State Constitutions' (n 2).

30 Peters, 'Compensatory Constitutionalism' (n 12) 580.

31 Peters, 'Global Constitutionalism' (n 28) 2.

32 Peters, 'Compensatory Constitutionalism' (n 12) 580.

33 See Betsy Schwarm and Linda Cantoni, 'The Barber of Seville', *Encyclopedia Britannica* <https://www.britannica.com/topic/The-Barber-of-Seville-opera-by-Rossini> accessed 5 March 2019.

34 Sterbini's aria reads: '"My wig here!" - "My beard here!" - "Here, bleed me!!" - "Quick, the note!" Figaro! Figaro! Figaro!' See Erwin H Ackerknecht, 'From Barber-Surgeon to Modern Doctor' (1984) 58 Bulletin of the History of Medicine 545.

both domestic and interstate affairs. Interestingly, similarly to what has happened to the one-time multifaceted profession of the barber, the state too has progressively lost its societal centrality. Functions once exclusively exercised by the state are today delegated to transnational entities. Consequently, as we have seen, constitutional law is no longer exclusively national, rooted in a territory, linked to a specific people. Conversely, it is necessarily plural, it appears as a complex conglomerate of several legal sources also emerging beyond the state dimension.

The explanation of such a phenomenon provided by legal sociologists reflects the dynamics underlying the evolution of the role of the barber in the last three centuries. In the globalised society, boundaries no longer follow national frontiers but are defined according to functional specialisation.[35] One can identify 'a multiplicity of autonomous subsystems'.[36] The economy, media, health, science: each one represents an independent regime. The barber is no longer, at the same time, the clock repairer, dentist, and surgeon because these figures have emerged as autonomous, specialised professions. In the same way, vis-à-vis global phenomena which engender a sectoral differentiation, some prerogatives once concentrated in the hands of the state are today assumed by specialised transnational entities.

As we have seen, this displacement of power at transnational level generates a series of constitutional questions to which national constitutional law cannot, alone, provide an answer. Niklas Luhmann argued that the emergence of a 'world society' is not compensated by the emergence of a world politics, and this circumstance would generate a twilight of constitutionalism at global level.[37] Conversely, David Sciulli contended that in spite of a rampant authoritarianism at societal level a constitutionalising trend was emerging in a plurality of societal institutions, such as those setting norms for specific professions in a collegial way.[38] Following this line, Gunther Teubner insisted that the functional differentiation of society would generate a 'societal' constitutionalisation: each societal subsystem would be able to develop its own constitutional norms.[39] According to this vision,

35 See Niklas Luhmann, *Theory of Society*, vol 1 (Rhodes Barrett tr, Stanford University Press 2012); Teubner, 'Societal Constitutionalism; Alternatives to State-Centred Constitutional Theory?' (n 16).

36 Teubner, 'Societal Constitutionalism; Alternatives to State-Centred Constitutional Theory?' (n 16) 8; for an overview of Teubner's position, see also Bianchi (n 5) ch 3.

37 Niklas Luhmann, *Law as a Social System* (Fatima Kastner and others eds, Klaus Ziegert tr, Oxford University Press 2004).

38 See David Sciulli, *Theory of Societal Constitutionalism: Foundations of a Non-Marxist Critical Theory* (Cambridge University Press 1992); David Sciulli, *Corporate Power in Civil Society* (NYU Press 2001).

39 See Teubner, 'Societal Constitutionalism; Alternatives to State-Centred Constitutional Theory?' (n 29); Teubner, *Constitutional Fragments* (n 9); Angelo Golia and Gunther Teubner, 'Societal Constitutionalism (Theory Of)' (2021) Max Planck Institute for Comparative Public Law & International Law (MPIL) Research Paper No 2021-08 ID 3804094 <https://

constitutional law-making would not only involve traditional centres of power but would flood into the 'peripheries of law'.[40] Constitutional law would no longer be relegated to the state dimension. Contrariwise, domestic constitutions would become 'a sub-constitution among others'.[41]

A socio-legal perspective allows us to understand that the 'fragments' of this plural constitutional scenario are not only represented by norms developed in a state-centric dimension, be they at national or supranational level, but also by principles shaped in the social context.[42] Teubner talks of the emergence of 'civil constitutions'.[43] A world unitary constitution is a utopia, as is to think that the activities of states and supranational organisations exhaust the potential articulations of global society's constitutionalisation. Such a process would be incremental, but, above all, hybrid and composite: 'a mix of autonomous and heteronomous law-making'.[44] Constitutionalisation is therefore understood as a legal *and* social process.[45] Teubner articulates it into several steps.[46]

The constitutional norms self-produced by autonomous subsystems of society, such as the economy, media, health, or science, would be initially only of 'constitutive', and not 'limitative', nature: they would amount to the fundamental rules which do not limit, but articulate the power of the dominant actors (e.g., private corporations), what Teubner calls the 'organised-professional' sphere of the society.[47] This situation triggers a reaction from its societal counterpart, the 'spontaneous' sector, which includes governmental agencies, civil society groups, trade unions, consumer protection organisations, and alike. The latter generates 'constitutional

papers.ssrn.com/abstract=3804094> accessed 26 May 2021; cf. Karl-Heinz Ladeur, 'The evolution of the law and the possibility of a "global law" extending beyond the sphere of the state – simultaneously, a critique of the "self-constitutionalisation" thesis' [2012] Ancilla Iuris 220.

40 Teubner, 'Societal Constitutionalism; Alternatives to State-Centred Constitutional Theory?' (n 16) 17.

41 Teubner, 'Societal Constitutionalism; Alternatives to State-Centred Constitutional Theory?' (n 16) 15.

42 See Teubner, *Constitutional Fragments* (n 1).

43 Teubner, 'Societal Constitutionalism; Alternatives to State-Centred Constitutional Theory?' (n 16).

44 Teubner, 'Societal Constitutionalism; Alternatives to State-Centred Constitutional Theory?' (n 16) 17.

45 Teubner even argues that constitutionalisation is 'primarily a social process': see Teubner, *Constitutional Fragments* (n 1) 104.

46 See Teubner, *Constitutional Fragments* (n 1); for a clear schematisation of Teubner's conception of constitutionalisation, see Christoph B Graber, 'Bottom-up Constitutionalism: The Case of Net Neutrality' (2016) 7 Transnational Legal Theory 524.

47 Teubner, *Constitutional Fragments* (n 1) 75 ff; see also Gunther Teubner, 'Self-Constitutionalizing TNCs? On the Linkage of "Private" and "Public" Corporate Codes of Conduct' (2011) 18 Indiana Journal of Global Legal Studies 617; cf. Nicolas Suzor, *Lawless. The Secret Rules That Govern Our Digital Lives* (Cambridge University Press 2019).

learning impulses' by manifesting its expectations.[48] In a variety of ways, the spontaneous societal sphere exercises pressure on the organised-professional sector until those impulses are 'reflected', translated in 'limitative' constitutional norms, rules which aim to restrict the power of dominant actors.[49]

Subsequently, the constitutional principles generated at societal level are progressively 'juridified' under the form of secondary norms, rules about rule-making.[50] They become an integral part of the legal system through a process which Teubner defines as 'reflexive' due to a 'structural coupling' between law and society.[51] In other words, legal norms start to mirror societal rules, which, at their turn, reflect societal expectations. Lastly, legal rules, within their own legal system, can surge to the level of constitutional norms,[52] either by directly being inserted in the text of the constitution or by testing in court their compatibility with the constitution.

Teubner's reconstruction therefore reveals that the process of constitutionalisation is characterised by a 'double reflexivity'.[53] The social and legal systems are mutually interwoven: their interaction could be metaphorically illustrated as 'an exchange of fluids between porous and permeable materials', at the same time bottom-up and top-down.[54] Not only the national and transnational dimensions, but also the social and legal planes, are part of a unique set of communicating vessels.[55] In contrast to natural law theory, one realises that constitutional principles are the product of a process of societal elaboration, and, at the same time, that social norms are shaped and oriented by legal rules.[56]

A single phenomenon

This brief overview of existing scholarship on phenomena of constitutionalisation helps us to contextualise and better define the phenomenon that we are analysing in the first part of this work: the emergence of constitutional counteractions to the challenges of digital technology.

48 Teubner, *Constitutional Fragments* (n 1) 94 ff.

49 Teubner, *Constitutional Fragments* (n 1) 94 ff; cf. the concept of 'inclusionary pressures' in Chris Thornhill, *A Sociology of Constitutions: Constitutions and State Legitimacy in Historical-Sociological Perspective* (Cambridge University Press 2011).

50 Teubner, *Constitutional Fragments* (n 1) 105 ff.

51 Teubner, *Constitutional Fragments* (n 1) 102 ff.

52 Teubner, *Constitutional Fragments* (n 1) 110 ff.

53 Teubner, *Constitutional Fragments* (n 1) 102 ff.

54 Edoardo Celeste, 'Digital Constitutionalism: A New Systematic Theorisation' (2019) 33 International Review of Law, Computers & Technology 76, 87; see Gunther Teubner, *Law as an Autopoietic System* (Blackwell 1993); Graber (n 46).

55 See Graber (n 46) 551.

56 See Teubner, *Constitutional Fragments* (n 1) 112; on the same line, see also Norberto Bobbio, *The Age of Rights* (Allan Cameron tr, Polity 1996).

The digital revolution is an integral part of the process of globalisation, not to say that it represents one of its main triggers.[57] The incessant development of digital technology generates a series of challenges which are no longer confined in a specific territorial dimension but involve global realities. In this context, nation-states do not hold the monopoly of power anymore because global issues require forms of cooperation with a multiplicity of transnational actors, both supranational organisations and multinational private entities.

This complex, layered governance system is reflected at constitutional level. National constitutions are no longer able, alone, to face the challenges of the digital revolution. The dispersion of power in the transnational dimension triggers the emergence of constitutional mechanisms beyond the state. Constitutional pluralism is a direct consequence of the phenomenon of globalisation. There is no single constitution of the digital society. The constitutional discourse is necessarily composite because no constitutional fragment, singularly taken, is able to address all the different portions of power. However, precisely this fragmentation becomes a new technique to provide a constitutional response to the issues of the global digital society.[58] The multifarious constitutional counteractions which are emerging to face the challenges of the digital revolution can eventually be regarded as the miscellaneous tesserae of a single mosaic. The different levels of this complex constitutional picture complement each other: like in a puzzle, the holes, and bulges of each piece.

The previous chapter has provided a snapshot of the variety of these constitutional counteractions. Now, if one were able to gain an aerial view of this phenomenon in motion, one would not simply see the static image of a set of constitutional fragments, but one would observe a lively and effervescent scenario. What at this stage, in light of the terminology used in the field of international law, EU law and legal sociology, one could call a phenomenon of 'constitutionalisation'.

The legal scholarship has used the notion of 'constitutionalisation' with a variety of different meanings.[59] This term has been referred to as the process of acquisition of constitutional relevance by a specific principle,

57 See Manuel Castells, *The Rise of the Network Society* (2nd edn, Blackwell 2000) ch 2; Manuel Castells, *The Power of Identity* (2. ed., Wiley-Blackwell 2010) ch 5; Ingolf Pernice, 'Die Verfassung der Internetgesellschaft: Zur Rolle von Staat und Verfassung im Zuge der digitalen Revolution' in Alexander Blankenagel (ed), *Den Verfassungsstaat nachdenken. Eine Geburtstagsgabe* (Duncker & Humblot 2014) <https://papers.ssrn.com/abstract=2964926> accessed 28 August 2018.

58 See Andrzej Jakubowski and Karolina Wierczyńska (eds), *Fragmentation vs the Constitutionalisation of International Law: A Practical Inquiry* (Routledge 2016) pt 3 who talk of 'constitutionalisation through fragmentation' in the context of international law.

59 For instance, for an overview of the various meanings of the concept of constitutionalisation in international law, see Kleinlein (n 7) ch 1.

circumstance or object.[60] It has been considered as a synonym of codification when constitutional norms were involved.[61] Or, as seen in the previous sections, constitutionalisation has also been intended as the process of introduction of constitutional values and principles in a dimension which formerly did not possess them.[62] There is certainly some overlap among these interpretations of the concept of constitutionalisation, however the last one, which definitively appears to be the broadest of the three, better reflects the phenomenon that we are analysing in the first part of this work. Embracing this perspective, the constitutional counteractions that are emerging to face the challenges of digital technology can be regarded as the core components

60 For example, with reference to the constitutionalisation of the Internet, see Gaetano Azzariti, 'Internet e Costituzione' [2011] Politica del diritto 367; Francesco Amoretti and Enrico Gargiulo, 'Dall'appartenenza Materiale All'appartenenza Virtuale? La Cittadinanza Elettronica Fra Processi Di Costituzionalizzazione Della Rete e Dinamiche Di Esclusione' [2010] Politica del diritto 353; See also Mark A Lemley, 'The Constitutionalization of Technology Law' (2000) 15 Berkeley Technology Law Journal 529 who talks of the constitutionalisation of technology law.

61 See, for example, on the constitutionalisation of the EU in a formal sense, Francis Snyder, 'The Unfinished Constitution of the European Union: Principles, Processes and Culture' in JHH Weiler and Marlene Wind (eds), *European Constitutionalism Beyond the State* (Cambridge University Press 2003); Pernice, 'Multilevel Constitutionalism and the Treaty of Amsterdam: European Constitution-Making Revisited' (n 26); in relation to international law, see Garrett Wallace Brown, 'The Constitutionalization of What?' (2012) 1 Global Constitutionalism 201, 210: 'constitutionalization, when used as a descriptive and reflective device, is meant to denote the processes of legal codification toward the establishment and incorporation of entities into a coherent and legally objectified body of law, where legal parties, legal rights, legal obligations and legitimate centres of adjudicating power are specified'; Karolina Milewicz, 'Emerging Patterns of Global Constitutionalisation: Towards a Conceptual Framework' (2009) 16 Indiana Journal of Global Legal Studies 413: 'Constitutionalization implies that a legal text can acquire or may eventually lose constitutional properties in a feedback process and can thus be a long-lasting development. It indicates a process encompassing the emergence, creation, and identification of constitution-like elements. In short, it denotes a constitution-in-the-making'.

62 On this point, in the context of international law, see also Aoife O'Donoghue, *Constitutionalism in Global Constitutionalisation* (Cambridge University Press 2014): constitutionalisation is 'a process, extending constitutional structures to fora and layers of governance other than nations'; Wiener and others (n 49): constitutionalisation denotes the 'process by which institutional arrangements in the non-constitutional global realm have taken on a constitutional quality'; Anne-Claire Jamart, 'Internet Freedom and the Constitutionalization of Internet Governance' in Roxana Radu, Jean-Marie Chenou and Rolf H Weber (eds), *The Evolution of Global Internet Governance* (Springer Berlin Heidelberg 2014): 'By constitutionalization I mean the process by which a constitution is being introduces in a legal order, whether domestic, or as in the case at hand, international'; Martin Loughlin, 'What Is Constitutionalisation?' in Petra Dobner and Martin Loughlin (eds), *The Twilight of Constitutionalism?* (Oxford University Press 2010): 'Constitutionalisation involves the attempt to subject all governmental action within a designated field to the structures, processes, principles, and values of a 'constitution'.

of a complex phenomenon of constitutionalisation of the digital society.[63] Let us explore its main characteristics.

Plurality and fragmentation

Firstly, such a phenomenon would not be uniform and unitary, but articulated, plural and fragmented. In the previous chapters, we have seen how the series of constitutional counteractions which have so far emerged do not share the same level of elaboration. They materialise in a variety of contexts, adopting a multiplicity of forms, and involving different actors. Nevertheless, one cannot ignore that this composite scenario rotates around a common aim. All these different constitutional counteractions share a common denominator: instilling constitutional principles and values in the mutated context of the digital society. In light of this observation, a more accurate analysis of this phenomenon reveals that these constitutional counteractions do not simply emerge spontaneously in different contexts, as in an extemporaneous mushrooming phenomenon. One can argue that they are all necessary components of a single, coordinated system. Indeed, drawing inspiration from the multilevel theory developed in international law and EU law, one could claim that each of these constitutional fragments is needed to complement the action of the other constitutional instruments.[64] They would represent the pieces of a single puzzle, in which each one interacts with, informs and complements the others.

The existing scholarship analysed many of these counteractions singularly, sometimes normatively claiming in favour of their allegedly pivotal role in constitutionalising the digital society.[65] For instance, Berman advocated the importance of national constitutions in this context;[66] Fitzgerald and Suzor recognised the significance of private law as a way to instil constitutional values in the rules of private actors;[67] Karavas praised the ability of digital communities to self-constitutionalise themselves;[68] and Redeker,

63 On the same line, cf. Jamart (n 62); Viktor Mayer-Schönberger and John Crowley, 'Napster's Second Life?: The Regulatory Challenges of Virtual World' (2006) 100 Northwestern University Law Review 1775, who talk of constitutionalisation in the context of virtual communities.

64 On the same line, see Pernice, 'Global Constitutionalism and the Internet. Taking People Seriously.' (n 26); Pernice, 'Risk Management in the Digital Constellation – A Constitutional Perspective' (n 26).

65 See Celeste (n 54).

66 Paul Berman, 'Cyberspace and the State Action Debate: The Cultural Value of Applying Constitutional Norms to "Private" Regulation' (2000) 71 University of Colorado Law Review 1263.

67 Brian Fitzgerald, 'Software as Discourse? The Challenge for Information Law' (2000) 22 European Intellectual Property Review 47; Nicolas Suzor, 'The Role of the Rule of Law in Virtual Communities' (2010) 25 Berkeley Technology Law Journal 1817.

68 Vagias Karavas, 'Governance of Virtual Worlds and the Quest for a Digital Constitution' in Christoph B Graber and Mira Burri-Nenova, *Governance of Digital Game Environments and Cultural Diversity: Transdisciplinary Enquiries* (Edward Elgar Publishing 2010).

Gill, and Gasser, lastly, underlined the potential constitutionalising function of Internet bills of rights.[69] Conversely, the reconstruction presented in this work does not support any hierarchical vision.[70] The constitutional counteractions to the challenges of the digital revolution would work in tandem. Their ultimate value could only be appreciated if globally assessed in conjunction with the achievements of the other constitutional counteractions involved.

Progressive translation

Secondly, the phenomenon of constitutionalisation of the digital society would not merely consist in a transfer of constitutional values and principles from a context to another. Such a phenomenon would unavoidably presuppose a progressive adaptation, translation of those values, and principles in light of the characteristics of their context of destination. Teubner talks of a process of 'generalisation' and 'respecification'.[71] Key principles of contemporary constitutionalism cannot be simply transplanted in the transnational, global context to address the challenges of the digital revolution. One first needs to identify their quintessence and then implement it in the context of the digital society.

It is therefore apparent that the phenomenon of constitutionalisation does not temporally denote a *fait accompli*, but rather describes – as the suffix -isation shows – a process. Chapter 3 has illustrated how some constitutional counteractions such as, for instance, the protection of personal data, have evolved, and are still evolving. More generally, constitutional counteractions do not end with their conceptual spring, but constantly ripe, develop, and change themselves. Consequently, the process of constitutionalisation does not merely correspond to the phase of formal codification of legal principles. It encompasses a broader process, which does not necessarily end with a codification in a formal constitution, but could involve the stabilisation of a norm within different sets of rules, such as, for instance, at the level of corporate policy.

Societal input

Finally, the process of constitutionalisation of the digital society is not uniquely top-down but also implicates bottom-up instances.[72] As the

69 Dennis Redeker, Lex Gill and Urs Gasser, 'Towards Digital Constitutionalism? Mapping Attempts to Craft an Internet Bill of Rights' (2018) 80 International Communication Gazette 302.

70 See Celeste (n 54).

71 Teubner, 'Societal Constitutionalism; Alternatives to State-Centred Constitutional Theory?' (n 16).

72 See Graber (n 46).

socio-legal scholarship on the phenomena of constitutionalisation shows, constitutional norms are first elaborated at societal level. Law and society are not two airtight containers. The evolution of the law is closely connected to societal developments: it represents the result of the juridification of social norms, which are at their turn a reflection of societal pressures. As we have seen, if one adopts an empirical-functional approach, looking beyond what is formally constitutional, it is possible to identify the emergence of constitutional counteractions even at societal level. The process of constitutionalisation, therefore, cannot be exclusively confined to what is formally legal or, conversely, be uniquely characterised as a societal phenomenon.[73] Such a compartmentalisation would simply not correspond to the reality. In this work, the concept of constitutionalisation of the digital society pragmatically encompasses the full range of possible constitutional counteractions. Not only those emerging in the legal dimension but also mere societal initiatives: all the tesserae of the contemporary constitutional mosaic.

73 Further on this point, see Celeste (n 86).

6 Digital constitutionalism

Constitutionalism vs constitutionalisation

A complex process of constitutionalisation is currently under way within contemporary society. A multiplicity of normative counteractions is emerging to address the challenges of the digital revolution. However, there is no single constitutional framer. As in a vast construction site there are several contracting companies working at the same time, so, in a globalised environment, constitutionalisation simultaneously occurs at different societal levels. This is not only in the institutional perimeter of nation-states but also beyond: on the international plane, in the fiefs of the private actors, within the civil society. The sense of this Gordian knot of normative responses can be deciphered only if these emerging constitutional fragments are interpreted as complementary tesserae of a single mosaic. Each one surfacing with a precise mission within the constitutional ecosystem, each one compensating the shortcomings of the others in order to achieve a common aim: translating the core principles of contemporary constitutionalism in the context of the digital society.

Constitutionalisation and constitutionalism are not two interchangeable concepts. Unfortunately, the scholarship sometimes uses these two terms as synonyms.[1] Several authors attempted to systematically define the meanings of the trio constitution-constitutionalism-constitutionalisation.[2] Yet, it seems that a certain nebulosity on the matter still persists.[3] Undoubtedly,

1 Rossana Deplano, 'Fragmentation and Constitutionalisation of International Law: A Theoretical Inquiry' (2013) European journal of legal studies.

2 See Paul Craig, 'Constitutions, Constitutionalism, and the European Union' (2001) 7 European Law Journal 125; Anne Peters, 'Compensatory Constitutionalism: The Function and Potential of Fundamental International Norms and Structures' (2006) 19 Leiden Journal of International Law 579; Karolina Milewicz, 'Emerging Patterns of Global Constitutionalisation: Towards a Conceptual Framework' (2009) 16 Indiana Journal of Global Legal Studies 413.

3 See Deplano (n 1); Peer Zumbansen, 'Comparative, Global and Transnational Constitutionalism: The Emergence of a Transnational Legal-Pluralist Order' (2012) 1 Global Constitutionalism 16; Anne Peters and Klaus Armingeon, 'Introduction: Global Constitutionalism from an Interdisciplinary Perspective' (2009) 16 Indiana Journal of Global

DOI: 10.4324/9781003256908-6

the absence of a common definition of the notion of constitution does not help.[4] Moreover, the application of these terms in the fields of international law and legal sociology has amplified their degree of semantic flexibility and further nuanced the boundaries of their expressive contours.[5] However, it is possible to present a basic distinction between the two concepts, on which the scholarship seems to generally agree.

The concept of constitutionalisation denotes a process.[6] The suffix –isation, as already highlighted in the previous chapter, characterises a procedure, an operation; it implies the idea of advancement, progression, and evolution. It may have occurred in the past, be still ongoing or be advocated in a normative sense for the future. Conversely, constitutionalism is a 'theory',[7] a 'movement of thought',[8] a 'conceptual framework',[9] a 'set of values',[10]

Legal Studies 385; Aoife O'Donoghue, *Constitutionalism in Global Constitutionalisation* (Cambridge University Press 2014).

4 See Herbert John Spiro, 'Constitution', *Encyclopedia Britannica* (2018) <https://www.britannica.com/topic/constitution-politics-and-law> accessed 23 October 2018; Roger A Shiner, 'Constitutions' in Enrico Pattaro (ed), *A Treatise of Legal Philosophy and General Jurisprudence*, vol 3 'Legal Institutions and Sources of Law' (Springer 2005); Dieter Grimm, *Constitutionalism: Past, Present, and Future* (Oxford University Press 2016); Giovanni Sartori, 'Constitutionalism: A Preliminary Discussion' (1962) 56 The American Political Science Review 853.

5 See Federico Fabbrini, 'The Constitutionalization of International Law: A Comparative Federal Perspective' (2013) 6 European journal of legal studies 7; Jan Klabbers, Anne Peters and Geir Ulfstein, *The Constitutionalization of International Law* (Oxford University Press 2009); Christoph B Graber, 'Bottom-up Constitutionalism: The Case of Net Neutrality' (2016) 7 Transnational Legal Theory 524; Chris Thornhill, *A Sociology of Constitutions: Constitutions and State Legitimacy in Historical-Sociological Perspective* (Cambridge University Press 2011); Gunther Teubner, *Constitutional Fragments: Societal Constitutionalism and Globalization* (Oxford University Press 2012).

6 See Girardeau A Spann, 'Constitutionalization' [2004] Saint Louis University Law Journal 709; Milewicz (n 2); Garrett Wallace Brown, 'The Constitutionalization of What?' (2012) 1 Global Constitutionalism 201; Aoife O'Donoghue, 'Alfred Verdross and the Contemporary Constitutionalization Debate' (2012) 32 Oxford Journal of Legal Studies 799; Antje Wiener and others, 'Global Constitutionalism: Human Rights, Democracy and the Rule of Law' (2012) 1 Global Constitutionalism 1; Anne-Claire Jamart, 'Internet Freedom and the Constitutionalization of Internet Governance' in Roxana Radu, Jean-Marie Chenou and Rolf H Weber (eds), *The Evolution of Global Internet Governance* (Springer Berlin Heidelberg 2014).

7 Jeremy Waldron, 'Constitutionalism: A Skeptical View' (2010) Philip A. Hart Memorial Lecture <https://scholarship.law.georgetown.edu/hartlecture/4>; see also Ingolf Pernice, 'Global Constitutionalism and the Internet. Taking People Seriously.' in Stefan Kadelbach and Rainer Hofmann (eds), *Law Beyond the State: Pasts and Futures* (Campus Verlag 2016) 7 <http://ssrn.com/abstract=2576697.>, according to whom constitutionalism is a form of 'theoretical thinking'.

8 Marco Bani, 'Crowdsourcing Democracy: The Case of Icelandic Social Constitutionalism' (Social Science Research Network 2012) SSRN Scholarly Paper ID 2128531 <https://papers.ssrn.com/abstract=2128531> accessed 15 August 2019.

9 Zumbansen (n 3); see also Perry Keller, 'Sovereignty and Liberty in the Internet Era' in Richard Rawlings, Peter Leyland and Alison Young (eds), *Sovereignty and the Law* (Oxford University Press 2013).

10 O'Donoghue (n 3).

an 'ideology'.[11] Again, an analysis of the term itself can be of help. The suffix -ism does not imply the idea of process; it denotes a more static concept.[12] An ism is a 'a distinctive practice, system, or philosophy, typically a political ideology or an artistic movement'.[13] Neglecting for a moment the question of what the actual principles of constitutionalism are, one could argue that, *lato sensu*, constitutional-*isation* is the *process* of implementation of constitutional-*ism*. Constitutionalisation would put into effect the values of constitutionalism or, regarded the other way around, constitutionalism would provide the principles that permeate, guide, inform constitutionalisation.[14]

The normative counteractions that have emerged so far to restore a condition of relative equilibrium in the constitutional ecosystem are driven by the values of contemporary constitutionalism. They do not surface in a legal vacuum. They aim to complement, adjust, and renovate existing constitutional safeguards. The multiple patterns of the process of constitutionalisation that is currently ongoing cannot depart from the foundational principles of the constitutional system that they seek to preserve in the mutated context of the digital society. The values of constitutionalism pervade both the old constitutional norms of the analogue world and the new mechanisms designed for the digital age.[15] The constitutionalisation of the digital society implies their process of translation in light of the characteristics of the digital society. Abstract values in this way become concrete norms that are able to effectively communicate their prescriptive message to the actors of the virtual environment.

11 Edoardo Celeste, 'Digital Constitutionalism: A New Systematic Theorisation' (2019) 33 International Review of Law, Computers & Technology 76: 'The term "ideology" is often used in a pejorative sense, following Marx's concept of ideology as "false consciousness", i.e. as "a set of beliefs with which people deceive themselves", or like in politics, as a non-practical attitude. In this paper, this descriptor is used in a neutral way, as a structured set of values and ideals. The advantage of thinking of digital constitutionalism as an ideology, and, therefore, as a purely theoretical concept, lies in the possibility to distinguish it from its implementation, its translation into reality'; see Maurice Cranston, 'Ideology' <https://www.britannica.com/topic/ideology-society> accessed 30 August 2018; cf. Lars Viellechner, 'Constitutionalism as a Cipher: On the Convergence of Constitutionalist and Pluralist Approaches to the Globalization of Law' (2012) 4 Goettingen Journal of International Law 599.

12 See Waldron (n 7); Milewicz (n 2).

13 *Oxford Dictionary of English* (3rd edn, Oxford University Press 2010).

14 Celeste, 'Digital Constitutionalism' (n 11); on the same line, but more concretely, Martin Loughlin, 'What Is Constitutionalisation?' in Petra Dobner and Martin Loughlin (eds), *The Twilight of Constitutionalism?* (Oxford University Press 2010).

15 See JHH Weiler and Marlene Wind (eds), *European Constitutionalism beyond the State* (Cambridge University Press 2003) 3, according to whom, constitutionalism 'embodies the values, often non-stated, which underlie the material and institutional provisions in a specific constitution'.

The values of constitutionalism

Constitutionalism evolves. This concept does not denote a process, as we have seen, but this does not contradict the fact that its underlying values, ideals, and principles have changed over time. The notion of constitutionalism emerged at the end of the eighteenth century as a response to absolute monarchy and popular despotism.[16] It advocated the adoption of a constitution, a written legal text establishing the fundamental law of a country, and, at the same time, its primacy over the discretion of rulers.[17] The power of the government should be legitimated by the constitution, an expression of popular sovereignty, and should be bound by the constitution, which represents its ultimate limit.[18] No actor in society should detain at the same time the legislative, executive, and judiciary power.[19] No ruler should be *ab-solutus*, unrestricted from the control of other institutional organs whose power derives from the constitution.[20] At the outset, constitutionalism was an ideology, a movement of thought that claimed the values of the rule of law and the separation of power.

This normative vision of society championed by the original constitutionalism was subsequently enriched with other ideals. Democracy definitively supplanted other forms of government and established itself as a foundational value.[21] Besides a negative, limitative approach, claiming the restriction of the power of rulers by law and the institution of a system of checks and balances, constitutionalism also developed a positive aspect, pivoting around individual empowerment.[22] In this way, the ultimate mission of constitutionalism, the limitation of power, was re-oriented towards the protection of fundamental rights and, ultimately, the safeguarding of human dignity.[23]

16 András Sajó and Renáta Uitz, *The Constitution of Freedom: An Introduction to Legal Constitutionalism* (Oxford University Press 2017) ch 1; Harold J Berman, *Law and Revolution. The Formation of the Western Legal Tradition* (Harvard University Press 1983); Graber (n 5).

17 See Milewicz (n 2); Sajó and Uitz (n 16) chs 1 and 8; Berman (n 16); Peters (n 2).

18 See Waldron (n 7); András Sajó, *Limiting Government: An Introduction to Constitutionalism* (Central European University Press 1999); Wil Waluchow, 'Constitutionalism' in Edward N Zalta (ed), *The Stanford Encyclopedia of Philosophy* (Spring 2018, Metaphysics Research Lab, Stanford University 2018) <https://plato.stanford.edu/archives/spr2018/entries/constitutionalism/> accessed 16 August 2019; Peters (n 2).

19 See Richard Bellamy, 'Constitutionalism', *Encyclopædia Britannica* (2019) <https://www.britannica.com/topic/constitutionalism> accessed 16 August 2019.

20 Cf. Nicholas Henshall, *The Myth of Absolutism: Change & Continuity in Early Modern European Monarchy* (Routledge 1992).

21 See Sajó and Uitz (n 16) ch 3; Nicholas W Barber, *The Principles of Constitutionalism* (Oxford University Press 2018) ch 6; see also Pernice (n 7).

22 See Barber (n 21) ch 1; Waldron (n 7).

23 See Sajó and Uitz (n 16) chs 1 and 10; Milewicz (n 2); Pernice (n 7).

Looking back before the eighteenth century, one could identify forms of constitutionalism within other ages. One could talk of a Greek or Roman constitutionalism, for instance.[24] However, this intellectual exercise is only possible analogically and by extension. Gerhard Casper rightly observed that

> constitutionalism does not refer simply to having a constitution, but to having a particular kind of constitution.[25]

When one thinks of constitutionalism, one generally implies the values underlying contemporary constitutionalism, the ideology that progressively developed from the big revolutions of the end of the eighteenth century. Constitutionalism is today synonymous with the values of democracy, the rule of law, and the separation of powers. Constitutionalism is associated with the idea of the protection of all fundamental rights that have been gradually recognised over the past few centuries, be they civil, political, socio-economic, or cultural.[26] However, what today no longer holds true is the necessary connection of the idea of constitutionalism with the nation-state.

The values of constitutionalism historically ripened in the context of the state.[27] However, over the past few decades, in a society that has become increasingly more global, the centrality of the state has faded due to the emergence of other dominant actors in the transnational context.[28] The scholarship has therefore started to transplant the constitutional conceptual machinery beyond the state, including the concept of constitutionalism.[29] The myth of the compulsory link between constitutionalism and the state is debunked.[30] As Hamann and Ruiz Fabri state, today 'it appears that any polity can be endowed with or can acquire constitutional features'.[31] Consequently, the constitutional ecosystem becomes plural, composite, and

24 See Charles Howard McIlwain, *Constitutionalism: Ancient and Modern* (Amagi, originally published by Cornell University Press, 1947, 2007); cf. Sartori (n 4); cf. Graham Maddox, 'A Note on the Meaning of `Constitution'' (1982) 76 The American Political Science Review 805; see also Raymond Polin, *Plato and Aristotle on Constitutionalism: An Exposition and Reference Source* (Ashgate 1998).

25 Gerhard Casper, 'Constitutionalism' in Leonard W Levy, Karst L Kenneth and Dennis J Mahoney (eds), *Encyclopedia of the American Constitution* (1986th edn, Macmillan) 474.

26 See Sajó and Uitz (n 16) chs 1 and 10.

27 See Grimm (n 4).

28 See Petra Dobner and Martin Loughlin (eds), *The Twilight of Constitutionalism?* (Oxford University Press 2010).

29 See Grimm (n 4) ch VII and VIII.

30 See Ulrich K Preuss, 'Disconnecting Constitutions from Statehood: Is Global Constitutionalism a Viable Concept?' in Petra Dobner and Martin Loughlin (eds), *The Twilight of Constitutionalism?* (Oxford University Press 2010).

31 A Hamann and H Ruiz Fabri, 'Transnational Networks and Constitutionalism' (2008) 6 International Journal of Constitutional Law 481, 503.

fragmented.[32] If the values of constitutionalism remain the same in their essence, their articulation in specific contexts, within and beyond the state, necessarily becomes 'polymorphic'.[33]

Constitutionalism in the digital age

Contemporary constitutionalism was not extracted from the rock of history as a monolithic marble block. Constitutionalism developed more like an onion. Its inner fundamental values progressively shaped further external layers: principles budding to face the emerging complexities of the society. In the words of Chris Thornhill:

> Constitutional norms are constructed as layers within the evolving inclusionary structure of the political system; new constitutional norms are articulated, progressively, as society's political system is exposed to challenges and demands, which it cannot absorb, and as it requires additional normative complexity to sustain its functions of inclusion. The key to understanding constitutions, in consequence, is to examine constitutional norms as a historically constructed, adaptive apparatus, which is closely correlated with distinct *inclusionary pressures* in society.[34]

Today, existing constitutional principles cannot anymore solve all the challenges of contemporary society. The external shape of constitutionalism necessarily changes again. New constitutional layers are progressively added to those already in existence. Novel principles emerge to articulate the fundamental values of constitutionalism in light of the problematic issues of contemporary society, including, but not limited to, the challenges of the digital revolution.[35] Constitutionalism is undergoing a mutation on multiple fronts. However, the scale of transformation prompted by the advent of the digital revolution is such that one can neatly distinguish the multiplicity

32 Neil Walker, 'The Idea of Constitutional Pluralism' (2002) 65 The Modern Law Review 317; Teubner (n 5); see also Paul Blokker, 'Modern Constitutionalism and the Challenges of Complex Pluralism' in Gerard Delanty and Stephen P Turner (eds), *Routledge International Handbook of Contemporary Social and Political Theory* (Routledge 2011) <https://papers.ssrn.com/abstract=1719258> accessed 22 August 2018.

33 See Walker (n 32).

34 Thornhill (n 5) 9, original emphasis; for a similar view on the historicism of constitutional principles, see Norberto Bobbio, *The Age of Rights* (Allan Cameron tr, Polity 1996); Teubner (n 5).

35 An example is the constitutionalisation of principles related to the protection of the environment, see David Marrani, 'The Second Anniversary of the Constitutionalisation of the French Charter for the Environment: Constitutional and Environmental Implications' (2008) 10 Environmental Law Review 9; see also Stefano Rodotà, *Il diritto di avere diritti* (Laterza 2012) 70.

of new normative layers addressing this phenomenon. A fresh sprout within the constitutionalist theory: what one could call 'digital constitutionalism'.

Digital constitutionalism is a useful shorthand to denote the theoretical strand that advocates for the translation of the core values of constitutionalism in the context of the digital society.[36] At first sight, however, such a descriptor could appear as misleading.[37] The adjective 'digital' does not directly qualify the substantive 'constitutionalism'. It is not akin to expressions such as 'democratic constitutionalism' or 'liberal constitutionalism' in which, respectively, democracy and liberalism characterise a newly acquired orientation of the theory of constitutionalism.[38] 'Digital' is rather an adverbial conveying the idea that one is referring to that strand of the constitutional theory that seeks to articulate principles for the digital society.[39] Similarly, the scholarship has talked of 'global' or 'international' constitutionalism, which Anne Peters defines as:

> a strand of thought (an outlook or perspective) and a political agenda which advocate the application of constitutional principles, such as the rule of law, checks and balances, human rights protection, and democracy, in the international legal sphere in order to improve the effectivity and the fairness of the international legal order.[40]

36 First formulated in this sense in Edoardo Celeste, 'Digital Constitutionalism: Mapping the Constitutional Response to Digital Technology's Challenges' (2018) HIIG Discussion Paper Series No 2018-02 <https://papers.ssrn.com/abstract=3219905> accessed 23 August 2018; subsequently revised and amplified in Celeste, 'Digital Constitutionalism' (n 11). In this last paper, at 88, I defined 'digital constitutionalism' as 'the ideology which aims to establish and to ensure the existence of a normative framework for the protection of fundamental rights and the balancing of powers in the digital environment'.

37 See Edoardo Celeste, 'What Is Digital Constitutionalism?' (*HIIG Science Blog*, 31 July 2018) <https://www.hiig.de/en/what-is-digital-constitutionalism/> accessed 31 August 2018.

38 See Blokker (n 32); Paul Blokker, 'Grassroots Constitutional Politics in Iceland' (Social Science Research Network 2012) SSRN Scholarly Paper ID 1990463 <https://papers.ssrn.com/abstract=1990463> accessed 19 August 2019; Michael W Dowdle and Michael Wilkinson (eds), *Constitutionalism beyond Liberalism* (Cambridge University Press 2016).

39 In these terms, Celeste, 'What Is Digital Constitutionalism?' (n 37); Celeste, 'Digital Constitutionalism' (n 11).

40 Peters (n 2) 583. Digital constitutionalism and global constitutionalism have different points in common, such as the identification of constitutional patterns beyond the state. On the same point, see Edoardo Celeste, 'Terms of Service and Bills of Rights: New Mechanisms of Constitutionalisation in the Social Media Environment?' (2019) 33 International Review of Law, Computers & Technology 122, para 4.1 ff. However, they remain distinct concepts with a different focus: the first one on the digital society, while the latter on the international legal sphere. On this point, see Vagias Karavas, 'Review Essay - Some Remarks on the Constitutionalisation of Cyberspace' (2012) 3 German Law Journal <http://www.germanlawjournal.com/index.php?pageID=11&artID=219>. More generally on global and international constitutionalism, see, ex multis, Jan Klabbers, 'Constitutionalism Lite' (2004) 1 International Organizations Law Review 31; Ronald MacDonald and Douglas Johnston (eds), *Towards World Constitutionalism: Issues in the Legal Ordering*

The notion of 'digital constitutionalism', and, more broadly, the idea of projecting constitutionalism in the context of the digital environment, is not new. However, the scholarship employed this concept in an inconsistent way.[41] Fitzgerald talked of 'informational constitutionalism' to denote state law, in particular in the fields of intellectual property, competition, contracts, and privacy, aiming to limit the power of tech companies to self-regulate.[42] For Berman, 'constitutive constitutionalism' advocates for an expansion of the reach of US constitutional law to encompass those private actors.[43] In Suzor, 'digital constitutionalism' is a project seeking to articulate a set of limits on private powers that affect how individuals can enjoy their rights in the digital world. The values of state constitutional law would inform the adoption of ordinary statutes imposing a series of minimal guarantees that tech companies should respect in self-regulating their products and services.[44] Karavas praised a form of digital constitutionalism without the state, or, at least, with its intervention kept to a minimum. The communities of cyberspace should be able to self-constitutionalise themselves in a bottom-up and incremental way. State judges should play only a maieutic role, socratically teaching what the basic rules in creating valid constitutional norms are.[45] Redeker, Gill, and Gasser, lastly, employed the notion of digital constitutionalism to connect the emergence of a series of non-binding declarations of Internet rights which aim to set limits on both public and private power in the digital context.[46]

---

of the World Community (Brill 2005); Peters (n 2); CEJ Schwöbel, 'Situating the Debate on Global Constitutionalism' (2010) 8 International Journal of Constitutional Law 611; Thomas Kleinlein, 'Between Myths and Norms: Constructivist Constitutionalism and the Potential of Constitutional Principles in International Law' (2012) 81 Nordic Journal of International Law 79; Anne Peters, 'Global Constitutionalism' in Michael T Gibbons (ed), *The Encyclopedia of Political Thought* (John Wiley & Sons 2014).

41 For a comprehensive and detailed analysis of the literature on the topic, see Celeste, 'Digital Constitutionalism' (n 11).

42 See Brian Fitzgerald, 'Software as Discourse? A Constitutionalism for Information Society' (1999) 24 Alternative Law Journal 144.

43 Paul Berman, 'Cyberspace and the State Action Debate: The Cultural Value of Applying Constitutional Norms to "Private" Regulation' (2000) 71 University of Colorado Law Review 1263. According to the so-called 'state action doctrine', US constitutional law only applies to the conduct of public actors.

44 See Nicolas Suzor, 'Digital Constitutionalism and the Role of the Rule of Law in the Governance of Virtual Communities' (phd, Queensland University of Technology 2010) <https://eprints.qut.edu.au/37636/> accessed 30 August 2018; Nicolas Suzor, 'The Role of the Rule of Law in Virtual Communities' (2010) 25 Berkeley Technology Law Journal 1817.

45 See Vagias Karavas, 'Governance of Virtual Worlds and the Quest for a Digital Constitution' in Christoph B Graber and Mira Burri-Nenova, *Governance of Digital Game Environments and Cultural Diversity: Transdisciplinary Enquiries* (Edward Elgar Publishing 2010).

46 Dennis Redeker, Lex Gill and Urs Gasser, 'Towards Digital Constitutionalism? Mapping Attempts to Craft an Internet Bill of Rights' (2018) 80 International Communication Gazette 302; cf. also the first version of their paper: Lex Gill, Dennis Redeker and Urs Gasser, 'Towards Digital Constitutionalism? Mapping Attempts to Craft an Internet Bill

At first sight, all of these interpretations of digital constitutionalism appear different. However, they are not incompatible as, if comprehensively regarded, they reveal themselves as multiple facets of a broader unitary picture.[47] They all deal with the issue of the limitation of power of dominant actors and, when considered together, they recognise the existence of a plurality of normative instruments translating constitutional values in the digital society, both emerging in the state context, such as constitutional and ordinary law, and beyond, as in the case of private companies' self-regulation.

Ultimately, these various readings provide plausibility for the wider vision presented in this work that sees digital constitutionalism as the theoretical strand of contemporary constitutionalism that is adapting core constitutional values to the needs of the digital society. Digital constitutionalism advocates the perpetuation of foundational principles, such as the rule of law, the separation of powers, democracy, and the protection of human rights, in the mutated scenario of the digital society. It triggers a complex process of constitutionalisation of the virtual environment, which occurs through a multiplicity of constitutional counteractions, both within and beyond the state. Century-old values are translated in normative principles that can speak to the new social reality. Digital constitutionalism reiterates that digital technology does not create any secluded world where individuals are not entitled to their quintessential guarantees.

A new constitutionalism?

Digital constitutionalism represents the conceptual lymph of the current constitutional moment. It normatively advocates a reconfiguration of the constitutional framework. Analogue norms are no longer able to address the full range of complexities of the virtual environment. A series of normative counteractions are emerging to implement the principles of a constitutionalism rethought for the digital age. The current constitutional moment, too, has a 'transformative impact'.[48] Core constitutional values are generalised and subsequently re-specified in light of the characteristics of the contemporary society.[49] Constitutionalism is translated in a language that

of Rights' (2015) Berkman Center Research Publication No 2015-15 <https://papers.ssrn.com/abstract=2687120> accessed 30 August 2018; adopting the same approach, see Claudia Padovani and Mauro Santaniello, 'Digital Constitutionalism: Fundamental Rights and Power Limitation in the Internet Eco-System' (2018) 80 International Communication Gazette 295; for a critical analysis, see Celeste, 'Digital Constitutionalism' (n 11).

47 See Celeste, 'Digital Constitutionalism' (n 11) para 4.

48 JHH Weiler, *The Constitution of Europe: 'Do the New Clothes Have An Emperor?' And Other Essays on European Integration* (Cambridge University Press 1999) 4.

49 The idea of a process of generalisation and re-specification of constitutional principles was first advanced in Gunther Teubner, 'Societal Constitutionalism; Alternatives to State-Centred Constitutional Theory?' in Christian Joerges, Inger-Johanne Sand and

speaks to the actors of the virtual environment. In this way, old principles become more easily applicable in new societal contexts. Further corollaries, and even novel norms emerge to express foundational constitutional values in the digital society.

This process of constitutionalisation is still ongoing; yet, it is legitimate to ask: are we facing an evolution or a *r*-evolution of contemporary constitutionalism? Is reshaping constitutionalism for the digital age merely a way to enhance its fitness vis-à-vis the mutated conditions of the social reality? Or does it imply a more radical change of paradigm?

Two decades ago, Fitzgerald wrote:

> Once upon a time it was thought (and taught) that constitutionalism was a legal and political concept that defined the exercise of power by national public institutions. So much has changed. Nowadays constitutionalism must be defined more broadly to encompass the exercise of power in the private sphere by, amongst others, corporations, groups and individuals and the growing significance of international institutions (including multinational corporations (MNCs)) to our daily lives.[50]

The extended scope of digital constitutionalism in comparison with its analogue version could be mentioned as apparent evidence of the revolutionary nature of the current constitutional moment. Constitutionalism is no longer anchored to the nation-state. In the digital age, it promotes ways to limit the power of all dominant actors, be they public or private. Overlooking the capability of non-state actors to affect individual rights would be anachronistic, and would ultimately fail to safeguard human dignity, which can be equally violated by public and private hands.[51] According to Suzor, the present circumstances would necessarily require

> [...] a new constitutionalism – a new way of thinking about the power that technology companies wield and the discretion they exercise over our lives. To constitutionalize power means to impose limits on how rules are made and enforced. Constitutionalism is the difference between lawlessness and a system of rules that are fairly, equally, and predictably applied. We should expect the technology companies that rule

Gunther Teubner (eds), *Transnational Governance and Constitutionalism. International Studies in the Theory of Private Law* (Hart 2004); see also Teubner (n 5); Celeste, 'Digital Constitutionalism' (n 11).

50 Fitzgerald (n 42).

51 Celeste, 'Digital Constitutionalism' (n 11) para 3.5 and 4.2; see also Redeker, Gill and Gasser (n 46); cf. Gill, Redeker and Gasser (n 46), where a conception of digital constitutionalism still anchored to the idea of limitation of power of public actors is present.

> over us to take on the hard work, now, to develop their own constitutional protections that can help ensure that *our* rights are protected.[52]

One is also tempted to evoke the advent of a new form of constitutionalism because constitutional moments generally represent the apex of a transformative process. Adaptations and transformations have always been integral components of the vital cycle of constitutionalism. However, today, constitutional counteractions emerge in response to a digital revolution that is violently shaking the existing constitutional architecture. Existing constitutional norms, which were shaped for an analogue society, are under unprecedented stress. One therefore envisages the need for immediate, drastic transformations. Digital constitutionalism would represent an appeal to urgently take a remedial action: a last minute, normative SOS. Teubner indeed observes:

> The functionally differentiated society appears to ignore earlier chances of self-correction; to ignore the fact that sensible observers draw attention to the impending danger with warnings and incantations. In the self-energizing processes of maximizing sub-rationalities, self-correction seems to be possible only at the very last minute. The similarity with individual addiction therapies is obvious: 'Hit the bottom!' It must be one minute before midnight. Only then, today's addiction society has a chance of self-correction. Only then is the understanding lucid enough, the suffering severe enough, the will to change strong enough, to allow a radical change of course. […] The Kuhnian paradigm shift in science appears to be a similar phenomenon, where aberrations from the current dominant paradigms are dismissed as anomalies until the point where the 'theory-catastrophe' forces a paradigm shift.[53]

If the digital revolution is regarded as a looming and inexorable cataclysm, the extent of the constitutional change is dramatised too. The constitutional ecosystem has still to fully realise the severity of the storm that it has started to navigate. It has waited until the last minute to understand the necessity to react against the challenges of the digital revolution, and now one has the impression that the normative transformations needed will represent a Copernican revolution. Certainly, the emergence of constitutional counteractions is not evidence that supports the vision of a constitutional ecosystem that is riding the digital revolution on the crest of the wave – this is true. However, the present work argues that, from an objective standpoint, the current constitutional moment does not represent a radical upheaval.[54]

52 Nicolas Suzor, *Lawless. The Secret Rules That Govern Our Digital Lives* (Cambridge University Press 2019) 9, original emphasis.

53 Teubner (n 5) 82.

54 See Celeste, 'Digital Constitutionalism' (n 11) para 2.

We are not facing a change of paradigm that is indelibly transforming the shape of our constitutional identity. We are not witnessing a transition from democracy to technocracy, for example.[55] Digital constitutionalism does not advocate a *tabula rasa* of our core constitutional values. On the contrary, it is deeply rooted in these foundational principles. Digital constitutionalism champions their translation in the context of the digital society. Innovation, of course, occurs – it suffices to think to the fact that digital constitutionalism seeks to limit the power of private actors too. The societal context unavoidably imposes similar changes. However, as the second part of this work will show, this does not subvert the original constitutional paradigm founded on the values of democracy, the rule of law, the separation of powers, and the protection of human rights. Digital constitutionalism perpetuates these constitutional principles in a mutated social reality: in the digital society, the DNA of contemporary constitutionalism is ultimately preserved.

55 See Emilio Castorina, 'Scienza, tecnica e diritto costituzionale' (2015) Rivista AIC <http://www.rivistaaic.it/la-scienza-costituzionalistica-nelle-transizioni-istituzionali-e-sociali.html>.

7 Towards an Internet constitution?

'Bytes can never hurt me'

In William Golding's *Lord of the Flies*, a plane carrying a group of young boys crashes on a remote island in the Pacific Ocean.[1] Stranded on an uninhabited atoll, without any adults, the schoolboys become the protagonists of a socio-legal experiment. They have the possibility to found a new society, establishing its rules, structure, and aims.

At the beginning, the symbol of this enterprise is represented by a conch shell found in the lagoon. 'We can use this to call the others. Have a meeting. They'll come when they hear us', says Piggy, a bespectacled and overweight boy personifying the voice of wisdom and prudence of the group.[2] The shell is used as a horn to call the assemblies of the survivors. It epitomises the boys' attempt to create a democratic society based on agreed rules. However, this egalitarian élan – what Golding lyrically calls the 'dignity of the conch' – fades in a few pages.[3] The teenagers, oblivious to the values of the society in which they used to live, surrender soon to their will to power, superstitions, and rivalries.

In this socio-legal experiment, the feral law eventually prevails on centuries of civilisation. At the end of the novel, an officer disembarked on the island observes with disappointment the tragic end of the boys' adventure. The tropical forest is gone in flame and two young boys are dead. In the last lines, one of the protagonists weeps for 'the end of innocence' of the group and the consequent twilight of its original democratic dream.[4]

A similarly despairing story characterises the development of the virtual world created by the advent of the Internet. Early Internet literati considered cyberspace as a recently discovered, uninhabited island, a place where

1 William Golding, *Lord of the Flies* (Faber & Faber 1954).
2 Golding (n 1) 17.
3 Golding (n 1) 216.
4 Golding (n 1) 223.

DOI: 10.4324/9781003256908-7

a new beginning was possible.[5] In 1994, Esther Dyson, George Gilder, George Keyworth, and Alvin Toffler published an article solemnly titled 'Cyberspace and the American Dream: A Magna Carta for the Knowledge Age'.[6] Cyberspace was celebrated as the 'land of knowledge' whose exploration would represent 'civilization's truest, highest calling'. The border between the physical and virtual worlds was considered as the 'electronic frontier' delimiting a new prosperous Far West. The advent of digital technology would mark the dawn of the 'Third Wave' economy, no longer based on physical matter, but exclusively consisting of knowledge. In the authors' magniloquent words:

> The central event of the 20th century is the overthrow of matter. In technology, economics, and the politics of nations, wealth -- in the form of physical resources -- has been losing value and significance. The powers of mind are everywhere ascendant over the brute force of things.[7]

In 1996, John Perry Barlow wrote the famous 'Declaration of the Independence of Cyberspace'.[8] This text reiterated the idea of cyberspace as the 'home of Mind', a 'global social space' where anyone 'may express his or her beliefs, no matter how singular, without fear of being coerced into silence or conformity'. As its title clearly evokes, the aim of the Declaration was to assert the independence of cyberspace from nation-states, defined as 'weary giants of flesh and steel', on the basis of its 'natural' autarky. Cyberspace was indeed seen as an independent space, distinct from the physical world. As Barlow lyrically put it:

> Ours is a world that is both everywhere and nowhere, but it is not where bodies live.[9]

This worldview, subsequently dubbed 'cyberlibertarianism', posited that cyberspace was a 'speech-dominated' world where no physical 'harm' was

5 See Andrew D Murray, *The Regulation of Cyberspace: Control in the Online Environment* (Routledge 2006) 5 ff; David J Bell and others, *Cyberculture: The Key Concepts* (Routledge 2004) 35 ff.

6 "Cyberspace and the American Dream: A Magna Carta for the Knowledge Age", Future Insight, Aug. 1994' <http://www.pff.org/issues-pubs/futureinsights/fi1.2magnacarta.html> accessed 30 April 2019; cf. Stéphane Marchand and Michel Bourdeau, 'Une Magna Carta pour Internet, 20 ans après' (2015) 141 Cahiers philosophiques 104.

7 "Cyberspace and the American Dream: A Magna Carta for the Knowledge Age", Future Insight, Aug. 1994' (n 6) Preamble.

8 John Perry Barlow, 'A Declaration of the Independence of Cyberspace' (1996) <https://www.eff.org/cyberspace-independence> accessed 11 December 2018.

9 Barlow (n 8).

conceivable.[10] 'Sticks and stones can break my bones but bytes can never hurt me' would have been their adage, as Boyle reports.[11] This assumption would have justified the argument of Internet exceptionalism, i.e. that nation-states do not have the right to apply their rules to cyberspace, but that conversely the digital world could find its very own system of governance.[12]

The end of innocence

A second group of scholars, at their turn dubbed 'cyberpaternalists', strongly rejected this vision of cyberspace as an intrinsically distinct world of pure speech, capable of self-regulation.[13] They argued that purely cyberlibertarian and cyberanarchist views were utopian. Similarly to the plot of *Lord of the Flies*, these ideals would be destined to surrender to the supremacy of the feral law of the Internet environment. In cyberspace, the 'invisible hand' would not be guided by democratic and egalitarian archetypes, but by the dominant pair of 'government' and 'commerce'.[14] The Internet would degenerate from the ideal 'home of Mind' into a space of commercial profit and government surveillance.[15] For this reason, cyberspace could not be considered as an autonomous space, fully distinct from the physical world but should be subject to regulation.[16] As stated by the German Federal Constitutional Court, 'even the Internet cannot create a legal vacuum'.[17]

Unfortunately, over the past few years, a series of events has inexorably infringed two central tenets of the cyberlibertarian vision. Firstly, it suffices to recall the mass surveillance programmes unveiled by Edward Snowden in 2013 and the recent Cambridge Analytica scandal involving Facebook to understand that cyberspace is not the utopian, self-regulating realm of the mind advocated by the cyberlibertarians.[18]

10 For a critical reconstruction of the cyberlibertarian account, see James Boyle, 'Foucault in Cyberspace: Surveillance, Sovereignty, and Hardwired Censors' (1997) 66 University of Cincinnati Law Review 177.

11 Boyle (n 10) 180.

12 See David R Johnson and David G Post, 'Law and Borders: The Rise of Law in Cyberspace' (1996) 48 Stanford Law Review; See also Barlow (n 8).

13 See Murray (n 5); as representative examples, see Jack L Goldsmith, 'Against Cyberanarchy' (1998) 65 The University of Chicago Law Review 1199; Lawrence Lessig, *Code: And Other Laws of Cyberspace, Version 2.0* (Basic Books 2006); Boyle (n 10); Joel R Reidenberg, 'Yahoo and Democracy on the Internet' (2002) 42 Jurimetrics 251.

14 Lessig (n 13) 4 ff.

15 See Lessig (n 13); Boyle (n 10).

16 See Murray (n 5).

17 *Vorratsdatenspeicherung (Data retention)* BVerfGE 125, 260 [260].

18 On the Snowden revelations, see David Lyon, *Surveillance after Snowden* (Polity Press 2015); on online surveillance, see Christian Fuchs and others (eds), *Internet and Surveillance: The Challenges of Web 2. 0 and Social Media* (Routledge 2011); Shoshana Zuboff, *The Age of Surveillance Capitalism: The Fight for a Human Future at the New Frontier of Power* (PublicAffairs 2019); for a comprehensive account of the Cambridge Analytica

Secondly, today it is apparent that cyberspace is not a remote island: a distinct, autonomous, watertight environment separable from the physical reality theorised by those early Internet thinkers.[19] Recent technological developments have contributed to bind physical and virtual existence together in a way that, today, for many, these two are complementary and inseparable. The use of digital technology has become an integral part of our daily life.[20] Reading news, communicating, searching for a job, professing one's own political or religious faith are all examples of activities that many individuals habitually perform online.

Today, digital technology does not merely represent one of the many instruments available to exercise a broad range of fundamental rights rotating around the exchange of information but has even become the most important catalyst of these rights. In 2017, the US Supreme Court in the case *Packingham v. North Carolina* held that:

> While in the past there may have been difficulty in identifying the most important places (in a spatial sense) for the exchange of views, today the answer is clear. It is cyberspace – the "vast democratic forums of the Internet" in general, […] and social media in particular.[21]

In this case, the Supreme Court found unconstitutional a national statute preventing a registered sex offender to access a broad range of social media. For the Court, the argument that such an individual does have other means to access and impart information other than through social media was not

---

scandals, see Patrick Greenfield, 'The Cambridge Analytica Files: The Story so Far' *The Guardian* (25 March 2018) <https://www.theguardian.com/news/2018/mar/26/the-cambridge-analytica-files-the-story-so-far> accessed 30 April 2019.

19 See Barlow (n 8); for a comprehensive analysis of Internet legal order, cf. Matthias C Kettemann, *The Normative Order of the Internet: A Theory of Rule and Regulation Online* (Oxford University Press 2020).

20 See Tero Karppi, *Disconnect* (University of Minnesota Press 2018); Gilles Dowek, *Vivre, aimer, voter en ligne et autres chroniques numériques* (Le Pommier 2017); see also, although more dated, Sherry Turkle, *Life on the Screen* (Simon and Schuster 1995); Annette N Markham, *Life Online: Researching Real Experience in Virtual Space* (Rowman Altamira 1998).

21 *Packingham v North Carolina* (2017) US Supreme Court 582 U.S. ___ 4; for a more detailed overview of the facts and the arguments of the court, see Alan Butler, 'US Supreme Court Finds Broad Restrictions on Access to Social Media Sites Unconstitutional' (2017) 4 European Data Protection Law Review 555; Katie Miller, 'Constitutional Law - Sex Offenses and Free Speech: Constitutionality of Ban on Sex Offenders' Use of Social Media: Impact on States with Similar Restrictions' (2018) 93 North Dakota Law Review 129; Madeleine Burnette-McGrath, 'Packingham v. North Carolina' (2019) 44 Ohio Northern University Law Review 117; see also Edoardo Celeste, 'Packingham v North Carolina: A Constitutional Right to Social Media?' (2018) 17 Cork Online Law Review 116 commenting on the existence of a right to social media; for an analysis of the application of the public forum doctrine to social media, see 'First Amendment -- Freedom of Speech -- Public Forum Doctrine -- Packingham v. North Carolina' (2017) 131 Harvard Law Review 233.

relevant, given the significance that these online platforms today play in our society as an essential instrument to exercise our fundamental rights.[22]

A constitution for the Internet

The Internet environment is not a *terra nullius* and does not lie anymore at the peripheries of our lives. It is a context where nation states well exercise their sovereignty, albeit in a complex way, due to the emergence of other dominant transnational private actors.[23] It is an ecosystem that plays a central role in determining the extent to which we can exercise a broad array of our fundamental freedoms. The *Packingham* case perfectly exemplifies the Janus-faced, yet crucial function of digital technology vis-à-vis fundamental rights. As illustrated in Chapter 2, on the one hand, the virtual world has increased the standard to which we are accustomed to exercise our rights. Digital technology offers unprecedented opportunities that are not equated by other existing media. On the other hand, the example of the North Carolina statute preventing sex offenders from accessing social media epitomises the risks deriving from the use of digital technology. Contrary to what the cyberlibertarians argued, it is not true that 'bytes can never hurt me': cyberspace can indeed be an instrument to perpetrate crimes with direct repercussions in the physical world.[24]

The Internet environment has not only acquired a legal but even an apparent constitutional relevance. In the first part of this work, we have seen the extent to which the digital revolution affects the constitutional ecosystem, and the complex reaction that this has triggered at various societal levels. Protecting fundamental rights and regulating the exercise of power in the digital environment has become one of the major challenges of contemporary constitutionalism. Everyone should have the right to exercise their rights according to the standard that new technology allows, and, at the same time, be protected against potential fundamental rights infringements. In the previous chapters, we have seen as this need has informed a multilevel process of constitutionalisation involving multiple normative counteractions, ranging from the adoption of more traditional constitutional instruments to more innovative tools emerged even beyond the state

22 *Packingham v. North Carolina* (n 21) 4, 8; see also Edoardo Celeste, Amélie Heldt and Clara Iglesias Keller (eds), *Constitutionalising Social Media* (Hart 2022); Edoardo Celeste, 'Digital Punishment: Social Media Exclusion and the Constitutionalising Role of National Courts' [2021] International Review of Law, Computers & Technology 1.

23 On the concept of digital sovereignty, see, ex multis, Edoardo Celeste, 'Digital Sovereignty in the EU: Challenges and Future Perspectives' in Federico Fabbrini, Edoardo Celeste and John Quinn (eds), *Data Protection Beyond Borders: Transatlantic Perspectives on Extraterritoriality and Sovereignty* (Hart 2021); Stephane Couture and Sophie Toupin, 'What Does the Notion of "Sovereignty" Mean When Referring to the Digital?' (2019) 21 New Media & Society 2305.

24 As was already evident in the initial phases of cyberspace: see Goldsmith (n 13).

dimension. In the second part of this work, we will focus on one peculiar solution: the appeal to adopt a 'constitution' for the Internet. An ambitious demand, originally advocated at academic level, which, as we will see, interestingly had a significant following, especially among civil society groups.

Lessig: The constitution in the Internet

In his seminal book *Code*, the American legal scholar Lawrence Lessig highlights the role of the Internet architecture as a powerful and effective regulatory mechanism.[25] Technology companies would have the ability to directly shape the code of software, in this way determining how users can interact in the digital world. Joel Reidenberg had already analysed this form of private rule-making through technical solutions under the name of *lex informatica*.[26] Lessig uses the slogan 'code is law'.[27] The legal norm somehow becomes invisible, embedded in the structure of the Internet. Internet users are no longer offered the possibility to infringe the law because respecting it is the only action still available to them.

The code, as a form of physical constraint, nullifies the space between law and law enforcement. Code is law in action and, as highlighted by Lessig, could also be constitution in action.[28] The Internet architecture enshrines constitutional values, in principle those determined by technology companies. Code in this way would represent the Internet's material constitution, its factual constitutional order.

However, Lessig rejects the idea of code's determinism: the Internet architecture should not remain that which is shaped by technology companies, completely subject to their economic interests. Code – he argues – would be malleable. He warns against the 'fallacy of "is-ism"': one should not think that how the Internet is now corresponds to how it should be.[29] In contrast to the views of cyberlibertarianism, he mistrusts the capability of cyberspace to self-regulate. In order to protect fundamental rights in the digital environment, he proposes to correct code by incorporating in it the values of the constitution, in his case, the US constitution.[30] Rather than praising the existing constitution *of* the Internet, Lessig advocates a constitution *in* the Internet.[31]

25 Lessig (n 13).
26 Joel Reidenberg, 'Lex Informatica: The Formulation of Information Policy Rules through Technology' (1998) 76 Texas Law Review 553.
27 Lessig (n 13).
28 See Lessig (n 13) 4 ff.
29 Lessig (n 13) 31 ff.
30 Lessig (n 13) 4 ff.
31 Cf. Laurence H Tribe, *The Constitution in Cyberspace: Law and Liberty Beyond the Electronic Frontier* (American Humanist Association 1991).

Teubner: Civil constitutions

Lessig wisely recognises that instilling the constitution in the code is not a straightforward task. It implies a complex work of 'translation' of constitutional values, a problematic process of selection, interpretation, transformation of principles entrusted both to the legislator and to the judiciary.[32] The issue of translation of traditional constitutional values in the context of the digital society is also pivotal in the works of Gunther Teubner. The German legal scholar generally questions the effectiveness of national constitutional law vis-à-vis three major trends of the twenty-first century: digitisation, privatisation, and globalisation.[33] The challenge of constitutional theory would be to 'generalise its nation-state tradition in contemporary terms and re-specify it'.[34] This operation, according to Teubner, would necessarily imply to disconnect constitutional law from the state dimension and eventually theorise a constitutionalism without the state.

Teubner moves a step forward in comparison with Lessig. He shares the view that the *lex electronica*, what in the previous paragraph was called the Internet's material constitution, is 'corrupted' by the economic interests of technology companies.[35] The *lex electronica* is for Teubner merely the heir of the *lex mercatoria* in the context of the cyberspace. He argues that 'it is here that the constitutional question of the Internet arises'.[36] The set of constitutional rules self-produced by dominant societal actors, such as technology companies, would suffer from a structural bias: they would only be of a 'constitutive', and not 'limitative', nature.[37] This structural corruption would, in turn, trigger a reaction from what Teubner calls the 'spontaneous sectors' of society, such as governmental agencies, civil society groups, trade unions, consumer protection organisations, and alike. The interaction between dominant players and this category of actors would engender

32 Lessig (n 13) 157 ff, 315 ff and 325 ff.

33 Gunther Teubner, 'Societal Constitutionalism; Alternatives to State-Centred Constitutional Theory?' in Christian Joerges, Inger-Johanne Sand and Gunther Teubner (eds), *Transnational Governance and Constitutionalism. International Studies in the Theory of Private Law* (Hart 2004).

34 Teubner, 'Societal Constitutionalism; Alternatives to State-Centred Constitutional Theory?' (n 33) 4.

35 Teubner, 'Societal Constitutionalism; Alternatives to State-Centred Constitutional Theory?' (n 33) 21.

36 Teubner, 'Societal Constitutionalism; Alternatives to State-Centred Constitutional Theory?' (n 33) 20.

37 Gunther Teubner, *Constitutional Fragments: Societal Constitutionalism and Globalization* (Oxford University Press 2012) 75 ff; see also Gunther Teubner, 'Self-Constitutionalizing TNCs? On the Linkage of "Private" and "Public" Corporate Codes of Conduct' (2011) 18 Indiana Journal of Global Legal Studies 617; cf. Nicolas Suzor, *Lawless. The Secret Rules That Govern Our Digital Lives* (Cambridge University Press 2019).

a process of 'constitutionalisation' and, ultimately, the emergence of new constitutional norms.[38]

Given the transnational nature of the digital society, for Teubner the digital constitution cannot derive from classical political processes of constitutionalisation. The alternative he proposes is a 'societal constitutionalism': subsectors of society would autonomously produce constitutional norms that would subsequently be absorbed by the legal system in a process of mutual influence.[39] Therefore, in contrast to Lessig, Teubner does not advocate a direct translation of constitutional principles drawn from national constitution into the Internet code but rather theorises a complementary constitutional process: the emergence of a multiplicity of 'civil constitutions'.[40]

Even if one could argue that for Teubner the ultimate mission of a digital constitution remains the same – the protection of fundamental rights in the digital society, its intrinsic characteristics would be very different from Lessig's archetype of constitution *in* the Internet. Teubner's digital constitution emerges beyond the state. It is potentially plural, resulting from a multiplicity of societal interactions. It is 'civil', in the sense that it is issued by the civil society, and it is not the result of institutionalised political processes. It is crowd-sourced, since its elaboration involves a variety of different actors. And, lastly, it is characterised by an unconventional nature, being something between a 'legal text' and a 'de facto structure of social systems'.[41]

Pernice: The constitution of the Internet society

Pernice shares one of the fundamental premises of Teubner's thought: the insufficiency of state-centred constitutionalism to address the challenges of contemporary society. A series of global issues, such as international terrorism, climate change, global financial regulation, Internet governance, and world peace-keeping, cannot be efficiently addressed at national or regional level.[42] Policies concerning these problems, when developed at local level, unavoidably produce external effects, structurally lack democratic

38 See Teubner, *Constitutional Fragments* (n 36) 94 ff; see also, *supra*, Chapter 5.

39 See Teubner, *Constitutional Fragments* (n 37).

40 For a critique to Teubner's theorisation was harshly criticised: see Stefano Rodotà, 'Una Costituzione per Internet?' [2010] Politica del diritto 337; Francesco Amoretti and Enrico Gargiulo, 'Dall'appartenenza Materiale All'appartenenza Virtuale? La Cittadinanza Elettronica Fra Processi Di Costituzionalizzazione Della Rete e Dinamiche Di Esclusione' [2010] Politica del diritto 353; Gaetano Azzariti, 'Internet e Costituzione' (2011) Politica del diritto 367.

41 Teubner, 'Societal Constitutionalism; Alternatives to State-Centred Constitutional Theory?' (n 33) 19.

42 Ingolf Pernice, 'Global Constitutionalism and the Internet. Taking People Seriously.' in Stefan Kadelbach and Rainer Hofmann (eds), *Law Beyond the State: Pasts and Futures* (Campus Verlag 2016) <http://ssrn.com/abstract=2576697>.

legitimacy, and are capable of undermining people's self-determination.[43] The power architecture no longer exclusively pivots on the states but is more similar to a 'constellation' of dominant actors, including private entities acting across a multiplicity of national territories.[44] In order to preserve our fundamental constitutional values in this mutated societal scenario, a global model of constitutional governance is needed.[45]

Pernice analyses existing paradigms of regulation beyond the state, such as the EU, the UN, the WTO, the so-called Rio Process on sustainable development, and Internet governance, concluding that none of them, taken singularly, provides a universal remedy for all the challenges of contemporary society.[46] For Pernice, the solution consists in a form of multilevel global constitutionalism, a complex architecture where all these partial legal systems would complement each other in order to shape a 'global constitutional framework'.[47] In such a setting, state constitutionalism is not absent. In contrast to Teubner's vision, it crucially lies at the basis of this fragmented and pluralistic construction, and, to this end, it is necessarily rethought. Pernice interprets the constitution in a 'postnational' sense, no longer uniquely anchored to the state, but opened up to the participation of individuals, and recognising the important co-regulatory role of private actors.[48]

Pernice's recent works highlight the twofold role that the Internet plays in this scenario. Firstly, the digital revolution is seen both as one of the transformative elements of contemporary society and as a unique opportunity to achieve a global constitutional framework. The Internet is not only a source of threat to our fundamental rights but it is also pivotal in allowing individuals to share information, participate in democratic life, and in enhancing transparency within the polity. For Pernice, the current impact of the digital revolution is so significant that he denotes contemporary society as the 'Internet society'.[49] Digital technologies create a 'global community' of individuals and shape a 'global public sphere' of political interaction.[50] In this

43 Pernice, 'Global Constitutionalism and the Internet. Taking People Seriously.' (n 42).

44 Ingolf Pernice, 'Risk Management in the Digital Constellation – A Constitutional Perspective' (2017) HIIG Discussion Paper Series No 2017-07 <https://papers.ssrn.com/abstract=3051124> accessed 18 October 2018. Cf. Jürgen Habermas, *The Postnational Constellation: Political Essays* (MIT Press 2001).

45 Pernice, 'Global Constitutionalism and the Internet. Taking People Seriously.' (n 42).

46 See Pernice, 'Global Constitutionalism and the Internet. Taking People Seriously.' (n 42).

47 See Pernice, 'Global Constitutionalism and the Internet. Taking People Seriously.' (n 42); Ingolf Pernice, 'Die Verfassung der Internetgesellschaft: Zur Rolle von Staat und Verfassung im Zuge der digitalen Revolution' in Alexander Blankenagel (ed), *Den Verfassungsstaat nachdenken. Eine Geburtstagsgabe* (Duncker & Humblot 2014) 33 <https://papers.ssrn.com/abstract=2964926> accessed 28 August 2018.

48 Pernice, 'Die Verfassung der Internetgesellschaft' (n 47).

49 Pernice, 'Die Verfassung der Internetgesellschaft' (n 47).

50 Pernice, 'Global Constitutionalism and the Internet. Taking People Seriously.' (n 42) 6.

way, the Internet becomes the driver of the new global constitutional framework, what Pernice also calls 'the constitution of the Internet society'.[51]

However, in this context, the Internet is not only the catalyst to a form of multilevel global constitutionalism but, as said before, it is also the object of a global model of governance. Pernice therefore adopts the expression 'constitution of the Internet' to specifically denote the basic legal order of Internet governance.[52] Such a constitution would emerge through an autonomous process of self-constitutionalisation carried out by a plurality of actors beyond the state.[53] The emerging constitution of the Internet would represent one of the several partial constitutions composing the multilevel mosaic of the global constitutional framework. In contrast to the broader notion of the 'constitution for the Internet society', its mission would therefore be to preserve the open, free, and interoperable character of the Internet, its variegated institutional framework, and the multistakeholder character of the processes of deliberation characterising its governance.

According to Pernice, the constitution of the Internet will not be realistically enshrined in an international treaty.[54] As with Lessig and Teubner, it could embody a basic legal order without being expressed in a written text.[55] Echoing Teubner, Pernice argues that the constitution of the Internet could remain fragmentary, thus very dissimilar from the traditional idea of constitution.[56] Nevertheless, these characteristics do not diminish the role of the Internet constitution in a broader context. In contrast to Teubner, Pernice offers a wider vision. The constitution of Internet governance can provide useful examples to understand how to craft constitutional norms for the global society.[57] He considers the constitution of the Internet as one of the many 'interwoven partial constitutions' whose elements, be they principles or institutional mechanisms, can be successfully harnessed to build the global constitutional framework of the Internet society.[58]

Rodotà: A charter of rights for the Internet

While Teubner theorises the progressive emergence of a digital constitution from the societal substratum through a complex process of interactions occurring outside traditional political processes, Stefano Rodotà directly

51 Pernice, 'Die Verfassung der Internetgesellschaft' (n 47).
52 Pernice, 'Die Verfassung der Internetgesellschaft' (n 47).
53 Pernice, 'Die Verfassung der Internetgesellschaft' (n 47) 22.
54 Ingolf Pernice, 'Vom Völkerrecht des Netzes zur Verfassung des Internets: Privacy und Digitale Sicherheit im Zeichen eines schrittweisen Paradigmenwechsels' (Social Science Research Network 2017) SSRN Scholarly Paper ID 2959257 <https://papers.ssrn.com/abstract=2959257> accessed 19 October 2019.
55 Pernice, 'Vom Völkerrecht des Netzes zur Verfassung des Internets' (n 53) 23.
56 Pernice, 'Vom Völkerrecht des Netzes zur Verfassung des Internets' (n 53).
57 See Pernice, 'Global Constitutionalism and the Internet. Taking People Seriously.' (n 42).
58 Pernice, 'Die Verfassung der Internetgesellschaft' (n 47) 26.

advocates a cooperation of all the relevant stakeholders in order to draft an Internet constitution.[59]

In 2005, the Italian legal scholar first wrote about the need to draft a 'Charter of Rights' to harness the development of the Internet.[60] Both states and powerful corporations would threaten fundamental rights online. The Internet would become an instrument to control, monetise, discriminate individuals and to reduce their specificity and autonomy. As the Parisians (re) discovered the importance of Mona Lisa when the famous Da Vinci painting was stolen from the museum of Louvre in 1911, so too would these series of new threats allow us to perceive the lack of guarantees for the digital society.[61] Therefore, at the moment, what would be most needed for Rodotà is a series of guiding principles. In his words:

> Time is come to affirm the principles of the new global people: freedom of access, freedom of use, right to knowledge, right to privacy, protection of the commons. Time is come to recognise these principles in a new Charter of Rights.[62]

Rodotà does not believe in a spontaneous natural reaction of the Internet. Invoking the original libertarian nature of cyberspace to reject the possibility to craft a charter of rights for the Internet would represent a 'position of rearguard' – writes Rodotà in another article.[63] It would be short-sighted not to take into account the multifarious situations in which, today, our fundamental rights are restricted in the online sphere by both nation-states and private corporations, as in the early cyberlibertarian charters. For the Italian scholar, elaborating a charter of rights for the Internet does not mean caging the freedom of the digital environment: conversely, charters and declarations have traditionally been the basis for an expansion of rights.[64] The formal recognition of rights in a written document would never be the end of the story: the (written) rights are instruments to fight for the (real) rights.[65]

Rodotà therefore abandons the innovative schemes proposed by Lessig, Teubner, and Pernice to stress the crucial role that a classical constitutional

59 Rodotà, 'Una Costituzione per Internet?' (n 40).

60 Stefano Rodotà, 'L'uomo nuovo di Internet' *La Repubblica* (28 October 2005) <https://ricerca.repubblica.it/repubblica/archivio/repubblica/2005/10/28/uomo-nuovo-di-internet.html> accessed 2 May 2019.

61 Stefano Rodotà, *Il diritto di avere diritti* (Laterza 2012) 16; Rodotà himself draws this example from Dominique Rousseau, 'La démocratie ou le vol de La Joconde' in Bertrand Mathieu and others (eds), *Nouvelles questions sur la démocratie* (Dalloz 2010).

62 Rodotà, 'L'uomo nuovo di Internet' (n 60), my translation.

63 Stefano Rodotà, 'Perché Internet Ha Bisogno Di Una Carta Dei Diritti' *La Repubblica* (14 November 2006) <http://www.repubblica.it/2006/11/sezioni/scienza_e_tecnologia/internet-30-milioni/carta-diritti-internet/carta-diritti-internet.html> accessed 2 May 2019.

64 Rodotà, 'Perché Internet Ha Bisogno Di Una Carta Dei Diritti' (n 63).

65 Rodotà, *Il diritto di avere diritti* (n 61) 32.

instrument, such a charter of rights, could play in the digital society. For Rodotà, the idea of an Internet constitution reacquires its traditional meaning of a written document: it neither refers to the code nor to a constitution as is intended in the common law systems, as normative 'architecture' resulting from the combination of various legal sources.[66]

Declarations of rights are texts that have marked epochal revolutions in the history of human rights. Rodotà rediscovers their power. He decides to exploit the evocative value that they have progressively acquired over the past few centuries to convey the new message of digital rights. In an article written in English and published in 2008, Rodotà employs for the first time the term 'Internet Bill of Rights', and explains:

> The choice of the old formula of the Bill of Rights has a symbolic force, it underlines that the aim is not to restrict freedom on the web but, on the contrary, to maintain the conditions for letting it continue to prosper. To do so, "constitutional" guarantees are required.[67]

The identification of a suitable instrument to promote fundamental rights in the digital environment is central for Rodotà. Like Lessig, Teubner, and Pernice, he understands that the current major challenges of the online worlds directly affect the constitutional dimension of the protection of individual rights. Rodotà's solution seems therefore to be the most conventional: he proposes to use a classical constitutional instrument to solve a constitutional problem.[68] Nevertheless, the idea of a charter of rights for the Internet, even though it appears at first sight in line with the constitutional tradition, presents some original aspects.

Rodotà clarifies that the use of the descriptors 'charter' or 'bill of rights' does not imply that the digital constitution should be the output of processes of elaboration similar to those that have brought about the adoption of those documents in the past. For the Italian scholar, the charter of rights for the Internet should not be the result of top-down processes analogous to those that led to the so-called 'constitutions octroyées', the charters graciously granted by enlightened princes in the nineteenth century, or to the constitutions deliberated by constituent assemblies in the twentieth century.[69] Sharing Pernice's scepticism, Rodotà contends that the digital

66 In the first sense, see Lessig (n 13); in the second sense, see Henry H Perritt, 'The Internet at 20: Evolution of a Constitution for Cyberspace' (2012) 20 William and Mary Bill of Rights Journal 1115.

67 Stefano Rodotà, 'A Bill of Rights for the Internet Universe' (2008) 21 The Federalist Debate <http://www.federalist-debate.org/index.php/current/item/250-a-bill-of-rights-for-the-internet-universe> accessed 2 May 2019.

68 Cf. Azzariti (n 40), who argues that using the descriptor 'Internet bill of rights' is legitimate in so far as it evokes the symbolic values of this concept but cannot lead to think that such a document has the same qualities of traditional constitutions.

69 Rodotà, 'Perché Internet Ha Bisogno Di Una Carta Dei Diritti' (n 63).

constitution cannot derive from traditional processes of international law making but would require the participation of all the relevant stakeholders: therefore not only states but also corporations, and – especially – citizens.[70] Only in this way the digital constitution could reflect the participatory and open nature of the Internet, 'the largest public space that the humankind has ever known'.[71]

Consequently, for Rodotà, the charter of rights for the Internet should be necessarily global. In his book 'Il diritto di avere diritti' (The right to have rights), he wrote:

> Landless rights wander in the global world in search of a constitutionalism that, being it global as well, could offer them a safe mooring. Today, rights are orphans of a land where they had their roots: national sovereignty once offered them a solid protection. Today, rights are dissolved in a world without borders, dominated by unrestrained power.[72]

Rodotà reports the legend of the man who owned a mill in Sanssouci, very close to the royal residence of Frederick the Great. The German king, disturbed by the proximity of the building, would have threatened the miller to seize his property using his royal prerogatives.[73] However, the humble man would have politely reminded the king of the existence of a high court in Berlin, which had the power to assess the justness of the royal order. Rodotà draws a comparison with the current global context in which rights and individuals have lost their reference points, and wonders: 'Who is the king and where are the judges today?'[74]

For Rodotà, we now live in a global society where we do not know what our guiding principles are and, even less, where we can obtain judicial redress. He argues that a global charter of rights for the Internet presupposes a rethinking of the relationship between public and private. He favours an overtaking of strategies of pure 'vertical domestication', where supranational norms are, in turn, incorporated and implemented at lower levels. He advocates a 'horizontal', expanding construction of norms, stressing in particular the role that judges will have in the future to interpret the general principles of the charter.[75]

70 Rodotà, 'Perché Internet Ha Bisogno Di Una Carta Dei Diritti' (n 63); see also Rodotà, 'Una Costituzione per Internet?' (n 40). Rodotà in particular praises the model of the 'dynamic coalitions' of the Internet Governance Forum; see, infra, ch 7. Cf. Pernice, 'Vom Völkerrecht Des Netzes Zur Verfassung Des Internets' (n 54).

71 Rodotà, 'L'uomo nuovo di Internet' (n 60), my translation.

72 Rodotà, *Il diritto di avere diritti* (n 61) 3, my translation.

73 See Wikipedia, 'Historische Mühle von Sanssouci' (2019) <https://de.wikipedia.org/w/index.php?title=Historische_M%C3%BChle_von_Sanssouci&oldid=185619946> accessed 3 May 2019.

74 Rodotà, *Il diritto di avere diritti* (n 61) 3, my translation.

75 Rodotà, 'Una Costituzione per Internet?' (n 40).

Following Rodotà's model

Rodotà's idea of a charter of rights for the Internet attracted a significant following among the scholarship. The model of an Internet bill of rights was considered as a suitable solution to limit the powers of predominant players in the digital environment and to protect the fundamental rights of individuals, in particular by updating or re-contextualising existing principles.[76] A few scholars further stressed that this instrument should also create new institutions.[77]

Giovanna De Minico considered the question of which 'legislative body' or 'constituent power' should draft the Internet bill of rights.[78] After having rejected the idea of a charter drafted by one single state or by a coalition of states, she concludes that the best solution would be to create a 'public supranational authoritative body'. This entity, according to De Minico, should legislate in a way that resembles the American 'notice and comment' procedure, i.e. by preliminary gathering the opinions of all the stakeholders involved before making its final decision.

Kinfe Micheal Yilma made a case for a declaration of Internet rights adopted by the UN General Assembly.[79] The structure of the existing UN organs would suitably fit the process of elaboration of a similar document. In particular, he praised the potential input that the General Assembly could receive from existing crowd-sourced mechanisms headed by the Office of the High Commissioner for Human Rights in the phase of drafting. Furthermore, a similar declaration would have a strong normative impact, at the same time avoiding hard legislation.

However, in the scholarship, there is no consensus on the role of states in drafting the charter of rights for the Internet. As seen, De Minico and Yilma, while recognising the global dimension of the digital environment, entrusted a central role to states and intergovernmental organisations. Conversely, Andreas Fischer-Lescano, echoing Teubner, stated that the

76 See David Casacuberta, Max Senges and Josep-Maria Duart, 'Privacy and the Need for an Internet Bill of Rights: Are There New Rights in Cyberspace?' (Social Science Research Network 2007) <https://papers.ssrn.com/abstract=2798298> accessed 3 May 2019; Francesca Musiani, 'The Internet Bill of Rights: A Way to Reconcile Natural Freedoms and Regulatory Needs?' (2009) 6 SCRIPTed 504; Azzariti (n 40); Giovanna De Minico, 'Towards an Internet Bill of Rights' (2015) 37 Loyola of Los Angeles International and Comparative Law Review 1; Andreas Fischer-Lescano, 'Struggles for a Global Internet Constitution: Protecting Global Communication Structures against Surveillance Measures' (2016) 5 Global Constitutionalism 145; Kinfe Micheal Yilma, 'Digital Privacy and Virtues of Multilateral Digital Constitutionalism—Preliminary Thoughts' (2017) 25 International Journal of Law and Information Technology 115.

77 See Casacuberta, Senges and Duart (n 76); Musiani (n 76); De Minico (n 76).

78 De Minico (n 76).

79 Yilma (n 76).

peculiarities of the digital environment impose a constitutional solution that necessarily overtakes the traditional nation-state dimension.[80]

Lastly, it is interesting to report Azzariti's development of the idea of a charter of rights for the Internet.[81] The Italian scholar recognised that an effective response to the issue of the protection of fundamental rights on the Internet should have a global nature. Nevertheless, he argued that a digital constitution should not necessarily be conceived as a single, 'cosmopolitan' document addressing the entire humankind. This would amount to a deplorable form of 'constitutional colonialism'. For Azzariti, the route to follow is longer and more complex. He supports the view of a slow process of elaboration of a multiplicity of charters and declarations by a variety of actors, including the civil society. This multitude of charters would persuade, influence, create a dialogue. Only in this way, the definition of the fundamental rights for the digital society could be really achieved in a democratic and participatory way. Though criticising Teubner, Azzariti eventually theorises a pluralisation of the idea and the process of elaboration of an Internet constitution, somehow echoing the archetype of civil constitutions proposed by the German scholar.

Internet bills of rights

Azzariti's idea of a multiplicity of charters of rights for the Internet emerging simultaneously is not a purely academic proposal, a utopian theoretical abstraction.[82] When suggesting a plural process of elaboration of fundamental principles for the digital society, he probably drew his inspiration from the reality. The idea of a written charter of rights for the Internet, indeed, did not remain a theoretical prototype, subject of discussion for academics and Internet literati. It was translated into practice, and, interestingly, we can identify not only one or few single texts that attempted to translate this idea of an Internet constitution. We observe a significant phenomenon, the emergence of numerous charters of rights for the Internet, very similarly to what Azzariti preconised.

Over the past few years, many civil society groups published their proposal for a charter of digital rights. Just to mention some recent examples, in 2014, the African Declaration Group issued the 'African Declaration on Internet Rights and Freedoms'[83] and the Just Net Coalition promoted the

80 Fischer-Lescano (n 76); cf. on the point Lessig (n 13), who opts for a residual role of states, which would be called to intervene only when the risk of adverse public consequences emerges; see also Teubner, 'Societal Constitutionalism; Alternatives to State-Centred Constitutional Theory?' (n 33).

81 Azzariti (n 40).

82 See Azzariti (n 40).

83 African Declaration Group, 'African Declaration on Internet Rights and Freedoms' <https://africaninternetrights.org/sites/default/files/African-Declaration-English-FINAL.pdf>.

'Delhi Declaration for a Just and Equitable Internet'.[84] In 2015, Rodotà himself chaired a commission composed of politicians, academics, representatives of private companies and NGOs, which issued a 'Declaration of Internet Rights', subsequently endorsed by the Italian Chamber of Deputies.[85] In 2016, a German working group supported by the Zeit-Stiftung proposed a 'Charter of Digital Fundamental Rights of the European Union'.[86]

A significant number of individuals, including academics, politicians, and technology experts, also proposed their own draft of Internet bill of rights. Robert Gelman published his 'Declaration of Human Rights in Cyberspace' back in 1997.[87] In 2010, Andrew Murray advanced 'A Bill of Rights for the Internet'.[88] In 2015, Mike Godwin wrote 'The Great Charter for Cambodian Internet Freedom'.[89]

Interestingly, there have been discussions at national level too on the need to incorporate a charter of Internet rights into domestic legislation.[90] In 2014, the Brazilian parliament was the first to approve a statute establishing 'principles, guarantees, rights and obligations for the use of Internet'.[91] In 2019, the Nigerian national assembly voted in a favour of a Digital Rights and Freedom Bill, which was however eventually not signed into law by the President.[92]

84 Just Net Coalition, 'The Delhi Declaration for a Just and Equitable Internet' <https://justnetcoalition.org/delhi-declaration> accessed 7 May 2019.

85 Camera dei Deputati, 'Mozione concernente iniziative per la promozione di una carta dei diritti in Internet e per la governance della rete' <http://www.camera.it/leg17/995?sezione=documenti&tipoDoc=assemblea_allegato_odg&idlegislatura=17&anno=2015&mese=11&giorno=03> accessed 7 May 2019.

86 'Charta der Digitalen Grundrechte der Europäischen Union' <https://digitalcharta.eu/> accessed 7 May 2019.

87 Robert Gelman, 'Draft Proposal-Declaration of Human Rights in Cyberspace' <http://www.be-in.com/10/rightsdec.html> accessed 17 June 2019.

88 Andrew Murray, 'A Bill of Rights for the Internet' <http://theitlawyer.blogspot.com/2010/10/bill-of-rights-for-internet.html> accessed 17 June 2019.

89 Mike Godwin, 'The Great Charter for Cambodian Internet Freedom' <https://www.linkedin.com/pulse/great-charter-cambodian-internet-freedom-mike-godwin> accessed 21 May 2019.

90 Green Party (New Zealand), 'Internet Rights and Freedoms Bill' (2014) <https://home.greens.org.nz/sites/default/files/internet_rights_and_freedoms_bill_accompanying_document_0.pdf>; UK Liberal Democrats, 'Creating a "Digital Bill of Rights": Why Do We Need It, and What Should We Include?' (2015) Consultation Paper <https://d3n8a8pro7vhmx.cloudfront.net/libdems/pages/8730/attachments/original/1428513286/Digital_Bill_of_Rights_Consultation_Paper_FINAL.pdf?1428513286>.

91 'Marco Civil Da Internet, Lei No. 12.965, de 23 de Abril de 2014.' <http://www.planalto.gov.br/ccivil_03/_ato2011-2014/2014/lei/l12965.htm> accessed 7 May 2019.

92 Ujam Chukwuemeka, Digital Rights and Freedom Bill 2016; see 'Nigeria's President Refused to Sign Its Digital Rights Bill, What Happens Now?' (*Techpoint.Africa*, 27 March 2019) <https://techpoint.africa/2019/03/27/nigerian-president-declines-digital-rights-bill-assent/> accessed 17 June 2019.

Even international organisations issued a series of declarations proclaiming rights and principles for the digital society. In particular, one can mention the Recommendation of the Committee of Ministers of the Council of Europe on Internet freedom of 2016,[93] the Code of EU Online Rights, published by the European Commission in 2012,[94] and the Code of ethics for the information society, adopted by the UNESCO in 2011.[95] More recently, the EU Commission announced its plan to adopt a proposal for a joint inter-institutional solemn declaration on digital rights and principles.[96]

Rodotà wrote that the contemporary digital society is witnessing a 'blossoming of declarations of rights'.[97] To get a more accurate idea of the dimension of this phenomenon, all the declarations mentioned by the existing scholarship have been listed.[98] In this way, a total of 172 documents has been gathered, dating between 1986 and 2016. As the following sections will show, by performing an Internet search of similar texts, the number of charters grows up to almost 200.

As one can notice from the examples mentioned above, these documents have different names. Mass media generally refer to these initiatives with a variety of denominations, such as 'Internet bill of rights', 'online Magna Carta', or 'Internet constitution'.[99] The next section will illustrate that the existing scholarship does not show greater terminological consistency either.

93 Council of Europe, 'Recommendation of the Committee of Ministers to Member States on Internet Freedom' (2016) CM/Rec(2016)5 <https://search.coe.int/cm/Pages/result_details.aspx?ObjectId=09000016806415fa>.

94 European Commission, 'Code of EU Online Rights' (2012) <https://ec.europa.eu/digital-single-market/sites/digital-agenda/files/Code%20EU%20online%20rights%20EN%20final%202.pdf>.

95 UNESCO, 'Code of Ethics for the Information Society Proposed by the Intergovernmental Council of the Information for All Programme (IFAP)' (2011) <https://unesdoc.unesco.org/ark:/48223/pf0000212696> accessed 17 June 2019.

96 EU Commission, 'Consultation Results: Europeans Express Strong Support for Proposed Digital Rights and Principles | Shaping Europe's Digital Future' (23 November 2021) <https://digital-strategy.ec.europa.eu/en/consultation-results-europeans-express-strong-support-proposed-digital-rights-and-principles> accessed 24 December 2021.

97 Rodotà, 'Una Costituzione per Internet?' (n 40) 344, my translation.

98 See Appendix B, available at <https://bit.ly/3lH6KDN>. An updated version of this database is now available on the website of the Digital Constitutionalism Network: <https://digitalconstitutionalism.org/database/>.

99 See Alex Howard, 'We the People Need Our Existing Bill of Rights to Apply in the Digital Domain' (*Radar*, 14 July 2012) <http://radar.oreilly.com/2012/07/digital-bill-of-rights-internet-freedom.html> accessed 7 May 2019; Tim Berners-Lee, 'We Need a Magna Carta for the Internet' *The Huffington Post* (5 June 2014) <https://www.huffpost.com/entry/internet-magna-carta_b_5274261?guccounter=1> accessed 7 May 2019; Jenima Kiss, 'An Online Magna Carta: Berners-Lee Calls for Bill of Rights for Web' *The Guardian* (12 March 2014) <https://www.theguardian.com/technology/2014/mar/12/online-magna-carta-berners-lee-web> accessed 7 May 2019; Pedro Abramovay, 'Brazil's Internet Constitution' *The Huffington Post* (5 June 2014) <https://www.huffpost.com/entry/brazils-internet-constitution_b_5274633> accessed 7 May 2019.

In 2015, a research paper of the Berkman Center for Internet and Society of Harvard University proposed 'digital constitutionalism' as a common term to connect these disparate documents.[100] However, as Chapter 6 has explained more extensively, this work posits that 'digital constitutionalism' is an expression more appropriate to denote the set of ideals and values underpinning these declarations rather than to describe these texts as a group. This book, reflecting the use established by some scholars, prefers to adopt the descriptor 'Internet bills of rights'.

Constitutional tone

From a cursory view of the examples of Internet bills of rights reported in the previous paragraph, one can immediately perceive that these documents, already from their title, aim to evoke the constitutional dimension. The majority of them refers to 'rights' and 'freedoms', the protection of which is traditionally one of the primary objectives of a constitution. It suffices to recall what the Abbé Sieyès and the Marquis de Lafayette wrote in Article 16 of the Declaration of the Rights of Man and of the Citizens of 1789:

> Any society in which no provision is made for guaranteeing rights or for the separation of powers, has no Constitution.[101]

In particular, these documents articulate rights and freedoms in the context of the digital age, 'digital rights' as some of these texts say. For example, the Declaration of Internet Rights endorsed by the Italian Chamber of Deputies in 2015 include a 'Right to Internet access' (Article 2), a 'Right to online knowledge and education' (Article 3), a right to 'Net neutrality' (Article 4), a right to 'Protection of personal data' (Article 5), just to mention some of them.[102]

Also in terms of structure, Internet bills of rights manifestly imitate traditional constitutional texts. Taking the example of the Italian Declaration of Internet Rights again, one can notice that the text is opened by a Preamble and is articulated in 14 articles, further divided in paragraphs. Moreover, it is apparent that these texts adopt a legal style, characterised by the use of present tense, modal and passive verbs, simple and concise sentences, and,

100 Lex Gill, Dennis Redeker and Urs Gasser, 'Towards Digital Constitutionalism? Mapping Attempts to Craft an Internet Bill of Rights' (2015) Berkman Center Research Publication No 2015-15 <https://papers.ssrn.com/abstract=2687120> accessed 30 August 2018.

101 Conseil constitutionnel (France), 'Declaration of Human and Civic Rights of 26 August 1789' <https://www.conseil-constitutionnel.fr/sites/default/files/as/root/bank_mm/anglais/cst2.pdf>; see the seminal Georg Jellinek, *The Declaration of the Rights of Man and of Citizens. A Contribution to Modern Constitutional History* (Max Farrand tr, Henry Holt 1901).

102 Camera dei Deputati, 'Mozione concernente iniziative per la promozione di una carta dei diritti in Internet e per la governance della rete' (n 85).

more specifically, a constitutional jargon, as is possible to understand from the employment of expressions such as 'everyone has the right to'.[103]

However, notwithstanding this apparent 'constitutional tone', Internet bills of rights are not generally texts with a constitutional value within any legal system.[104] They do not represent superior legal sources and, in the majority of the cases, they are not even considered as legal sources at all.[105] It is not a coincidence that many of these texts are titled 'declaration', a denomination that, even more so than 'charter', traditionally conveys the idea of a text that is not legally binding. To offer a known example, one could mention the Universal Declaration of Human Rights adopted by the United Nations General Assembly in 1948, a document that in principle does not have any binding legal value, although today some scholars consider it as part of customary international law.[106]

The lack of binding legal force of Internet bills of rights can be easily justified by identifying the sources of these texts. The majority of them are issued by civil society organisations, which are not vested with any institutional role. Internet bills of rights are usually elaborated outside traditional political contexts, through deliberative processes which are at times innovative.[107] The first draft of the Italian Declaration of Internet Rights, for example, was issued by an *ad hoc* committee established by the then President of the Italian Chamber of Deputies, composed of politicians, academics, and experts.[108] Such a draft was subsequently opened to comment by the general public on an online platform called CIVI.CI between October 2014 and March 2015, before being further modified and definitively endorsed by the Italian lower house in July 2015.[109]

103 See again, e.g., Camera dei Deputati, 'Mozione concernente iniziative per la promozione di una carta dei diritti in Internet e per la governance della rete' (n 85).

104 On the concept of 'constitutional tone', see also Edoardo Celeste, 'Terms of Service and Bills of Rights: New Mechanisms of Constitutionalisation in the Social Media Environment?' (2019) 33 International Review of Law, Computers & Technology 122.

105 Azzariti (n 40); Oreste Pollicino and Marco Bassini (eds), *Verso Un Internet Bill of Rights* (Aracne 2015); Gill, Redeker and Gasser (n 100); Yilma (n 76).

106 See Gordon Brown (ed), *The Universal Declaration of Human Rights in the 21st Century: A Living Document in a Changing World* (Open Book Publishers 2016); Johannes Morsink, *The Universal Declaration of Human Rights: Origins, Drafting, and Intent* (University of Pennsylvania Press 1999); cf. Frederick Mari van Asbeck, *The Universal Declaration of Human Rights and Its Predecessors (1679-1948)*, vol 10 (E J Brill 1949).

107 See *infra* Chapter 10.

108 For the minutes of the first Committee's meeting, see Camera dei Deputati, 'XVII Legislatura - XVII Legislatura - Deputati e Organi - Commissione diritti e doveri per l'uso di internet - Resoconti' <http://www.camera.it/leg17/1175> accessed 8 May 2019.

109 See Camera dei Deputati <http://camera.civi.ci/discussion/proposals/partecipa_alla_consultazione_pubblica_bill_of_rights>; Camera dei Deputati, 'Mozione concernente iniziative per la promozione di una carta dei diritti in Internet e per la governance della rete' (n 85).

Limited scholarship

Despite the size of such a phenomenon, its evident evocation of the constitutional dimension and its singularity, the study of the emergence of Internet bills of rights has not attracted significant attention from the scholarship, especially in the legal field.[110] Some scholars commented on single documents, in particular the Charter of Human Rights and Principles for the Internet developed in the context of the World Summits on the Information Society (WSIS) and the subsequent Internet Governance Forums,[111] the Brazilian law dubbed 'Marco civil da Internet' adopted in 2014,[112] and the Declaration of Internet Rights endorsed by the Italian Chamber of Deputies in 2015.[113]

Occasionally, Internet bills of rights were the object of study within broader research works. In these cases, the purpose of such analyses was to generate evidence to support arguments related to different research topics.[114] In particular, it is worth mentioning one of these studies. In 2015, UNESCO, the United Nations agency specialised in Education, Science and Culture, published a report conducted by Rolf H. Weber on '52 declarations, guidelines, and frameworks containing Internet Governance principles'.[115] This study is significant for the purposes of the present work because it provides one of the biggest selection of Internet bills of rights. However, the primary aim of Weber's work was not to analyse these documents generally but

110 In similar terms, Gill, Redeker and Gasser (n 100); see also Rolf H Weber, *Principles for Governing the Internet: A Comparative Analysis* (UNESCO 2015) 82 <https://unesdoc.unesco.org/ark:/48223/pf0000234435>.

111 See Joanna Kulesza, 'Freedom of Information in the Global Information Society: The Question of the Internet Bill of Rights' (2008) 1 University of Warmia and Mazury in Olsztyn Law Review 81; Musiani (n 76); Rikke Frank Jørgensen, 'An Internet Bill of Rights?' in Ian Brown (ed), *Research Handbook on Governance of the Internet* (Edward Elgar 2013).

112 See Francis Augusto Medeiros and Lee A Bygrave, 'Brazil's Marco Civil Da Internet: Does It Live up to the Hype?' (2015) 31 Computer Law & Security Review 120.

113 See Pollicino and Bassini (n 105).

114 See Giovanni Ziccardi, *Resistance, Liberation Technology and Human Rights in the Digital Age* (Springer 2013) ch 4 which focuses on 'Digital resistance, digital liberties and human rights'. In this context Ziccardi analysed four projects of 'Bill of Rights'. The purpose of such an investigation was to demonstrate that there is no clear correlation between these initiatives and activities of digital resistance; see Todd Davies, 'Digital Rights and Freedoms: A Framework for Surveying Users and Analyzing Policies' in Luca Maria Aiello and Daniel McFarland (eds), *Social Informatics: 6th International Conference, SocInfo 2014, Barcelona, Spain, November 11-13, 2014. Proceedings* (Springer 2014) who analysed ten 'digital rights', and showed the results of a survey conducted to demonstrate their importance for web users. To complement this investigation, 'four policy frameworks [Internet bills of rights] that have been proposed over the past twenty years [to secure] rights for users' were analysed to assess whether the ten selected principles were present, and to compare their content with the results of the survey. Davies eventually argued that the freedoms related to software platforms were generally overlooked by these texts.

115 Weber (n 110) 24.

more specifically to assess the presence in these texts of principles related to the UNESCO's notion of 'Internet Universality'.[116] Weber eventually concluded that none of the analysed documents encompassed entirely all the basic components of the UNESCO's concept of 'Internet Universality', encouraging the UN agency to formally adopt this principle and operationalise it more effectively in the context of its policies.

Only a restricted group of scholars with different academic backgrounds has conducted a comparative analysis of existing Internet bills of rights. In a 2009 article, Francesca Musiani, Claudia Padovani, and Elena Pavan, performed a lexicon-content analysis of 'ten documents that have been elaborated between 1996 and 2006 by different stakeholders and promoted as constitution-like documents for the digital age through an explicit self-proposing as Charters of civic rights or Bills of Rights for the Internet'.[117] The aim of this investigation was to assess if a 'consistent normative vision' of human rights in the digital age was emerging or, conversely, a trend of fragmentation and diversity both in terms of language used and issues identified prevailed. The World Summit on the Information Society (WSIS) held in 2003 was considered 'a turning point in the identification and emergence of a number of issues pertaining to human rights in the digital age'.[118] The ten selected Internet bills of rights were accordingly divided into pre-WSIS texts, WSIS texts, and post-WSIS texts. The results of this analysis showed that the human rights machinery developed in the last 60 years was not acknowledged in these documents. The multiplicity of levels and contexts where Internet bills of rights emerged did not favour the convergence or the coordination of these initiatives. Although one cannot yet talk of a consistent normative vision, some common issues and principles were identified. The three scholars concluded that it is more likely that this emerging

116 As explained in the report: 'UNESCO has been involved in the development of Internet Governance principles mainly through its «Internet Universality» concept, encompassing four key pillars, namely Rights, Openness, Accessibility, and Multistakeholder Participation (called R.O.A.M.). To assist in strengthening the role of UNESCO in this field, this study provides a comprehensive overview of the core documents about Internet Governance principles developed and adopted by various other stakeholders. [...] The analyzed documents are put into the historical, political, economic and social context, assessed in view of a potential normative use as well as accountability, and evaluated in respect of their compatibility and completeness in light of UNESCO's mandate and positions.' See Weber (n 110) 7.

117 Francesca Musiani, Elena Pavan and Claudia Padovani, 'Investigating Evolving Discourses on Human Rights in the Digital Age: Emerging Norms and Policy Challenges' (2009) 72 International Communication Gazette 359.

118 Musiani, Pavan and Padovani (n 117); in these terms, see also Anne-Claire Jamart, 'Internet Freedom and the Constitutionalization of Internet Governance' in Roxana Radu, Jean-Marie Chenou and Rolf H Weber (eds), *The Evolution of Global Internet Governance* (Springer Berlin Heidelberg 2014).

normative framework will develop in a plurality of soft law instruments rather than turning into a formalised constitutional document.[119]

In 2015, Sarah Oates authored a chapter entitled 'Towards an Internet Bill of Rights'. The work was part of the book 'The Onlife Manifesto. Being Human in a Hyperconnected Era', edited by Luciano Floridi, collecting the results of the so-called 'Onlife Initiative'.[120] Collecting a group of philosophers, social scientists, and artificial intelligence scholars, the purpose of the Onlife Initiative was to understand how to 're-engineer' essential concepts of human life altered by the advent of ICTs. Promoted under the auspices of the DG Connect of the European Commission, the main output of the initiative was summarised in a short document, the 'Onlife Manifesto', published in the mentioned book together with a series of commentaries authored by the different scholars involved. Oates observed that fundamental rights are not sufficiently articulated and protected in the online sphere. She identified 21 'manifestoes and other documents that articulate rights (and responsibilities) in the online sphere' dating from 1986 to 2015.[121] These texts were not analytically analysed but some of them were selected to provide examples of cyber-utopian ideals and to demonstrate that the rules that these documents propose presuppose an ecosystem far different from the existing online world dominated by capitalistic norms. Oates argued that there is an increasing informational asymmetry between online users, internet service providers and states. Individuals do not have sufficient awareness of their rights in the online sphere. For this reason, Oates advocated the need to promote a digital bill of rights and identified six core principles that should be promoted at policy level. Finally, the chapter encouraged a more active role of states in sheltering private self-regulation of the online sphere from potential infringements of the rights of users.

In 2015, a group of scholars from the Berkman Center for Internet & Society at Harvard University, Lex Gill, Urs Gasser, and Dennis Redeker, published a research paper entitled 'Towards Digital Constitutionalism? Mapping Attempts to Craft an Internet Bill of Rights'.[122] This work proposed 'digital constitutionalism' as an umbrella term to connect a 'constellation of initiatives that have sought to articulate a set of political rights, governance norms, and limitations on the exercise of power on the Internet'.[123] The paper conducted both a qualitative and a quantitative lexical analysis on 30

119 Cf. Teubner, 'Societal Constitutionalism; Alternatives to State-Centred Constitutional Theory?' (n 33); Azzariti (n 40).

120 Sarah Oates, 'Towards an Online Bill of Rights' in Luciano Floridi (ed), *The Onlife Manifesto: Being Human in a Hyperconnected Era* (Springer 2015).

121 Oates (n 120) 230.

122 Gill, Redeker and Gasser (n 100); subsequently published as Dennis Redeker, Lex Gill and Urs Gasser, 'Towards Digital Constitutionalism? Mapping Attempts to Craft an Internet Bill of Rights' (2018) 80 International Communication Gazette 302.

123 Gill, Redeker and Gasser (n 100) 2.

documents dating between 1999 and 2015. In particular, they studied the content of these texts identifying common principles and themes, concluding that the relationship between digital rights and traditional human rights machinery has not yet been fully defined. The paper subsequently analysed the political communities addressed by these texts and the key actors involved in their process of deliberation. Open and multistakeholder participatory mechanisms were identified as a common feature of these documents. Moreover, a series of tendencies over time were observed: firstly, that the targeted audience of these initiatives is shifting from public institutions to private actors; secondly, that the content of these documents is becoming more issue-specific; thirdly, that the initially international scope of these initiatives is narrowing towards the regional/national level; and fourthly, that there is a trend towards an increased degree of formalisation. Finally, the quantitative lexical analysis performed on the selected texts allowed the scholars to detect the presence of some trends in content over time and to discover that specific political developments, such as the Snowden revelations, had an impact on the principles enshrined in these texts.

In 2017, Kinfe Micheal Yilma published an article entitled 'Digital privacy and virtues of multilateral digital constitutionalism – preliminary thoughts'.[124] Yilma argued that, as an effect of the impact of the Snowden revelations on digital privacy, civil society renewed its effort to produce an Internet bill of rights. Drawing on the research performed by Gill, Redecker, and Gasser, Yilma examined to what extent Internet bills of rights are the appropriate instruments to uphold digital privacy.[125] In particular, Yilma moved three major critiques to these documents. Firstly, he argued that Internet bills of rights risk producing a phenomenon of 'rights inflation'. There would not be evidence that the existing human rights machinery is failing to protect digital rights, the main issue being rather the enforcement of such rights. Secondly, he criticised the fragmented and uncoordinated nature of these initiatives that would eventually make civil society and national efforts less influential. Thirdly, he underlined the fact that the majority of proposals originate from Western countries and that it could consequently be more difficult for developing countries whose needs are not represented to digest their content.[126]

Finally, there is a last source to report: it does not represent an analysis of existing Internet bills of rights, but a database of documents. 'Mapping Global Media Policy' was a project managed by a partnership between McGill University, the University of Padua, the Central European University, and the

124 Yilma (n 76).

125 Gill, Redeker and Gasser (n 100).

126 See Kinfe Micheal Yilma, '"Bill of Rights for the 21st Century: Some Lessons from the Internet Bill of Rights Movement"' [2021] The International Journal of Human Rights 1, in which the author also criticises the potential lack of legitimacy of Internet bills of rights.

International Association for Media and Communication Research.[127] The project 'serves to monitor, categorize and analyze key issues, significant developments and recent trends in the governance of media, information and communication on a global level'.[128] In particular, a section of the project aims to list 'legal and policy documents focusing on Internet rights and freedoms'.[129] The documents listed are 59 and date from 1997 to 2016. The project's website allows one to use filters to generate statistics on the data available according to 'organisations', 'people', 'resources', and 'policy documents' involved.

A constitutional role?

Reviewing the literature on Internet bills of rights, it emerges that the scholarship, particularly legal, that has investigated this phenomenon is very limited. None of the sources mentioned in the previous section has performed a systematic analysis of all the existing Internet bills of rights mentioned in the literature. As will be shown in the next section, every author has adopted a slightly different definition of Internet bill of rights and has consequently investigated different datasets. No source has combined a systematic empirical investigation of Internet bills of rights with a theoretical-normative analysis of this phenomenon.[130] In particular, it is not clear from a legal and, more specifically, constitutional point of view what the role, contribution and ultimate message of Internet bills of rights is.

The second part of this book intends to address this gap by analysing the phenomenon of the emergence of Internet bills of rights from a legal perspective. More specifically, it aims to investigate the value of these instruments from a constitutional point of view, understanding to what extent they contribute to the process of constitutionalisation described in the previous chapters by shaping fundamental rights for the Internet age. It is argued that Internet bills of rights play an important role within the constitutional ecosystem. They advance the discourse on rights, principles and obligations in the digital society. Using the language of human rights, the structure and jargon of legal texts, and evoking the imaginary of constitutions, they aim to translate our fundamental values in a mutated social reality. They represent – one could say – a proto-constitutional discourse. Often stemming from non-institutionalised processes, these documents are able to gather instances from a broader number of actors, in a wider social

127 See 'Mapping Global Media Policy' <http://www.globalmediapolicy.net> accessed 18 December 2018.

128 'Mapping Global Media Policy' <http://www.globalmediapolicy.net/node/20> accessed 18 December 2018.

129 'Mapping Global Media Policy' <http://www.globalmediapolicy.net/node/15288> accessed 18 December 2018.

130 With the exception of Yilma (n 76), who however focused more specifically on digital privacy.

dimension. Not being caged in the formalities of legally binding sources, Internet bills of rights have the power to experiment. These documents convey avant-garde ideas on how to shape the constitutional principles of our society in the digital age.

The number of Internet bills of rights and their protean nature are proof of their experimental character. It would be short-sighted to overlook their role simply because of their non-binding legal character or because of their spontaneous and uncoordinated emergence. Their potential lies precisely in their informal essence. Internet bills of rights can propose innovative principles and suggest unconventional solutions as they are not anchored to any particular legal order and not restricted by any formal ties.

A legal analysis of Internet bills of rights is therefore useful because these documents can reveal which principles our societies need in order to preserve their fundamental values in the digital age. Internet bills of rights are the litmus test of the health of our constitutional systems. When these documents adapt an existing constitutional right, they are telling us that there is a divergence between the legal rule and the social reality. Internet bills of rights indicate a potential way to translate traditional constitutional values in the context of the digital society so that a legal provision is able to continue 'speaking' in the coming years.

Datasets

The following chapters will also perform a textual analysis on a selection of Internet bills of rights. The aim of this investigation is not to offer an exhaustive directory of all the existing charters of rights for the Internet. This collection of texts has been nevertheless created starting from an examination of all the documents mentioned in the existing literature on Internet bills of rights.

The scholarship to date has not adopted a common definition of Internet bill of rights. Each source analysed a different dataset of texts, and a single document rarely recurred in more than one source. Appendix B collects all the documents to which the existing scholarship referred.[131] This list has been integrated with a series of analogous texts found through a web search using keywords such as 'internet bill of rights', 'charter of digital rights', 'digital magna carta', and similar. As a minimal condition, all these documents articulate rights and principles for the digital society. This dataset includes very different types of texts: soft law of international organisations, such as declarations, recommendations, guidelines, codes of conduct, and reports; policy statements from a multiplicity of actors, including non-institutional stakeholders; documents published on given topics to stimulate discussion, such as the Green Papers issued by the European Commission;

131 Appendix B is available at <https://bit.ly/3lH6KDN>. An updated version of this database is now available on the website of the Digital Constitutionalism Network: <https://digitalconstitutionalism.org/database/>.

national laws, bills, and legislative projects; multistakeholders declarations, and manifestoes.

All the texts listed in Appendix B could be said to contribute to the conversation on the rights and principles for the digital society. As the first part of this work has claimed, the digital revolution has triggered a phase of reflection on the suitability of the existing constitutional framework to address the challenges generated by the development of digital technology. A new discourse on how to rethink the constitutional ecosystem in the digital age is emerging. Appendix B captures a variety of contexts – certainly not all, as we have seen in the previous chapters – in which this conversation is taking place.

However, only a narrower group of the texts more closely reflects the characteristics of Rodotà's archetype of a comprehensive charter of rights for the digital age: as we have seen in the previous sections, a model deliberately imitating the old declarations of rights, adopting a normative style and, more specifically, espousing the language and the concepts of constitutional law, which emerges as the output of a multistakeholder deliberative process. As the next chapter will explore in more detail, this work advances the thesis that this narrower category of texts is particularly suited to advance the conversation on how to articulate constitutional rights and principles in the digital society. They provide comprehensive proposals for a constitutional framework for the digital age. By adopting the *lingua franca* of constitutions, they enhance the degree of accessibility, understanding, and comparability of the ongoing constitutional reflection on issues generated by the digital revolution. Often free from the formalism of institutionalised deliberative processes, these documents are able to involve a greater number of stakeholders. Lastly, their lack of legally binding value provides wider scope to innovate and experiment with new solutions on how to adapt the constitutional framework to the needs of the digital society.

Without pretending to establish a rigid taxonomy, the documents that most closely reflect Rodotà's archetype of a charter of Internet rights have been collected in Appendix A, which is reproduced at the end of this volume. To this end, the text of the Italian Declaration of Internet Rights, authored by Rodotà himself among others, has been used as a model.[132] The majority of texts in Appendix A are civil society declarations, but the dataset also includes some soft law documents issued by international organisations and one legally binding legislation, the Brazilian Marco civil da Internet. The following chapters will primarily analyse this dataset, at times drawing comparisons with the documents listed in Appendix B.

132 To this end, the text of the Italian Declaration of Internet Rights, authored by Rodotà himself among others, has been used as a model. See Camera dei Deputati, 'Mozione concernente iniziative per la promozione di una carta dei diritti in Internet e per la governance della rete' (n 85). The creation of two datasets, one reflecting a minimal definition of Internet bill of rights and one reflecting the characteristics of the ideal-type of Internet bill of rights, has been inspired by John Gerring, *Social Science Methodology: A Unified Framework* (Cambridge University Press 2012) 65 ff.

8 The force of declarations

Proto-constitutional discourses

The emergence of a multiplicity of Internet bills of rights does not represent an isolated phenomenon in the contemporary constitutional landscape. As seen in the first part of this work, we are currently witnessing a new constitutional moment. The digital revolution generates a series of changes at societal level, which ultimately ferment under a vault of constitutional norms shaped for an analogue society. The constitutional ecosystem is gradually reacting to face the challenges created by the advent of digital technology. The core values of contemporary constitutionalism are progressively translated in the context of the digital society. However, the constitutional discourse is no longer uniform. It resembles a normative conglomerate. It is fragmented, and acts on multiple, intersecting levels. It involves public and private, dominant and weak actors. Constitutional norms flow beyond the state dimension to reflect societal dynamics occurring in a transnational and virtual space.

Internet bills of rights are an integral part of the constitutional response to the challenges of digital technology. The emergence of these texts, too, is a component of the process of constitutionalisation that, at multiple levels, is adapting the main principles and values of contemporary constitutionalism to the needs of the digital society. However, their role in such a dynamic is generally neglected, as the limited presence of legal scholarship on this phenomenon shows. The reason for this disregard can be easily explained by looking at the legal value of these texts. As seen in the previous chapter, the majority of Internet bills of rights are not issued from political processes, but emerge through civil society or, more generally, non-institutionalised initiatives.[1] Not only they do not have any binding legal value from a formal perspective but they can hardly be regarded as exercising any legal influence

1 As first recognised in Lex Gill, Dennis Redeker and Urs Gasser, 'Towards Digital Constitutionalism? Mapping Attempts to Craft an Internet Bill of Rights' (2015) Berkman Center Research Publication No 2015-15 <https://papers.ssrn.com/abstract=2687120> accessed 30 August 2018.

DOI: 10.4324/9781003256908-8

from a substantial point of view as well.[2] They do not have, for example, the 'high status of soft law' that the Charter of Fundamental Rights of the European Union was recognised to have in the first years of its existence before the Treaty of Lisbon affirmed its primary value.[3] Nor can they be considered to play any role as customary international law, similarly to the Universal Declaration of Human Rights.[4]

Most of the scholarship exclusively saw the value of Internet bills of rights in their future legal transformation, codification or incorporation into a (more) binding legal source. Some authors, for example, emphasised the role that international institutions, such as the United Nations, could play in this regard by formally including an Internet bill of rights within their body of rules.[5] Nevertheless, none of them argued in favour of the future independent development of an Internet bill of rights from a mere civil society initiative to an international convention, on the model of the International Committee of the Red Cross, which, although born as a non-institutional association of private citizens, led to the adoption of a series of international conventions.[6] Interestingly, Belli, commenting on the Italian Declaration of

2 In relation to the Italian Declaration of Internet Rights, see Oreste Pollicino and Marco Bassini (eds), *Verso Un Internet Bill of Rights* (Aracne 2015), in particular the chapters by Belli, Melzi d'Eril and Vigevani, and Nannipieri.

3 Joseph A Cannataci and Jeanne Pia Mifsud-Bonnici, 'Data Protection Comes of Age: The Data Protection Clauses in the European Constitutional Treaty' (2005) 14 Information & Communications Technology Law 5, 8; on the evolution of the legal value of the Charter, see Giacomo Di Federico, *The EU Charter of Fundamental Rights: From Declaration to Binding Instrument* (Springer 2011); Steve Peers and others (eds), *The EU Charter of Fundamental Rights: A Commentary* (Hart Publishing 2014).

4 See Gordon Brown (ed), *The Universal Declaration of Human Rights in the 21st Century: A Living Document in a Changing World* (Open Book Publishers 2016); Johannes Morsink, *The Universal Declaration of Human Rights: Origins, Drafting, and Intent* (University of Pennsylvania Press 1999); cf. Frederick Mari van Asbeck, *The Universal Declaration of Human Rights and Its Predecessors (1679-1948)*, vol 10 (E J Brill 1949).

5 See Luca Belli, 'Dichiarazione Dei Diritti in Internet. Cuius Regio Eius Religio?' in Marco Bassini and Oreste Pollicino (eds), *Verso un Internet Bill of Rights* (Aracne 2015); Monica Alessia Senor, 'La Forma Della Dichiarazione Dei Diritti in Internet' in Marco Bassini and Oreste Pollicino (eds), *Verso un Intenet Bill of Rights* (Aracne 2015); Kinfe Micheal Yilma, 'Digital Privacy and Virtues of Multilateral Digital Constitutionalism—Preliminary Thoughts' (2017) 25 International Journal of Law and Information Technology 115; cf. Giovanna De Minico, 'Towards an Internet Bill of Rights' (2015) 37 Loyola of Los Angeles International and Comparative Law Review 1, who, from a theoretical perspective, suggests the idea of a supranational legislator.

6 See Stefan Kadelbach and Thomas Kleinlein, 'International Law - A Constitution for Mankind: An Attempt at a Re-Appraisal with an Analysis of Constitutional Principles Focus Section: Typisch Deutsch: Is There a German Approach to International Law: German Obsessions' (2007) 50 German Yearbook of International Law 303, 325 ff.; for a history of the Red Cross, see David P Forsythe, *The Humanitarians: The International Committee of the Red Cross* (Cambridge University Press 2005); see also Caroline Moorehead, *Dunant's Dream: War, Switzerland and the History of the Red Cross* (Harper Collins 1998).

Internet Rights, proposed to integrate it within the Italian Constitution as a separate instrument, taking as a prototype the French 'Charte de l'environnement', a document enshrining a series of rights and principles related to the protection of the environment that was formally incorporated into French constitutional law in 2005.[7]

The majority of the authors, in sum, considered the potential of Internet bills of rights to lie exclusively in their *future* capability of acquiring a greater binding legal force within the (inter-) state dimension. However, the *current* role of Internet bills of rights in the process of constitutionalisation of the digital society has been generally downplayed.

The emergence of Internet bills of rights is an integral part of a new constitutional moment. These documents represent a unique component of the multilevel mosaic of norms that address the constitutional issues of the global society and are currently reacting against the challenges of the digital revolution. Only few scholars highlighted their utility as an intermediary step to enhance consensus and promote discussion in view of the adoption of an international normative framework on the topic or, more generally, as an instrument with a 'cultural and political' value, yet always underlining their lack of binding legal force.[8]

However, it is precisely in their non-legally binding value – this work argues – that the 'force' of Internet bills of rights lies.[9] It is their flexibility and ductility that enhance their capacity to experiment, to represent the avant-garde of the constitutional discourse that is translating our core fundamental rights and principles in the new context of the digital society.

Internet bills of rights are *proto*-constitutional discourses because, by linking society and law, they translate societal needs in the language of constitutional norms and transmit such impulses to the other components of

7 Belli (n 5); on the legal status of the Charte de l'environnement in France, see Michel Prieur, 'La Charte de l'environnement et La Constitution Française' (2005) 35 Environmental Policy and Law 134; Marie-Anne Cohendet and Marine Fleury, 'Chronique de droit constitutionnel sur la Charte de l'environnement' (2018) 43 Revue Juridique de l'Environnement 749.

8 See Nicolò Zingales, 'Mettiamo La Dichiarazione Dei DIritti in Internet in Prospettiva' in Marco Bassini and Oreste Pollicino (eds), *Verso un Internet Bill of Rights* (Aracne 2015), who compares the Italian Declaration of Internet Rights with atypical sources of international law with exhortatory value, such as the reports of the UN Special Rapporteurs; see Marco Bassini and Oreste Pollicino, 'Carta Dei Diritti in Internet Verso Una Missione Culturale. Né Costituzione Né Legge.', *Verso un Internet Bill of Rights* (Aracne 2015), who stress the 'cultural and political value' of the Italian Declaration of Internet Rights in 'guiding' the future choices of the Italian legislator. see Claudia Padovani and Mauro Santaniello, 'Digital Constitutionalism: Fundamental Rights and Power Limitation in the Internet Eco-System' (2018) 80 International Communication Gazette 295, who highlight the political mission of Internet bills of rights.

9 Cf. Jacques Derrida, 'Force of Law: The "Mystical Foundation of Authority"' in Drucilla Cornell, Michel Rosenfeld and David Carlson (eds), *Deconstruction and the Possibility of Justice* (Routledge 1992).

the constitutional dimension.[10] They are *proto*-constitutional because they advance the elaboration of constitutional principles for the digital society, and, as a part of the porous constitutional conglomerate of norms, they allow new formulations of values and ideals to flow between constitutional layers, as between communicating vessels. These texts are also *proto*-constitutional because, as we will see at the end of this work, they help highlight latent constitutional diseases, areas of constitutional law that no longer reflect the society and need new lymph to be revitalised.

In this way, the same characteristics of Internet bills of rights that have often been criticised, such as the fact that they lack binding legal value because they are issued from civil society, non-institutionalised processes, that they adopt a constitutional tone without having any formal constitutional value within national legal systems, and their significant number, can be read as the source of force of these declarations.[11]

Experimentalism

From a cursory look at the authors of our selection of Internet bills of rights listed in Appendix A, it is easily detectable that most of them are not issued from institutional processes but are rather the output of civil society organisations or even single individuals.[12] Even when they are adopted by international institutions, such as the OECD or the Council of Europe, these documents do not have any biding legal value, being presented in the form of a recommendation or declaration.[13] At first sight, Internet bills of rights appear as a weak instrument within the mosaic of norms which are addressing

10 Cf. Gunther Teubner, *Constitutional Fragments: Societal Constitutionalism and Globalization* (Oxford University Press 2012) 94 ff, who in similar terms describes the process of 'self-constitutionalisation of corporations' as a 'translation process' of supra-national soft law into the normative dynamics of corporations.

11 For a critical account on the Internet bills of rights, see in particular Pollicino and Bassini (n 2); Yilma (n 5).

12 See, e.g., Ryan Lytle, 'Explore Mashable's Crowdsourced Digital Bill of Rights' (*Mashable*) <https://mashable.com/2013/08/12/digital-bill-of-rights-crowdsource/> accessed 21 May 2019; Social Innovation Society, 'Carta Internazionale Dei Diritti Digitali' <http://www.soinsociety.org/carta-internazionale-dei-diritti-digitali/> accessed 7 May 2019; Jeff Jarvis, 'A Bill of Rights in Cyberspace' (*BuzzMachine*, 27 March 2010) <https://buzzmachine.com/2010/03/27/a-bill-of-rights-in-cyberspace/> accessed 21 May 2019; Katie Rogers, 'Congressman Drafts "Digital Bill of Rights" – What Would You Add?' *The Guardian* (13 June 2012) <https://www.theguardian.com/technology/us-news-blog/2012/jun/13/digital-bill-of-rights-sopa> accessed 21 May 2019; Mike Godwin, 'The Great Charter for Cambodian Internet Freedom' <https://www.linkedin.com/pulse/great-charter-cambodian-internet-freedom-mike-godwin> accessed 21 May 2019.

13 See, e.g., OECD, 'Principles for Internet Policy Making" <https://www.oecd.org/sti/ieconomy/oecd-principles-for-internet-policy-making.pdf>; Council of Europe, Committee of Ministers, 'Declaration by the Committee of Ministers on Internet Governance Principles' (21 September 2011) <https://search.coe.int/cm/Pages/result_details.aspx?ObjectID=09000016805cc2f6> accessed 21 May 2019.

constitutional issues in the digital society.[14] There is no doubt that, if contrasted to the internal rules of private actors or to state law, for instance, these documents cannot bear the comparison in terms of enforceability.

However, this view takes the legal force as a unique parameter to assess the role of these documents within the constitutional ecosystem. In this way, one would neglect the very reason as to why Internet bills of rights are emerging. We have seen that these documents are not the only ones seeking to translate our fundamental values and principles to address the challenges of the digital technology. Internet bills of rights are part of a conglomerate of norms emerging at multiple levels. Therefore, it is not unreasonable to posit that their peculiarity, their lack of legal force, is also one of the main factors at the basis of their emergence.

In contrast to the other normative instruments which are currently conveying constitutional counteractions against the challenges of digital technology, Internet bills of rights, being non-legally binding, appear to be particularly ductile, plastic, malleable. These texts are unaffected by the formalisms and constraints that would ensue from an institutional adoption. Internet bills of rights, as other normative instruments are currently doing, aim to translate our constitutional values and principles in the context of the digital society, but, in contrast to them, they are freer to experiment and innovate.[15]

For example, as Chapter 12 will show, these texts enshrine innovative rights and principles on which there is no consensus and that have not been incorporated into other constitutional instruments yet. In this way, Internet bills of rights are advancing the discourse of constitutionalism in the digital age.[16] As the declarations of rights of the eighteenth century, they are proclaiming new principles, a necessary step to nourish the conversation on their content and shape, which, in the longer term, will lead to their factual enforcement. Indeed, as Rodotà wrote, even the mere action of declaring rights is a first move towards their substantial recognition.[17]

Beyond enhancing their experimentalist character, the lack of binding legal force of Internet bills of rights also allows a higher level of plasticity in their processes of elaboration and deliberation. As Chapter 10 will illustrate, Internet bills of rights are often the output of innovative procedures

14 See *supra* Chapters 4 and 5.

15 Cf. Gráinne de Búrca, 'Human Rights Experimentalism' (2017) 111 American Journal of International Law 277, who sees the emergence of an experimentalist approach in the context of international human rights law and institutions. On the concept of constitutional experimentalism, see also Günter Frankenberg, *Comparative Constitutional Studies: Between Magic and Deceit* (E Elgar 2019) 156 ff, who describes nineteenth-century constitutions as a 'laboratory' of constitutionalism.

16 See, e.g., Praxis, 'Guiding Principles of Internet Freedom' <http://www.praxis.ee/fileadmin/tarmo/Projektid/Valitsemine_ja_kodanikeühiskond/Praxis_Theses_Internet.pdf>, Preamble.

17 Stefano Rodotà, *Il diritto di avere diritti* (Laterza 2012) 32, 75.

involving a plurality of actors. Not only traditional institutional players but also representatives from the technology industry, NGOs, civil society groups, and single individuals. Advancing the discourse of constitutionalism in the digital age through non-legally binding instruments allows for the adoption of more inclusive processes of deliberation, which may not be offered through traditional political channels. The procedures which lead to Internet bills of rights are tailored to reflect a global, transnational society in which, as seen in the first part of this work, private corporations managing the access to digital technology have emerged as new dominant actors besides states.

Internet bills of rights offer a way to convey the instances of what Teubner calls the 'spontaneous' sphere of the society, such as NGOs and advocacy groups, and, as we will see in the next paragraph, to put them in dialogue with the powerful actors of politics and the economy.[18] The elaboration of these documents recreates a political dimension, *le politique*, in a global context, where the traditional political world, *la politique*, anchored to the state dimension, could no longer be of help.[19] Internet bills of rights bring the conversation on constitutionalism in the digital age closer to the civil society. Bespoke and innovative processes of deliberation enhance the proximity of this discussion to the people and ensure greater inclusiveness. In this way, these documents emerge as a counteraction to the progressive phenomenon of privatisation of the law in the digital society.[20] Internet bills of rights ultimately aim to foster democracy in a context even more dominated by the *lex digitalis* of powerful multinational corporations and by a declining, distant politics.[21]

18 See Teubner, *Constitutional Fragments* (n 10) 91 ff; Christoph B Graber, 'Bottom-up Constitutionalism: The Case of Net Neutrality' (2016) 7 Transnational Legal Theory 524, 546 ff.

19 See Teubner, *Constitutional Fragments* (n 10), who analyses the dichotomy 'la politique versus le politique' in the context of societal constitutionalism; see also, more generally, Oliver Marchart, *Post-Foundational Political Thought: Political Difference in Nancy, Lefort, Badiou and Laclau* (Edinburgh University Press 2007); cf. Niklas Luhmann, *Law as a Social System* (Fatima Kastner and others eds, Klaus Ziegert tr, Oxford University Press 2004) 487, who argues that 'the structural coupling of the political system and the legal system through constitutions does not have an equivalent at the level of global society'; see also, commenting on Luhmann's position, Graber (n 18) 529 ff.

20 On the phenomenon of privatisation of law in the digital society, see Gunther Teubner and Andreas Fischer-Lescano, 'Regime-Collisions: The Vain Search for Legal Unity in the Fragmentation of Global Law' (2004) 25 Michigan Journal of International Law 999; Nicolas Suzor, *Lawless. The Secret Rules That Govern Our Digital Lives* (Cambridge University Press 2019); Brian Fitzgerald, 'Software as Discourse? The Challenge for Information Law' (2000) 22 European Intellectual Property Review 47; Rikke Frank Jørgensen and Anja Møller Pedersen, 'Online Service Providers as Human Rights Arbiters' in Mariarosaria Taddeo and Luciano Floridi (eds), *The Responsibilities of Online Service Providers* (Springer 2017).

21 See Gunther Teubner, 'Societal Constitutionalism; Alternatives to State-Centred Constitutional Theory?' in Christian Joerges, Inger-Johanne Sand and Gunther Teubner (eds),

Communicability

Internet bills of rights explicitly evoke the constitutional dimension by adopting a constitutional tone. As illustrated in the previous chapter, the denominations of these texts refer to traditional constitutional instruments: the charters and declarations of rights. They reproduce the structure of constitutional texts; they employ their typical jargon and rhetoric. Yet, as we have seen, Internet bills of rights do not exercise any legal force. They do not have the typical superior value of constitutional texts within the hierarchy of legal sources.

However, once again, in line with what has been argued in the previous section, one cannot overlook such a clear reference to the constitutional dimension, simply because the form of Internet bills of rights is not reflected in their legal force. These documents adopt a constitutional tone to become part of a specific conversation. Internet bills of rights tend to evoke the normative style of constitutional texts because their message is intrinsically constitutional. They seek to articulate and translate the core values and principles of contemporary constitutionalism in the context of the digital society. They deal with rights and the balancing of power: the two cardinal missions of constitutional law.[22]

By adopting a constitutional tone, Internet bills of rights aim to make visible the ongoing process of defining constitutional values of the digital society that would otherwise risk remaining concealed in the complex meanders of corporate policies, in the impenetrability of the code of software, and in recondite conclaves of national and international politics.[23] As Chapter 10 will explore more in depth, these documents strive to bring the conversation on digital rights and principles to the attention of global citizens. The language of constitutions is traditionally closer to civil society than the

---

Transnational Governance and Constitutionalism. International Studies in the Theory of Private Law (Hart 2004); Lee A Bygrave, 'Lex Facebook', *Internet Governance by Contract* (Oxford University Press 2015).

22 See Conseil constitutionnel (France), 'Declaration of Human and Civic Rights of 26 August 1789' <https://www.conseil-constitutionnel.fr/sites/default/files/as/root/bank_mm/anglais/cst2.pdf>, in particular Article 16 that reads 'Any society in which no provision is made for guaranteeing rights or for the separation of powers, has no Constitution'; see also Anne Peters, 'Compensatory Constitutionalism: The Function and Potential of Fundamental International Norms and Structures' (2006) 19 Leiden Journal of International Law 579, 585.

23 Cf. Teubner, 'Societal Constitutionalism; Alternatives to State-Centred Constitutional Theory?' (n 21), who highlights the latent character of the process of emergence of civil constitutions in comparison with the 'blinding glare' of political constitutions. Reflecting on Teubner's point, we could argue that the Internet bills of rights, by evoking the dimension of political constitutions, would indirectly reflect part of this glare, becoming more visible than the concealed processes of definition of constitutional norms of private corporations, for example.

obscure jargon of ordinary legislation and corporate terms.[24] Embracing a constitutional tone is therefore a way to enhance the communicability of a message.[25]

Internet bills of rights adopt the *lingua franca* of constitutional rights and principles, at the same time, to nourish a debate on a specific topic and to address a particular audience. These documents convey through a common language a series of societal instances, ultimately unifying a discourse otherwise fragmented in the multiplicity of normative dialects of corporations and institutions.[26] The objective of Internet bills of rights is to foster a conversation on how to translate core constitutional values in the context of the digital society and the language of constitutions offers a fertile field of exchange to this end, allowing the interlocutors to reflect and react by using the same language.[27]

In a time when the digital revolution generates a climate of legal incertitude and axiological dilemmas in relation to core constitutional aspects, Internet bills of rights aim to develop orienting principles.[28] Traditionally, constitutions are created to transmit foundational societal values from

24 See Giovanni Sartori, 'Constitutionalism: A Preliminary Discussion' (1962) 56 The American Political Science Review 853, who talks about the positive meaning that the notion of constitution has in our minds.

25 Cf. JHH Weiler and Marlene Wind (eds), *European Constitutionalism beyond the State* (Cambridge University Press 2003) 2, who explain that the idea of a Constitution for Europe became suddenly popular because the constitutional language was 'a fashionable code work, like "governance", for the need to engage in a more profound institutional reform in view of enlargement'.

26 See Evgeny Morozov, 'The Case for Publicly Enforced Online Rights' (*Financial Times*, 27 September 2018) <https://www.ft.com/content/5e62186c-c1a5-11e8-84cd-9e601db069b8> accessed 22 May 2019, who argued that digital rights would not be expressed in the texts of our constitutions but would rather be the result of a 'bundle of permissions of technology platforms'; cf. Carl Friedrich von Gerber, *Über öffentliche Rechte* (H Laupp 1852); and Georg Jellinek, *System der subjektiven öffentlichen Rechte* (Mohr 1892), who, respectively, intended individual rights as 'reflex rights' and output of the self-limitation of the state power.

27 See, on the same line, Jason Pielemeier, 'AI & Global Governance: The Advantages of Applying the International Human Rights Framework to Artificial Intelligence' (*Centre for Policy Research at United Nations University*) <https://cpr.unu.edu/ai-global-governance-the-advantages-of-applying-the-international-human-rights-framework-to-artificial-intelligence.html> accessed 22 May 2019; see also Access Now et al., 'The Human Rights Principles for Connectivity and Development' <https://www.accessnow.org/cms/assets/uploads/2016/10/The-Human-Rights-Principles-for-Connectivity-and-Development.pdf>; cf. Olympe de Gouges, 'Declaration of the Rights of Women and Female Citizens', *The Declaration of the Rights of Women: The Original Manifesto for Justice, Equality and Freedom* (Hachette 2018), who paraphrases the Declaration of the Rights of Man and of the Citizen in order to highlight the question of women's rights.

28 See Lawrence Lessig, *Code: And Other Laws of Cyberspace, Version 2.0* (Basic Books 2006), who talks of the 'latent ambiguity' of constitutional texts; see David Casacuberta, Max Senges and Josep-Maria Duart, 'Privacy and the Need for an Internet Bill of Rights: Are There New Rights in Cyberspace?' (Social Science Research Network 2007) <https://

generation-to-generation. Internet bills of rights similarly seek to articulate lasting guidelines that could work as reference points in the future: the most valuable normative contribution in the fast-changing digital society.[29] As seen in Chapter 4, for example, the code of digital technology products can play a constitutional function. However, in contrast to Internet bills of rights, it cannot offer an active guidance. It directly regulates, it does not provide any orienting principles. Internet bills of rights instead enshrine guidelines, generating the possibility to debate on their suitability for the digital society.

Lastly, the language of constitutions purveys a rich cultural baggage. Internet bills of rights can benefit from concepts, terminology, ideals, values, and mechanisms that have been developed over centuries to address issues of the protection of individual rights and the balancing of power.[30] Evoking this conceptual universe means that the conversation of Internet bills of rights does not start from scratch. It posits itself in a precise scenario. It aims to continue an old discourse relating to rights and powers, this time involving more people, addressing a more composite audience and speaking to global actors.

Gradualism

In the seminal case from the United States Supreme Court *Reno v American Civil Liberties Union*, in which the highest federal judges for the first time identified the quintessential tenets of the relationship between the Internet and First Amendment's rights, Justice Stevens, for the majority, wrote:

> Through the use of chat rooms, any person with a phone line can become a town crier with a voice that resonates farther than it could from any soapbox. Through the use of Web pages, mail exploders, and newsgroups, the same individual can become a pamphleteer.[31]

---

papers.ssrn.com/abstract=2798298> accessed 3 May 2019, who analyse the problem of rights clashes in the context of the digital society.

29 On the necessity to establish orienting principles instead of detailed norms that could not follow the pace of societal changes in the digital society, see Rodotà (n 17) 60; cf. Martti Koskenniemi, 'Constitutionalism as Mindset: Reflections on Kantian Themes About International Law and Globalization' (2006) 8 Theoretical Inquiries in Law 9, 13, who talks of 'deformalization' as the process whereby the law retreats solely to the provision of procedures or broadly formulated directives to experts and decision-makers for the purpose of administering international problems by means of functionally effective solutions and "balancing interests"'.

30 See Teubner, 'Societal Constitutionalism; Alternatives to State-Centred Constitutional Theory?' (n 21), who recognises the significance of political constitutions as 'historical model for civil constitutions'. Teubner however warns against the risks of 'over-hastily' transposing the 'stock of historical experience' of political constitutions, overlooking the peculiarities of the global society.

31 *Reno v American Civil Liberties Union* [1997] US Supreme Court 521 U.S. 844 870.

This vision of the Internet as an extraordinary catalyst of freedom of expression, which reflects the reality of 1997 as it does today, reaches its apex with the emergence of Internet bills of rights. These documents are evidence that in contemporary times 'any person with a phone line' can even become a constitutional author. Internet bills of rights, of course, are not printed texts, manuscripts signed with ink and sealed with wax. These modern declarations of rights are simply published online, a practice so easy and accessible today, that really everyone, from civil society groups to single individuals, can draft one's own charter and spread it on the web. It is therefore not surprising to see a broad array of non-institutional actors involved in initiatives seeking to draft these documents. Nor it is unexpected to observe a high number of Internet bills of rights. The 'parchment' of these declarations is largely available and affordable, and this partially explains why so many Internet bills of rights have emerged over the past few years.

Part of the scholarship has criticised such a 'fragmented' and 'uncoordinated' way in which the discourse on digital constitutionalism is conveyed by Internet bills of rights.[32] However, in light of the experimentalist value of these documents that has been emphasised in the previous sections, considering their purpose of nourishing a discussion on rights and principles for the digital age through an accessible normative language, it is possible to read the multiplicity of Internet bills of rights as a positive form of gradualism. These declarations are progressively advancing the discourse on constitutional values for the digital society. They are testing new solutions, contributing to a debate, they are dialoguing and generating dialogue.

Teubner, developing his theory of societal constitutionalism, wrote:

> Civil constitutions will not be produced by some sort of big bang, a spectacular revolutionary act of the constituent assembly on the American or French model. Nor do the global regimes of economy, research, health, education, the professions have a single great original text embodied as a codification in a special constitutional document. Instead, civil constitutions are formed in underground evolutionary processes of long duration in which the juridification of social sectors also incrementally develops constitutional norms, although they remain as it were embedded in the whole set of legal norms.[33]

Internet bills of rights are halfway between political constitutions and Teubner's civil constitutions. On the one hand, they adopt the language of political constitutions, and they evoke the constitutional dimension to become a visible discussion on how to translate constitutional principles in the digital

32 Yilma (n 5) 126 ff.

33 Teubner, 'Societal Constitutionalism; Alternatives to State-Centred Constitutional Theory?' (n 21).

society. On the other hand, Internet bills of rights emerge outside institutionalised political processes, and they are issued from novel combinations of institutional actors, civil society, corporations, and single individuals. In a similar way to Teubner's civil constitutions, Internet bills of rights do not boastfully claim their primacy as if they were *the* unique charter of rights for the Internet. As Chapter 10 will explore more in depth, there is no single, solemn constituent assembly in charge of drafting the Internet constitution. Internet bills of rights emerge with the awareness to add, each one singularly, a small brick to the conversation on digital rights and principles. There is no doubt that the level of visibility, be it economic or social, of the promoters of these initiatives may affect their specific weight in such a debate. Yet, one could argue that, comprehensively regarded, every Internet bill of rights increments and nourishes this dialogue, without pretending to declare the final word.[34]

As briefly outlined in the previous chapter, Azzariti advocated for a similar pluralism of initiatives in order to reach a consensus on a constitution for the digital society.[35] He criticised the idea of creating, in the present phase, a legally binding constitutional text articulating digital rights and principles. Such a global *lex superior* would risk becoming a form of 'cultural colonialism' and would tend to weaken the power of existing constitutional instruments.[36] Conversely, the appropriate route to follow is, for Azzariti, a 'laborious and slow' process of defining foundational principles for the digital society through the elaboration of non-binding international charters, promoted by a multiplicity of stakeholders and having a persuasive value. In this way – he rightly observes – 'building a virtual democracy could come back to be a political objective of real citizens'.[37] Indeed, the multiplicity of Internet bills of rights is not only a positive factor in allowing for experimentalism and gradualism in the discourse on digital rights and principles but also because such pluralism implies a higher level of involvement by civil society and, ultimately, greater democracy.

34 Cf. 'About the People's Communication Charter' <http://www.pccharter.net/about.html> accessed 6 October 2019: 'The People's Communication Charter is a first step in the development of a permanent movement concerned with the quality of our communication environment. The initiators of the PCC think it is time for individual citizens and their organisations to take an active role in the shaping of the cultural environment and to focus on the production and distribution of information and culture. The People's Communication Charter provides the common framework for all those who share the belief that people should be active and critical participants in their social reality and should be able to communicate their ideas and opinions. The Charter is not an end in itself. It provides the basis for a permanent critical reflection on those world-wide trends that determine the quality of our lives in the third millennium'.

35 Gaetano Azzariti, 'Internet e Costituzione' [2011] Politica del diritto 367.

36 Azzariti (n 35).

37 Azzariti (n 35) 378.

Gradualism, of course, naturally entails time. Internet bills of rights do not generate a coherent and immediately applicable set of principles, as – borrowing Teubner's words – in a sort of normative 'big bang'.[38] They slowly advance a reflection, offering stakeholders involved the possibility to cogitate about the most appropriate way to translate core values and principles of contemporary constitutionalism in the context of the digital society. Internet bills of rights are not the output of a multiplicity of Solon, the Athenian lawmaker who drafted a new constitution for his city and then voluntarily went into exile in order to avoid the modification of his own laws.[39] The authors of Internet bills of rights, as we will see more in depth in Chapter 10, propose their own declarations to partake in a dialogue; they do not leave the constitutional agora. The emergence of each of these texts does not singularly represent a transient constitutional moment. Internet bills of rights are part of an unfinished, continuous phenomenon of cogitation about digital rights and principles. A Sisyphean labour – one could say – but not in a pessimistic sense. The journey that leads to the definition of the constitutional principles for the digital age is certainly more relevant than the ephemeral instant of their solemn proclamation. In this context too, the lesson taught by Albert Camus in *The Myth of Sisyphus* is true:

> The struggle itself toward the heights is enough to fill a man's heart. One must imagine Sisyphus happy.[40]

The extended temporality of the phenomenon of emergence of Internet bills of rights not only allows for gradual experimentalism and enhances the level of cogitation but it is also a necessary ingredient to generate far-sighted constitutional principles. The declarations of Internet rights aim to translate the core values and ideals of contemporary constitutionalism in a way that they can speak and last in the context of the fast-changing digital society. It would be of scarce utility to elaborate a series of principles exclusively tailored to the current societal scenario. The speed of digital years no longer seems to reflect Gregorian calendar's units, but it is somehow similar to a cats' age. In one calendar year, the digital society moves forward six times. However, we do not have any crystal ball to foresee how our society will appear in the coming decades. It is then crucial to craft future-proof constitutional rules. They do not have to last forever. It would be naive to think it possible to do as Solon did in Athens: to establish our law and go into exile to never modify it. However, taking time to understand what the

38 Cf. Teubner, 'Societal Constitutionalism; Alternatives to State-Centred Constitutional Theory?' (n 21).

39 See Arnold Wycombe Gomme, Theodore John Cadoux and PJ Rhodes, 'Solon', *The Oxford Companion to Classical Civilization* (Oxford University Press 2014); see also John Lewis, *Solon the Thinker: Political Thought in Archaic Athens* (Duckworth 2006).

40 Albert Camus, *The Myth of Sisyphus* (Justin O'Brien tr, Penguin Classics 2000) 111.

core principles of contemporary constitutionalism are and how to re-specify them in the context of the digital society is a good strategy to elaborate a far-sighted and future-proof set of norms.

Espousing this perspective, the gradual process of emergence of Internet bills of rights is not necessarily disoriented or disorganised. It is running a long 'slow and steady' race, in the hope of achieving a better and long-lasting result. If history can teach us something, it is worth remembering Cicero's words:

> Cato used to say that our constitution was superior to those of other States on account of the fact that almost every one of these other commonwealths has been established by one man, the author of their laws and institutions; for example, Minos in Crete, Lycurgus in Sparta, [...]; on the other hand, our own commonwealth was based upon the genius, not of one man, but of many; it was founded, not in one generation, but in a long period of several centuries and many ages of men.[41]

Compensation and stimulation

In conclusion, by highlighting the peculiar features in which the force of Internet bills of rights lies, we gain a better understanding of the role these declarations play within the constitutional ecosystem. Internet bills of rights do not emerge in a legal vacuum but are an integral part of a conglomerate of constitutional mechanisms which are seeking to translate our constitutional values and principles in the context of the digital society.[42] In contrast to most other constitutional instruments, often caged in rigid institutional processes or subject to the influence of a single societal actor, these declarations represent a ductile instrument allowing a multiplicity of stakeholders to participate in a reasoned conversation on digital rights and principles. Internet bills of rights adopt the *lingua franca* of constitutions to foster a debate, gradually experimenting new ideas through a cogitated process of generalisation and re-specification.

As seen in Chapter 5, Peters regarded the emergence of transnational constitutional instruments as an expression of 'compensatory constitutionalisation on the international plane'.[43] Similarly, in light of what has been argued in the previous paragraphs, one could posit that Internet bills of rights emerge to play a 'compensatory' role within the constitutional ecosystem.[44] Freed from institutional constraints, they aim to complement the lack of plasticity, the slow and rigid institutional processes of deliberation,

41 Marcus Tullius Cicero, *De Re Publica* (Clinton Walker Keys tr, William Heinemann 1928), Book II, I, 2; 110-113.

42 See *supra* Chapter 4.

43 Peters (n 22) 580.

44 I first advanced this theory in Edoardo Celeste, 'Terms of Service and Bills of Rights: New Mechanisms of Constitutionalisation in the Social Media Environment?' (2019) 33 International Review of Law, Computers & Technology 122.

the innate caution and absence of experimentalist tendency of other constitutional mechanisms by courageously promoting the conversation on digital rights and principles. Internet bills of rights surface to counterbalance a static and conservatory tendency within the constitutional ecosystem. They represent – one could say – the most innovative layer of the process of constitutionalisation of the digital society.

However, compensation should not be intended as implying that Internet bills of rights and other instruments composing the constitutional conglomerate are *de facto* airtight containers. As previously seen, the constitutional ecosystem is more similar to a porous material which allows its internal fluids to circulate as in a system of communicating vessels.[45] The relationship between Internet bills of rights and other constitutional instruments is therefore not only compensatory but – one could add – 'stimulatory' at the same time. The tissue of the other constitutional mechanisms, such as national and supranational constitutions and laws or internal rules of private actors, is permeable and, although partially soaked, it reacts when it comes in contact with the innovative fluids synthetised in the Internet bills of rights' conversation.[46]

These declarations are pushing forward the debate on how to translate the core principles of contemporary constitutionalism in the context of the digital society. The ideas that emerge from this exchange unavoidably come in contact and, potentially, persuade other societal layers, such as politics or the economy, that time has come and sufficient consensus has been reached to incorporate them in their own constitutional mechanisms. Internet bills of rights can therefore play a litmus test function within the constitutional ecosystem. When compared to other constitutional instruments, these declarations allow for the measurement of its health. They highlight areas of constitutional 'anaemia', in which the discrepancy between legal rules and social reality has reached its apex, and consequently stimulate the

45 I first expressed this idea in Edoardo Celeste, 'Digital Constitutionalism: A New Systematic Theorisation' (2019) 33 International Review of Law, Computers & Technology 76; see Graber (n 18), at 551, who argues that the formal and social constitution should be regarded as two "interconnected vessels"; cf. Teubner's conception of porous law in Gunther Teubner, *Law as an Autopoietic System* (Blackwell 1993).

46 Cf. the concepts of 'permeability' and 'responsivity' developed in the context of European constitutional law and transnational law, respectively, by Mattias Wendel, *Permeabilität Im Europäischen Verfassungsrecht*, vol 4 (1st edn, Mohr Siebeck 2011); Lars Viellechner, *Transnationalisierung des Rechts* (Velbrück 2013); see also Ingolf Pernice, 'Die Verfassung der Internetgesellschaft: Zur Rolle von Staat und Verfassung im Zuge der digitalen Revolution' in Alexander Blankenagel (ed), *Den Verfassungsstaat nachdenken. Eine Geburtstagsgabe* (Duncker & Humblot 2014) <https://papers.ssrn.com/abstract=2964926> accessed 28 August 2018, who mentions these characteristics of contemporary constitutional law to argue that a constitution of the Internet society could only emerge as a plural constitutional system.

emergence of constitutional counteractions in other parts of the constitutional ecosystem.

In light of these observations, the next four chapters will analyse the material scope of application of Internet bills of rights (Chapter 9), the actors involved in their processes of elaboration (Chapter 10), and, finally, their substantive content (Chapters 11 and 12). This investigation will be persistently approached considering the question of which problematic issues the emergence of Internet bills of rights aims to highlight in the contemporary constitutional ecosystem, and ultimately what it is possible learn from these instruments. The conversation on digital constitutionalism that these declarations are nourishing will not be merely studied in isolation. The key to truly understand the force of these instruments will be to read them in the context of the composite process of constitutionalisation of the digital society. Only in this way – this work argues – can one fully appreciate the real didactic force of Internet bills of rights.

9 Understanding the digital society

A new law of the horse?

A cursory look at the titles of Internet bills of rights listed in Appendix A unavoidably evokes the famous debate between Frank Easterbrook and Lawrence Lessig on whether cyber law is nothing more than the 'law of the horse'.[1] By reading titles such as 'Declaration of Human Rights in Cyberspace', 'Charter of Rights of Citizens in the Knowledge Society', or 'A Bill of Rights for the Internet', it is apparent that these documents, in contrast to the declarations of rights of the eighteenth century, do not aim to articulate rights and principles for the present society at large. Instead, they target a specific context, situation, and characterisation of this society, focusing for example on 'cyberspace',[2] 'the Internet',[3] the 'online' world,[4] the 'knowledge society',[5] and the 'digital' dimension.[6] In particular, they aim to articulate a series of principles addressing the challenges generated by the digital revolution.

More than 20 years ago, Frank Easterbrook, a then United States Circuit judge and academic at the Chicago Law School, argued that teaching too specific 'Law and...' courses would amount to 'multidisciplinary

1 See Frank H Easterbrook, 'Cyberspace and the Law of the Horse' [1996] The University of Chicago Legal Forum 207; Lawrence Lessig, 'The Law of the Horse: What Cyberlaw Might Teach' (1999) 113 Harvard Law Review 501.

2 See, e.g. Robert Gelman, 'Draft Proposal-Declaration of Human Rights in Cyberspace' <http://www.be-in.com/10/rightsdec.html> accessed 17 June 2019.

3 See, e.g. Andrew Murray, 'A Bill of Rights for the Internet' <http://theitlawyer.blogspot.com/2010/10/bill-of-rights-for-internet.html> accessed 17 June 2019.

4 See, e.g. European Commission, 'Code of EU Online Rights' (2012) <https://ec.europa.eu/digital-single-market/sites/digital-agenda/files/Code%20EU%20online%20rights%20EN%20final%202.pdf>.

5 See, e.g. EUROCITIES Knowledge Society Forum – TeleCities, 'Charter of Rights of Citizens in the Knowledge Society' <https://www.comune.modena.it/storiaretecivica/Materiale_PDF_2_marzo/Brugi_Miranda2.pdf>.

6 See, e.g. Ryan Lytle, 'Explore Mashable's Crowdsourced Digital Bill of Rights' (*Mashable*) <https://mashable.com/2013/08/12/digital-bill-of-rights-crowdsource/> accessed 21 May 2019.

DOI: 10.4324/9781003256908-9

dilettantism' and would risk leading towards a 'cross-sterilisation of ideas'.[7] For Easterbrook:

> [...] the best way to learn the law applicable to specialized endeavors is to study general rules. Lots of cases deal with sales of horses; others deal with people kicked by horses; still more deal with the licensing and racing of horses, or with the care veterinarians give to horses, or with prizes at horse shows. Any effort to collect these strands into a course on "The Law of the Horse" is doomed to be shallow and to miss unifying principles. Teaching 100 percent of the cases on people kicked by horses will not convey the law of torts very well.[8]

Easterbrook argued that specifically studying cyber law would equate to delving into a course on the law of the horse: in his opinion, not only a scarcely useful endeavour but even one at risk of becoming counterproductive for our economy, by stifling innovation with rules without a proper rationale. The American judge contended that there was still much work to do in order to understand whether existing law – i.e., for him, pre-digital law – is 'optimal' for the current economy. Studying and researching which kind of regulation would be appropriate for the fast-galloping digital world would be therefore a naïve and vain task. In Easterbrook's words:

> If we are so far behind in matching law to a well-understood technology such as photocopiers - if we have not even managed to create well-defined property rights so that people can adapt their own conduct to maximize total wealth - what chance do we have for a technology such as computers that is mutating faster than the virus in *The Andromeda Strain?* Well, then, what can we do? By and large, nothing. If you don't know what is best, let people make their own arrangements.[9]

Easterbrook then suggested that we should not 'struggle to match an imperfect legal system to an evolving world that we understand poorly'.[10] Far less complex technologies of yesterday should have taught us that this is almost impossible. What conversely the regulator should do is to 'let the world of cyberspace evolve as it will, and enjoy the benefits'.[11]

In response to these claims, a couple of years later, in 1999, Lawrence Lessig, one of Easterbrook's former colleagues at the Chicago Law School, published a paper on 'What Cyberlaw Might Teach'.[12] Summarising the

7 Easterbrook (n 1) 207.
8 Easterbrook (n 1) 207.
9 Easterbrook (n 1) 210.
10 Easterbrook (n 1) 215.
11 Easterbrook (n 1) 215.
12 Lessig, 'The Law of the Horse' (n 1).

arguments almost simultaneously published in his famous monograph *Code and Other Laws of Cyberspace*,[13] Lessig did not contest the apparent lack of interest in teaching the 'law of the horse'. However, he made a case for the specificity and unicity of cyber law.[14] In cyberspace, even more ostensibly than in real space, it is apparent that 'more than law alone enables legal values, and law alone cannot guarantee them'.[15] Legal norms would represent only one of the regulatory modalities available to enforce values in cyberspace. Social norms, market forces, and, particularly, the architecture of cyberspace, its code, are important regulatory tools not to be underestimated. A successful regulatory strategy simultaneously utilises these instruments of enforcement in a complementary way. As seen in the introduction, Lessig contended that the code of cyberspace, in particular, is not immutable by nature, but it is conversely a ductile regulatory tool that can be shaped by law.[16] Unlike Easterbrook, he did not suggest remaining inactive, waiting for a magical self-regulation of cyberspace.

In contrast to the law of the horse, the study of cyberspace does teach a series of lessons which are generalisable and may also inform the regulation of real space.[17] Cyberspace highlights the limited role of law and the consequent relevance of social norms, market forces, and architecture. It allows us to reflect on the degree of transparency that a regulatory tool can achieve, certainly higher in relation to legal norms, but definitively lower when legal values are embodied in the code of software and hardware. Lastly, cyber law represents a good case study to assess the proportionality of regulation, its width, and its capability to involuntarily impinge on legal behaviour, if not sufficiently narrowly tailored.

Such a scholarly debate can help us to better reflect on the role of Internet bills of rights. A critique similar to Easterbrook's also emerged with regard to these documents. Some authors questioned the utility of drafting a charter of rights for 'the Internet', 'the information society', the 'online' world, the 'digital' dimension, etc.[18] Such a set of principles would exclusively focus on one specific technology, on one single aspect, or connotation of the present society. Similarly to Easterbrook, their argument hinged on the fast

13 Lawrence Lessig, *Code and Other Laws of Cyberspace* (Basic Books 1999); See also Lawrence Lessig, *Code: And Other Laws of Cyberspace, Version 2.0* (Basic Books 2006).

14 Lessig, 'The Law of the Horse' (n 1) 502 ff.

15 Lessig, 'The Law of the Horse' (n 1) 546; see also Andrew D Murray, *The Regulation of Cyberspace: Control in the Online Environment* (Routledge 2006).

16 See Lessig, 'The Law of the Horse' (n 1) 505 ff; see also Lessig, *Code* (n 13).

17 Lessig, 'The Law of the Horse' (n 1) 503 ff.

18 See Carlo Blengino, 'Non i Diritti in Internet, Ma Internet Nei Diritti' in Marco Bassini and Oreste Pollicino (eds), *Verso un Internet Bill of Rights* (Aracne 2015); Kinfe Micheal Yilma, 'Digital Privacy and Virtues of Multilateral Digital Constitutionalism—Preliminary Thoughts' (2017) 25 International Journal of Law and Information Technology 115; cf. Giovanna De Minico, 'Towards an Internet Bill of Rights' (2015) 37 Loyola of Los Angeles International and Comparative Law Review 1, 12 ff.

evolution of the Internet as a technology, a factor that would potentially increase the risk of early obsolescence of a set of rights designed exclusively for it.[19] The scholarship also more generally highlighted the risk of duplicating or inflating existing rights, consequently diminishing their overall relevance.[20] Following this line of argumentation, a charter of rights for the Internet would be nothing but a 'constitution of the horse' – one could say paraphrasing Easterbrook – a vain and counterproductive endeavour. By replicating the arguments of the American federal judge, one could affirm that we have already enough questions to solve in our existing constitutions before tackling the issue of a charter of rights for the Internet. Moreover, building on Easterbrook, one could contend that studying those specialist documents would not teach us anything potentially generalisable from a broader constitutional perspective.

Litmus test

A partial answer to this critique has already been provided in the previous chapters. As we have just seen, Lessig underscored the unicity and specificity of cyber law. He affirmed:

> We see something when we think about the regulation of cyberspace that other areas would not show us.[21]

Similarly, Chapter 2 has made the case for the centrality of the digital revolution within the current constitutional moment. The recent development of digital technology has largely affected the constitutional ecosystem, putting under strain existing norms that regulate its two central tenets: the protection of fundamental rights and the balancing of powers. Digital technologies have enhanced our possibilities to exercise fundamental rights and, at the same time, they have increased the risk of fundamental rights violations. The digital revolution has magnified the capability of the state to control our digital lives and, simultaneously, it has vested extended powers in the hands of multinational private companies managing and selling digital products and services. Chapter 3 then showed that, in response to these challenges, a series of constitutional counteractions are emerging in order to restore a condition of relative equilibrium in the constitutional ecosystem. This work has analysed, as examples, the ongoing elaboration of a right to access governmental information via electronic means, the emergence of due process

19 On this point, see, in particular, Blengino (n 18).

20 On this point, see, in particular, Yilma (n 18); cf. Edoardo Celeste, 'Terms of Service and Bills of Rights: New Mechanisms of Constitutionalisation in the Social Media Environment?' (2019) 33 International Review of Law, Computers & Technology 122, para 3.2.1.1.

21 Lessig, 'The Law of the Horse' (n 1) 502.

principles in the context of online content moderation, the debate around a right to Internet access, and the development of the right to data protection.

The extent to which the digital revolution is affecting the constitutional ecosystem and the relevance of the answers that have been consequently produced allows us to reject the critique on the pettiness of the constitutional question related to the digital society in comparison with the entirety of constitutional law. Internet bills of rights undoubtedly deal with a topic which is central and crucial in the current constitutional landscape. They are not discussing rights and principles of the horse, but, as Rodotà said, of 'the largest public space that the humankind has ever known'.[22]

It seems far too simplistic to espouse Easterbrook's view that, since we have not yet understood how to solve the problems of the past, we should renounce exploring the potential constitutional solutions for the digital age. One could argue that the dichotomy digital/analogue in the present society is merely theoretical.[23] Today, digital and analogue components are melded in our life. It would not make sense to isolate the analogue 'side' of a constitutional issue, without considering the interplay with digital technology. Taking Easterbrook's example, it does not appear particularly useful to deal with the issue of intellectual property related to photocopiers, first, before delving into the problems associated with the Internet.[24] It would be inappropriate, today, to think of the action of photocopying as a merely analogue action. For example, one could photocopy using a smartphone app, or one could still use a photocopier, but one could send the digitalised version of the copied document via email, instead of printing the physical copy. These are both circumstances that would radically change any consideration of the problem of photocopying and the protection of intellectual property in our society.

Lessig also made a general point about the utility of studying cyber law to appraise the existence of regulatory modalities other than law.[25] Similarly, the analysis of Internet bills of rights allowed us to explore, in Chapters 3 and 4, the conglomerate of layers composing the constitutional dimension. Not only national and supranational constitutional instruments but also normative tools embedded in the code of software, incorporated in the private laws of corporations, and, last but not least, in civil society declarations. The constitutional discourse is no longer uniform but plural and stratified, which does not necessarily mean that it is chaotic too. Each of

22 Stefano Rodotà, 'L'uomo nuovo di Internet' *La Repubblica* (28 October 2005) <https://ricerca.repubblica.it/repubblica/archivio/repubblica/2005/10/28/uomo-nuovo-di-internet.html> accessed 2 May 2019, my translation.

23 On the same point, see, generally, Gilles Dowek, *Vivre, aimer, voter en ligne et autres chroniques numériques* (Le Pommier 2017); Tero Karppi, *Disconnect* (University of Minnesota Press 2018); Blengino (n 18).

24 See Easterbrook (n 1) 208 ff.

25 See Lessig, 'The Law of the Horse' (n 1) 546.

these constitutional layers addresses a specific need and complements the other normative sources. One cannot really speak of 'rights inflation' when talking about Internet bills rights, because the aim of these documents is not to place themselves side-by-side with other constitutional instruments, nor to replace them.[26] Internet bills of rights, as seen in Chapter 8, aim to compensate and stimulate other constitutional instruments. Internet bills of rights do not emerge in a legal vacuum nor do they develop in an air-tight container. They adopt the *lingua franca* of constitutions to be part of the constitutional dimension. In this way, their principles are free to flow within the constitutional conglomerate and can be easily compared with other norms. Although they focus on the Internet, the digital dimension, the online world, and so on, Internet bills of rights contaminate other constitutional layers which are more comprehensive. Criticising the limited scope of these documents does not hold anymore if one puts them in context, bearing in mind that they are an integral part of a composite constitutional framework.

Following this line of argumentation, the narrow focus of Internet bills of rights can also be usefully read as an alarm sign for the entire constitutional ecosystem. The emergence of these documents would work as a sort of litmus test, highlighting an area of constitutional law that presents a series of problematic issues. In particular, the analysis of the scope of application of Internet bills of rights allows us to better understand which specific aspects of the digital society are in need of intervention. This chapter will provide the first concrete example of the didactic force of Internet bills of rights. Analysing the material scope of application of Internet bills of rights, that is, simply said, the subject matter to which these texts aim to apply, it will assess to what extent these documents have managed to successfully define the area of constitutional law in which it would be appropriate to intervene in facing the challenges of the digital revolution. In the following sections, we will see that such an endeavour is nothing but straightforward.

A complex delimitation

At first sight, and instinctively – it could be said, one has the impression that the analysis of the material scope of application of Internet bills of rights does not reveal any surprise. These documents, indeed, focus on the Internet by definition. However, it is worth reminding that 'Internet bill of rights' is a denomination that this work has attributed to a broad array of documents, on the basis of their content, and notwithstanding their formal characteristics. A cursory look at the titles of the documents, for example, already shows that these texts do not always refer to the Internet literarily.

26 See Yilma (n 18), who talks of a risk of rights inflation in relation to Internet bills of rights; cf. the counter-critique by Celeste (n 20).

Table 9.1 Material scope of application (Appendix A)

Material scope of application	*Number of texts (out of 26)*
Internet (22), Internet-related technologies (1)	23
Digital media (2), age (1), environment (1), platforms (1), world (1)	6
Information and communication technologies (2), services (1), society (2), systems (1)	6
Online (3), environment (1), networks and services (1)	5
Cyber environment (1), cyberspace (2)	3
New ecosystem (1), technologies (1)	2

If one performs a full textual analysis of these documents,[27] it is apparent that Internet bills of rights do not consistently define their subject matter, although the Internet represents their most recurring material scope of application.[28]

Table 9.1 visualises the results of the textual analysis performed on the material scope of application of the narrower dataset of Internet bills of rights listed in Appendix A. The column on the left lists the subject matter of these documents, and the column on right shows their recurrence. The results are arranged according to the latter parameter in a descending order. As is evident from the figures in Table 9.1, the analysed texts do not adopt a single material scope of application but often focus on more than one subject matter. Conceptually regrouping these results, one could say that 23 texts out of 26 identify the Internet as their material scope of application; six of them also refer to the 'digital' dimension; six also focus on 'information and communication' technologies; five of them on the 'online' environment; three on the 'cyber' space; and, finally, two also underline the 'new' character of the ecosystem to which they aim to apply.

In only four documents, the denomination 'Internet' is not employed at all to designate the material scope of application. The Declaration of Human Rights in Cyberspace edited by Robert B. Gelman in 1997 exclusively refers to the 'cyberspace'[29]; the Code of EU Online Rights issued by the European Commission in 2012 focuses only on 'online networks and services'[30]; the

27 A first textual analysis of the material scope of application of these texts was published in Edoardo Celeste, 'The Scope of Application of Digital Constitutionalism. Output from an Empirical Research' (Nexa Research Papers 2017) Nexa Research Papers <https://nexa.polito.it/nexacenterfiles/E.%20Celeste%20-%20Research%20Paper.pdf>.

28 From a methodological perspective, the material scopes of application of the documents listed in Appendix B have been derived from the analysis of relevant excerpts identified using a coding technique. On coding, see Johnny Saldaña, *The Coding Manual for Qualitative Researchers* (3rd ed., Sage 2016).

29 Gelman (n 2).

30 European Commission, 'Code of EU Online Rights' (n 4).

Table 9.2 Material scope of application (Appendix B)

Material scope of application	*Number of texts (out of 199)*
Internet (147), economy (1), ecosystem (1), environment (2), Internet-related technologies (2)	153
Information and communication technologies (37), industry (1), services/ systems/networks/society (6), environment (2), space (1)	47
Digital (7), age (7), computer and network technologies (1), economy (5), environment/ecosystem (10), marketplace (1), media (2), networks (1), revolution (1), services (1), technology (3), digitisation/digitalisation (3)	42
Online (10), environment (4), networks and services (2), technologies (1), world (3)	20
Cyber environment (1), cyberspace (17), cybersecurity (1)	19
Information highways (1), society (12), information society services (1), systems (2)	16
New ecosystem (1), media (3), technologies (5)	9
Social networks/social web	9
Electronic commerce (3), environment (2), marketplace (1), media (1)	7
Artificial intelligence (5), machine learning systems (1)	6
Communication technologies (4), surveillance (1), means of mass communication (1)	6
Web/websites/WWW/Web 2.0	6
Audiovisual and information services	3
Knowledge Society	3
Search Engines	2
Big data	1
Blogging websites	1
Broadband market/services	1
Computer network	1
Direct marketing	1
Global networks	1
Mobile app ecosystem	1

UNESCO's Code of Ethics for the Information Society, consistently with its title, mentions only the 'information society',[31] while the Declaration on Digital Freedom adopted by PEN International in 2012 chooses 'digital media' as its focal point.[32]

A similar terminological inconsistency is observable in relation to the material scope of application of the texts listed in Appendix B, those, more

31 UNESCO, 'Code of Ethics for the Information Society Proposed by the Intergovernmental Council of the Information for All Programme (IFAP)' (2011) <https://unesdoc.unesco.org/ark:/48223/pf0000212696> accessed 17 June 2019.

32 PEN International, 'Declaration on Internet Freedom' <https://pen-international.org/app/uploads/PEN-Declaration_INTERNATIONALweb.pdf>.

broadly speaking, representing the ongoing 'conversation' on rights and principles in the digital society. In this dataset too, the majority of the documents identify 'the Internet' as their material scope of application. The other most recurring scopes are similar to those just seen in relation to Appendix A. The dimension of 'information and communication' technologies is chosen by 47 texts out of 199; the 'digital' environment reaches a similar score (42 texts); the 'online' and 'cyber' worlds follow with 20 and 19 documents, respectively. In 50 texts, the denomination 'the Internet' is not employed to designate the material scope of application but is replaced by a variety of terms.[33]

This chapter suggests that such a terminological inconsistency, characterising not only the material scope of application of Internet bills of rights but also the broader ongoing conversation on rights and principles for the digital society witnesses that the borders of the societal context that require a constitutional intervention are not clearly defined yet. These documents are progressively identifying which aspects of contemporary society have been affected by the digital revolution and the magnitude to which it has modified our life. Ultimately, it is possible to say that Internet bills of rights are attempting to understand the digital society and its problematic issues.

The main evidence to prove this assertion is provided by the analysis of the recurrence of the material scope of application of the analysed texts over-time. Table 9.3 visualises terminological trends in the use of a specific subject matter from a chronological perspective. It reveals that, while notions such as 'the Internet' or 'information society' constantly recur over time, other scopes have been adopted only for a limited amount of time. For example, the 'electronic' environment was chosen as the material scope of application mainly in the 1990s, while references to the 'digital' and 'online' dimension, 'information and communications technologies', 'social media', and 'artificial intelligence' exclusively characterise more recent years.[34] Such terminological tendencies could be explained as progressive attempts

33 In 50 cases, the denomination 'Internet' is not employed to designate the material scope of application but is replaced, respectively, with 'artificial intelligence/machine learning systems' (5, i.e. interestingly, in all cases when this subject matter is chosen), 'big data', 'broadband', 'communication surveillance', 'communication systems and networks' (2), 'computer and computer network', 'cybersecurity', 'cyberspace' (3), 'digital', 'digital age', 'digital economy', 'digital marketplace', 'digital computer and network technologies', 'digital media' (2), 'digital network and computer technologies', 'digital environment' (4), 'electronic commerce' (2), 'ICTs/information and communication environment/industry/space' (11), 'information society/information society services' (4), 'information networks and digitalisation', 'knowledge society' (2), 'media' (2), 'mobile app ecosystem', 'online' (3), 'online networks and services', 'search engines', 'social web/social networks' (6), and 'web' (2). It is important to remind that each text can refer to more than one subject matter at the same time.

34 For a study on the emergence of principles related to artificial intelligence, see 'Artificial Intelligence & Human Rights' (*Berkman Klein Center*, 18 January 2019) <https://cyber.harvard.edu/publication/2018/artificial-intelligence-human-rights> accessed 3 July 2019.

Table 9.3 Recurrence of the material scopes of application over time (Appendix B)

Material scope of application	1992	1993	1994	1995	1996	1997	1998	1999	2000	2001	2002	2003	2004	2005	2006	2007	2008	2009	2010	2011	2012	2013	2014	2015	2016	2017	2018	2019
Artificial intelligence																										■	■	■
Cyberspace			■	■		■	■	■			■	■				■		■		■		■	■					
Communication	■				■												■	■		■			■					
Digital							■	■		■				■		■	■		■	■	■	■	■	■	■		■	
Electronic				■			■	■	■		■												■					
ICTs			■							■		■	■	■	■	■	■	■	■	■	■	■	■		■		■	■
Information society				■	■					■		■		■		■				■	■	■			■			
Internet			■	■	■	■	■	■		■	■	■	■	■	■	■	■	■	■	■	■	■	■	■	■	■		■
New media, technologies		■							■				■	■			■			■	■	■	■		■		■	■
Online					■								■	■	■		■				■	■	■	■		■	■	■
Social networks																■			■	■	■	■	■				■	
Web/websites/WWW															■			■		■	■	■					■	

to identify the best descriptor that would be able to capture the problematic issues to be addressed.

However, the terminological inconsistency that characterises the material scope of application of Internet bills of rights and, more broadly, the conversation on rights and principles in the digital age, is not uniquely the result of a definitional experimentalism. The scenario is more complex. On the one hand, this work posits that these documents are attempting to find a suitable terminological solution to delimit the societal dimension that needs a constitutional intervention. On the other hand, one has to also highlight that this definitional instability is amplified by a substantial lack of reference points from a conceptual point of view. Indeed, there are no univocal definitions for the majority of the material scopes of application that these texts adopt. There is no authority defining what, for instance, 'cyberspace', the 'information society', or 'new technologies' precisely mean. Moreover, the analysed documents themselves generally overlook defining their subject matter. Only 33 texts out of 199 listed in Appendix B, and 8 documents out of 26 included in Appendix A report a definition, and comprehensive explanations are ever rarer. A paradoxical and paradigmatic case is represented by the notion of 'the Internet'. As we will see in the next section, although the majority of Internet bills of rights identifies the Internet as their material scope of application, its definition is nothing but clear.

What is really 'the Internet'?

Datasets

Among the analysed texts, all the documents that attempt to define the Internet articulate their definition in a different way, highlighting different aspects. A large number of texts consider the Internet as 'a network of networks',[35] but it is possible to find other descriptors, such as 'computer network',[36] 'infrastructure',[37] and 'multi-media platform'.[38] Some sources also specify that the Internet uses a single language consisting in a set of protocols.[39] Godwin, in his proposal for a Great Charter of Cambodian Internet Freedom, one of the Internet bills of rights listed in Appendix A, describes the Internet as:

35 See "Cyberspace and the American Dream: A Magna Carta for the Knowledge Age," Future Insight, Aug. 1994 <http://www.pff.org/issues-pubs/futureinsights/fi1.2magnacarta.html> accessed 30 April 2019; European Commission, 'Green Paper on the Protection of Minors and Human Dignity in Audiovisual and Information Services' <http://aei.pitt.edu/1163/1/minors_info_soc_gp_COM_96_483.pdf>; European Parliament, 'Report on the Commission Communication on Illegal and Harmful Content on the Internet' (1997) COM(96)0487-C4-0592/96 <http://www.europarl.europa.eu/sides/getDoc.do?type=REPORT&reference=A4-1997-0098&language=EN#Contentd184264e1056>; Stephen J Page, 'IANA & Human Rights Declaration of Individual Rights in Cyberspace, July' (1998) <https://forum.icann.org/iana/comments/25july1998-31july1998/msg00015.html> accessed 2 July 2019; 'APC Internet Rights Charter' <https://www.apc.org/en/pubs/about-apc/apc-internet-rights-charter> accessed 17 December 2018; OECD, 'Communiqué on Principles for Internet Policy-Making' (2011) <http://www.oecd.org/internet/innovation/48289796.pdf>; OECD, 'Principles for Internet Policy Making" <https://www.oecd.org/sti/ieconomy/oecd-principles-for-internet-policy-making.pdf>; Panel on Global Internet Cooperation and Governance Mechanisms, 'Towards a Collaborative, Decentralized Internet Governance Ecosystem' (2014) <https://www.icann.org/en/system/files/files/collaborative-decentralized-ig-ecosystem-21may14-en.pdf>; Mike Godwin, 'The Great Charter for Cambodian Internet Freedom' <https://www.linkedin.com/pulse/great-charter-cambodian-internet-freedom-mike-godwin> accessed 21 May 2019.

36 See European Commission, 'Illegal and Harmful Content on the Internet' <http://aei.pitt.edu/5895/1/5895.pdf>; Godwin (n 35).

37 See European Parliament (n 35); 'APC Internet Rights Charter' (n 35).

38 See 'APC Internet Rights Charter' (n 35).

39 See European Parliament (n 35); WSIS, 'Civil Society Declaration to the World Summit on the Information Society – Shaping Information Societies for Human Needs' <https://www.itu.int/net/wsis/docs/geneva/civil-society-declaration.pdf>; 'Marco Civil Da Internet, Lei No. 12.965, de 23 de Abril de 2014.' <http://www.planalto.gov.br/ccivil_03/_ato2011-2014/2014/lei/l12965.htm> accessed 7 May 2019; Godwin (n 35).

> the myriad of computers and telecommunications facilities, including equipment and operating software, which *comprise* the interconnected worldwide network of networks.[40]

The functions of the Internet are variably detailed. Some texts assert that the Internet is a medium of transmission of 'electromagnetic energy'[41] or that it connects together 'a great number of computers',[42] while other sources specify that it is a communications infrastructure[43] or a commercial platform.[44] Most of the texts agree on the global[45] and decentralised[46] nature of the Internet, while there is less consensus on the fact that it is by definition an 'open architecture',[47] 'user-driven',[48] 'public',[49] and 'indestructible'.[50]

It is apparent that the definitions of the Internet provided by the analysed texts focus on different aspects of this concept. Only two definitions appear to be quite comprehensive and describe at the same time the substance, the attributes, and the functions of the Internet. In 1997, the European Parliament defined the Internet as:

> a shared infrastructure (the 'network of networks'), the joint creation of all those party to it, using a single language (the TCP/IP protocols)

40 Godwin (n 35), emphasis added. This definition reproduces that one adopted by the U.S. Code: see 15 USC § 6501(6), 15 USC § 6555(2), and 21 USC § 802(50) <https://www.law.cornell.edu/uscode/text>.

41 Page (n 35).

42 European Commission, 'Illegal and Harmful Content on the Internet' (n 36); European Parliament (n 35).

43 See European Commission, 'Illegal and Harmful Content on the Internet' (n 36); Open Society Institute – Regional Internet Program and Parliamentary Human Rights Foundation, 'Open Internet Policy Principles' <http://mailman.anu.edu.au/pipermail/link/1997-March/026302.html>; European Parliament (n 35); Page (n 35); 'Marco Civil Da Internet, Lei No. 12.965, de 23 de Abril de 2014.' (n 39); Panel on Global Internet Cooperation and Governance Mechanisms (n 35); Godwin (n 35).

44 Panel on Global Internet Cooperation and Governance Mechanisms (n 35).

45 See European Commission, 'Illegal and Harmful Content on the Internet' (n 36); 'APC Internet Rights Charter' (n 35); 'Marco Civil Da Internet, Lei No. 12.965, de 23 de Abril de 2014.' (n 39); Godwin (n 35).

46 See European Parliament (n 35); Open Society Institute – Regional Internet Program and Parliamentary Human Rights Foundation (n 43); OECD, 'Communiqué on Principles for Internet Policy-Making' (n 35); OECD, 'Principles for Internet Policy Making'' (n 35); WSIS (n 39).

47 Open Society Institute - Regional Internet Program and Parliamentary Human Rights Foundation (n 43); 'APC Internet Rights Charter' (n 35).

48 European Commission, 'Illegal and Harmful Content on the Internet' (n 36); European Parliament (n 35).

49 European Parliament (n 35); 'APC Internet Rights Charter' (n 35).

50 European Parliament (n 35).

> and linking up computers worldwide, thus enabling their users to communicate.[51]

Article 5 of the Brazilian act called 'Marco Civil da Internet', instead, provided the following definition:

> Internet: the system consisting of the set of logical protocols, structured on a global scale for public and unrestricted use, in order to enable communication of data between terminals, through different networks.[52]

Both definitions agree on the fact that the Internet is an interconnection of networks, it is global, based on a set of protocols, and enables communication. However, such an observation is of little help, if one considers that, except for these two cases, the other sources analysed do not adopt the same minimal definition and rather highlight different aspects of the Internet's nature.

Institutions

The absence of a consensus on what the Internet is, and more generally a lack of definitional effort among the analysed texts, is not surprising. Indeed, a common definition of the Internet does not exist.[53] The constitutionalist Paolo Passaglia compared the attempt to define the Internet with an *actio finium regundorum*, the Roman law procedure to define the contested boundaries of confining lands.[54] Even eminent players on the Internet governance scene avoid identifying a single definition. The Magna Carta for Philippine Internet Freedom, for example, explicitly states that:

> [w]hen possible, definitions shall be adopted from those established by the International Telecommunications Union (ITU), the Internet Engineering Task Force (IETF), the World Wide Web Consortium (WWWC), and the Internet Corporation for Assigned Numbers and Names (ICANN), and other international and transnational agencies governing the development, use, and standardization of information and communications technology and the Internet.[55]

51 European Parliament (n 35).

52 'Marco Civil Da Internet, Lei No. 12.965, de 23 de Abril de 2014.' (n 39).

53 See Vinton G Cerf and Robert E Kahn, 'What Is The Internet (and What Makes It Work)' (1999) <http://www.cnri.reston.va.us/what_is_internet.html> accessed 2 July 2019; cf. Matthias C Kettemann, *The Normative Order of the Internet: A Theory of Rule and Regulation Online* (Oxford University Press 2020) 22 ff.

54 Paolo Passaglia, 'Internet nella Costituzione italiana' Consulta Online <http://www.giurcost.org/studi/passaglia5.pdf>.

55 Miriam Defensor Santiago, The Magna Carta for Philippine Internet Freedom 2013.

However, the mentioned organisations, both singularly and collectively, do not firmly adopt a single definition of the Internet.

In a 2013 information document, the ITU stated that 'it would seem appropriate to use the term "Internet" in its broad sense, to refer to the applications and services as well as to the network itself', like in the definition adopted in 1995 by the US Federal Networking Council.[56] The latter defined the Internet as:

the global information system that

i is logically linked together by a globally unique address space based on the Internet Protocol (IP) or its subsequent extensions/follow-ons;
ii is able to support communications using the Transmission Control Protocol/Internet Protocol (TCP/IP) suite or its subsequent extensions/follow-ons, and/or other IP-compatible protocols; and
iii provides, uses, or makes accessible, either publicly or privately, high level services layered on the communications and related infrastructure described herein.[57]

Some authors, in particular Kahn and Cerf, two Internet pioneers, consider the US Federal Networking Council's definition as the most suitable.[58]

In a 1993 document addressed to the IEFT Network Working Group, Krol and Hoffman stated that the reason why the question 'what is the Internet?' is so frequently asked 'is because there's no agreed upon answer that neatly sums up the Internet'.[59] Nevertheless, one can find a definition of the Internet in two IEFT glossaries.[60] The IEFT Internet Users' Glossary, under the term 'internet', states that '[w]hile an internet is a network, the term "internet" is usually used to refer to a collection of networks interconnected with routers'. Interestingly, there is also a voice under the term 'Internet' with capital letter:

56 ITU, 'Document WTPF-13/INF/8-E, "Defining the Internet"' <https://www.itu.int/dms_pub/itu-s/md/13/wtpf13/inf/S13-WTPF13-INF-0008!!MSW-E.docx>

57 Federal Networking Council, 'Definition of "Internet"' <https://www.nitrd.gov/fnc/internet_res.pdf>.

58 Cerf and Kahn (n 53); see also Passaglia (n 54); ITU (n 56).

59 E Krol and E Hoffman, 'FYI on "What Is the Internet?"' (1993) <https://tools.ietf.org/html/rfc1462> accessed 2 July 2019; see also S Carl-Mitchell and J Quarterman, 'What Is the Internet, Anyway?' (1996) <https://tools.ietf.org/html/rfc1935> accessed 2 July 2019.

60 See Tracy LaQuey Parker and Gary Scott Malkin, 'Internet Users' Glossary' (1993) <https://tools.ietf.org/html/rfc1392> accessed 2 July 2019; Robert W Shirey, 'Internet Security Glossary, Version 2' (2007) <https://tools.ietf.org/html/rfc4949#page-7> accessed 2 July 2019. However, the latter includes the following disclaimer: 'The recommendations and some particular interpretations in definitions are those of the author, not an official IETF position'.

> [t]he Internet is the largest Internet in the world. Is a three levels hierarchy composed of backbone networks (e.g., NSFNET, MILNET), mid-level networks, and stub networks. The Internet is a multiprotocol Internet.[61]

The IEFT Internet Security Glossary, version 2, at its turn, adopts a different definition:

> The Internet is the single, interconnected, worldwide system of commercial, governmental, educational, and other computer networks that share (a) the protocol suite specified by the IAB (RFC 2026) and (b) the name and address spaces managed by the ICANN.[62]

Continuing with the institutions listed by The Magna Carta for Philippine Internet Freedom, the World Wide Web Consortium defines the Internet by referring to its Wikipedia definition:

> The Internet is a global system of interconnected computer networks that interchange data by packet switching using the standardized Internet Protocol Suite (TCP/IP).[63]

Finally, ICANN does not provide any definition of the Internet.[64] As a consequence of the divergence among those institutions, the Magna Carta for Philippine Internet Freedom itself eventually coined its own definition of the Internet.[65]

Reasons

From the analysis of these sources, it seems that there are two main reasons hindering the possibility of crafting a single definition of the Internet.

61 Parker and Malkin (n 60).

62 Shirey (n 60).

63 W3C, 'Help and FAQ - "What Is the Difference between the Web and the Internet?"' <https://www.w3.org/Help/#webinternet> accessed 2 July 2019.

64 No definition of the Internet is provided in the ICANN glossary: < https://www.icann.org/icann-acronyms-and-terms/en#i> accessed 2 July 2019. In the course 'Digital Trade and Global Internet Governance, provided in the ICANN learning platform, the Internet is defined by Professor S Aaronson as 'a network of network': <http://learn.icann.org/courses/> accessed 2 July 2019.

65 Miriam Defensor Santiago The Magna Carta for Philippine Internet Freedom (n 55). Section 3(40) reads '40. Internet - The global system of interconnected computer networks linked by various telecommunications technologies and that uses the standard Internet protocol suite'.

Firstly, the nature of the Internet is constantly evolving.[66] The Internet is 'a creature of the computer', and it will 'continue to change and evolve at the speed of the computer industry'.[67] This is why some authors tend to answer the question of 'what is the Internet?' with a history of the Internet's development over time.[68] The OECD, in a recommendation issued in 1992, already highlighted this issue more generally in relation to information and communication technologies:

> The dynamism of information and communication technologies dictates that this description of information systems may serve only to give an indication of the present situation and that new technological developments will arise to augment the potentialities of information systems.[69]

The second main explanation of the lack of a single definition lies in the composite and multi-function nature of the Internet. The latter can be regarded from two distinct, but complementary angles: from a technical perspective, and from a personal-functional perspective.[70] A definition of the Internet focusing on the technical aspect highlights the nature of its structure and its intrinsic mechanisms of functioning, that is, for instance, that it is a network of networks adopting a single language based on protocols. A definition of the Internet focusing on the personal-functional aspect conversely emphasises its functions in terms of personal liberties. The person, i.e., the human being, is taken as a filter to select the relevant functions of the Internet. In this way, the Internet is defined for example as a means of communication, an instrument of freedom of expression, rather than a means of packet switching.

66 See Barry M Leiner and others, 'Brief History of the Internet' (*Internet Society*) <https://www.internetsociety.org/resources/doc/2017/brief-history-internet/> accessed 2 July 2019; Krol and Hoffman (n 59).

67 Leiner and others (n 66).

68 See, e.g., Vinton G Cerf, 'Internet Governance' <https://www.icann.org/en/system/files/files/cerf-internet-publication-28oct04-en.pdf>.

69 OECD, 'Guidelines for the Security of Information Systems' (1992) <http://www.oecd.org/sti/ieconomy/oecdguidelinesforthesecurityofinformationsystems1992.htm> accessed 2 July 2019.

70 Cf. Passaglia (n 54). The Italian constitutionalist stresses the difference between the definitions of the Internet focusing on the technical structure and the functioning of the network, such as for example the one provided by the U.S. Federal Networking Council, and those mostly given by national courts emphasising the correlation with the principle of personal freedom of individuals. On the same line, see 'Internet Policy Politics - A Q&A with Marianne Franklin' (*Internet Policy Review*) <https://policyreview.info/articles/news/internet-policy-politics-qa-marianne-franklin/1349> accessed 2 July 2019. Cf. also the difference between narrow definitions only focusing on the network itself, and broad definitions including services provided through the network in ITU (n 56).

Relations

Moreover, the complexity deriving from the existence of this double perspective from which it is possible to describe the Internet magnifies the difficulty of fully understanding the relations between the Internet and the other material scopes of application adopted by the analysed documents and ultimately their effective scope.

Figure 9.1 attempts to visualise the conceptual links between the subject matter of the documents listed in Appendix B. The analysed texts offer little explicit information on the relationship between the Internet and the other scopes of application. To provide a full picture of this relational mosaic, this work has referred to the definitions provided by the Oxford English Dictionary.[71]

The diagram shows that the analysed texts focus both on a subject matter that is conceptually narrower than the Internet, such as on the 'web', 'social networks', and 'search engines' and on scopes that are far more encompassing, such as the 'digital environment', 'information and communication technologies', or the 'information society'. However, as is apparent from Figure 9.1, the relationship between the different material scopes of application is not exactly comparable with the structure of a Russian doll: one does not observe a set of concentric circles, but some variably overlapping and intersecting shapes. Therefore, by merely referring to this diagram, it is possible to exclude that the analysed texts identify, as a group, one single, encompassing scope of application, while referring in their body to different narrower aspects of the latter.

However, it is important to highlight that, in reality, the effective relation between each subject matter is even more complex than that represented in Figure 9.1. Such a bi-dimensional diagram, in fact, can only visualise the relation between two concepts in terms of breadth: wider or narrower. However, it does not represent the more sophisticated series of links between each subject matter. In fact, to complicate this scenario, as we have seen, there is the multifaceted nature of what we mean today by the term 'the Internet', interpretable both in a technical sense and from a personal-functional perspective. This circumstance certainly does not help to define a clearer picture of the material scope of application of these texts, ultimately blurring the boundaries of the main problematic areas of the contemporary digital society that these documents are trying to delineate.

71 'Oxford English Dictionary' <https://www.oed.com/> accessed 2 July 2019. The choice to refer to the definitions of a language dictionary is justified by the scope of the present analysis. Indeed, this work does not aim at assessing the validity of the definitions of the analysed material scopes from a technical perspective. Its purpose is rather to establish their mutual relationship from a semantic point of view. See, *amplius*, Celeste (n 27).

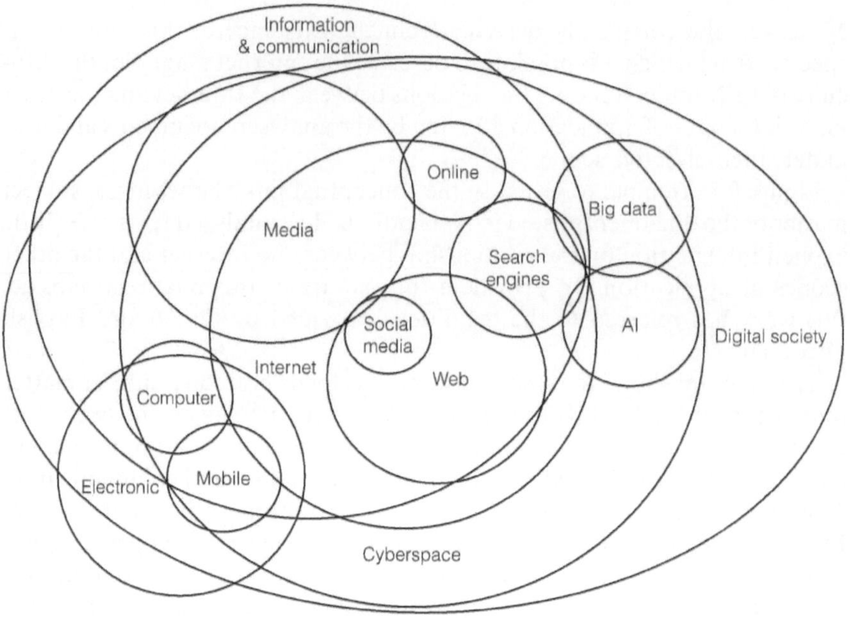

Figure 9.1 Relationship between the analysed material scopes.

Future-proof norms

At first sight, the analysis of the material scope of application of Internet bills of rights does not show encouraging results. We have observed that these texts, from a terminological point of view, inconsistently define their subject matter. Such differences emerge not only between different documents but also within the same text. Terms such as ‘the Internet’, ‘cyberspace’, and ‘information society’ are seemingly used in an interchangeable way, as if they were synonyms. Furthermore, these texts often neglect to define those concepts and, regrettably, if one also looks at external sources, agreed definitions do not exist.

We have explored more closely the notion of ‘the Internet’. It represents the most recurrent subject matter among the analysed documents. Nevertheless, it is seldom defined; when defined, there is no consensus among the different texts; and, what is even more worrisome, it appears that a commonly agreed definition of the Internet does not exist at all. It is extremely complex to define the conceptual boundaries between each subject matter adopted by the analysed texts, but what is clear is that the Internet does not represent the most encompassing notion. One cannot conclude that the observed terminological inconsistency in reality reflects a Russian doll-style architecture. Already drawing a simplified diagram visualising the relation between each subject matter, we have seen that they extensively overlap and intersect.

The fragmentation which is observable in relation to the material scope of application of Internet bills of rights does not represent an isolated phenomenon. In the previous paragraphs, we have more broadly taken into account the documents listed in Appendix B, a sample of the more general conversation on rights and principles for the digital society. Moreover, this issue does not seem to be new. In 1999, Cerf and Kahn had already pointed out the risk that the terminology currently employed at legislative level does not neatly define the boundaries of the subject matter to be regulated.[72] The terminological inconsistency highlighted in Internet bills of rights manifestly witnesses the persistence of what Cerf and Kahn called a pressing 'need of clarification' in the area of digital law- and policy-making.[73] Marchand and Bourdeau describe pessimistically the current scenario:

> The cyberspace remains a non-identified space. We are not able to figure out the right way to organise it, because it subverts all traditional national legal frameworks. Failing our understanding of this phenomenon, the cyberspace became a space of non-law, where everything, even the worst, is possible [...][74]

However, the results of the textual analysis of the material scope of application of Internet bills of rights can also be read more constructively – not to say, optimistically. In the previous chapter, we have seen that the emergence of these documents can be interpreted as a form of constitutional experimentalism, from which one can learn useful lessons for the entire constitutional dimension. From this viewpoint, Internet bills of rights would be seeking to identify the areas of contemporary society affected by the digital revolution, contexts in which a constitutional intervention is needed. At the beginning of this chapter, these documents have been compared with a sort of litmus test, which would allow us to understand where the current problematic issues exactly lie. Following this line of argumentation, the terminological inconsistency that we have observed in relation to their material scope of application can be seen as the positive evidence of works-in-progress in the context of an ongoing process of definition of the problematic aspects of our society. Internet bills of rights would be in search of the terminology best fitting their substantive content, which articulates rights and principles to address the challenges generated by the advent of the digital revolution.

From a more strictly legal point of view, this situation can be viewed as an attempt to find suitable concepts that would be, at the same time, technology-neutral and future-proof. Constitutional law does not aim for perpetuity, but it strives to define stable guiding principles that need not be amended

72 Cerf and Kahn (n 53).
73 Cerf and Kahn (n 53).
74 Stéphane Marchand and Michel Bourdeau, 'Une Magna Carta pour Internet, 20 ans après' (2015) 141 Cahiers philosophiques 104, 106, my translation.

at every change of legislature. The Italian legal scholar Piero Calamandrei, in an intervention before the Constituent Assembly created after the fall of the fascist regime, said that the Constitution should be 'presbyopic', far-sighted, and not 'myopic'.[75] Similarly, Internet bills of rights would be researching concepts and terms that are able to speak to the present and the future society.

The presence of trends in the use of certain terms to define their material scope of application shows this effort to articulate a future-proof discourse on digital rights and principles. Some scopes, such as those related to the 'electronic' dimension, have been abandoned, because they are no longer able to identify the problematic areas of our society that need constitutional intervention. At the same time, the existence of these trends warns us against the adoption of narrow scopes that reflect a particular technological moment. Recently, for example, the discourse on rights and principles for the digital society has focused on the challenges created by social media or artificial intelligence. On the one hand, it is certainly useful to reflect on the threats that those technological developments generate and to translate our existing fundamental rights and principles in those specific contexts. On the other hand, however, very technological-specific scopes risk being subject to early obsolescence after their initial momentum.

From the analysis of the material scope of application of Internet bills of rights, we recognise the future importance of establishing a series of stable definitional parameters to fully understand what each subject matter effectively encompasses and its relationship with other scopes. Terminological inconsistency among Internet bills of rights and in the broader constitutional conversation undermines the effectiveness of the dialogue and the reflection that these initiatives aim to promote. This problem will be solved only if greater consensus is reached on basic definitions among all the involved stakeholders, especially in light of the transnational character of the phenomenon to regulate. It will also be crucial to avoid using different descriptors in order to identify a single document's subject matter: this form of internal terminological inconsistency does not help the reader to appraise the scope of the text and magnifies an overall sense of normative imprecision and uncertainty.

We have seen that today the concept of 'the Internet' is approached both from a technical and a personal-functional perspective: in this way, the Internet would not only be a 'network of networks' based on the exchange of specific protocols but also, more generally, a means of communication, a space of deliberation, and ultimately an instrument to exercise a broad array of fundamental rights. In some contexts, it is possible to observe that

75 Piero Calamandrei, 'Intervento all'Assemblea costituente, 4 marzo 1947, seduta pomeridiana' <http://www.istitutodegasperi-emilia-romagna.it/pdf/seminari2014_calamandrei.pdf>, my translation.

the notion of the Internet has gradually shifted from an original technical meaning to a more functional-personal one. An apparent example is Internet governance, where the discussion on technical aspects has been manifestly overtaken by the broader social, economic, legal, and political dimensions related to the Internet.[76] A suggestion that one could infer from this observation is that, in order to nourish a more future-proof conversation on digital rights and principles, it is better to focus on how the personal-functional aspects of technology, rather than its transient technical features, affect contemporary society. When defining what the Internet is, it would be better to offer a less detailed description of its technical aspects and, instead, highlight more clearly its functions in society.

Probably, taking this argumentation to the extreme, one could be led to think that the material scope of application of Internet bills of rights itself loses its centrality in the economy of these documents. It would not be so important to assess in relation to which specific technology we are articulating rights and principles, but it would be crucial to understand which social changes these technologies have generated in our society. However, in reality, this is a false dichotomy: we cannot fully appraise the extent to which our society is being transformed, if we do not previously clarify what the source and the trends of contemporary mutations are. These two intellectual stages are closely linked. The ongoing process of elaboration of the material scope of application of Internet bills of rights, comprehensively regarded as a single phenomenon, has taken this route. These documents are promoting a constitutional reflection on specific aspects of our society. Identifying what is changing established societal patters and what is challenging existing constitutional norms ultimately aims to better understand the contemporary society at large, its peculiarities, why it is different from the past, the powers from which we will need to be protected, and the new sources of threat for our fundamental rights. Only in this way, the constitutional ecosystem will produce effective and long-lasting norms, targeting those areas of our society that are more in need of intervention.

76 See 'Internet Policy Politics - A Q&A with Marianne Franklin' (n 70).

10 Empowering global people

Universal reach

'Cyberspace does not lie within your borders' wrote John Barlow, in 1996, in his famous *Declaration of the Independence of Cyberspace*, resolutely claiming that the virtual world overtakes physical boundaries.[1] National frontiers would not demarcate the digital environment. Cyberspace, the 'new home of Mind', would be a 'global social space' escaping from the jurisdiction of states.[2] Over the past two decades, this claim has been largely debated.[3] Today, there seems to be a broad consensus on the fact that our action in the virtual realm does not enjoy any special immunity from the law of the states.[4] Notwithstanding the complexity that acting in the cyberspace engenders, the Internet does not lie in a 'legal vacuum'.[5]

However, recognising that the virtual world is subject to the law of nation-states does not automatically prevent the argument that the nature of the social dimension created by the Internet is intrinsically transnational

1 John Perry Barlow, 'A Declaration of the Independence of Cyberspace' (1996) <https://www.eff.org/cyberspace-independence> accessed 11 December 2018.

2 Barlow (n 1).

3 See David R Johnson and David G Post, 'Law and Borders: The Rise of Law in Cyberspace' (1996) 48 Stanford Law Review; Jack L Goldsmith, 'Against Cyberanarchy' (1998) 65 The University of Chicago Law Review 1199; Joel R Reidenberg, 'Yahoo and Democracy on the Internet' (2002) 42 Jurimetrics 251; Joel R Reidenberg, 'Technology and Internet Jurisdiction' (2005) 153 University of Pennsylvania Law Review 1951; Uta Kohl, *Jurisdiction and the Internet: Regulatory Competence over Online Activity* (Cambridge University Press 2007); Jack Goldsmith and Tim Wu, *Who Controls the Internet? Illusions of a Borderless World* (Oxford University Press 2008); Thomas Schultz, 'Carving up the Internet: Jurisdiction, Legal Orders, and the Private/Public International Law Interface' (2008) European Journal of International Law 799; cf. Milton Mueller, *Will the Internet Fragment? Sovereignty, Globalization and Cyberspace* (Polity 2017), who accurately distinguishes the problem of technical fragmentation of the Internet and the issue of network-states alignment.

4 See, in particular, Goldsmith and Wu (n 3); Schultz (n 3); cf. Mueller (n 3).

5 *Vorratsdatenspeicherung (Data retention)* BVerfGE 125, 260 260.

DOI: 10.4324/9781003256908-10

and global.[6] A similar analysis of the application of state law in the digital realm witnesses that the digital environment overtakes national boundaries. The recent debate in Europe around the extraterritorial implications of the so-called 'right to be forgotten' may be mentioned as an example in this regard: the very existence of the question of whether a search engine result should be delisted globally, or only nationally/regionally, whatever position is eventually taken, shows that the boundaries of the digital society are not in principle aligned with those of nation-states.[7] As another example, the General Data Protection Regulation, the data protection legislation that entered into force in May 2018 in all the member states of the European Union, has an explicitly extraterritorial scope of application: a symptom that, if one really wants to protect the right to data protection in Europe, it is necessary to regulate a series of activities that technically occur beyond its territorial boundaries.[8]

Milton Mueller warned not to overemphasise the phenomenon of Internet 'fragmentation' or 'balkanisation', at least from a technical perspective.[9] 'The Internet is not breaking apart', he wrote referring to the alleged trend

6 See Milton L Mueller, *Networks and States: The Global Politics of Internet Governance* (MIT Press 2013) 4 ff.

7 See Federico Fabbrini and Edoardo Celeste, 'The Right to Be Forgotten in the Digital Age: The Challenges of Data Protection Beyond Borders' (2020) 21 German Law Journal 55; Brendan Van Alsenoy and Marieke Koekkoek, 'Internet and Jurisdiction after Google Spain: The Extraterritorial Reach of the "Right to Be Delisted"' (2015) 5 International Data Privacy Law 105; Paul De Hert and Vagelis Papkonstantinou, 'Google Spain: Addressing Critiques and Misunderstandings One Year Later Comment' (2015) 22 Maastricht Journal of European and Comparative Law 624; see also Christopher Wolf, 'Impact of the CJEU's Right to Be Forgotten: Decision on Search Engines and Other Service Providers in Europe' (2014) 21 Maastricht Journal of European and Comparative Law 547; Hielke Hijmans, 'Right to Have Links Removed: Evidence of Effective Data Protection' (2014) 21 Maastricht Journal of European and Comparative Law 555; cf. *Google LLC v Commission nationale de l'informatique et des libertés (CNIL)* [2019] ECJ C-507/17, ECLI:EU:C:2019:772.

8 See Federico Fabbrini, Edoardo Celeste and John Quinn (eds), *Data Protection beyond Borders: Transatlantic Perspectives on Extraterritoriality and Sovereignty* (Hart 2021); Paul de Hert and Michal Czerniawski, 'Expanding the European Data Protection Scope beyond Territory: Article 3 of the General Data Protection Regulation in Its Wider Context' (2016) 6 International Data Privacy Law 230; cf. Dan Jerker B Svantesson, 'Extraterritoriality and Targeting in EU Data Privacy Law: The Weak Spot Undermining the Regulation' (2015) 5 International Data Privacy Law 226; more specifically in relation to international data transfer, Christopher Kuner, 'Extraterritoriality and Regulation of International Data Transfers in EU Data Protection Law' (2015) 5 International Data Privacy Law 235; focusing on the old data protection directive, Lokke Moerel, 'The Long Arm of EU Data Protection Law: Does the Data Protection Directive Apply to Processing of Personal Data of EU Citizens by Websites Worldwide?' (2011) 1 International Data Privacy Law 28; see also Christopher Kuner, 'Data Protection Law and International Jurisdiction on the Internet (Part 1)' (2010) 18 International Journal of Law and Information Technology 176.

9 See Mueller (n 3) 11 ff.

of nation-states' assertion of sovereignty in cyberspace.[10] This apparent fragmentation would in reality conceal a 'mismatch' between the Internet's global nature and the Westphalian concept of territorial sovereignty characterising existing politico-legal entities.[11] In Mueller's words:

> [...] the rhetoric of fragmentation can be used to camouflage the more important issue, which is the question of alignment, the perceived need to re-align control of communication with the jurisdictional boundaries of national states.[12]

If, on the one hand, it is true that digital technology is not immune from state law, on the other hand, the digital ecosystem, broadly intended as the social reality where we act with the help of digital technology, remains geographically unbound and, in principle, globally open.

It is therefore not surprising to observe that the majority of Internet bills of rights do not restrict their territorial scope of application to any specific physical territory.[13] A universal reach is often implied.[14] They generally

10 Mueller (n 3) 18.

11 Mueller (n 3) 11; see also Mueller (n 6); cf. Edoardo Celeste, 'Digital Sovereignty in the EU: Challenges and Future Perspectives' in Federico Fabbrini, Edoardo Celeste and John Quinn (eds), *Data Protection Beyond Borders: Transatlantic Perspectives on Extraterritoriality and Sovereignty* (Hart 2021); for a concise outline of the Westphalian system, see Gerry Simpson, 'Westphalian System', *The New Oxford Companion to Law* (Oxford University Press 2008); on the recent debate on the concept of Westphalian sovereignty, see Martin Loughlin, 'Why Sovereignty?' in Richard Rawlings, Peter Leyland and Alison Young (eds), *Sovereignty and the Law: Domestic, European and International Perspectives* (Oxford University Press 2013); Neil Walker, 'Sovereignty Frames and Sovereignty Claims' in Richard Rawlings, Peter Leyland and Alison Young (eds), *Sovereignty and the Law: Domestic, European and International Perspectives* (Oxford University Press 2013); with particular focus on freedom of expression in the digital era, see Perry Keller, 'Sovereignty and Liberty in the Internet Era' in Richard Rawlings, Peter Leyland and Alison Young (eds), *Sovereignty and the Law* (Oxford University Press 2013).

12 Mueller (n 3) 18.

13 As for the analysis of the material scope of application presented in the previous chapter, the territorial scope of application of all the documents listed in Appendix A has been analysed using a coding technique. Both the explicit and the aspirational territorial scope of application have been considered.

14 See, e.g., 'Digital Bill of Rights' (*reddit*) <https://www.reddit.com/r/fia/comments/vuj37/digital_bill_of_rights_1st_draft/> accessed 5 July 2019. The Preamble of this document reads: 'We, the People of the Free World and Users of the Internet, in recognition of our Digital Rights; in order to promote Freedom *throughout the world*, to guard ourselves against oppressors motivated solely by greed; to ensure peace and prosperity to all through innovation unhindered; and to preserve our social and cultural progress *throughout the Earth*, do establish this Declaration of Digital Rights and Freedoms to protect this, the largest repository of human knowledge and most important invention known to the *People of Earth*.', emphasis added.

refer to the Internet dimension as 'global'.[15] Even documents with a national or regional focus, in which the territorial scope of application is explicitly limited to a particular state or region, acknowledge the universal nature of the Internet,[16] or at least recognise the transnational implications of its development.[17] Analogous trends are also observable in the sample of texts collected in Appendix B, which represent a broader conversation on rights and principles in the digital society.[18]

15 See, e.g., Open Society Institute – Regional Internet Program and Parliamentary Human Rights Foundation, 'Open Internet Policy Principles' <http://mailman.anu.edu.au/pipermail/link/1997-March/026302.html>; NETmundial, 'Internet Governance Principles - NETmundial Multistakeholder Statement' <http://netmundial.br/wp-content/uploads/2014/04/NETmundial-Multistakeholder-Document.pdf>.

16 See, e.g., Council of Europe, Committee of Ministers, 'Declaration by the Committee of Ministers on Internet Governance Principles' (21 September 2011) <https://search.coe.int/cm/Pages/result_details.aspx?ObjectID=09000016805cc2f6> accessed 21 May 2019. Although this declaration is addressed to the member states of the Council of Europe, it includes at para. 5 a provision on the 'Universality of the Internet', which reads: 'Internet-related policies should recognise the global nature of the Internet and the objective of universal access'. See also 'Marco Civil Da Internet, Lei No. 12.965, de 23 de Abril de 2014.' <http://www.planalto.gov.br/ccivil_03/_ato2011-2014/2014/lei/l12965.htm> accessed 7 May 2019. The territorial scope of application of this act is restricted to the Republic of Brazil. However, Article 2 provides that: 'The discipline of internet use in Brazil is founded on the basis of respect for freedom of expression, as well as: I – the recognition of the global scale of the network.'

17 See, e.g., Miriam Defensor Santiago, The Magna Carta for Philippine Internet Freedom 2013. This bill has been presented before the Philippine Congress and it is supposed to bind exclusively the Republic of Philippines. Nevertheless, Section 2, para. 5 recognises that the '[...] development, invention, and innovation for the Internet and for information and communications technology are pursuits of both the public and the private sector, and can be local, national, international, and transnational in effort. Therefore, the State shall endeavor to develop plans, policies, programs, measures, and mechanisms to encourage development, invention, and innovation through and for the Internet and for information and communications technology, in cooperation with other nations and international bodies'. Moreover, Section 2, para. 6 reads: 'Recognizing that the growth of the Internet and information and communications technologies affect peace and order and the enforcement of law within the national territory and across other nations, the State reaffirms its policy of cooperation and amity with all nations, and its adoption of generally accepted principles of international law as part of the law of the land, in the pursuit of peace and order and in the enforcement of law'. See also Mike Godwin, 'The Great Charter for Cambodian Internet Freedom' <https://www.linkedin.com/pulse/great-charter-cambodian-internet-freedom-mike-godwin> accessed 21 May 2019. Article 3 of this document focuses on the 'scope of application' and in particular its section A reads: 'The Great Charter of Cambodian Internet Freedom applies to all governmental actions that may damage or limit the Citizens' Internet rights and freedoms regardless of where the actions occur, regardless whether the source of the harm arises inside or outside of the territory of the Kingdom of Cambodia.'

18 See, e.g., European Commission, 'Green Paper on the Protection of Minors and Human Dignity in Audiovisual and Information Services' <http://aei.pitt.edu/1163/1/minors_info_soc_gp_COM_96_483.pdf>: 'Certain facets of these issues require European, indeed global solutions.'; European Commission, 'Illegal and Harmful Content on the Internet'

Looking at their territorial scope of application, one can therefore argue that Internet bills of rights articulate a series of principles for the digital society in a way that is more similar to international human rights conventions than to national constitutions. Their provisions echo the global breadth of the Universal Declaration of Human Rights. They do not reflect a physical rooting to the state-centric dimension. Rights are not claimed from the hands of specific, physical leviathans. They are established at a universal level. Internet bills of rights proclaim 'landless' rights that 'wander in the global world'.[19]

Restricting private power

In such a universal social space created by the advent of digital technology, the Westphalian logic anchored to sovereignty and state territories unavoidably loses its centrality.[20] Of course, as we have seen, nation-states maintain their relevance. However, the dynamics of power no longer reflect the exclusively binary relation between the state and its citizens. In the new global territory generated by digital technology, new dominant actors emerge besides nation-states. Powerful multinational corporations producing, managing, or selling digital technology products and services act as sovereigns in their own private fiefdoms.[21] Global people become subject to the rules of these 'silicon giants' as soon as they access their virtual premises.[22] The dominance that these private actors exercise on individuals is sometimes less visible.[23] It is certainly not as tangible as the power of physical coercion in the hands of nation-states. Nevertheless, these corporations *de facto* affect individual rights in a way not dissimilar from how nation-states do.

Interestingly, Internet bills of rights reflect this alteration of societal dynamics of power. The analysis of their personal scope of application shows

---

<http://aei.pitt.edu/5895/1/5895.pdf>: 'The symbol of the convergence between telecommunications, computer, and content industries, and one of its main drivers, the Internet has established itself as one of the main building blocks of the Global Information Infrastructure and as an essential enabler of the Information Society in Europe.'; Global Ethics Network for Applied Ethics, 'Ethics in the Information Society: The Nine 'P's' <https://www.globethics.net/documents/4289936/14121854/InformationEthics_Texts-Series_04_WSIS_EN_text.pdf/8492ed8f-0818-4a18-8c3e-d1a61221f8ac>: 'In a globalized multicultural world these values have to be global values while at the same time respecting the diversity of contextual values.'; OECD, 'Principles for Internet Policy Making'' <https://www.oecd.org/sti/ieconomy/oecd-principles-for-internet-policy-making.pdf>: 'The Internet economy depends crucially on the global free flow of information'.

19 Stefano Rodotà, *Il diritto di avere diritti* (Laterza 2012) 3, my translation.

20 See Mueller (n 3); Celeste (n 11).

21 See, more extensively, *supra* Chapter 2.

22 Stefano Rodotà, 'Una Costituzione per Internet?' [2010] Politica del diritto 337, 339, my translation.

23 See on the same point Monika Zalnieriute and Stefania Milan, 'Internet Architecture and Human Rights: Beyond the Human Rights Gap' (2019) 11 Policy & Internet 6.

that they address a wider circle of actors in comparison to traditional constitutional texts. These documents create obligations not only for states but also for multinational private corporations.[24] Internet bills of rights do not exclusively focus on the binary relation between state/s and its/their citizens. This would not make sense in the context of the global digital society, where the idea of territorial sovereignty is no longer the cornerstone of the power architecture. These documents re-interpret their constitutional mission by reading the contemporary society in a functional way, going beyond the traditional archetypes of power relations. They overtake the dichotomy of state/citizens on which the modern constitutionalism has been built and pragmatically appraise the present dynamics of power. The territorial scope of these documents is global, as we have seen. In this enlarged environment, Internet bills of rights understand that the big technology corporations today play a dominant role besides nation-states. By restricting the power of private corporations, these texts aim to suggest constitutional solutions that better mirror the stakeholders of the digital society and their internal dynamics.

More precisely, such an expanded personal scope of application of Internet bills of rights can be read as an alarm sign for the current state of the constitutional ecosystem. The creation of direct obligations for private actors clearly represents a choice going against the grain among contemporary constitutional instruments. The theory which sees the state as the ultimate holder of responsibility to enforce human rights represents one of the canons of constitutional law.[25] Internet bills of rights however highlight how in the digital society the issue of fundamental rights violations perpetrated by non-state actors has exacerbated.[26] Even those texts with a more traditional

24 See, e.g., Council of Europe, Committee of Ministers (n 16): 'public and private actors should recognise and uphold human rights and fundamental freedoms in their operations and activities, as well as in the design of new technologies, services and applications'; Godwin (n 17): 'Article 3: Scope of Application B. This Charter applies to all Persons conducting business regardless of whether they are formed as profit-making organizations, non-profit organizations or charitable organizations, including Business Operators engaged in production or supply of Public Utility products or services or Business Operators conducting business in Government Monopoly industries and sectors.'; Robert Gelman, 'Draft Proposal-Declaration of Human Rights in Cyberspace' <http://www.be-in.com/10/rightsdec.html> accessed 17 June 2019: 'to secure their universal and effective recognition and observance, among service providers, individual and organizational users, and the institutions of humanity at large.'; 'Charter of Human Rights and Principles for the Internet' <http://internetrightsandprinciples.org/site/wp-content/uploads/2018/10/IRPC_english_5thedition.pdf> accessed 17 December 2018: 'Every individual and every organ of society shall act to promote respect for these rights and freedoms and, by local and global measures, to secure their universal and effective recognition and observance'.

25 See Andrew Clapham, *Human Rights Obligations of Non-State Actors* (Oxford University Press 2006) ch 1.

26 On the point, cf., e.g., Emily B Laidlaw, *Regulating Speech in Cyberspace: Gatekeepers, Human Rights and Corporate Responsibility* (Cambridge University Press 2015); Frank

approach, while maintaining a central role for the state, recognise the risks to fundamental rights that private corporations can engender today. The Preamble of the Charter of Human Rights and Principles for the Internet, for example, echoes the Universal Declaration of Human Rights and states that 'every organ of society', therefore not only the state, shall protect human rights.[27] The document containing the Charter however explains:

> Human rights govern the relationship between the State and the individual, so human rights obligations bind states. The Charter is based on existing human rights and so in practice most of its provisions will only be binding on the State. However, there is a growing recognition that the private sector does have obligations under human rights law, as authoritatively outlined in the UN "Protect, Respect and Remedy" Framework. [...] Thus, while the primary responsibilities under the Charter remain with governments, the Charter also provides guidance to governments about how they must ensure that private companies are respecting human rights, and guidelines to companies about how they should behave so as to respect human rights in the Internet environment.[28]

The attention given by Internet bills of rights to the role and the responsibilities of private actors warns us about the existence of a 'human rights gap' in the constitutional ecosystem.[29] A grey zone, not to say a true legal 'vacuum', is emerging from the dis-alignment between norms that are tailored on states and the digital environment, in which the protection of individual rights is *de facto* entrusted to private actors.[30] Some authors have talked

Pasquale, *The Black Box Society: The Secret Algorithms That Control Money and Information* (Harvard University Press 2015); Rikke Frank Jørgensen and Anja Møller Pedersen, 'Online Service Providers as Human Rights Arbiters' in Mariarosaria Taddeo and Luciano Floridi (eds), *The Responsibilities of Online Service Providers* (Springer 2017); Luca Belli, Pedro Augusto P Francisco and Nicolo Zingales, 'Law of the Land or Law of the Platform? Beware of the Privatisation of Regulation and Police', *Platform regulations: how platforms are regulated and how they regulate us* (FGV Direito Rio 2017) <http://hdl.handle.net/10438/19402> accessed 8 July 2019; Nicolas Suzor, *Lawless. The Secret Rules That Govern Our Digital Lives* (Cambridge University Press 2019); Shoshana Zuboff, *The Age of Surveillance Capitalism: The Fight for a Human Future at the New Frontier of Power* (PublicAffairs 2019); Edoardo Celeste, Amélie Heldt and Clara Iglesias Keller (eds), *Constitutionalising Social Media* (Hart 2022); see also, supra, ch. 2.

27 'Charter of Human Rights and Principles for the Internet' (n 24); cf. Council of Europe, 'Recommendation of the Committee of Ministers to Member States on Internet Freedom' (2016) CM/Rec(2016)5 <https://search.coe.int/cm/Pages/result_details.aspx?ObjectId=09000016806415fa>, para. 5.4.

28 'Charter of Human Rights and Principles for the Internet' (n 24) 2, 9.

29 Zalnieriute and Milan (n 23).

30 Zalnieriute and Milan (n 23).

of a 'privatisation' of human rights.[31] Multinational companies, sometimes even vested by the states themselves, unavoidably shape the way individuals exercise their fundamental rights according to the values or the exigencies of their business models.[32] The solution that the majority of Internet bills of rights envisage to tame the 'new governors' of the online fiefs is to impose direct obligations on these private actors.[33] Thus, complex constitutional stratagems, such as the third party effect of fundamental rights, are no longer needed.[34] These documents coherently adopt the same solution to restrict the power of all the dominant actors, be they states or not.

An enlarged social contract

In the global social environment connected through the use of digital technology, nation-states, at times, are vested only with a formal suzerainty: they claim and are deemed to be the overlord of the digital environment too, but *de facto* allow multinational private corporations to reign sovereign in their fiefs.[35] In the dynamics of the digital society, the power of corporations is magnified and, consequently, the centrality of the binary relation between state and citizens fades. Another area of tension emerges: that between multinational private corporations and single individuals.

In the previous section, we have seen that Internet bills of rights pragmatically appraise the mutated power dynamics of the digital society by directly imposing obligations both on states and private corporations. In this way, these documents acknowledge the role of multinational companies, refusing to be bound by traditional constitutional archetypes. They do not resort to constitutional stratagems, which would continue to see states as the only dominant power. They broaden the scope of their constitutional norms by considering both states and private corporations as the effective holders of power in the digital society.

At the same time, Internet bills of rights understand that it is no longer the 'citizen' of a specific territory who is subject to the power of this complex

31 See L DeNardis and AM Hackl, 'Internet Governance by Social Media Platforms' (2015) 39 Telecommunications Policy 761; Emily Taylor, 'The Privatization of Human Rights: Illusions of Consent, Automation and Neutrality' (2016) 24 Global Commission on Internet Governance Paper Series <https://www.cigionline.org/publications/privatization-human-rights-illusions-consent-automation-and-neutrality> accessed 8 July 2019; Zalnieriute and Milan (n 23).

32 Belli, Francisco and Zingales (n 26).

33 Kate Klonick, 'The New Governors: The People, Rules, and Processes Governing Online Speech' 131 Harvard Law Review 1598.

34 See, e.g., Eric Engle, 'Third Party Effect of Fundamental Rights (Drittwirkung)' (2009) 5 Hanse Law Review 165.

35 See Bruce Schneier, 'Power in the Age of the Feudal Internet' [2013] MIND 16; on the concept of 'suzerainty', see John P Grant and J Craig Barker, 'Suzerainty', *Encyclopaedic Dictionary of International Law* (Oxford University Press 2009).

conglomerate of dominant actors. They functionally identify the generic 'individual' as the weak actor of the constitutional landscape. Analysing the personal scope of application of these texts, such a choice is apparent from the use of specific terminology. These charters do not establish rights only for the 'citizens' of a specific state but for all 'persons', all 'individuals', 'everyone'.[36] In this way, these documents claim their support for the long-established view of international human rights law affirming the existence of a series of inalienable rights of the human being, which are independent from the status of the citizen.[37] The UNESCO's *Code of Ethics for the Information Society* explicitly states:

> Every person irrespective of where they live, their gender, education, religion, social status shall be able to benefit from the Internet and use of ICTs. Everyone shall be able to connect, access, choose, produce,

36 See, e.g., Gelman (n 24): 'We, the citizens of cyberspace proclaim THIS DECLARATION OF HUMAN RIGHTS in CYBERSPACE as a common standard of achievement to the end that every individual and every organization of the information infrastructure, keeping this Declaration in mind, shall strive by teaching and education to promote respect for these rights and freedoms and by progressive measures, online and in the physical world, to secure their universal and effective recognition and observance, among service providers, individual and organizational users, and the institutions of humanity at large'; Open Society Institute – Regional Internet Program and Parliamentary Human Rights Foundation (n 15): 'Access to the global Internet and other interactive communications infrastructures is essential for all citizens of the world to enable full participation in the global society and developing digital economy'; CGI.br – Comitê Gestor da Internet no Brasil, 'Principles for the Governance and Use of the Internet' (*CGI.br – Comitê Gestor da Internet no Brasil*, 2009) <https://cgi.br> accessed 5 July 2019: 'the Internet must be based on open standards that facilitate interoperability and enable all to participate in its development.'; 'Charter of Human Rights and Principles for the Internet' (n 24): 'We bring this Charter of Human Rights & Principles for the Internet as a common standard of achievement for all stakeholders in the Internet environment. Every individual and every organ of society shall act to promote respect for these rights and freedoms and, by local and global measures, to secure their universal and effective recognition and observance.' and see also Article 20; UNESCO, 'Code of Ethics for the Information Society Proposed by the Intergovernmental Council of the Information for All Programme (IFAP)' (2011) <https://unesdoc.unesco.org/ark:/48223/pf0000212696> accessed 17 June 2019: 'Emphasizing that ethical principles are relevant to all stakeholders of the information society, collectively or individually, and that existence and implementation, at all levels, of the ethical principles is essential to ensure an all-inclusive information society'.

37 See, seminally, Hannah Arendt, *The Origins of Totalitarianism* (Harcourt Brace Jovanovich 1979), ch 9, 267 ff; on the theory of universality of human rights, see Stefan-Ludwig Hoffmann, *Human Rights in the Twentieth Century* (Cambridge University Press 2010) 83 ff; Gerhard Ernst and Jan-Christoph Heilinger, *The Philosophy of Human Rights: Contemporary Controversies* (De Gruyter 2012) 211 ff; on the complex relationship between human rights and citizenship, see David Weissbrodt, *The Human Rights of Non-Citizens* (Oxford University Press 2008); Alison Brysk and Gershon Shafir, *People out of Place: Globalization, Human Rights, and the Citizenship Gap* (Routledge 2004); David Owen, 'On the Right to Have Nationality Rights: Statelessness, Citizenship and Human Rights' (2018) 65 Netherlands International Law Review 299.

communicate, innovate and share information and knowledge on the Internet.[38]

Internet bills of rights aim to craft – one could say – a new, enlarged 'social contract' overtaking territorial boundaries and encompassing all the actors of the digital society.[39] Such a pact would still be rooted in, and mirror, societal power relations: a compromise emerging to strike a balance between dominant and weak actors. However, this time, it would be no longer founded on a physical bond. It is the social environment generated by the advent of digital technology that virtually unifies the individuals which are subject to the power of states and multinational private companies. The territory of the state loses its centrality. It is no longer the exclusive parameter for the recognition of rights.

Interestingly, the concept of citizenship survives but acquires a new meaning, unbound from any territorial characterisation. Internet bills of rights are the voice of the 'citizens of cyberspace',[40] the 'People of the Internet',[41] and the 'citizens of an Internet-mediated world'.[42] Such a novel form of citizenship is independent from nation-states. It is global: it exclusively relies on the abstract possibility of an individual to claim access to the digital society. By enlarging the social contract, recognising rights and responsibilities for all the stakeholders of the digital society, notwithstanding their formal legal status, Internet bills of rights contribute to consolidate the distinctiveness of the global digital community,[43] a group of actors that does not aim to reconfigure the contours of territorial identities, but which acts as a necessary pre-condition to establishing the guiding principles for the digital society.

38 UNESCO (n 36), Article 2.

39 See Rolf Weber and Romana Weber, 'Social Contract for the Internet Community? Historical and Philosophical Theories as Basis for the Inclusion of Civil Society in Internet Governance?' (2009) 6 SCRIPT-ed 90; cf. the idea of Sir Tim Berners Lee of a 'contract for the Web': '30 Years on, What's next #ForTheWeb?' (*World Wide Web Foundation*) <https://webfoundation.org/2019/03/web-birthday-30/> accessed 9 July 2019.

40 Gelman (n 24).

41 Ryan Lytle, 'Explore Mashable's Crowdsourced Digital Bill of Rights' (*Mashable*) <https://mashable.com/2013/08/12/digital-bill-of-rights-crowdsource/> accessed 21 May 2019.

42 Just Net Coalition, 'The Delhi Declaration for a Just and Equitable Internet' <https://justnetcoalition.org/delhi-declaration> accessed 7 May 2019.

43 See Mueller (n 3); Ingolf Pernice, 'Die Verfassung der Internetgesellschaft: Zur Rolle von Staat und Verfassung im Zuge der digitalen Revolution' in Alexander Blankenagel (ed), *Den Verfassungsstaat nachdenken. Eine Geburtstagsgabe* (Duncker & Humblot 2014) <https://papers.ssrn.com/abstract=2964926> accessed 28 August 2018; cf. John Keane, *Global Civil Society?* (Cambridge University Press 2003).

Participatory deliberation

Considering the wide scope of application of Internet bills of rights, aiming to articulate rights and principle for all the stakeholders of the digital society and, on top of that, on a global scale, a central question emerges. In the words of De Minico:

> which legislative body should write this Bill? [...] which Authority should be legitimated to write the fundamental Charter of the Internet?[44]

Internet bills of rights claim to articulate values and principles for the global digital community. However, this implies that the elaboration of these charters cannot merely rely on existing mechanisms of deliberation. Traditionally, constitutions were graciously granted by the monarch, elaborated by restricted constituent assemblies of citizens, or, on the international plane, negotiated by government representatives.[45] Embracing one of these traditional models of deliberation to craft a charter of rights for the Internet would mean to conclude a social contract *in absentia*. Some of the relevant stakeholders of the digital society would not be represented and, consequently, would not be able to defend their respective interests while deliberating the set of fundamental principles for the digital society.[46]

Moreover, Internet bills of rights are not merely declarations of independence, unilateral assertions of rights, and liberties against an external source of power.[47] These documents clearly evoke the constitutional dimension in which the dynamics of power between dominant and weak actors of a society are balanced. A social contract for the digital society would not be such

44 Giovanna De Minico, 'Towards an Internet Bill of Rights' (2015) 37 Loyola of Los Angeles International and Comparative Law Review 1, 2, 20.

45 For an overview of the most frequent mechanisms of constitution-making, see Tom Ginsburg, Zachary Elkins, and Justin Blount, 'Does the Process of Constitution-Making Matter?' (2009) 5 Annual Review of Law and Social Science 201; John M Carey, 'Does It Matter How a Constitution Is Created?' in Robert G Moser and Zoltan Barany (eds), *Is Democracy Exportable?* (Cambridge University Press 2009); for a historical overview on the role of granted constitution in Europe, see Luigi Lacchè, 'Granted Constitutions. The Theory of Octroi and Constitutional Experiments in Europe in the Aftermath of the French Revolution' (2013) 9 European Constitutional Law Review 285; on constituent assemblies, see Andrew Arato, 'Conventions, Constituent Assemblies, and Round Tables: Models, Principles and Elements of Democratic Constitution-Making' (2012) 1 Global Constitutionalism 173; cf. also Jon Elster, 'Legislatures as Constituent Assemblies' in Richard W Bauman and Tsvi Kahana (eds), *The Least Examined Branch: The Role of Legislatures in the Constitutional State* (Cambridge University Press 2006).

46 See, e.g., African Declaration Group, 'African Declaration on Internet Rights and Freedoms' 1 <https://africaninternetrights.org/sites/default/files/African-Declaration-English-FINAL.pdf>: 'the policy and legislative processes in most African countries lack meaningful mechanisms for inclusive participation, with the result that many critical stakeholders, particularly from civil society, are frequently excluded'.

47 Cf. Barlow (n 1).

if it were simply proclaimed by a restricted group of actors. A constitution stipulated exclusively among states and citizens, for example, would overlook the central role that private companies today play as dominant actors. A charter of rights for the Internet would not be a true act of self-constraint if all the dominant players, both states and multinational corporations, were not included in the constitutional negotiations.[48] The broad scope of application of Internet bills of rights encompassing individuals, states, and private corporations on a global basis reclaims more suitable mechanisms of deliberation.

Theoretical models

Rodotà was an active supporter of a multistakeholder method of deliberation, not only involving governmental representatives but also the private sector and civil society.[49] He strenuously defended the idea that the 'route to follow' to elaborate a charter of rights for the Internet cannot be the same adopted in the past to craft similar documents.[50] Historically, constitutional processes were top-down, but now such a model does not fit the 'very nature of the Internet' anymore. In Rodotà's words:

> The Internet is the realm of open discussions, of initiatives that want and can involve a huge number of people, the domain of shared creation. One cannot conceive the elaboration of its Charter of Rights

48 On the idea of constitutions as acts of self-constraint of the dominant actor, see Jon Elster, *Ulysses Unbound: Studies in Rationality, Precommitment, and Constraints* (Cambridge University Press 2000); see also Gunther Teubner and Anna Beckers, 'Expanding Constitutionalism' (2013) 20 Indiana Journal of Global Legal Studies 523; András Sajó and Renáta Uitz, *The Constitution of Freedom: An Introduction to Legal Constitutionalism* (Oxford University Press 2017).

49 See Rodotà, 'Una Costituzione per Internet?' (n 22); Stefano Rodotà, 'Perché Internet Ha Bisogno Di Una Carta Dei Diritti' *La Repubblica* (14 November 2006) <http://www.repubblica.it/2006/11/sezioni/scienza_e_tecnologia/internet-30-milioni/carta-diritti-internet/carta-diritti-internet.html> accessed 2 May 2019. On multi-stakeholderism in Internet governance, see Bertrand de La Chapelle, 'Multistakeholder Governance - Principles and Challenges of an Innovative Political Paradigm' [2011] *MIND # 2 - Internet Policy Making* <http://en.collaboratory.de/w/MIND_2_-_Internet_Policy_Making>; William Drake, 'Multistakeholderism: Internal Limitations and External Limits' [2011] *MIND # 2 - Internet Policy Making* <http://en.collaboratory.de/w/MIND_2_-_Internet_Policy_Making>; Mikkel Flyverbom, *The Power of Networks: Organizing the Global Politics of the Internet* (Edward Elgar 2011) chs 3–4; Eric Brousseau, Meryem Marzouki and Cécile Méadel (eds), *Governance, Regulation and Powers on the Internet* (Cambridge University Press 2012); Francesca Musiani, 'WSIS+10: The Self-Praising Feast of Multi-Stakeholderism in Internet Governance' (2013) 2 Internet Policy Review; Françoise Massit-Folléa, 'Internet et Les Errances Du Multistakeholderism' (2014) 79 Politique étrangère 29; see, more generally, Laura DeNardis, *The Global War for Internet Governance* (Yale University Press 2014); cf. Mueller (n 3) 114 ff.

50 See Rodotà, 'Perché Internet Ha Bisogno Di Una Carta Dei Diritti' (n 49).

> through traditional mechanisms of international treaty-making, with the Sherpas of the ministers of foreign affairs preparing a draft to discuss before the UN General Assembly. The Charter for the Internet can be nothing but the result of a more complex process [...][51]

De Minico too excludes that the role of 'legislator' of a charter of rights for the Internet could be taken up by 'one or more national States' or by an 'international body'.[52] These two models would remain excessively anchored to a state-centric paradigm and, consequently, would not be able to reflect the core features of a plural and global digital community. At the same time, De Minico also rejects 'the idea of an Internet Bill of Right written by its own people', what she defines 'an endogenous process of self-organization'.[53] In similar circumstances, she argues, constitutional norms risk being deviated by the predominant interests of private corporations. The Italian constitutionalist therefore advances an intermediary solution. She envisages the creation of a 'public supranational authoritative body' that would lead and coordinate a participatory process of decision-making involving all categories of private actors, on the model of the American notice and comment procedure.[54] According to this paradigm, the public authority would be called to mediate and find a common denominator from the input received by the relevant stakeholders.

Along the same lines, Kinfe Michael Yilma proposes vesting the UN organs with the duty to draft and enforce a 'Declaration of Internet Rights'.[55] The Human Rights Council would be charged with the drafting of the document. The Office of High Commissioner for Human Rights would seek feedback from societal actors on the text of the declaration. Lastly, the actual enforcement of the provisions articulating Internet rights would be entrusted to the Human Rights Committee.[56]

Looking at the deliberative models underlying existing Internet bills of rights, one can observe that none of these initiatives has led to the same degree of institutionalisation envisaged by De Minico and Yilma.[57] So far, no 'public supranational authoritative body' has been created, nor has any formal duty to craft a Declaration of Internet Rights' been entrusted to any

51 Rodotà, 'Perché Internet Ha Bisogno Di Una Carta Dei Diritti' (n 49), my translation.
52 De Minico (n 44) 20.
53 De Minico (n 44) 21.
54 De Minico (n 44) 22.
55 Kinfe Micheal Yilma, 'Digital Privacy and Virtues of Multilateral Digital Constitutionalism—Preliminary Thoughts' (2017) 25 International Journal of Law and Information Technology 115, 129 ff.
56 Yilma (n 55) 138.
57 Cf. Nanette S Levinson and Meryem Marzouki, 'Internet Governance Institutionalization: Process and Trajectories' in Michèle Rioux and Kim Fontaine-Skronski (eds), *Global Governance Facing Structural Changes: New Institutional Trajectories for Digital and Transnational Capitalism* (Palgrave Macmillan 2015).

UN organ. However, as suggested in the normative reconstructions of these two legal scholars, almost all the analysed Internet bills of rights present a participatory element, directly involving or aiming to involve all the stakeholders of the digital society in the process of elaboration of its foundational rights and principles.

Individuals

Some Internet bills of rights were authored by single individuals.[58] In these cases, the participatory element is not present in the phase of drafting, specifically, but informs the whole initiative of proposing a charter of rights for the Internet. The authors of these documents do not aim to declare the final word on what the rights and principles for the digital society should be. They explicitly present their initiatives as part of a broader discussion. For example, in 1997, Robert Gelman, in the introduction of his *Declaration of Human Rights in Cyberspace*, stated:

> You are invited to participate in our discussion forum about this document and also to bring it to the attention of individuals, companies, social organizations and political groups you are connected with. By involving ALL who use the Net or who may have the need or desire to do so in the future, we can make cyberspace a place that fosters the best of human thought and ideals.[59]

In this sense, each Internet bill of rights advanced by a single individual can be seen as an instance of a wider multistakeholder process of deliberation. In contrast to the past, today, the use of digital technology allows any individual to become a 'pamphleteer' or, as one may say in this case, a constitutional 'framer'.[60] Single individuals perceive to be an integral part of the social contract that should regulate the digital society. New technologies enhance the possibility to intervene in the constitutional debate. Individuals therefore spontaneously propose their visions on rights and principles for the digital society as if they were part of a global constituent assembly.

Internet bills of rights re-substantiate in the digital society the old concept of *isegoria*. One of the three pillars of democratic life in ancient Athens

58 See, in Appendix B, the second column from the left.

59 Gelman (n 24).

60 Cf. *Reno v American Civil Liberties Union* [1997] US Supreme Court 521 U.S. 844 870: 'Through the use of chat rooms, any person with a phone line can become a town crier with a voice that resonates farther than it could from any soapbox. Through the use of Web pages, mail exploders, and newsgroups, the same individual can become a pamphleteer'; on the concept of 'framers' in the US legal history, see James H Charleton, Robert G Ferris and Mary C Ryan (eds), *Framers of the Constitution* (National Archives and Records Administration 1986).

together with the principle of *isonomia*, the equality before the law, and *isokrateia*, the equality or equilibrium of powers, the concept of *isegoria* established that each citizen had an equal right of speech before the assemblies.[61] In Athens, everyone could take the floor and share with the city their personal thoughts. Today, we conversely live in a time when the citizens formally intervene in the political life of their countries only to vote for their representatives. In this context, individuals who elaborate and publish their personal vision for an Internet bill of rights reassert their right to equally contribute to the political speech that is currently taking place in the global digital community.

Civil society

Similar to these individual framers, some civil society organisations published their own bill of rights online to foster a participated debate on the topic. The Estonian think-tank Praxis, for example, in its *Guiding Principles of Internet Freedom*, states:

> The theses were drafted in order to foster discussion in society about the basic rights of Internet users that governments and citizens should follow in creating new laws, entering into foreign agreements, developing new e-services and using the Internet. It is not a legally binding document and does not try to resolve any legal issues related to the protection of intellectual property online. [...] Individuals, organizations, companies and government departments are invited to take part in the discussion. We look forward to receiving your comments and contributions [...].[62]

Certain civil society initiatives even created customised websites to discuss their own charters. In the German version of the website https://digitalcharta.eu, for example, one can read and interactively comment each article of the *Charter of Digital Fundamental Rights of the European Union*.[63]

In the process of elaboration of other civil society-led Internet bills of rights, the participatory moment is even anticipated to the phase of drafting itself. Both the *Geneva Declaration on Internet Freedom* and the *Delhi Declaration for a Just and Equitable Internet*, for example, were the output

61 See JD Lewis, 'Isegoria at Athens: When Did It Begin?' (1971) 20 Historia: Zeitschrift für Alte Geschichte 129.

62 Praxis, 'Guiding Principles of Internet Freedom' <http://www.praxis.ee/fileadmin/tarmo/Projektid/Valitsemine_ja_kodanikeühiskond/Praxis_Theses_Internet.pdf>.

63 For the last, German version of the Charter, see 'Charta der Digitalen Grundrechte der Europäischen Union' <https://digitalcharta.eu/> accessed 7 May 2019.

of two international conferences involving a variety of civil society actors.[64] The *African Declaration on Internet Rights and Freedoms* was adopted after a period of online public consultation.[65] The Italian civil society groups Social Innovation Society and Stati Generali dell'Innovazione asked their communities and other national and international associations to comment and modify the text of their *International Charter of Digital Rights* directly through a collaborative Wiki website.[66]

Interestingly, there are also examples of Internet bills of rights which have been directly drafted online by a plurality of civil society actors in a collaborative way and not simply commented upon at a later stage. In 2012, for example, the Free Internet Activism sub-group on the social media site Reddit collectively drafted its first *Digital Bill of Rights*.[67] One year later, the news website Mashable created a Google document to crowdsource a Digital Bill of Rights from its community.[68]

64 The *Geneva Declaration on Internet Freedom* was adopted in 2010 by a group of 'Human Rights Defenders and Civil Society Representatives' at the 2nd Geneva Summit for Human Rights, Tolerance and Democracy. For the text of the Declaration, see Geneva Summit for Human Rights and Democracy, 'Geneva Declaration on Internet Freedom' (2010) <http://atlarge-lists.icann.org/pipermail/lac-discuss-es/2010/001287.html> accessed 11 July 2019; for more details on the summit, visit 'Geneva Summit for Human Rights and Democracy' (*Geneva Summit for Human Rights and Democracy*) <https://www.geneva-summit.org> accessed 11 July 2019. The *Delhi Declaration for a Just and Equitable Internet* was adopted in 2014 at a meeting organised by the civil society organisation Just Net Coalition in Delhi. For the text of the Declaration, see Just Net Coalition (n 42); for additional information on its promoters, see 'Who Are We? | Just Net Coalition' <https://justnetcoalition.org/> accessed 11 July 2019.

65 'African Declaration on Internet Rights and Freedoms | About the Initiative' <https://africaninternetrights.org/about/> accessed 11 July 2019.

66 See Social Innovation Society, 'Carta Internazionale Dei Diritti Digitali' <http://www.soinsociety.org/carta-internazionale-dei-diritti-digitali/> accessed 7 May 2019. According to 'Wiki', *Wikipedia* (2019) <https://en.wikipedia.org/w/index.php?title=Wiki&oldid=903687785> accessed 11 July 2019, a Wiki is 'a knowledge base website on which users collaboratively modify content and structure directly from the web browser.'; see also Bo Leuf and Ward Cunningham, *The Wiki Way: Quick Collaboration on the Web* (Addison-Wesley Professional 2001).

67 'Digital Bill of Rights' (n 14).

68 See Ryan Lytle, 'Let's Write a Digital Bill of Rights' (*Mashable*) <https://mashable.com/2013/07/01/digital-bill-of-rights/> accessed 11 July 2019; for the final text of the bill, see Lytle (n 41).This initiative was not, strictly speaking, led by a civil society actor, being Mashable a private corporation. However, the text of the Digital Bill of Rights was *de facto* generated from the input of the Mashable's community, which could be considered as a civil society group *lato sensu*.

National parliaments

In 2013, a bill to introduce a *Magna Carta for Philippine Internet Freedom* was presented to the Philippine Congress.[69] In 2019, in Nigeria, a *Digital Rights and Freedom Bill*, originally proposed in 2016, after being voted by the majority of both houses of the parliament, was sent to the President, who however refused to sign it into law.[70] Brazil therefore remains the only country in the world to have successfully passed an act including a comprehensive set of digital rights and principles: the so-called *Marco civil da Internet.* Interestingly, this legislation was not purely the output of parliamentary discussions but originated from a multistakeholder project that envisaged the participation of the general public too.

In 2007, the Brazilian professor Ronaldo Lemos advanced for the first time the idea of a 'marco regulatório civil' for the Internet, a civil rights framework that would have been complementary to the so-called Azeredo bill focusing on cybercrime.[71] In 2009, the Brazilian Ministry of Justice and the Centre for Technology and Society of the Getulio Vargas Foundation launched the initiative 'marco civil da Internet', opening a public consultation on a first draft of text including civil rights for the Internet.[72] The bill was subsequently sent to the Congress and was given the status of 'constitutional urgency' by the then Brazilian President Dilma Rousseff.[73] The proposal was intensely debated over the Internet and discussed among Brazilian political forces, especially after the Snowden's revelations on the NSA's mass surveillance programme involving President Rousseff herself.[74] The *Marco civil da Internet* was eventually enacted as law by the Brazilian parliament in 2014[75] and presented at the Global Multistakeholder Meeting

69 Miriam Defensor Santiago The Magna Carta for Philippine Internet Freedom (n 17). The bill was the output of online crowdsourcing: see Jonathan de Santos, 'The Wisdom of Crowds: Crowdsourcing Net Freedom' (*Vera Files*) <http://ph.news.yahoo.com/blogs/the-inbox/wisdom-crowds-crowdsourcing-net-freedom-042242158.html> accessed 17 July 2019.

70 See Victor Ekwealor, 'Nigeria's President Refused to Sign Its Digital Rights Bill, What Happens Now?' (*Techpoint.Africa*, 27 March 2019) <https://techpoint.africa/2019/03/27/nigerian-president-declines-digital-rights-bill-assent/> accessed 11 July 2019; for the text of bill, see Ujam Chukwuemeka, Digital Rights and Freedom Bill 2016.

71 Ronaldo Lemos, 'Internet Brasileira Precisa de Marco Regulatório Civil' *UOL* (22 May 2007) <https://tecnologia.uol.com.br/ultnot/2007/05/22/ult4213u98.jhtm> accessed 11 July 2019.

72 Francis Augusto Medeiros and Lee A Bygrave, 'Brazil's Marco Civil Da Internet: Does It Live up to the Hype?' (2015) 31 Computer Law & Security Review 120; on the public consultative process on the first draft of the Marco civil, see João Carlos Magalhães, 'Critically Imagining Internet Governance: A Content Analysis of the Marco Civil Da Internet Public Consultation' (London School of Economics 2015).

73 Medeiros and Bygrave (n 72).

74 Medeiros and Bygrave (n 72).

75 'Marco Civil Da Internet, Lei No. 12.965, de 23 de Abril de 2014.' (n 16).

on the Future of Internet Governance (so-called NetMundial Initiative) that took place in Brazil in 2014.[76]

A similarly mixed participatory process of deliberation, involving both civil society and national political institutions, characterised the elaboration of the Italian *Declaration of Internet Rights.*[77] In 2014, the President of the Italian Chamber of Deputies Laura Boldrini created an *ad hoc* committee on 'Internet Rights and Duties' composed of parliamentarians, academics, and civil society experts and chaired by professor Rodotà.[78] The committee heard 46 representatives from the public and the private sector as well as from civil society.[79] It subsequently issued a first draft of declaration of rights for the Internet, which, from October 2014 to March 2015, was opened to public consultation through the online platform CIVI.CI.[80] In July 2015, the Commission eventually adopted the definitive text of the declaration, and the Italian Chamber of Deputies subsequently endorsed the proposal in a parliamentary motion.[81] In September 2015, the committee signed a joint declaration with the *Commission de reflexion et de propositions sur le droit et les libertés à l'âge numerique* of the French National Assembly, reiterating a series of common values and principles.[82] The following year, the Italian

76 For more details on the Net Mundial multi-stakeholder meeting, see 'Net Mundial | Global Multistakeholder Meeting on the Future of Internet Governance' <http://netmundial.br/> accessed 11 July 2019.

77 Mixed participatory processes of deliberation were also adopted in relation to broader constitution-making. See, e.g., Silvia Suteu, 'Constitutional Conventions in the Digital Era: Lessons from Iceland and Ireland' (2015) 38 Boston College International and Comparative Law Review 251; Tofigh Maboudi and Ghazal P Nadi, 'Crowdsourcing the Egyptian Constitution: Social Media, Elites, and the Populace' (2016) 69 Political Research Quarterly 716.

78 For the minutes of the committee's sessions, see Camera dei Deputati, 'Resoconti della Commissione per i diritti e i doveri relativi ad Internet' <https://www.camera.it/leg17/1175> accessed 11 July 2019.

79 See Camera dei Deputati, 'Elenco Soggetti Auditi' <https://www.camera.it/leg17/1195> accessed 11 July 2019.

80 For the results of the public consultation, see Camera dei Deputati, 'Commenti e Proposte Di Modifica Della Bozza Della Dichiarazione Dei Diritti in Internet' <https://www.camera.it/application/xmanager/projects/leg17/attachments/upload_file/upload_files/000/000/230/TAF_audiz.pdf>.

81 Camera dei Deputati, 'Declaration of Internet Rights' <https://www.camera.it/application/xmanager/projects/leg17/commissione_internet/testo_definitivo_inglese.pdf>; see also Camera dei Deputati, 'Mozione concernente iniziative per la promozione di una carta dei diritti in Internet e per la governance della rete' (11 March 2015) <https://www.camera.it/leg17/995?sezione=documenti&tipoDoc=assemblea_allegato_odg&idlegislatura=17&anno=2015&mese=11&giorno=03> accessed 11 July 2019.

82 Camera dei Deputati, 'Dichiarazione Congiunta Con La Commissione Dell'Assemblea Nazionale Francese' <https://www.camera.it/application/xmanager/projects/leg17/commissione_internet/testo_definitivo_ita.pdf>.

committee started a phase of dissemination of the *Declaration of Internet Rights* among Italian schools.[83]

International organisations

Other Internet bills of rights have been promoted by international organisations, such as UNESCO and the Council of Europe.[84] At first sight, one has the impression that these documents are merely the output of intergovernmental negotiations. UNESCO's *Code of Ethics for the Information Society*, for example, was elaborated by the Intergovernmental Council of the Information for All Programme (IFAP), and the Council of Europe's *Declaration on Internet governance principles* was adopted by the respective Committee of Ministers.[85] However, a more careful analysis of these texts interestingly reveals that both institutions, before issuing their position on rights and principles for the digital society, preliminary consulted other stakeholders.

UNESCO, in the 'background' section of its *Code of Ethics for the Information Society*, explains that its document was elaborated 'through an extensive consultation process', as part of a wider multistakeholder process aiming to address the 'ethical dimensions of the Information society', and to implement a mandate conferred by a multistakeholder community at the World Summit on the Information Society (WSIS).[86] As a result, the *Code of Ethics* 'is addressed to all stakeholders of the information and knowledge societies and outlines a number of universal values and guiding principles'.[87]

The Council of Europe opens its *Declaration on Internet governance principles* acknowledging that:

> States, the private sector, civil society and individuals have all contributed to build the dynamic, inclusive and successful Internet that we know today.[88]

The Council explicitly sees the principles set out in its *Declaration* as building on the work carried out over the past years by all stakeholders.[89] The *Declaration* itself is presented 'as a contribution to this ongoing, inclusive, collaborative and open process'.[90]

83 See Camera dei Deputati, 'La Commissione Internet nelle scuole' <https://www.camera.it/leg17/1308> accessed 11 July 2019.
84 See, in Appendix B, the second column from the left.
85 UNESCO (n 36); Council of Europe, Committee of Ministers (n 16).
86 UNESCO (n 36) paras 3–4. On the World Summit on the Information Society (WSIS), see *infra* in this chapter.
87 UNESCO (n 36) para 5.
88 Council of Europe, Committee of Ministers (n 16) para 1.
89 Council of Europe, Committee of Ministers (n 16) para 6.
90 Council of Europe, Committee of Ministers (n 16) para 6.

Global multistakeholder forums

International organisations also played an important role in supporting the creation of a series of global multistakeholder forums of discussion on Internet governance issues that led to the adoption of the *Charter of Human Rights and Principles for the Internet* and inspired the drafting of other Internet bills of rights.[91]

In 2001, the General Assembly of the United Nations endorsed the International Telecommunication Union (ITU)'s proposal to hold a World Summit on the Information Society with representatives of national governments, international organisations, NGOs, and civil society.[92] The WSIS was held in two phases: in December 2003, in Geneva, and in November 2005, in Tunis.[93] The first phase reaffirmed the application of existing human rights in the information society and led to the adoption of a Declaration of principles and a Plan of Action.[94] After the first WSIS, UN Secretary-General Kofi Annan established the Working Group on Internet Governance (WGIG), a multistakeholder caucus aimed at bringing the discussion on Internet governance further before the second WSIS in 2005.[95] The first Summit, indeed, had failed to agree on a common definition of Internet Governance: the WGIG worked on this topic and in 2005 eventually proposed a broad definition of Internet governance.[96] According to Jørgensen, the effect of such a comprehensive definition was to increase 'the number of contact points between human rights standards and Internet governance policies and programmes'.[97]

91 The *African Declaration on Internet Rights and Freedoms*, for example, originated from the African Internet Governance Forum held in Nairobi in 2013, a regional version of the global multi-stakeholder forum IGF. See 'African Declaration on Internet Rights and Freedoms | About the Initiative' (n 65). On the IGF, see *infra* in this section. More in detail on the relationship between international organisations and global multi-stakeholder forums, see Levinson and Marzouki (n 57). More generally on Internet governance, inter alia, see Roxana Radu, *Negotiating Internet Governance* (Oxford University Press 2019); DeNardis (n 49); Mueller (n 6); Brousseau, Marzouki and Méadel (n 49).

92 United Nations, General Assembly, 'Resolution A/RES/56/183, "World Summit on the Information Society"' <https://www.itu.int/net/wsis/docs/background/resolutions/56_183_unga_2002.pdf>.The ITU is the UN specialised agency that deals with information and communication technologies. For more detailed information, see 'About ITU' <https://www.itu.int/en/about/Pages/default.aspx> accessed 12 July 2019.

93 See 'World Summit on the Information Society: About WSIS' <https://www.itu.int/net/wsis/basic/about.html> accessed 12 July 2019.

94 WSIS, 'Declaration of Principles' (12 December 2003) <https://www.itu.int/net/wsis/docs/geneva/official/dop.html> accessed 12 July 2019; WSIS, 'Plan of Action' (12 December 2003) <https://www.itu.int/net/wsis/docs/geneva/official/poa.html> accessed 12 July 2019.

95 WGIG, 'Report of the Working Group on Internet Governance' <http://www.wgig.org/docs/WGIGREPORT.pdf>.

96 WGIG (n 95).

97 Rikke Frank Jørgensen, 'An Internet Bill of Rights?' in Ian Brown (ed), *Research Handbook on Governance of the Internet* (Edward Elgar 2013) 358.

The second phase of WSIS took place in 2005 in Tunis and focused on the most debated issues of Internet governance, such as the control on the Internet root file, and the organisation of the Internet Corporation for Assigned Names and Numbers (ICANN).[98] The aim of the second phase was to get the Geneva Plan of Action in operation, and, to this end, the Tunis Commitment and the Tunis Agenda for the Information Society were signed in November 2005.[99] In this last document, the participants to the Tunis WSIS asked the UN Secretary-General to convoke a meeting called Internet Governance Forum (IGF) in order to facilitate a dialogue between the different stakeholders on Internet governance issues.[100] The first IGF took place in Athens in 2006, then followed by annual meetings which were held in Rio de Janeiro (2007), Hyderabad (2008), Sharm El Sheikh (2009), Vilnius (2010), Nairobi (2011), Baku (2012), Bali (2013), Istanbul (2014), João Pessoa (2015), Jalisco (2016), Geneva (2017), Paris (2018), Berlin (2019), virtually in 2020, and Katowice (2021).[101]

It was in 2005, during the Tunis WSIS, that Stefano Rodotà, at that time President of the Italian data protection authority, submitted an appeal for the creation of a 'Charter of the Rights of the Net'.[102] This demand was subsequently endorsed by the Italian government and led to the creation of a group of discussion on human rights protection on the Internet named 'Internet Bill of Rights dynamic coalition'.[103] In 2009, after the Hyderabad IGF, this working group merged with the Framework of Principles for the Internet coalition, a caucus focusing more on Internet governance principles, forming the Internet Rights and Principles Dynamic Coalition (IRP-C).[104] In 2010, at the Vilnius IGF, a first draft (Version 1.0) of the *Charter*

98 For additional details, see Jørgensen (n 97); Anne-Claire Jamart, 'Internet Freedom and the Constitutionalization of Internet Governance' in Roxana Radu, Jean-Marie Chenou and Rolf H Weber (eds), *The Evolution of Global Internet Governance* (Springer Berlin Heidelberg 2014).

99 WSIS, 'Tunis Commitment' (18 November 2005) <https://www.itu.int/net/wsis/docs2/tunis/off/7.html> accessed 12 July 2019; WSIS, 'Tunis Agenda for the Information Society' (18 November 2005) <https://www.itu.int/net/wsis/docs2/tunis/off/6rev1.html> accessed 12 July 2019.

100 WSIS, 'Tunis Agenda for the Information Society' (n 99); see also Francesca Musiani, 'The Internet Bill of Rights: A Way to Reconcile Natural Freedoms and Regulatory Needs?' (2009) 6 SCRIPTed 504.

101 See the 'archived content' section at 'Internet Governance Forum' (*Internet Governance Forum*) <http://www.intgovforum.org/multilingual/> accessed 12 July 2019.

102 Jørgensen (n 97).

103 Jørgensen (n 97); see 'Charter of Human Rights and Principles for the Internet' (n 24); on the work of the dynamic coalitions, see 'Dynamic Coalitions' (*Internet Governance Forum*, 15 June 2010) <https://www.intgovforum.org/multilingual/content/dynamic-coalitions-4> accessed 12 July 2019; see also Musiani (n 100); Levinson and Marzouki (n 57).

104 Subsequently joined by the Freedom of Expression Coalition; see 'Charter of Human Rights and Principles for the Internet' (n 24); Musiani (n 100); Joanna Kulesza, 'Freedom of Information in the Global Information Society: The Question of the Internet Bill of Rights' (2008) 1 University of Warmia and Mazury in Olsztyn Law Review 81.

of Human Rights and Principles for the Internet was released. A few months later, a second draft (Version 1.1) was published, and a consultation phase on the text was opened to the general public.[105] In 2011, the content of the Charter was condensed into ten principles and published as the *10 Internet Rights & Principles*.[106] The present edition of the Charter (7th edition, 2019) is the output of several revisions occurring after the launch of the phase 2.0 of the Charter at the UNESCO First WSIS+10 Review Meeting in 2013.[107]

A new constituent power

Openness, collaboration, participation, and multistakeholderism manifestly emerge as the leitmotivs of the deliberative models adopted to elaborate Internet bills of rights. These documents are not conceived as Solonian constitutions, unmodifiable charters drafted by single individuals. They are not definitive declarations solemnly proclaimed by constituent assemblies. Internet bills of rights are more akin to preparatory works, evolving drafts that nourish a conversation on rights and principles for the digital society. This open constituent process aims to craft a new, enlarged social contract, no longer based on territorial bounds, nor merely reflecting the binary relation states/citizens. A pact that ensures a balancing of power between all the stakeholders of the global digital society, and that, consequently, normatively claims to be concluded by all its parties. In this way, Internet bills of rights, attempting to generate a constitutional answer to the challenges of the digital society through an inclusive and collaborative process, contribute to shape the identity of the global digital community as a new constituent power.[108]

Recurrent references to 'we' in the preambles of Internet bills of rights witness the progressive emergence of new forms of selfhood, an expression of a-territorial communities unified by the use of digital technology.[109]

105 'Charter of Human Rights and Principles for the Internet' (n 24).

106 '10 Internet Rights and Principles' <http://internetrightsandprinciples.org/site/wp-content/uploads/2017/12/IRPC_10RightsandPrinciples_28May2014-1.pdf>.

107 'Charter of Human Rights and Principles for the Internet' <https://drive.google.com/file/d/1dyhXJLBLKJ0v_0sUHHRNEaUzKzp2dFr_/view> accessed 17 December 2021.

108 Cf. Mueller (n 3) 138 ff., who considers the question of whether 'the community connected via cyberspace [is] capable of the kind of solidaristic identity sufficient to forge a political unit'; among the endless scholarship on the topic of constituent power, see Martin Loughlin and Neil Walker, *The Paradox of Constitutionalism: Constituent Power and Constitutional Form* (Oxford University Press 2008); HK Lindahl, 'Collective Self-Legislation as an Actus Impurus: A Response to Heidegger's Critique of European Nihilism' (2008) 41 Continental Philosophy Review 323; Joel I Colon-Rios, *Weak Constitutionalism: Democratic Legitimacy and the Question of Constituent Power* (Routledge 2012); Andrew Arato, *The Adventures of the Constituent Power: Beyond Revolutions?* (Cambridge University Press 2017).

109 Cf. Hans Lindahl, 'We and Cyberlaw: The Spatial Unity of Constitutional Orders' (2013) 20 Indiana Journal of Global Legal Studies 697, who analyses Barlow's Declaration of

These first-persons plural represent global 'users', the whole 'people of the Internet'.[110] Sometimes, their meaning seems to be even broader, as if these 'we' encompassed all the parties to this new enlarged social contract, all the actors of the global digital community: not only individuals but also the public and private sectors.[111] Using Mueller's words, one could talk of a 'cyber-version of nationalism, an Internet nation so to speak, that forges its own political identity'.[112] Internet bills of rights would not amount to a top-down form of constitutionalisation, but would be an expression of a renovated and wide-ranging form of 'popular sovereignty in cyberspace'.[113]

The digital revolution is shaping a global community, where individuals are subject to the power of a multitude of states and private corporations. The emergence of Internet bills of rights alerts the constitutional ecosystem to the need to renovate its core architecture. These documents propose to modernise the anatomy of fundamental rights, by imposing obligations on all dominant actors, independently from their public or private nature and from their territorial location. Secluding the conversation on individual rights exclusively into the precincts of nation-states would manifestly neglect the plurality of issues that today emerge at transnational level. The unrestricted territorial scope of Internet bills of rights suggests that a global constitutional perspective is necessitated too. To this end, openness, participation, and multistakeholderism are recommended as the new North Star to follow in future constitution-making. Internet bills of rights fully acknowledge the unprecedented possibility that today's digital technology offers to participate in deliberative processes and highlight innovative mechanisms of legal drafting that promote collaboration and diversity. In order to conclude a new social contract for the digital society, the question of *how* constitutional norms should be created is as important as that of *which* fundamental principles should be established.

Independence of Cyberspace as a form of self-constitutionalisation and reflects on the implications of the use of the first-person plural 'we' in such a text. By the same author, more broadly on the relationship between constituent power and collective selfhood, see Hans Lindahl, 'Constituent Power and Reflexive Identity: Towards an Ontology of Collective Selfhood' in Martin Loughlin and Neil Walker (eds), *The Paradox of Constitutionalism: Constituent Power and Constitutional Form* (Oxford University Press 2008).

110 See, e.g., 'Digital Bill of Rights' (n 14); Lytle (n 41).

111 See, e.g., 'Charter of Human Rights and Principles for the Internet' (n 24); Godwin (n 17).

112 Mueller (n 3) 20.

113 Cf. Mueller (n 3) ch 6.

11 Translating fundamental rights

An aerial view

The tourist who visits the Roman Forum for the first time is often disoriented. Especially if just catapulted from an air-conditioned coach, the traveller struggles to acquire a sense of the surrounding space. What today is called the *forum romanum* is in reality a complex amalgam of multiple fora, Roman temples, basilicas, arches, medieval monasteries, and Renaissance churches, crossed by centuries-old lanes and at times overlapped by modern roads.[1] Simply wandering in the Forum, one hardly understands the anatomy of what, for over a millennium, was the *umbilicus* of Rome: its political, economic, and social centre, even considered the geographical 'navel' of the city, from which all the distances of the known world were calculated.[2] However, if one patiently takes the steps that lead to the top of the close Palatine Hill, the layout of the Forum suddenly becomes clearer. Observed from above, this maze of laying columns, capitals, and remnants of walls unexpectedly unveils the contours of the first public square of the Eternal City.

Towards the end of this work, we are virtually back in Italy. This second 'postcard' highlights the importance of getting a panoramic view. Internet bills of rights emerge in multiple forms. They are not identical xylographic reproductions of a single text. They articulate in multifarious ways how fundamental rights and principles should be shaped to address the challenges of the Internet age. Singularly analysed, these declarations are similar to the lying columns of the Roman forum: the reader risks missing the overall topography of the area that she is exploring. To understand what Internet bills of rights aim to communicate within the constitutional conglomerate – the

1 See, ex multis, Gilbert Gorski and James E Packer, *The Roman Forum: A Reconstruction and Architectural Guide* (Cambridge University Press 2015).

2 On the 'Umbilicus Urbis Romae', see L Richardson, *A New Topographical Dictionary of Ancient Rome* (Johns Hopkins University Press 1992); more broadly, on the social functions of the Forum, see Amy Russell, *The Politics of Public Space in Republican Rome* (Cambridge University Press 2016).

DOI: 10.4324/9781003256908-11

legacy of these documents, thoroughly examined as a single phenomenon within the broader constitutional conversation on the rights and principles for the digital society – a comprehensive reading is crucial.

To this end, Chapter 11 and 12 will provide a panoramic overview of the constitutional message of Internet bills of rights. The present chapter will focus on rights and principles that have already emerged in the analogue society but have been reiterated, articulated, or translated by Internet bills of rights to reflect the specificities of the Internet age. Chapter 12 will instead analyse innovative principles that have surfaced in the texts of Internet bills of rights as new solutions to the challenges of the digital revolution. The final part of this book, thus, does not aim to provide a detailed analysis of which fundamental rights are materialising as a response to the digital revolution, in general. Nor to analyse the relationship between these norms and existing constitutional law instruments. Without pretending to offer an exhaustive study of how all the various expressions of digital constitutionalism are articulating the values of contemporary constitutionalism to face the challenges of the Internet age, this part will focus on the specific constitutional message of Internet bills of rights.

Common roots

First of all, a panoramic picture of the content of Internet bills of rights confirms that these texts are not subverting the central tenets of contemporary constitutionalism. These documents explicitly affirm that their source of inspiration and reference point lies within existing international human rights law.[3] The Universal Declaration of Human Rights is the most cited text,[4] but Internet bills of rights also refer to the International Covenant on

3 The Italian *Declaration of Internet Right* also refers to fundamental rights enshrined in national constitutions. The *Carta internazionale dei diritti digitali* issued by the Social Innovation Society even mentions the *Déclaration des droits de la femme et de la citoyenne* (Declaration of the Rights of Woman and of the [Female] Citizen), a pamphlet published in 1791 by Olympe de Gauges as a response to the adoption of the Declaration of the Rights of Man and the Citizen. For the original text of de Gauges' declaration, see Olympe de Gauges, 'Déclaration Des Droits de La Femme et de La Citoyenne' <https://fr.wikisource.org/wiki/D%C3%A9claration_des_droits_de_la_femme_et_de_la_citoyenne> accessed 6 August 2019. For a commentary on the declaration, see Joan Wallach Scott, 'French Feminists and the Rights of "Man": Olympe de Gouges's Declarations' [1989] History Workshop 1.

4 See Robert Gelman, 'Draft Proposal-Declaration of Human Rights in Cyberspace' <http://www.be-in.com/10/rightsdec.html> accessed 17 June 2019; Andrew Murray, 'A Bill of Rights for the Internet' <http://theitlawyer.blogspot.com/2010/10/bill-of-rights-for-internet.html> accessed 17 June 2019; Open Society Institute – Regional Internet Program and Parliamentary Human Rights Foundation, 'Open Internet Policy Principles' <http://mailman.anu.edu.au/pipermail/link/1997-March/026302.html>; 'Charter of Human Rights and Principles for the Internet' <http://internetrightsandprinciples.org/site/wp-content/uploads/2018/10/IRPC_english_5thedition.pdf> accessed 17 December 2018;

Civil and Political Rights,[5] the International Covenant on Economic, Social and Cultural Rights,[6] the Convention on the Rights of Persons with Disabilities,[7] the Convention on the Rights of the Child,[8] the UNESCO Universal Declaration on Cultural Diversity,[9] the European Convention on Human Rights,[10] and the Charter of Fundamental Rights of the European Union.[11] Internet bills of rights, therefore, are not revolutionising contemporary constitutional foundations. They manifestly share their roots in existing human rights law, presenting themselves as a logical continuum and, as we will see more in detail in the next sections, as a translation, a re-contextualisation of our fundamental rights and principles in light of the challenges of the digital society.

Human dignity

The genetic heritage of international human rights law deeply permeates the DNA of Internet bills of rights. The human being remains the cornerstone of the system of values that these declarations of rights articulate. Article 1 of the *Charter of Digital Fundamental Rights of the European Union* is paradigmatic in this sense. It reads:

Geneva Summit for Human Rights and Democracy, 'Geneva Declaration on Internet Freedom' (2010) <http://atlarge-lists.icann.org/pipermail/lac-discuss-es/2010/001287.html> accessed 11 July 2019; NETmundial, 'Internet Governance Principles - NETmundial Multistakeholder Statement' <http://netmundial.br/wp-content/uploads/2014/04/NETmundial-Multistakeholder-Document.pdf>; Camera dei Deputati, 'Declaration of Internet Rights' <https://www.camera.it/application/xmanager/projects/leg17/commissione_internet/testo_definitivo_inglese.pdf>; Social Innovation Society, 'Carta Internazionale Dei Diritti Digitali' <http://www.soinsociety.org/carta-internazionale-dei-diritti-digitali/> accessed 7 May 2019; 'Charta der Digitalen Grundrechte der Europäischen Union' <https://digitalcharta.eu/> accessed 7 May 2019.

5 See NETmundial (n 4); Social Innovation Society (n 4); Council of Europe, 'Recommendation of the Committee of Ministers to Member States on Internet Freedom' (2016) CM/Rec(2016)5 <https://search.coe.int/cm/Pages/result_details.aspx?ObjectId=09000016806415fa>. It is interesting to notice that the Universal Declaration of Human Rights, the International Covenant on Civil and Political Rights with its two optional Protocols, and the International Covenant on Economic, Social and Cultural Rights form together the so-called 'International Bill of Human Rights'. On the topic, see Christopher NJ Roberts, *The Contentious History of the International Bill of Human Rights* (Cambridge University Press 2015).

6 See NETmundial (n 4); Social Innovation Society (n 4).

7 See NETmundial (n 4).

8 See Social Innovation Society (n 4).

9 See Social Innovation Society (n 4).

10 See Council of Europe (n 5).

11 See Social Innovation Society (n 4); Camera dei Deputati (n 4).

> Human dignity shall remain inviolable in the digital age. Human dignity must be respected and safeguarded. No technological development may be allowed to encroach upon it.[12]

This provision echoes the concept of human dignity enshrined in the first article of the Universal Declaration of Human Rights and manifestly paraphrases Article 1 of the Charter of Fundamental Rights of the European Union.[13] However, interestingly, it adds a new principle, establishing that technological developments shall not violate human dignity. At first sight, it seems almost redundant to specify it. Human dignity is – as the Charter of Fundamental Rights of the European Union affirms – and 'remains', as its digital correspondent reiterates – inviolable. However, it is precisely in this apparent repetition that the added value of the Internet bills of rights lies. One has to read it as an alarm sign. The drafters of the *Charter of Digital Fundamental Rights of the European Union* felt the need to include this sentence to stress the prevalence of the human beings and their dignity above all and, in particular, over technology. In the digital age, where one cannot live without technologies and many choices are entrusted to 'intelligences' which are by now increasingly artificial, it is crucial to remember that the human beings and their dignity should remain the pivot of our fundamental values. Far-sightedly, Article 12 of the constitution of the German state of Bremen already established that 'Human beings outrank technologies and machines'.[14] Similarly, Internet bills of rights become the champions of this principle. Even if not always explicit through their provisions, they vigorously reiterate the centrality of humanity and dignity in a society invaded by 'technologies and machines'.

Life, liberty, and security

Some declarations of rights, echoing Article 3 of the Universal Declaration of Human Rights, enshrine a right to life, liberty, and security on the

12 'Charta der Digitalen Grundrechte der Europäischen Union' (n 4).

13 Article 1 of the Universal Declaration of Human Rights states that: 'All human beings are born free and equal in dignity and rights. [...]'. Article 1 of the Charter of Fundamental Rights of the European Union reads: 'Human dignity is inviolable. It must be respected and protected'. The *Charter of Digital Fundamental Rights of the European Union* also reminds the first two paragraphs of Article 1 of the German Basic Law, which provide: '(1) Human dignity shall be inviolable. To respect and protect it shall be the duty of all state authority. (2) The German people therefore acknowledge inviolable and inalienable human rights as the basis of every community, of peace and of justice in the world'.

14 Article 12, section 1 of the constitution of the Free State of Bremen. For the original text, see 'Landesverfassung Der Freien Hansestadt Bremen Vom 21. Oktober 1947' <https://www.transparenz.bremen.de/sixcms/detail.php?gsid=bremen2014_tp.c.75088.de&asl=bremen203_tpgesetz.c.55340.de&template=20_gp_ifg_meta_detail_d> accessed 6 August 2019.

Internet.[15] Human dignity is not only imperilled when facing a physical threat. Online harms can be immaterial but may not necessarily be less tangible than those occurring in the real world. Cyberbullying, disinformation, revenge porn, or online child pornography, for instance, may directly impact the psycho-physical wellness of the individual.[16] Identity thefts and other forms of cybercrime affect our digital body, intruding our personal life and violating our sphere of intimacy.[17] By establishing a right to life, liberty, and security online, Internet bills of rights ultimately aim to safeguard the dignity of the individual and confirm the centrality of the person in the constitutional ecosystem.

Protection of children and disabled people

The protection of human dignity is also the red thread of a series of provisions relating to the rights of children, the disabled, and, more generally, vulnerable persons. The Internet is recognised as an essential tool for the personal development and the education of the children, but, at the same time, Internet bills of rights highlight the risks that the online world can generate for minors.[18] Disabled people are guaranteed a right to access to the Internet and public institutions are vested with the obligation to remove all types of barriers, be they economical or technical, hampering the effective use of digital technology by this category of individuals.[19]

15 See 'Charter of Human Rights and Principles for the Internet' (n 4), Article 3; Mike Godwin, 'The Great Charter for Cambodian Internet Freedom' <https://www.linkedin.com/pulse/great-charter-cambodian-internet-freedom-mike-godwin> accessed 21 May 2019, Section 2.6; Praxis, 'Guiding Principles of Internet Freedom' <http://www.praxis.ee/fileadmin/tarmo/Projektid/Valitsemine_ja_kodanikeühiskond/Praxis_Theses_Internet.pdf>, Principle no. 6; Social Innovation Society (n 4), Article 9.

16 On these issues, see, ex multis, Bernadette H Schell, *Online Health and Safety: From Cyberbullying to Internet Addiction* (Greenwood 2016); Fabio Tagliabue, Luca Galassi and Pierpaolo Mariani, 'The "Pandemic" of Disinformation in COVID-19' (2020) 2 SN Comprehensive Clinical Medicine 1287; Jenna K Stokes, 'The Indecent Internet: Resisting Unwarranted Internet Exceptionalism Combating Revenge Porn' (2014) 29 Berkeley Technology Law Journal 929; Yaman Akdeniz, *Internet Child Pornography and the Law: National and International Responses* (Ashgate 2008).

17 On these issues, see, ex multis, Angus M Marshall and Brian C Tompsett, 'Identity Theft in an Online World' (2005) 21 Computer Law & Security Review 128; Susan W Brenner, *Cybercrime and the Law: Challenges, Issues, and Outcomes* (Northeastern University Press 2012).

18 See 'Charter of Human Rights and Principles for the Internet' (n 4), Article 12; European Commission, 'Code of EU Online Rights' (2012) <https://ec.europa.eu/digital-single-market/sites/digital-agenda/files/Code%20EU%20online%20rights%20EN%20final%202.pdf>, Section 1, Chapter 2, paragraph 4; Miriam Defensor Santiago, The Magna Carta for Philippine Internet Freedom 2013, Section 33, letter C.1 ff.

19 See 'Charter of Human Rights and Principles for the Internet' (n 4), Article 13; EUROCITIES Knowledge Society Forum – TeleCities, 'Charter of Rights of Citizens in the Knowledge Society' <https://www.comune.modena.it/storiaretecivica/Materiale_PDF_2_marzo/

Right to a healthy environment

Furthermore, the respect of human dignity can also be read as implying the protection of the context in which people live. In this sense, the environment, being the place where the individuals have the right to freely develop their personality, deserves special protection. The *Charter of Human Rights and Principles for the Internet* is the only document which articulates a right to a healthy environment in the context of the digital society. Article 4(b) reads:

> The Internet must be used in a sustainable way. This relates to the disposal of e-waste and to the use of the Internet for the protection of the environment.[20]

Any individual, in order to enjoy their fundamental rights, should live in a healthy environment. Digital technology can play a Janus-faced role in this context. On the one hand, it could help promoting respect for the environment; on the other hand, the production and use of digital tools implies the generation of waste and a significant need for electricity. The *Charter of Human Rights and Principles for the Internet*, by including a similar provision, further articulates the principle that technological developments should not outrank the individual.[21] The safeguarding of the environment in which we live is a necessary condition to guarantee our free development and, ultimately, the respect of our dignity.

Economic freedom

Finally, Internet bills of rights recognise that the core values of international human rights law such as human dignity, liberty, and equality should represent the main parameters to balancing competing rights.[22] Particularly, many declarations articulate this principle in relation to economic freedom. While recognising the fundamental role that digital technology plays in fostering innovation and nourishing economic growth, Internet bills of rights require that technological developments shall be constantly accompanied

---

Brugi_Miranda2.pdf>, Article 7; Murray (n 4), Article 3; UNESCO, 'Code of Ethics for the Information Society Proposed by the Intergovernmental Council of the Information for All Programme (IFAP)' (2011) <https://unesdoc.unesco.org/ark:/48223/pf0000212696> accessed 17 June 2019, Paragraph 4; European Commission (n 18), Section 1, Chapter 1; NETmundial (n 4); Camera dei Deputati (n 4), Article 2.5; 'Charta der Digitalen Grundrechte der Europäischen Union' (n 4), Article 13; Ujam Chukwuemeka, Digital Rights and Freedom Bill 2016, Section 16(9).

20 'Charter of Human Rights and Principles for the Internet' (n 4).

21 See *supra* in relation to human dignity.

22 See Camera dei Deputati (n 4), Article 1.3.

by an assessment of their impact on human rights.[23] In this exercise of balancing, the principles of dignity, liberty, and equality help to define the hard kernel of such conflicting rights, even if the latter have not yet been definitively defined.[24] In this regard, in the *Declaration on Internet governance principles*, the Council of Europe explicitly states:

> 1. [...] All public and private actors should recognise and uphold human rights and fundamental freedoms in their operations and activities, as well as in the design of new technologies, services and applications. They should be aware of developments leading to the enhancement of, as well as threats to, fundamental rights and freedoms, and fully participate in efforts aimed at recognising newly emerging rights.[25]

Internet bills of rights thus affirm that existing human rights should be applied from the phase of design of new technologies. Public and private actors are required to preventively assess potential negative consequences that the use of digital technology could ensue in terms of disrespecting human rights.[26] However, interestingly, the panorama of these fundamental values and principles is not seen as static. Dominant stakeholders are encouraged to be particularly sensitive to a landscape in continuous mutation, where old rights can acquire a new look, and even novel rights can emerge.

Online as offline

In 1992, in his book *Technopoly: The Surrender of Culture to Technology*, Neil Postman reflected on the consequences that technological developments have always generated in our language and, more broadly, in our way of conceiving the surrounding world. He wrote:

> New things require new words. But new things also modify old words, words that have deep-rooted meanings. The telegraph and the penny press changed what we once meant by "information." Television changes what we once meant by the terms "political debate," "news," and "public opinion." The computer changes "information" once again. Writing changed what we once meant by "truth" and "law"; printing changed

23 See Camera dei Deputati (n 4), Preamble; Geneva Summit for Human Rights and Democracy (n 4), Article 8; Council of Europe, Committee of Ministers, 'Declaration by the Committee of Ministers on Internet Governance Principles' (21 September 2011) <https://search.coe.int/cm/Pages/result_details.aspx?ObjectID=09000016805cc2f6> accessed 21 May 2019, Para 1; PEN International, 'Declaration on Internet Freedom' <https://pen-international.org/app/uploads/PEN-Declaration_INTERNATIONALweb.pdf>, Point 4.C.

24 See Camera dei Deputati (n 4); Council of Europe, Committee of Ministers (n 23).

25 Council of Europe, Committee of Ministers (n 23).

26 Cf. Miriam Defensor Santiago The Magna Carta for Philippine Internet Freedom (n 18), Section 9(3); Camera dei Deputati (n 4), Article 14.4.

> them again, and now television and the computer change them once more. Such changes occur quickly, surely, and, in a sense, silently. Lexicographers hold no plebiscites on the matter. No manuals are written to explain what is happening, and the schools are oblivious to it. The old words still look the same, are still used in the same kinds of sentences. But they do not have the same meanings; in some cases, they have opposite meanings. [...] [T]echnology imperiously commandeers our most important terminology. It redefines "freedom," "truth," "intelligence," "fact," "wisdom," "memory," "history"—all the words we live by.[27]

The law, being expressed in words, is unavoidably affected by this phenomenon. Technological developments introduce new terms that are not mentioned by the law and, at the same time, the 'old words' of the law are reshaped by new technologies. However, if it is true, as Postman observes, that such words acquire new, and sometimes very different meanings, one cannot automatically imply that their old sense is lost. Especially in phases of rapid technological change, old and new significations of a word can cohabit. In the same way, the text of the law can be interpreted in different manners. If common people are sensitive to this change and are still able to read the norm in light of the mutated technological context, the law is not ineluctably destined to succumb to technological developments. It can survive, speaking both to the old and the new societal context.

It is therefore apparent that a crucial issue in a time of fast technological developments is to assess the level of accessibility of a norm, its communicative capacity. In other words, one has to appraise whether the existing law is still perceived as applicable in a scenario that has been intrinsically transformed by the advent of new technologies. In the case of digital rights, the main issues are: are existing constitutional values and principles still valid in the virtual world? Are analogue constitutional norms still able to transmit their meaning in the digital society?

When one analyses the content of Internet bills of rights, one can understand that the drafters of these declarations globally perceive that the communicative power of analogue constitutional norms is fading. There is increasing difficulty in understanding the meaning of constitutional values in the digital environment. The *Code of EU online rights*, for instance, states:

> This Code compiles the basic set of rights and principles enshrined in EU law that protect citizens when acceding and using online networks and services. These rights and principles are not always easy to grasp because they are not exclusive to the digital environment and are scattered across various directives, regulations and conventions in the areas of electronic communications, e-commerce and consumer protection.

27 Neil Postman, *Technopoly: The Surrender of Culture to Technology* (Vintage Books 1993) 8.

> [...] While the majority of these rights are not in themselves new, due to the complexity of the legal framework many online consumers might not be aware of them. This is precisely the reason for establishing this Code: to make citizens aware of their minimum rights and the principles recognised in EU law when going online, being online, and when buying and consuming services online.[28]

Internet bills of rights, comprehensively regarded, thus appear as a work of translation of principles.[29] They start from the assumption that all existing analogue rights are equally applicable in the digital society.[30] However, they reiterate those fundamental values in a form that speaks to the present social reality which has been profoundly affected by the advent of digital technology. Such an endeavour of interpretation and conversion of norms is not carried out in a unitary way. It is a matter of degree. As the following sections will show, sometimes analogue constitutional principles are generalised and subsequently re-specified in the new societal reality, in this way giving a new shape to the legal norm. In some circumstances, old constitutional values are so transformed through this process that even novel, independent rights emerge.[31] However, there are also cases where the work of translation that existing constitutional principle necessitate in order to be communicated in the digital society is far lighter. Some rights are simply reaffirmed in the digital context. Internet bills of rights aim to highlight that those principles are valid online as much as offline.

Freedom of expression

As in several declarations, the *NETmundial Multistakeholder Statement* opens its list of 'Internet governance principles' with the right to freedom of expression.[32] It reads:

> Everyone has the right to freedom of opinion and expression; this right includes freedom to hold opinions without interference and to seek, receive and impart information and ideas through any media and regardless of frontiers.[33]

28 European Commission (n 18) 2.
29 See the introduction of 'Charter of Human Rights and Principles for the Internet' (n 4), where the centrality of 'translating' rights is particularly emphasised.
30 See NETmundial (n 4); Camera dei Deputati (n 4), Article 1; Godwin (n 15); Gelman (n 4); 'Charter of Human Rights and Principles for the Internet' (n 4), Preamble.
31 See *infra* Chapter 12.
32 See also Gelman (n 4); PEN International (n 23); 'Digital Bill of Rights' (*reddit*) <https://www.reddit.com/r/fia/comments/vuj37/digital_bill_of_rights_1st_draft/> accessed 5 July 2019; 'Marco Civil Da Internet, Lei No. 12.965, de 23 de Abril de 2014.' <http://www.planalto.gov.br/ccivil_03/_ato2011-2014/2014/lei/l12965.htm> accessed 7 May 2019.
33 NETmundial (n 4).

This formulation corresponds exactly to the text of Article 19 of the Universal Declaration of Human Rights, punctuation included. Such wording survives unchanged through the challenge of the time thanks to its farsighted technology-neutral ('through *any* media') and global ('*regardless* of frontiers') approach. As Postman observed, technological developments have changed the meaning that we nowadays associate with the term 'media'.[34] At the time of the adoption of the Universal Declaration, in 1948, one would have thought of the press, the radio or the telephone. Today, one imagines computers and smartphones. Freedom of expression, as established 70 years ago, is a fundamental principle which is still valid today, in the digital society.

Internet bills of rights reiterate that this constitutional norm, as it is, is able to address the challenges of the virtual world.[35] Freedom of expression implies the right to spread online all ideas, including religious beliefs,[36] and even if they 'shock, offend or disturb'.[37] Everyone can 'organise and engage in online [...] protest' like one would make offline.[38] Anonymous freedom of speech, without fear of being surveilled, should be guaranteed.[39] The right to express one's own opinion is paralleled by the freedom to 'receive' and 'search' information in the digital realm too.[40]

The principle of freedom of expression does not seem to require a particular adaptation to the needs of the contemporary society. Internet bills of rights just make more explicit what some 'old words' can mean today. For example, in relation to the potential limitations of the right to freedom of expression, the *African Declaration on Internet Rights and Freedoms* explains that:

34 See Postman (n 27).

35 See, for instance, 'Charta der Digitalen Grundrechte der Europäischen Union' (n 4), Article 2; European Commission (n 18), Section 1, Chapter 2, Paragraph 5; Miriam Defensor Santiago The Magna Carta for Philippine Internet Freedom (n 18), Section 33, B.1; Just Net Coalition, 'The Delhi Declaration for a Just and Equitable Internet' <https://justnetcoalition.org/delhi-declaration> accessed 7 May 2019, Article 15.

36 See 'Charter of Human Rights and Principles for the Internet' (n 4), Article 6; Murray (n 4), Article 8.

37 See Ujam Chukwuemeka Digital Rights and Freedom Bill (n 19), Article 13(2); see also African Declaration Group, 'African Declaration on Internet Rights and Freedoms' 15 <https://africaninternetrights.org/sites/default/files/African-Declaration-English-FINAL.pdf>. See *Handyside v The United Kingdom* [1976] European Court of Human Rights 5493/72 [49].

38 See 'Charter of Human Rights and Principles for the Internet' (n 4), Article 5; Murray (n 4), Article 10; Praxis (n 15), Principle no. 4; Miriam Defensor Santiago The Magna Carta for Philippine Internet Freedom (n 18), Article 8.

39 See 'Digital Bill of Rights' (n 32), Article II, Section 1; Ujam Chukwuemeka Digital Rights and Freedom Bill (n 19), Section 4(1); PEN International (n 23), Article 3.

40 See Praxis (n 15), Principle no. 2; 'Charter of Human Rights and Principles for the Internet' (n 4), Article 5(c).

> Mandatory blocking of entire websites, IP addresses, ports, network protocols or types of uses (such as social networking) is an extreme measure – analogous to banning a newspaper or broadcaster – which can only be justified in accordance with international standards, for example where necessary to protect children against sexual abuse.[41]

In this regard, the Nigerian *Digital Rights and Freedoms Bill* is even more drastic:

> Censorship on the Internet, which usually takes the form of laws allowing for the total or partial banning of certain web pages and in certain extreme circumstances, where the State resorts to the complete disconnection of the Internet network, thus isolating a whole region from the rest of the country and the world at large, is a violation of freedom of expression.[42]

The term 'censorship' in the online world acquires new meanings. Internet bills of rights highlight how blocking or taking down materials from the Web is in essence not dissimilar from banning a newspaper or a book. Freedom of expression is not an absolute right, but its compression should be contemplated only in limited circumstances. Internet bills of rights focus particularly on the issues of hate speech online and the protection of intellectual property rights. The incitement to hatred and violence, as in the offline world, violates the dignity of the individual.[43] Along with the protection of minors, national security and public order, morality, and data protection, it remains a reason of public interest capable of restricting the right to freedom of expression.[44] Intellectual property rights are also recognised,[45] but generally Internet bills of rights underline the need to balance

41 African Declaration Group (n 37) 14; see also Open Society Institute – Regional Internet Program and Parliamentary Human Rights Foundation (n 4) para IV.A.

42 See Ujam Chukwuemeka Digital Rights and Freedom Bill (n 19), Article 13(17); see, in the same sense, Council of Europe (n 5) para 2.1.5; PEN International (n 23), Article 2(c); cf. Ujam Chukwuemeka Digital Rights and Freedom Bill (n 19), Article 2(c), which states that 'disconnection from access to the Internet on ground of copyright infringement is always a disproportionate restriction of the right to freedom of expression'.

43 See, in particular, Praxis (n 15), Principle no. 2.

44 See UNESCO (n 19) para 14; PEN International (n 23), Article 2(b); Camera dei Deputati (n 4), Article 13.2; Ujam Chukwuemeka Digital Rights and Freedom Bill (n 19), Articles 13(14) and 14(11); Council of Europe (n 5) para 2.4.1 ff.

45 See 'Charter of Human Rights and Principles for the Internet' (n 4), Article 11(d); Gelman (n 4), Article 21; Steve Peers and others (eds), *The EU Charter of Fundamental Rights: A Commentary* (Hart Publishing 2014), Article 6; Geneva Summit for Human Rights and Democracy (n 4), Article 4; Praxis (n 15), Principle no. 3; cf. 'Digital Bill of Rights' (n 32), Article II, Section 2, Subsection 3; Ryan Lytle, 'Explore Mashable's Crowdsourced Digital Bill of Rights' (*Mashable*) <https://mashable.com/2013/08/12/digital-bill-of-rights-crowdsource/> accessed 21 May 2019, Article 6; Miriam Defensor Santiago The Magna

their protection with the interests of individuals, who now live in a world characterised by the possibility of transmitting information instantaneously and at a global scale.[46]

Freedom and secrecy of correspondence

Internet bills of rights also restate the old principle of freedom and secrecy of correspondence, which conceptually shares its roots with the right to freedom of expression and the right to privacy. These declarations highlight how this constitutional right should, and can, be easily applied in the context of the digital society. Mashable's *Digital Bill of Rights* clearly outlines an equation between the offline and online dimension:

> The user's online user data and personal communications, including but not limited to email, instant messages, social media and audio and video conferences shall have the same legal protections as a user's traditional letters, phone calls and any other physical correspondence or records.[47]

Internet bills of rights demonstrate that the digital revolution has not undermined the communicative capacity of the analogue formulation of this right. Today, the term 'correspondence' has certainly acquired new meanings, encompassing not only the physical dispatch of mails but also all forms of online communication between a restricted number of individuals. However, emails, for instance, are commonly interpreted as today's equivalent of traditional letters. In this way, the right to freedom and secrecy of correspondence is instinctively and easily translated in the digital context.

It is however interesting to notice that some Internet bills of rights introduce a new limitation to the principle of freedom of correspondence. In 1997, Robert Gelman, in his *Declaration of Human Rights in Cyberspace*, already wrote:

> Without prior agreement, no one should be subjected to unsolicited mass email, server-clogging file-attachments, or invasive applets.[48]

Unsolicited commercial communications are arguably classifiable as correspondence given the large number of addressees that they usually have.

Carta for Philippine Internet Freedom (n 18), Section 12; NETmundial (n 4); Camera dei Deputati (n 4), Article 3; Godwin (n 15), Article 10; 'Charta der Digitalen Grundrechte der Europäischen Union' (n 4), Article 16.

46 See UNESCO (n 19) para 17; Social Innovation Society (n 4).

47 Lytle (n 45), Article 7.

48 Gelman (n 4), Article 5; see also European Commission (n 18), Section 1, Chapter 4, Paragraph 4.

However, notwithstanding their qualification, Internet bills of rights establish that so-called spam does not enjoy the same protections as other types of correspondence.

Lastly, Internet bills of rights stress the importance of establishing clear procedural safeguards in circumstances where public authorities need to access private communications.[49] From an analysis of the terminology used, it appears that these declarations are reinforcing the idea that the digital tools used to transmit online correspondence enjoy a status of inviolability similar to that traditionally accorded to the personal domicile.[50] Private correspondence is not simply qualified as 'secret' but becomes in principle 'inviolable'.[51]

Freedom of association and assembly

Digital technologies not only offer an unprecedented possibility to communicate but also generate a new virtual space of social interaction. Today, individuals can create online communities and virtually meet in the digital realm.[52] Internet bills of rights highlight how these new possibilities are protected by the existing rights to freedom of association and peaceful assembly, both principles which equally apply online as offline.[53] The Council of Europe, for example, in its Recommendation on Internet freedom recognises that:

> 1 Individuals are free to use Internet platforms, such as social media and other ICTs in order to associate with each other and to establish associations, to determine the objectives of such associations, to form trade unions, and to carry out activities within the limits provided for by laws that comply with international standards.

49 See, in particular, 'Marco Civil Da Internet, Lei No. 12.965, de 23 de Abril de 2014.' (n 32), Article 7.II; Godwin (n 15), Articles 8(c) and 9(a); see also Council of Europe (n 5) para 4.1.7.

50 See, for example, Article 7 of Camera dei Deputati (n 4), entitled 'Inviolability of electronic systems, devices and domiciles'.

51 See 'Marco Civil Da Internet, Lei No. 12.965, de 23 de Abril de 2014.' (n 32), Article 7; Camera dei Deputati (n 4), Article 7.

52 See, e.g., the recent project by Facebook of creating a 'metaverse': 'Connect 2021: Our Vision for the Metaverse' (*Facebook Technology*, 28 October 2021) <https://tech.fb.com/connect-2021-our-vision-for-the-metaverse/> accessed 15 November 2021.

53 See 'Charter of Human Rights and Principles for the Internet' (n 4), Article 7; Murray (n 4), Article 10; NETmundial (n 4); African Declaration Group (n 37), Article 5; Just Net Coalition (n 35), Article 15; Godwin (n 15), Article 7; Ujam Chukwuemeka Digital Rights and Freedom Bill (n 19), Section 15; cf. Gelman (n 4), Article 6; Open Society Institute - Regional Internet Program and Parliamentary Human Rights Foundation (n 4) para C.1.

2 Associations are free to use the Internet in order to exercise their right to freedom of expression and to participate in matters of political and public debate.
3 Individuals are free to use Internet platforms, such as social media and other ICTs in order to organise themselves for purposes of peaceful assembly.[54]

In relation to this last point, the UNESCO's *Code of ethics for the information society* adds that individuals can not only use the Internet as an instrument to 'organise' peaceful assemblies but have also the right to use digital technology itself to assemble in virtual space.[55] In this case too, therefore, it is apparent that existing constitutional norms are still able to convey their principles in the context of the digital society. Social media platforms and other means of online communication are instinctively seen as natural instruments to exercising the rights of association and peacefully assembly, the essence of which remain unaltered in the contemporary digital society. Internet bills of rights limit themselves to reiterate their applicability in the online world.

Generalisation and re-specification

The work of translating fundamental principles operated by Internet bills of rights is not confined to a conceptual make-up. These declarations do not merely specify the applicability of existing constitutional guarantees in the digital society. If one talks of a right to freedom of expression online, one instinctively grasps the idea that communication through digital technology means is guaranteed. The same, as we have observed, can be said for the freedom and secrecy of correspondence and for the freedom of association and peacefully assembly. The development of digital technology has provided new instruments to exercise these rights. The communicative power of these constitutional provisions is generally preserved because the individual is instinctively led to consider new technologies as the heir of old means of communication. Internet bills of rights thus tend to simply restate the applicability of analogue constitutional provisions in the context of the contemporary society by making reference to digital communication tools.

A similar intervention of superficial stuccoing, however, does not always suffice. A series of fundamental rights, which were designed for an analogue world, struggles to permeate and inform the virtual reality. Their current formulation does not immediately speak to the actors of the digital society. Individuals as well as public and private actors do not instinctively grasp the implications of these fundamental values. Internet bills of

54 Council of Europe (n 5).
55 See UNESCO (n 19), Article 7.

rights intervene to extract their new meaning and their significance for the contemporary digital society. These declarations distil the quintessence of these constitutional values. They unfasten the pure essence of these rights from the accidentals of society in which they emerged. The ultimate telos of the constitutional norm is at this point plunged into the context of the digital society, from which it resurfaces with a more specifically tailored layout. Teubner, dealing with the emergence of constitutional patterns beyond the state, similarly talks of a double process of 'generalisation' and 're-specification'.[56] The constitutional norm cannot be merely transplanted in a different societal context. One needs to preliminarily understand its ultimate aim, generalising its principle and purifying it from its original contextual contaminants, and then to re-specify it in light of the characteristics of the new social reality.

Non-discrimination

In this way, Internet bills of rights translate the right to non-discrimination into the principles of net neutrality and multilingualism of the net. The value of non-discrimination finds its conceptual roots in the principle of equality of all individuals.[57] Everyone shall enjoy their own rights without any form of discrimination based on their characteristics, be they their gender, sexual orientation, age, or political beliefs, for example. A principle which is reiterated in the online context too, thus banning all forms of discrimination that can also take place online, such as racism, ableism, misogyny, and all sorts of religious and sexual orientation phobias.[58] However, in addition to this principle, Internet bills of rights explicitly recognise that, as the Internet acts as an essential instrument in exercising our fundamental rights today, no one should be discriminated in accessing and using it.[59] All the actors involved in the management of the network, in particular Internet access and service providers, should strive to preserve a neutral, non-discriminatory environment.[60] More concretely, as the *Marco civil da Internet* puts it:

56 Gunther Teubner, 'Societal Constitutionalism; Alternatives to State-Centred Constitutional Theory?' in Christian Joerges, Inger-Johanne Sand and Gunther Teubner (eds), *Transnational Governance and Constitutionalism. International Studies in the Theory of Private Law* (Hart 2004).

57 Cf. 'Charter of Human Rights and Principles for the Internet' (n 4), in particular Article 1(d) that talks of 'net neutrality and net equality'.

58 See, e.g., 'Charter of Human Rights and Principles for the Internet' (n 4), Article 2.

59 See, in particular, Camera dei Deputati (n 4), Article 4.2.

60 See 'Charter of Human Rights and Principles for the Internet' (n 4), Article 1(d) and 2(a); 'Digital Bill of Rights' (n 32), Article I, Section 1 and Article II, section 2; European Commission (n 18), Section 1, Chapter 3; Lytle (n 45), Article 2; Miriam Defensor Santiago The Magna Carta for Philippine Internet Freedom (n 18), Section 5; African Declaration Group (n 37), Articles 1, 2 and 13; Council of Europe (n 5) para 2.2.3; CGI.br - Comitê Gestor da Internet no Brasil, 'Principles for the Governance and Use of the Internet' (*CGI.*

> The party responsible for the transmission, switching or routing has the duty to process, on an isonomic basis, any data packages, regardless of content, origin and destination, service, terminal or application.
>
> §1 The discrimination or degradation of traffic shall be regulated [...] and can only result from:
>
> I – technical requirements essential to the adequate provision of services and applications; and
> II – prioritization of emergency services.[61]

In the digital society, the guarantee of net neutrality is a necessary corollary of the right to non-discrimination, which, at its turn, is a precondition for an equal enjoyment of fundamental rights by all individuals. The right to non-discrimination does not lose its original sense in the virtual world. Internet bills of rights enrich its significance by re-contextualising this principle in the digital society. Besides providing a general condemnation of all forms of online discrimination, this principle today *also* implies the preservation of the neutrality of the Internet.

However, guaranteeing neutral access and use of the Internet by imposing an obligation not to discriminate transmitted data is not in and of itself enough to ensure that everyone can equally enjoy their fundamental rights online. Internet bills of rights recognise that in the digital society the right to non-discrimination additionally entails the guarantee of multilingualism on the net.[62] UNESCO, in its *Code of ethics for the information society*, formulates this principle as follows:

> Information should be made available, accessible and affordable across all linguistic, cultural and social groups and to both genders, including people with physical, sensory or cognitive disabilities, and people who speak minority languages. Internet and other ICTs shall serve to reduce digital divide and deploy technology and applications to ensure inclusion.[63]

Multilingualism is thus intended in a broad sense. It involves not only the use of different languages to avoid a cultural homogenisation but also the employment of technical means to ensure that people with disabilities can access and use the Internet. In this way, the right to non-discrimination online, implying both the principles of net neutrality and multilingualism,

br - Comitê Gestor da Internet no Brasil, 2009) <https://cgi.br> accessed 5 July 2019, Article 6; Gelman (n 4), Article 2; Murray (n 4), Article 2; 'Charta der Digitalen Grundrechte der Europäischen Union' (n 4), Article 11.

61 'Marco Civil Da Internet, Lei No. 12.965, de 23 de Abril de 2014.' (n 32), Article 9.

62 See, in particular, Council of Europe, Committee of Ministers (n 23) para 10; UNESCO (n 19) paras 4 and 6; Godwin (n 15), Article 2.7.

63 UNESCO (n 19) para 4.

ultimately aims to foster inclusion in the digital society.[64] Internet bills of rights stress that, paradoxically, to achieve a greater level of equality among all individuals, one needs to enhance the diversity of the virtual world.[65]

Right to privacy

The respect of individual privacy is another fundamental value that Internet bills of rights generalise and re-specify in the context of the digital society.[66] First of all, these declarations of rights restate that any form of surveillance affects the privacy of the individual.[67] However, in addition, they interestingly introduce a new principle. In the words of the *African Declaration on Internet Rights and Freedoms*:

> Mass or indiscriminate surveillance of individuals or the monitoring of their communications, constitutes a disproportionate interference, and thus a violation, of the right to privacy, freedom of expression and other human rights. Mass surveillance shall be prohibited by law. [...] In order to meet the requirements of international human rights law, targeted surveillance of online communications must be governed by clear and transparent laws which, at a minimum, comply with the following basic principles: first, communications surveillance must be both targeted and based on reasonable suspicion of commission or involvement in the commission of serious crime; second, communications surveillance must be judicially authorised and individuals placed under surveillance must be notified that their communications have been monitored as soon as practicable after the conclusion of the surveillance operation; third, the application of surveillance laws must be subject to strong parliamentary oversight to prevent abuse and ensure the accountability of intelligence services and law enforcement agencies.[68]

64 See, in particular, UNESCO (n 19) para 4; 'Charta der Digitalen Grundrechte der Europäischen Union' (n 4), Article 3.

65 See, in particular, Just Net Coalition (n 35), Article 9; Godwin (n 15), Article 2.7; Council of Europe, Committee of Ministers (n 23) para 10; 'Charter of Human Rights and Principles for the Internet' (n 4), Article 1(d).

66 Some declarations conversely limit themselves to restate the right to privacy in the online context. See 'Marco Civil Da Internet, Lei No. 12.965, de 23 de Abril de 2014.' (n 32), Article 7; UNESCO (n 19) paras 12 and 13; Praxis (n 15), Principle no. 9; Social Innovation Society (n 4), Article 8.

67 See 'Charter of Human Rights and Principles for the Internet' (n 4), Article 8; Godwin (n 15), Article 2.5; NETmundial (n 4); Open Society Institute - Regional Internet Program and Parliamentary Human Rights Foundation (n 4) para B.1; 'Charta der Digitalen Grundrechte der Europäischen Union' (n 4), Article 7; Murray (n 4), Article 7.

68 African Declaration Group (n 37) 18.

Only targeted forms of surveillance, subject to specific guarantees, can be tolerated as reasonable restrictions of the right to privacy.[69] Internet bills of rights affirm that mass and indiscriminate surveillance represents an inadmissible limitation of that right, which cannot be considered proportionate as a matter of principle.[70] These declarations, by re-contextualising the value of individual privacy in the digital society, take into account the unprecedented possibilities of surveillance that digital technologies today offer to dominant actors and, in light of the ultimate telos of that right, they shape a new principle, outlawing an extreme form of control over the individual.

From this process of translation of the right to privacy in the context of the digital society, Internet bills of rights also derive two other linked corollaries. Firstly, these declarations recognise that respect of individual privacy online today implies a right to communicate anonymously.[71] The Italian *Declaration of Internet rights* includes a specific provision on the 'protection of anonymity'. It reads:

1 Every person may access the Internet and communicate electronically using instruments, including technical systems, which protect their anonymity and prevent the collection of personal data, in particular with a view to exercising civil and political freedoms without being subject to discrimination or censorship.
2 Restrictions may be imposed only when they are based on the need to safeguard a major public interest and are necessary, proportional and grounded in law and in accordance with the basic features of a democratic society.
3 In the event of violations of the dignity and fundamental rights of any person, as well as in other cases provided for by the law, the courts may require the identification the author of a communication with a reasoned order.[72]

A right to online anonymity is perceived as a necessary precondition to preserve one's own privacy and, at the same time, to exercise freely one's own freedom of expression, without fear of repercussions. As a linked corollary,

69 See African Declaration Group (n 37) 18; Council of Europe (n 5) para 4.2.1; Open Society Institute - Regional Internet Program and Parliamentary Human Rights Foundation (n 4) para B.1.

70 See African Declaration Group (n 37) 18; Just Net Coalition (n 35) para 16; Ujam Chukwuemeka Digital Rights and Freedom Bill (n 19), Section 10(3).

71 See Godwin (n 15), Article 2.5; Ryan Lytle, 'Let's Write a Digital Bill of Rights' (*Mashable*) <https://mashable.com/2013/07/01/digital-bill-of-rights/> accessed 11 July 2019, Article 9; Council of Europe (n 5) para 4.1.7; African Declaration Group (n 37), Article 8; Geneva Summit for Human Rights and Democracy (n 4), Article 6; 'Digital Bill of Rights' (n 32), Article II, Section 1.

72 Camera dei Deputati (n 4), Article 10.

Internet bills of rights then derive the right of the individual to use encryption online.[73] According to the *Open Internet Policy Principles*:

> Users should have the right to use any form of cryptographic technology they choose to protect the privacy of their communications. Users should not be compelled to guarantee in advance law enforcement access to communications through key escrow, key recovery or other mechanisms.[74]

In order to guarantee their privacy online, Internet bills of rights stress that individuals should not only have the right to encrypt their communications but also not to be forced to disclose their credentials. Today, a significant portion of our private and family life occurs online. By protecting access to the content of our online activities, Internet bills of rights seek to safeguard the sphere of virtual personality that the individual develops online. The *Charter of Human Rights and Principles for the Internet*, in this regard, even establishes that 'digital signatures, usernames, passwords, PIN and TAN codes' are 'inviolable' and cannot be altered without the previous consent of the individual.[75]

Due process

Article 18 of the *Charter of Human Rights and Principles for the Internet* observes:

> It is increasingly common for the right to a fair trial and to an effective remedy to be violated in the Internet environment, for example with Internet intermediary companies being asked to make judgements about whether content is illegal and encouraged to remove content without a court order. It is therefore necessary to reiterate that procedural rights must be respected, protected and fulfilled on the Internet as they are offline.[76]

As seen in the previous chapters, in the digital society big multinational companies managing and selling products and services online emerge as

73 See Godwin (n 15), Article 2.5 and 8; Council of Europe (n 5) para 4.1.7; Murray (n 4), Article 5; Geneva Summit for Human Rights and Democracy (n 4), Article 7; 'Digital Bill of Rights' (n 32), Article IV; Miriam Defensor Santiago The Magna Carta for Philippine Internet Freedom (n 18), Section 10(2); African Declaration Group (n 37), Article 8.

74 Open Society Institute - Regional Internet Program and Parliamentary Human Rights Foundation (n 4) para C.2.

75 'Charter of Human Rights and Principles for the Internet' (n 4), Article 8(c).

76 'Charter of Human Rights and Principles for the Internet' (n 4).

new dominant actors.[77] Within their private online fiefs, these corporations administer their own justice, according to their internal rules and often with blatant disregard to basic fair trial rights. As such, Internet bills of rights advocate the respect of due process principles by private dominant actors, too.[78] In contrast to what Article 18 of the *Charter of Human Rights and Principles for the Internet* quoted above states, such an extension does not merely represent a reiteration of the applicability of procedural rights online as they are offline. In this way, Internet bills of rights are not simply reminding nation-states, the traditional holders of the obligation to ensure due process, to apply those guarantees in cases involving online activities.[79] These declarations of rights are remodelling the anatomy of the right of fair trial by extending its application to circumstances where private actors administer judicial functions. Internet bills of rights pragmatically acknowledge that, in the digital society, justice is no longer a prerogative of state authorities. Due process rights, re-contextualised in the virtual world, equally apply to private judges.

77 See *supra* Chapter 2 and 3.

78 See 'Charter of Human Rights and Principles for the Internet' (n 4), Article 18; Council of Europe (n 5) para 5.1.

79 Cf. African Declaration Group (n 37) 20; Just Net Coalition (n 35), Article 11; Council of Europe (n 5) para 5.1.

12 Constitutional innovation

New rights

The twofold process of generalisation and re-specification of fundamental values put in motion by Internet bills of rights does not always merely lead to the identification of new principles that conceptually still appear as corollaries, necessary implications of existing constitutional norms in the digital society. Sometimes, the re-contextualisation of fundamental principles in the virtual world gives birth to new rights. New, not in the sense of emerging from scratch. These rights do not materialise suddenly in the constitutional universe from an unexpected conceptual big-bang. One can rather observe a series of principles that become autonomous fundamental values, emancipating themselves from the constitutional rights from which they originated. Different from the examples analysed in the previous chapter, these new values are not merely a reverberation of a pre-existing analogue right in the context of the digital society. These principles start to shine on their own, generating, at their turn, a series of corollaries and implications that the global conversation on the rights and principles for the digital society is still defining.

Data protection

In some Internet bills of rights, the protection of personal data is still presented as a particular aspect of the right to privacy.[1] The *Carta internazionale*

1 See 'Charta der Digitalen Grundrechte der Europäischen Union' <https://digitalcharta.eu/> accessed 7 May 2019, Article 7; Council of Europe, 'Recommendation of the Committee of Ministers to Member States on Internet Freedom' (2016) CM/Rec(2016)5 para 4.1 <https://search.coe.int/cm/Pages/result_details.aspx?ObjectId=09000016806415fa>; UNESCO, 'Code of Ethics for the Information Society Proposed by the Intergovernmental Council of the Information for All Programme (IFAP)' (2011) para 13 <https://unesdoc.unesco.org/ark:/48223/pf0000212696> accessed 17 June 2019; African Declaration Group, 'African Declaration on Internet Rights and Freedoms' <https://africaninternetrights.org/sites/default/files/African-Declaration-English-FINAL.pdf>, Article 8.

DOI: 10.4324/9781003256908-12

dei diritti digitali issued by the Social Innovation Society, for example, establishes:

> Everyone has the right to the protection of his own intimacy and private sphere. Everyone has the right to fully and freely access all the data, information and documents related to such intimate and private sphere. Everyone has the right to rectify, modify, correct and erase all the data, information and documents related to that sphere.[2]

In those declarations, personal data are considered worthy of protection because they relate to the private life of the individual. However, a significant number of Internet bills of rights overtake such equation between personal and private.[3] Data which are to be protected become all those related to the individual, independently from the fact that they belong to her sphere of intimacy. Article 5 of the Italian *Declaration of Internet rights* exemplarily reads:

> 1. Everyone has the right to the protection of the data that concern them in order to ensure respect for their dignity, identity and privacy.[4]

The respect of privacy is no longer the exclusive value that informs data protection. Ensuring that the processing of personal data satisfies appropriate guarantees also aims to safeguard the dignity and the identity of the individual. The multiplicity of personal data scattered in the digital world represents the digital body of the individual, the immediate projection of her personality online. For this reason, Internet bills of rights restate the importance of respecting the principles of lawfulness, purpose limitation,

2 Social Innovation Society, 'Carta Internazionale Dei Diritti Digitali' <http://www.soin-society.org/carta-internazionale-dei-diritti-digitali/> accessed 7 May 2019, Article 8, my translation.

3 See Camera dei Deputati, 'Declaration of Internet Rights' <https://www.camera.it/application/xmanager/projects/leg17/commissione_internet/testo_definitivo_inglese.pdf>, Article 5; 'Charter of Human Rights and Principles for the Internet' <http://internetrightsandprinciples.org/site/wp-content/uploads/2018/10/IRPC_english_5thedition.pdf> accessed 17 December 2018, Article 9; 'Marco Civil Da Internet, Lei No. 12.965, de 23 de Abril de 2014.' <http://www.planalto.gov.br/ccivil_03/_ato2011-2014/2014/lei/l12965.htm> accessed 7 May 2019, Article 7; Praxis, 'Guiding Principles of Internet Freedom' <http://www.praxis.ee/fileadmin/tarmo/Projektid/Valitsemine_ja_kodanikeühiskond/Praxis_Theses_Internet.pdf>, Principle no. 5; European Commission, 'Code of EU Online Rights' (2012) <https://ec.europa.eu/digital-single-market/sites/digital-agenda/files/Code%20EU%20online%20rights%20EN%20final%202.pdf>, Section 1, Chapter 4; Ryan Lytle, 'Explore Mashable's Crowdsourced Digital Bill of Rights' (*Mashable*) <https://mashable.com/2013/08/12/digital-bill-of-rights-crowdsource/> accessed 21 May 2019, Article 4 and 8; Miriam Defensor Santiago, The Magna Carta for Philippine Internet Freedom 2013, Section 10.

4 Camera dei Deputati (n 3).

necessity, and proportionality, which are established by many data protection laws and represent the minimal safeguards that should apply to personal data processing.[5] Several declarations include detailed provisions limiting the possibility to retain personal data.[6] These rules, as a whole, emerge as the fundamental obligations that the dominant actors should respect when exercising their power on our digital selves.

In parallel, Internet bills of rights empower the individual with a series of rights, also in this case drawn from existing data protection laws: data subjects can ask to access, rectify, transfer, and even erase personal data.[7] Some charters even proclaim a right to data ownership.[8] Personal data, although fragmented in the virtual space in the hands of different actors, are considered as a part of a unique, inalienable body, whose ownership individuals permanently hold and, at their death, can even be transferred to their heirs.[9] Other declarations are less radical. They do not justify the control of individuals of their personal data as a consequence of her right to ownership. They more generally recognise a right of the person to informational self-determination.[10] Every individual is free to develop their own personality online. Personal data processed by digital technology means constitute the virtual image of the individual. Everyone should be entitled to freely determine their own representation online and, if necessary, to change it.

5 See Camera dei Deputati (n 3), Article 5.4 ff; 'Charter of Human Rights and Principles for the Internet' (n 3), Article 9(c); 'Digital Bill of Rights' (*reddit*) <https://www.reddit.com/r/fia/comments/vuj37/digital_bill_of_rights_1st_draft/> accessed 5 July 2019, Article IV; European Commission (n 3), Section 1, Chapter 4; Miriam Defensor Santiago The Magna Carta for Philippine Internet Freedom (n 3), Article 10; African Declaration Group (n 1) 17; Cf. Regulation (EU) 2016/679 (General Data Protection Regulation), Chapter 2.

6 See 'Marco Civil Da Internet, Lei No. 12.965, de 23 de Abril de 2014.' (n 3), Articles 10, 13, 15, 16, 17, 22, 23; Mike Godwin, 'The Great Charter for Cambodian Internet Freedom' <https://www.linkedin.com/pulse/great-charter-cambodian-internet-freedom-mike-godwin> accessed 21 May 2019, Article 13; Ujam Chukwuemeka, Digital Rights and Freedom Bill 2016, Article 6.

7 See Social Innovation Society (n 2), Article 8; Camera dei Deputati (n 3), Articles 5, 6 and 12; Council of Europe (n 1) para 4.1.4; 'Charter of Human Rights and Principles for the Internet' (n 3), Article 9; European Commission (n 3), Section 1, Chapter 4; cf. Regulation (EU) 2016/679 (General Data Protection Regulation), Chapter 3.

8 See Robert Gelman, 'Draft Proposal-Declaration of Human Rights in Cyberspace' <http://www.be-in.com/10/rightsdec.html> accessed 17 June 2019, Article 17; Just Net Coalition, 'The Delhi Declaration for a Just and Equitable Internet' <https://justnetcoalition.org/delhi-declaration> accessed 7 May 2019, Article 12; Ujam Chukwuemeka Digital Rights and Freedom Bill (n 6), Sections 7 and 8.

9 See Ujam Chukwuemeka Digital Rights and Freedom Bill (n 6), Article 8(2), which even broadly talks of 'digital assets'. It reads: 'The digital assets or data sets of an owner such as passwords, instructive memos, digital contracts, digital receipts, pictures, medical information, bank account, writings, social interactions or anything else that a user has access to primarily in the digital space is inheritable to be managed and owned by his heirs or next of kin'.

10 See, in particular, Camera dei Deputati (n 3), Article 5.4 and 6.

In order to do so, all persons shall know who detains their data and how those data are processed. At the same time, they shall be able to exercise a form of control on their personal information, should those data no longer be updated or in case individuals express their willingness to stop the processing or to change processor. The Italian *Declaration of Internet rights* encapsulates this principle in a provision on the right to online identity:

1 Every person has a right to the complete and up-to-date representation of his or her identities on the Internet.
2 The definition of identity regards the free construction of personality and cannot take place without the intervention and the knowledge of the data subject.[11]

From the principle of informational self-determination, which represents one of the most salient aspects of the right to data protection as emancipated from the right to privacy and re-contextualised in the digital environment, Internet bills of rights derive an additional corollary: the so-called right to be forgotten, recently recognised in the case-law of the European Court of Justice and incorporated in the data protection legislation currently in force in the European Union.[12] In the words of the Italian *Declaration of Internet rights*:

1 Every person has the right to obtain the removal from search engines of references to information that, due to their content or the time elapsed from the moment of collection, no longer have public relevance.
2 The right to be forgotten cannot restrict the freedom of search and the right of the public to be informed, which are necessary conditions for the functioning of a democratic society. This right may be exercised by public figures or those who hold public functions only if the data concerning them are irrelevant with regard to their activities or the public functions they perform.
3 Where a request to be removed from search engines is granted, any person may appeal the decision before the courts to ensure that the public interest in the information is preserved.[13]

The right to be forgotten originates from the need to preserve the autonomy of the individual to determine her online representation. Search engines publicly offer the image of the digital person, by recomposing the puzzle of

11 Camera dei Deputati (n 3), Article 9.
12 See Camera dei Deputati (n 3), Article 11; 'Charta der Digitalen Grundrechte der Europäischen Union' (n 1), Article 7(4); cf. *Google Spain v APED* [2014] ECJ C-131/12, ECLI:EU:C:2014:317; Regulation (EU) 2016/679 (General Data Protection Regulation), Article 17.
13 Camera dei Deputati (n 3), Article 11.

multiple webpages including information on the individual. By establishing this right, Internet bills of rights claim back the control of the individual on these virtual pictures. Provided that information is not of public interest and, therefore, worthy to be preserved, all persons acquire a right to a 'digital fresh start'.[14]

Interestingly, the right to be forgotten is not the only safeguard taken into consideration by Internet bills of rights to stem the proliferation of virtual representations of the individuals that could have negative consequences on the enjoyment of their fundamental rights and, more broadly, on their life. These declarations constitutionalise another principle derived from the European data protection legislation according to which decisions affecting the individual cannot be exclusively based on automated processing of data.[15] A human review is always necessary when a choice that could have negative effects on the person is based on a virtual reconstruction of her profile. The *Charter of Digital Fundamental Rights of the European Union* includes a detailed provision on the topic:

1 Ethical principles shall only be formulated by human beings, and decisions that impact fundamental rights shall only be made by human beings.
2 The responsibility for automated decisions must lie with a natural or legal person.
3 The criteria leading to automated decisions, in cases such as digital profiling, must be made transparent.
4 Every person subject to an automated decision that has a significant impact on his or her life shall have the right to have an independent review and ruling conducted by a human being.
5 Decisions about life and death, physical integrity, and the deprivation of liberty shall only be made by human beings.
6 The use of artificial intelligence and robotics in areas sensitive to possible fundamental rights violations must be subject to social debate and regulated by legislation.[16]

Internet bills of rights, in conclusion, stress the centrality of the right to data protection as an autonomous value which is functional to the safeguard of the digital body against the power of dominant actors and to the preservation of the autonomy of the development of personality online. For this reason, some declarations even affirm the necessity to constitutionalise the institution of data protection authorities as a new fundamental principle to

14 'Charta der Digitalen Grundrechte der Europäischen Union' (n 1), Article 7(4).

15 See Camera dei Deputati (n 3), Article 8; 'Charta der Digitalen Grundrechte der Europäischen Union' (n 1), Article 3 and 5; Council of Europe (n 1) para 4.1.4; European Commission (n 3), Section 1, Chapter 4, Paragraph 3.

16 'Charta der Digitalen Grundrechte der Europäischen Union' (n 1), Article 5.

ensure the balancing of powers of dominant actors and the respect of the rights of the individuals.[17]

E-democracy

In contemporary society, our identities and actions are translated by digital technologies in the form of data. Data related to individuals fuels the power of dominant actors, such as states and multinational corporations. However, the constitutional ecosystem attempts to rebalance this asymmetry of power by providing, at its turn, individuals with data about dominant actors. In the previous section, we have seen that Internet bills of rights recognise the right of individuals to access their personal data, to know who processes their personal information and how. Along the same lines, these declarations also affirm that individuals have the right to access governmental information through electronic means.[18] According to the formulation of the *Open Internet Policy Principles*:

> Governments should enable citizens access to legislative, judicial and executive branch information through the Internet. Such access should be backed up by a legal right to public information, without any showing of need or intended use. Such information should be available in standard formats to promote broad and effective access.[19]

Contrastingly from the right to access personal data, this principle only involves public actors. The individual, however, does not have to justify any particular link with the data requested. Everyone can in principle access *all* types of information held by public authorities.[20] The transmission via digital technology favours – not to say, substantiates – the possibility to effectively exercise this right. In this sense, this principle, although already

17 See 'Charter of Human Rights and Principles for the Internet' (n 3), Article 9(d); 'Charta der Digitalen Grundrechte der Europäischen Union' (n 1), Article 7(8); Council of Europe (n 1) para 4.1.6.

18 See 'Charter of Human Rights and Principles for the Internet' (n 3), Article 5(c); Open Society Institute - Regional Internet Program and Parliamentary Human Rights Foundation, 'Open Internet Policy Principles' <http://mailman.anu.edu.au/pipermail/link/1997-March/026302.html>, Article II.B; EUROCITIES Knowledge Society Forum – TeleCities, 'Charter of Rights of Citizens in the Knowledge Society' <https://www.comune.modena.it/storiaretecivica/Materiale_PDF_2_marzo/Brugi_Miranda2.pdf>, Article 6; Andrew Murray, 'A Bill of Rights for the Internet' <http://theitlawyer.blogspot.com/2010/10/bill-of-rights-for-internet.html> accessed 17 June 2019, Article 9; UNESCO (n 1) para 9; Camera dei Deputati (n 3), Article 14.6; 'Charta der Digitalen Grundrechte der Europäischen Union' (n 1), Article 6; Council of Europe (n 1) para 4.2.11.

19 Open Society Institute - Regional Internet Program and Parliamentary Human Rights Foundation (n 18), Article II.B.

20 Cf. Murray (n 18), Article 9; Council of Europe (n 1) para 4.2.11; 'Charta der Digitalen Grundrechte der Europäischen Union' (n 1), Article 6.

appearing long ago in its analogue form, acquires new force and independence in the digital context.[21]

In some Internet bills of rights, this principle is expanded into a right to open data.[22] The state is required not only to disclose the information in its possession once solicited by the individual but even to proactively publish online all the data held by public bodies and to make it reusable by individuals. In this form, the right to governmental information is transformed in the duty of the state to ensure full transparency. The Internet offers the chance to achieve what Bobbio called 'democracy in public', to transform the complex machine of the state, and particularly its arcana, into a transparent glasshouse.[23]

Moreover, Internet bills of rights do not limit themselves to empower the individuals with a new tool to monitor state's activities. These declarations also establish the duty of the state to use digital technologies to involve the citizens in public life.[24] In this regard, the UNESCO's *Code of ethics for the information society* states:

> Member States should support the use of the Internet and other ICTs to enhance the effectiveness of democracy and democratic institutions, providing to the public opportunities for effective public deliberation and participation in democratic process, and promoting transparency, accountability, responsiveness, engagement, inclusiveness, accessibility, participation, subsidiarity and social cohesion.[25]

In this way, the possibility of individuals to have access to the full panorama of the state's activities also becomes functional to the enhancement of direct participation in the democratic process. Lastly, Internet bills of rights complement this vision of a state where the citizen at the same time controls and takes part in democratic life through digital technologies by establishing the right of the individual to access public services via electronic means.[26] Digital technologies, in this context, considerably ease the citizen

21 See *supra* Chapter 3.

22 See African Declaration Group (n 1) 15; UNESCO (n 1) para 9; Camera dei Deputati (n 3), Article 14.6; Ujam Chukwuemeka Digital Rights and Freedom Bill (n 6), Section 14.

23 See Norberto Bobbio, *The Future of Democracy* (Richard Bellamy ed, Roger Griffin tr, University of Minnesota Press 1991).

24 See 'Charter of Human Rights and Principles for the Internet' (n 3), Articles 15 and 17; EUROCITIES Knowledge Society Forum – TeleCities (n 18), Articles 8 and 9; UNESCO (n 1) paras 3 and 16; Praxis (n 3), Principle no. 7; Camera dei Deputati (n 3), Preamble; Ujam Chukwuemeka Digital Rights and Freedom Bill (n 6), Article 17; 'Marco Civil Da Internet, Lei No. 12.965, de 23 de Abril de 2014.' (n 3), Article 24.III; cf. Universal Declaration of Human Rights 2015, Article 21.

25 UNESCO (n 1) para 16.

26 See 'Charter of Human Rights and Principles for the Internet' (n 3), Article 17; Praxis (n 3), Principle no. 7; Social Innovation Society (n 2), Article 10; 'Marco Civil Da Internet, Lei No. 12.965, de 23 de Abril de 2014.' (n 3), Article 24.III ff.

in this task and ultimately make the state closer to the individual. However, interestingly, some Internet bills of rights also take into consideration the opposite scenario where digital technology would represent an obstacle for the individual to access public services. The *Delhi Declaration for a Just and Equitable Internet*, for example, in this regard establishes:

> People must be able to enjoy all their rights and entitlements as citizens, even if they choose not to have Internet access. Access to and use of the Internet should not become a requirement for access to public services.[27]

In this way, these declarations comprehensively define the contours of a new right to e-democracy. Internet bills of rights highlight the central role that digital technology should play in a democratic society. New instruments of information and communication are enshrined as a fundamental tool to increase the level of transparency, enhance direct democracy, and facilitate the access to public services, ultimately rebalancing the asymmetry of power between the state and the individual.[28]

Internet access

The cornerstone of the constitutional ecosystem in the digital age is a new right to Internet access. Many Internet bills of rights list it first in their decalogue of principles.[29] The Internet is recognised as a new vital gateway to exercising fundamental rights.[30] Accessing it is a precondition to participation in social life according to the new standards that the advent of the digital technology has made possible. It represents the *sine qua non* of personal and collective development.[31] In the digital society, without the Internet, one

27 Just Net Coalition (n 8) para 17; see also 'Charta der Digitalen Grundrechte der Europäischen Union' (n 1), Article 9.

28 See Camera dei Deputati (n 3), Article 3.5.

29 See 'Charter of Human Rights and Principles for the Internet' (n 3); Open Society Institute - Regional Internet Program and Parliamentary Human Rights Foundation (n 18); EUROCITIES Knowledge Society Forum – TeleCities (n 18); Murray (n 18); Geneva Summit for Human Rights and Democracy, 'Geneva Declaration on Internet Freedom' (2010) <http://atlarge-lists.icann.org/pipermail/lac-discuss-es/2010/001287.html> accessed 11 July 2019; Praxis (n 3); European Commission (n 3); Lytle (n 3); Godwin (n 6).

30 See, in particular, Godwin (n 6); 'Charter of Human Rights and Principles for the Internet' (n 3), Article 1; Social Innovation Society (n 2); African Declaration Group (n 1), Article 2; see also 'Marco Civil Da Internet, Lei No. 12.965, de 23 de Abril de 2014.' (n 3), Article 4 and 7.

31 See Camera dei Deputati (n 3), Article 2; African Declaration Group (n 1), Article 2 and 7; NETmundial, 'Internet Governance Principles - NETmundial Multistakeholder Statement' <http://netmundial.br/wp-content/uploads/2014/04/NETmundial-Multistakeholder-Document.pdf>; Open Society Institute - Regional Internet Program and Parliamentary Human Rights Foundation (n 18) para A.1; Social Innovation Society (n 2), Article 5.

cannot fully enjoy her fundamental rights. The possibility of individuals to communicate and express their opinion would be limited; one could not exercise her right to association with the unprecedented number of users of the web; one could not access the large amount of government's documents with the same ease, receive a public service, or participate in the democratic life of her own country, just to make some examples. Internet access substantiates the 'right to have rights' of all individuals.[32]

For this reason, Internet bills of rights stress that Internet access should not merely remain a theoretical possibility, but 'must be ensured with respect to its substantive prerequisites'.[33] Restrictions to Internet access should be kept to a minimum; they should satisfy a legitimate interest and be proportionate.[34] Disconnection from the Internet or one of its services should be regarded as a solution of last resort and should be accompanied with adequate due process guarantees.[35] Public actors are called to remove all barriers favouring the persistence of the digital divide.[36] At the same time, they are urged to ensure that the use of digital technology should not become an indispensable requirement to access public services.[37] All individuals should be able to access the Internet on equal basis and without discrimination.[38] They should be able to do so by choosing their preferred device, software, or application.[39] Internet access should be offered at an affordable price.[40] However, in any case, the state is called to guarantee a public Internet access point to enhance inclusion in the digital world.[41]

The right to Internet access is not merely a right to connect, but is a right to 'make use of' the Internet, too.[42] Such use unavoidably implies that

32 Hannah Arendt, *The Origins of Totalitarianism* (Harcourt Brace Jovanovich 1979); see also Stefano Rodotà, *Il diritto di avere diritti* (Laterza 2012).

33 Camera dei Deputati (n 3), Article 2.3.

34 See Godwin (n 6), Article 11; 'Charter of Human Rights and Principles for the Internet' (n 3), Article 1.

35 See Gelman (n 8), Article 15; Murray (n 18), Article 1; Godwin (n 6), Article 9(b); PEN International, 'Declaration on Internet Freedom' <https://pen-international.org/app/uploads/PEN-Declaration_INTERNATIONALweb.pdf>, Article 2.c; Ujam Chukwuemeka Digital Rights and Freedom Bill (n 6), Section 13(17) ff; Council of Europe (n 1) para 2.1.5-7, 2.2.1, 2.2.2 and 2.2.5; African Declaration Group (n 1) 14.

36 See Social Innovation Society (n 2), Article 3; Camera dei Deputati (n 3), Article 2.5; Council of Europe (n 1) para 2.1.3.

37 See Just Net Coalition (n 8), Article 17; cf. 'Charta der Digitalen Grundrechte der Europäischen Union' (n 1), Article 9.

38 See Godwin (n 6), Article 2.8 and 5; Geneva Summit for Human Rights and Democracy (n 29), Article 1; Ujam Chukwuemeka Digital Rights and Freedom Bill (n 6), Section 15(5); African Declaration Group (n 1), Article 2; see also 'Charta der Digitalen Grundrechte der Europäischen Union' (n 1), Article 10; Murray (n 18), Article 2.

39 See, in particular, Camera dei Deputati (n 3), Article 2.4; Gelman (n 8), Article 14.

40 See UNESCO (n 1) para 3; African Declaration Group (n 1), Article 2.

41 See EUROCITIES Knowledge Society Forum – TeleCities (n 18), Article 1; NETmundial (n 31); Council of Europe (n 1) para 2.1.2.

42 See 'Charter of Human Rights and Principles for the Internet' (n 3), so the title of Article 1.

the individual has familiarity with digital technology tools, knows their functioning, their advantages and their risks. Internet bills of rights therefore specify that the right to Internet access necessarily entails a right to digital literacy.[43] Not a right to culture *through* the Internet, but a right to education *about* the Internet.[44] And not only a right to learn how digital technologies work but also how individuals can use them to exercise their rights.[45] The *Carta internazionale dei diritti digitali* talks of – my emphasis – '*civic* digital literacy':

> Everyone has the right to a civic digital literacy that enables to use all digital communication tools in order to become an active digital democratic citizen who is able to exercise his rights and freedoms in a conscious and informed way.[46]

Public actors play a special role in this context. Internet bills of rights vest them with the duty to educate the individual,[47] and to ensure that, in particular, vulnerable categories of people have all the necessary instruments to effectively use digital technologies.[48] Only an inclusive and diffuse digital literacy will really allow everyone to have a 'self-determined existence in the digital world'.[49]

A right to a digital forum

Internet bills of rights do not only establish the right of individuals to access *an* Internet, but they strive to define the architecture of how *the* Internet should be. Article 3 of the *Carta internazionale dei diritti digitali* paradigmatically reads:

43 See UNESCO (n 1), Article 10; Just Net Coalition (n 8), Article 13; Gelman (n 8), Article 19; EUROCITIES Knowledge Society Forum – TeleCities (n 18), Articles 3 ff; Murray (n 18), Article 3; Miriam Defensor Santiago The Magna Carta for Philippine Internet Freedom (n 3), Section 16.F; Social Innovation Society (n 2), Article 6; 'Marco Civil Da Internet, Lei No. 12.965, de 23 de Abril de 2014.' (n 3), Article 26; Camera dei Deputati (n 3), Article 3; Council of Europe (n 1) para 1.8.

44 Cf. UNESCO (n 1) para 10; Murray (n 18), Article 3; Ujam Chukwuemeka Digital Rights and Freedom Bill (n 6), Section 16(20); 'Charter of Human Rights and Principles for the Internet' (n 3), Article 11.

45 See Social Innovation Society (n 2), Article 6; 'Marco Civil Da Internet, Lei No. 12.965, de 23 de Abril de 2014.' (n 3), Article 26; Camera dei Deputati (n 3), Article 3.3.

46 Social Innovation Society (n 2), Article 6.

47 See Social Innovation Society (n 2), Article 6; 'Marco Civil Da Internet, Lei No. 12.965, de 23 de Abril de 2014.' (n 3), Article 26; Camera dei Deputati (n 3), Article 3.3; Council of Europe (n 1) para 1.8.

48 See Gelman (n 8), Article 19; EUROCITIES Knowledge Society Forum – TeleCities (n 18), Article 4; Murray (n 18), Article 3.

49 'Charta der Digitalen Grundrechte der Europäischen Union' (n 1), Article 14.

> Everyone has the right to freely access and participate in the digital public forum.[50]

One is instinctively led to simply read the term 'digital public forum' as 'the Internet', as a mere terminological variation. There is, however, a subtle difference between the two notions, which becomes clearer only from a comprehensive analysis of the content of Internet bills of rights.

These declarations translate the core values of contemporary constitutionalism in light of the characteristics of the digital society. Foundational constitutional principles, like equality, democracy and the rule of law, are in this way adapted to inform the 'largest public space that the humankind has never known', what we are accustomed to generally call 'the Internet'.[51] The digital public forum to which the provision quoted above refers is precisely that space, an Internet governed by such constitutional values. The *Carta internazionale dei diritti digitali* pledges that everyone should have the possibility to access and participate in *that* Internet.

Internet bills of rights comprehensively define the characteristics of this common space. They advocate for an Internet no longer at the mercy of the interests of the dominant actors, but a reality founded on determined essential values, roles, and principles of governance. A public space, which aims at the common good, where cultural diversity is preserved, which all individuals can use to exercise their fundamental rights. An instrument of democracy, and a democratic place at its turn. In this way, Internet bills of rights ultimately outline the contours of a new fundamental right: a right to a digital forum.[52]

Public service value

Today, the Internet is so crucial to the economy of fundamental rights that Internet bills of rights even claim its public service value.[53] Digital

50 Social Innovation Society (n 2), Article 3, my translation.

51 Stefano Rodotà, 'L'uomo nuovo di Internet' *La Repubblica* (28 October 2005) <https://ricerca.repubblica.it/repubblica/archivio/repubblica/2005/10/28/uomo-nuovo-di-internet.html> accessed 2 May 2019, my translation.

52 See Christoph Graber, 'Freedom and Affordances of the Net' (2018) 10 Washington University Jurisprudence Review 221, 251, who proposes a 'freedom of the Net' as a fundamental right protecting the Internet as an institution; see also Matthias C Kettemann, *The Normative Order of the Internet: A Theory of Rule and Regulation Online* (Oxford University Press 2020), who explains in detail the rationale of a protection of and from the Internet. Cf. Universal Declaration of Human Rights, Article 28, which reads: 'Everyone is entitled to a social and international order in which the rights and freedoms set forth in this Declaration can be fully realized'; see also 'Charter of Human Rights and Principles for the Internet' (n 3), Article 19; Gelman (n 8), Article 22.

53 See 'Charter of Human Rights and Principles for the Internet' (n 3), Article 11; UNESCO (n 1) para 1; African Declaration Group (n 1), Article 9; 'Marco Civil Da Internet, Lei No. 12.965, de 23 de Abril de 2014.' (n 3), Article 2; Just Net Coalition (n 8), Articles 1 ff.

technologies are defined as a key 'global resource which should be managed in the public interest'.[54] As a basic rule, the *Delhi Declaration for a Just and Equitable Internet* resolutely affirms:

> 2. The Internet must be maintained as a public space. Where a divergence emerges between the utility of the Internet for public interest purposes and the particular interests of Internet service or technology companies, the public interest must take priority, and the service must be subjected to regulation as a public utility.[55]

According to most Internet bills of rights, the digital public forum should be based on a 'secure, stable, resilient, reliable and trustworthy network'.[56] Beyond its integrity, the Internet should maintain a transparent, open, and decentralised architecture, so as to ensure free access, interoperability, innovation, and avoid the creation of concentrations of powers in the management of the network.[57] The use of free and open source software is encouraged in public institutions.[58] Research funded by public bodies should always be freely available online.[59] Internet bills of rights strongly advocate in favour of a non-proprietary vision of the Internet. Again, in the words of the *Delhi Declaration for a Just and Equitable Internet*:

> 3. The Internet's basic or essential functionalities and services, such as email, web search facilities, and social networking platforms, must be made available to all people as public goods.

54 NETmundial (n 31).

55 Just Net Coalition (n 8), Article 2.

56 African Declaration Group (n 1), Article 9; see also CGI.br - Comitê Gestor da Internet no Brasil, 'Principles for the Governance and Use of the Internet' (*CGI.br - Comitê Gestor da Internet no Brasil*, 2009) <https://cgi.br> accessed 5 July 2019, Article 8; Council of Europe, Committee of Ministers, 'Declaration by the Committee of Ministers on Internet Governance Principles' (21 September 2011) para 6 <https://search.coe.int/cm/Pages/result_details.aspx?ObjectID=09000016805cc2f6> accessed 21 May 2019; UNESCO (n 1) para 8; NETmundial (n 31); 'Marco Civil Da Internet, Lei No. 12.965, de 23 de Abril de 2014.' (n 3), Article 3; Camera dei Deputati (n 3), Article 13.

57 See Open Society Institute – Regional Internet Program and Parliamentary Human Rights Foundation (n 18), Preamble and Articles A.3, A.4; Geneva Summit for Human Rights and Democracy (n 29), Article 2; Council of Europe, Committee of Ministers (n 56) paras 7 and 8; Just Net Coalition (n 8), Article 8; UNESCO (n 1) paras 5 and 15; European Commission (n 3), Section 1, Chapter 2, Paragraph 2; Miriam Defensor Santiago The Magna Carta for Philippine Internet Freedom (n 3), Section 4; NETmundial (n 31); African Declaration Group (n 1), Article 1; CGI.br - Comitê Gestor da Internet no Brasil (n 56), Article 9; Camera dei Deputati (n 3), Article 14(2).

58 'Charter of Human Rights and Principles for the Internet' (n 3), Article 11(f).

59 'Charter of Human Rights and Principles for the Internet' (n 3), Article 11(e).

4. Community-owned and not-for-profit infrastructure, applications, services and content, must be encouraged and enabled including through access to public funding and by other means.[60]

Internet bills of rights also stress the necessity of an economically fairer and more equitable Internet whose wealth, also deriving from state taxation, is better distributed within single societies and at global level.[61] Lastly, objectives that should inform all policies aiming to promote the public service value of the Internet are the preservation of cultural and linguistic diversity on the network,[62] the maintenance of a peaceful purpose in the development of any digital technology[63] and, more broadly, the safeguard of a democratic society.[64]

Responsibilities

A digital forum should be based on a clear allocation of responsibilities. The *Charter of Human Rights and Principles for the Internet*, establishes as a basic rule:

> Everybody has the duty and responsibility to respect the rights of all individuals in the online environment.[65]

In particular, dominant actors hold special responsibilities. According to the UNESCO's *Code of ethics for the information society*:

> Member States are responsible for ensuring an inclusive, relevant, up-to-date and legal environment for the development of the information society.[66]

This obligation, however, does not exempt private companies from assessing the potential impact of their behaviour on fundamental rights. In this regard, the PEN *Declaration on Digital Freedom* states:

60 Just Net Coalition (n 8), Articles 3 and 4.
61 Just Net Coalition (n 8), Articles 6 and 7.
62 See 'Charta der Digitalen Grundrechte der Europäischen Union' (n 1), Article 12; Council of Europe, Committee of Ministers (n 56); NETmundial (n 31); African Declaration Group (n 1), Article 6; CGI.br - Comitê Gestor da Internet no Brasil (n 56), Article 4; 'Charter of Human Rights and Principles for the Internet' (n 3), Article 11.
63 See Just Net Coalition (n 8), Article 5.
64 See CGI.br - Comitê Gestor da Internet no Brasil (n 56), Article 1; Council of Europe, Committee of Ministers (n 56).
65 'Charter of Human Rights and Principles for the Internet' (n 3), Article 20(a).
66 UNESCO (n 1) para 18.

> c. Technology companies have the duty to determine how their products, services, and policies impact human rights in countries in which they intend to operate. If violations are likely, or violations may be inextricably linked to the use of products or services, the companies should modify or withdraw their proposed plans in order to respect human rights.[67]

There is however a shared consensus among Internet bills of rights on the opportunity to exempt some Internet intermediaries from secondary liability arising from the activity of their users.[68] The *Principles for the Governance and Use of the Internet* for example establish:

> All action taken against illicit activity on the network must be aimed at those directly responsible for such activities, and not at the means of access and transport, always upholding the fundamental principles of freedom, privacy and the respect for human rights.[69]

Of course, such an exemption does not free these intermediaries from any liability when a court or other national authority require them to perform a specific action, such as removing content from their platform.[70] At the same time, Internet bills of rights acknowledge that other kinds of intermediaries, such as those hosting social media websites, hold more responsibilities and should play an active role in guaranteeing the respect of fundamental rights on their platforms.[71] In this regard, the *African Declaration on Internet Rights and Freedoms* specifies:

> To the extent that intermediaries operate self-regulatory systems, and/or make judgement calls on content and privacy issues, all such decisions should be made taking into account the need to protect expression that is legitimate under the principles provided for under international human rights standards [...]. Processes developed by intermediaries should be transparent and include provisions for appeals.[72]

67 PEN International (n 35), Article 4(c).

68 See CGI.br - Comitê Gestor da Internet no Brasil (n 56), Article 7; NETmundial (n 31); African Declaration Group (n 1) 14; 'Marco Civil Da Internet, Lei No. 12.965, de 23 de Abril de 2014.' (n 3), Article 18.

69 CGI.br - Comitê Gestor da Internet no Brasil (n 56), Article 7.

70 See 'Marco Civil Da Internet, Lei No. 12.965, de 23 de Abril de 2014.' (n 3), Article 19.

71 See 'Charta der Digitalen Grundrechte der Europäischen Union' (n 1), Article 4(3); cf. African Declaration Group (n 1), Article 11.

72 African Declaration Group (n 1) 14.

Governance

The north star of the digital forum is not only the respect of fundamental rights but also the pursuit of specific governance principles.[73] Internet bills of rights shape them by re-contextualising the constitutional values of democracy and the rule of law.[74] These declarations do not include detailed norms of an organisational or institutional nature establishing how the digital forum should be governed.[75] In lieu of specific meta-rules, Internet bills of rights enshrine a general set of values that should inform Internet governance.[76] The *Charter of Human Rights and Principles for the Internet* summarises them in this way:

> Internet governance must be driven by principles of openness, inclusiveness and accountability and exercised in transparent and multilateral manner.[77]

The principles of openness, inclusiveness, and multilateralism translate the constitutional value of democracy. The digital world should not be subject exclusively to the rules of dominant actors.[78] The technical community, alone, cannot assume the responsibility to regulate the Internet.[79] Single individuals should be empowered to take an active part in the governance of the Internet, even those who have not access to it yet.[80] The digital forum should be governed according to a multistakeholder logic.[81] In the words of the Council of Europe:

73 See, in particular, 'Charter of Human Rights and Principles for the Internet' (n 3), Article 19(a); Godwin (n 6), see para on 'governance'.

74 See Council of Europe, Committee of Ministers (n 56) para 1.

75 See African Declaration Group (n 1), which limits itself to state that 'Independent, well-resourced, multistakeholder bodies should be established to guide Internet policy at the national level'.

76 See 'Charter of Human Rights and Principles for the Internet' (n 3), Article 19; Godwin (n 6), para on 'governance'; Praxis (n 3), Principle no 11; NETmundial (n 31); 'Marco Civil Da Internet, Lei No. 12.965, de 23 de Abril de 2014.' (n 3), Article 24; Council of Europe (n 1) para 1.4; Camera dei Deputati (n 3), Article 14(5); CGI.br - Comitê Gestor da Internet no Brasil (n 56), Article 2; Just Net Coalition (n 8), Article 18.

77 'Charter of Human Rights and Principles for the Internet' (n 3), Article 19(a).

78 See Camera dei Deputati (n 3), Article 14(2); cf. Just Net Coalition (n 8).

79 See Just Net Coalition (n 8), Article 20.

80 See Council of Europe, Committee of Ministers (n 56) para 4; Just Net Coalition (n 8).

81 See Council of Europe, Committee of Ministers (n 56) para 2; 'Charter of Human Rights and Principles for the Internet' (n 3), Article 19; Praxis (n 3), Principle no 11; NETmundial (n 31); Just Net Coalition (n 8), Articles 18 and 19; 'Marco Civil Da Internet, Lei No. 12.965, de 23 de Abril de 2014.' (n 3), Article 24; Council of Europe (n 1) para 1.4 and 7; Steve Peers, 'Internet Bill of Rights' <http://www.europarl.europa.eu/RegData/etudes/etudes/join/2009/408335/IPOL-LIBE_ET(2009)408335_EN.pdf>; Camera dei Deputati (n 3), Article 14; CGI.br - Comitê Gestor da Internet no Brasil (n 56), Article 2; African Declaration Group (n 1) 20 and Article 12.

> Internet governance arrangements should ensure [...] the full participation of governments, the private sector, civil society, the technical community and users, taking into account their specific roles and responsibilities.[82]

Such roles are not pre-determined[83]; they can vary according to the issue at stake but should always be exercised in a transparent and accountable manner. In light of the principle of the rule of law, Internet bills of rights require that Internet governance actors establish clear rules, procedures, and mechanisms of review.[84]

Within Internet bills of rights, the concept of popular sovereignty ultimately seems to acquire a new meaning.[85] All Internet stakeholders become the 'people' of the virtual environment. Popular sovereignty is not merely claimed in the constituent phase, and subsequently *de facto* delegated to a body of elected representatives.[86] It encompasses the process of governing the Internet too. Democracy, in the vision claimed by Internet bills of rights, means that all Internet actors have the right to directly shape the governance of the digital world. Only in this way can the Internet really become a true, democratic, digital forum.

82 Council of Europe, Committee of Ministers (n 56) para 2.
83 Cf. Praxis (n 3), Principle no 11; NETmundial (n 31).
84 See, in particular, NETmundial (n 31); Just Net Coalition (n 8), Article 18.
85 Cf. Milton Mueller, *Will the Internet Fragment? Sovereignty, Globalization and Cyberspace* (Polity 2017) 122 ff.
86 Cf. Dieter Grimm, *Sovereignty: The Origin and Future of a Political and Legal Concept* (Columbia University Press 2015).

13 Conclusion

Contrasting constitutional anaemia

Neil Postman opens his book *Technopoly* with the myth of Thamus and Theuth from Plato's *Phaedrus*.[1] Socrates tells that Theuth, the ibis-headed god of wisdom, magic and the dead, illustrated to the Egyptian king Thamus the advantages of many of his inventions, among which was writing. Thamus however realistically observed that 'the discoverer of an art is not the best judge of the good or harm which will accrue to those who practice it'.[2] The pharaoh then commented on each of Theuth's inventions, specifying if, to his eyes, they looked useful or not for the Egyptian people. In this way, writing, which was presented by Theuth as 'a sure receipt for memory and wisdom',[3] was surprisingly dismissed by Thamus as a source of forgetfulness and ignorance:

> Those who acquire it will cease to exercise their memory and become forgetful; they will rely on writing to bring things to their remembrance by external signs instead of by their own internal resources. What you have discovered is a receipt for recollection, not for memory. And as for wisdom, your pupils will have the reputation for it without the reality: they will receive a quantity of information without proper instruction, and in consequence be thought very knowledgeable when they are for the most part quite ignorant. And because they are filled with the conceit of wisdom instead of real wisdom they will be a burden to society.[4]

One of the multifarious teachings of this anecdote is that the impact of new technologies on our society needs to always be appraised, simultaneously, from multiple perspectives. Thamus would have prevented writing from

1 Postman (n 744) ch 1; Plato, *Phaedrus and Letters VII and VIII* (Walter Hamilton tr, Penguin Classics 1973).
2 Plato (n 880) 96.
3 Plato (n 880) 96.
4 Plato (n 880) 96.

DOI: 10.4324/9781003256908-13

spreading into Egypt. Theuth, however, neglected the negative aspects of introducing his invention. The souls of Thamus and Theuth have to be reconciled. One has to be Theuth and Thamus at the same time, assessing not only the benefits of innovation but also its drawbacks.

In the first part of this work, it has been essential to strike a balance between the enthusiasm of the Egyptian god of wisdom and the prudence of king Thamus in order to objectively analyse the impact of the digital revolution on the constitutional ecosystem. As explained in Chapter 2, digital technology, on the one hand, has provided individuals with an unprecedented possibility to exercise their fundamental rights, in particular those rotating around the exchange of information. Today, everyone can become a public speaker or a pamphleteer; every citizen can actively participate in the democratic life of their country by electronically accessing government information and reacting to it. Without Internet access, one would not be able to enjoy the same standard of rights that digital technology offers. However, on the other hand, digital technology has increased the power of states over our digital lives. Technology companies managing and selling digital products and services essentially determine the extent to which we can enjoy our fundamental rights online. The rate of violation of fundamental rights has dramatically increased due to a significant series of risks that stem from the capillary use of digital technology in multiple contexts of our life.

The equilibrium that constitutional norms pursue has been significantly affected by the advent of the digital revolution, both in a positive and negative sense. However, the constitutional ecosystem does not lie inert vis-à-vis these challenges. It reacts, generating a series of normative responses. Chapter 3 has examined examples of the progressive affirmation of a right to electronically access government information, the development of further principles related to the right to data protection, the debates on the opportunity to recognise a right to Internet access, and the elaboration of norms guaranteeing due process rights in the context of online content moderation. We are witnessing a new constitutional moment, and this is not something unusual.

Changes are an integral part of the cycle of all constitutional systems. Constitutional norms are historical products. Borrowing Allott's words, they represent 'the fruit of a society's contemplation of itself in time and space'.[5] This unavoidably implies that parts, or the whole constitutional architecture can become no longer updated due to societal changes. In those circumstances, constitutional mutations are required. However, a peculiarity of the present constitutional moment lies in its global reach. In the digital environment, the centrality of the nation-state as a dominant actor fades. Multinational corporations exercise their power within virtual fiefs that overtake Westphalian boundaries. The normative counteractions that

5 Philip Allott, *Eunomia: New Order for a New World* (Oxford University Press 2001) 133.

emerge to face the challenges of the digital revolution are therefore generated in multiple contexts: not only within the state but also beyond. In Chapter 4, we observed the materialisation of constitutional responses in traditional constitutions and in civil society declarations of rights, at the level of ordinary law and within the private regulations of non-state actors, in the decisions of conventional courts and in the judgments of private arbitrators.

The process of constitutionalisation of the digital society is multifaceted, intrinsically fragmented. There is no single constitutional discourse, but a plurality of overlapping constitutional layers is the only solution to address the complexities of a global society. As explained in Chapter 5, the answer of the constitutional ecosystem to the challenges of the digital revolution is consequently complex and multilevel. The process of constitutionalisation of the digital society is not a *fait accompli* but an ongoing, gradual process. It is not simply an operation of top-down codification but a broader process of elaboration of norms that includes bottom-up instances from different societal sectors.

The process of constitutionalisation of the digital society is articulated and fragmented, but at the same time unified by a shared willingness not to depart from the roots of contemporary constitutionalism. To restore a state of equilibrium in the society, it is not sufficient to transplant constitutional concepts and mechanisms that were designed for an analogue world into the digital galaxy. One has to undertake an operation of translation of constitutional values. The constitutional counteractions to the challenges of the digital society maintain their reference point in the principles of contemporary constitutionalism. They introduce new constitutional safeguards by adapting the core values of contemporary constitutionalism to the mutated context of the digital society. Chapter 6 proposed the notion of digital constitutionalism denoting this movement of thought that advocates the translation of the ideals and principles of contemporary constitutionalism in light of the exigencies of the digital environment. Digital constitutionalism would not represent a new, autonomous form of constitutionalism, rather it must be seen as an internal theoretical layer of contemporary constitutionalism. Digital constitutionalism aims to preserve the DNA of contemporary constitutionalism. It translates its foundational values, perpetuating them in the context of the digital society.

Reacting to the challenges of the digital society, adapting the principles of contemporary constitutionalism to the mutated social reality, ultimately means starting to contrast a looming state of constitutional anaemia. Today, the societal transformations prompted by the advent of the digital revolution ferment under a vault of constitutional norms shaped for an analogue society. The constitutional system struggles to encompass new social phenomena. At times, constitutional norms are dumb vis-à-vis the novel challenges of the digital environment. What are our fundamental rights in the digital environment? What are the guarantees that all dominant actors, be they public and private, should respect? Constitutional law fails to fully convey its prescriptive message to the actors of contemporary society. The constitutional dimension then gradually becomes anaemic: new societal lymph no longer circulates into the veins of its norms. It remains crystallised in an analogue time.

The growing mismatch between society and constitutional norms is enhancing a perception of the absence of rules for the digital world and worrisomely leads to a form of disorientation. In this way, the anaemic state of the constitutional system generates a sense of anomie within the society.[6] Existing constitutional law is perceived as obsolete because it is no longer a living instrument. Its centrality within the legal order progressively fades and, consequently, the individuals no longer understand which principles should guide their action in the digital environment.

The legacy of Internet bills of rights

The second part of this work has analysed one of the most peculiar answers to this phenomenon: the emergence of Internet bills of rights. As illustrated in Chapter 7, the ambitious idea of drafting a 'constitution' for the Internet, originally advocated at academic level, has had a significant following, resulting in the publication of dozens of charters. These documents aim to articulate constitutional rights and principles for the digital society but have been mostly neglected by the scholarship, given their lack of binding legal

6 On the concept of 'constitutional anomie', see Matthew Flinders, *Democratic Drift: Majoritarian Modification and Democratic Anomie in the United Kingdom* (Oxford University Press 2009) ch 1: here anomie is in the sense of disorientation characterising the strategy of a political party in the context of constitutional reform: 'Constitutional anomie is a debilitating condition. Its symptoms include the introduction of reforms in a manner bereft of any underlying logic or explicit principles combined with the inability to adopt a strategic approach which is sensitive to the inter-related nature of any constitutional configuration'; see also Matthew Flinders, 'Constitutional Anomie: Patterns of Democracy and "The Governance of Britain"' (2009) 44 Government and Opposition 385; cf. Paul Blokker, 'Constitutionalism and Constitutional Anomie in the New Europe' (2010) 53 Quaderni del Dipartimento di Sociologia e Ricerca Sociale 7 <https://papers.ssrn.com/abstract=1719095> accessed 21 August 2019: 'in contemporary Europe, there is arguably a situation of anomie in the sense that there seems to exist a profound mismatch between existing institutions, institutionalised models and norms, and imaginaries (here designated as modern, Westphalian constitutionalism based on a unitary nation-state) and a rapidly changing political and societal context that does in crucial ways not correspond to an institutionalised, Westphalian framework. In other words, there are a number of clear discrepancies between institutions and society'; Blokker, 'Grassroots Constitutional Politics in Iceland' (n 336) 2: 'Such constitutional frictions might be understood as forms of what I call "constitutional anomie", that is, a distance between existing, institutionalized constitutional orders, on the one hand, and wider societal perceptions, interpretations and tendencies, on the other'; cf. Emile Durkheim, *The Division of Labour in Society* (Steven Lukes ed, WD Halls tr, Palgrave Macmillan 2013): for Durkheim, anomie denotes the absence of regulation caused by the sudden advent of industrialisation in the economic context.

force. Most of them, indeed, stem from initiatives of single individuals or civil society groups. They are not the output of institutionalised processes but were simply published on the web. However, as argued in Chapter 8, these declarations are significant in better understanding the current constitutional moment precisely because they do not aim to set in stone unmodifiable tables of the law for the digital age. Internet bills of rights are in this way free to experiment and innovate. They become a ductile and plastic instrument through which different societal actors can express their needs, freed from the formalisms of institutionalised political processes. They can adopt more inclusive mechanisms of deliberation, ultimately fostering democracy and participation in the conversation on the rights and principles for the digital age.

At the same time, Internet bills of rights claim their belonging to the constitutional dimension by adopting the traditional language of constitutions. In this way, these declarations make visible a constitutional debate that would have otherwise risked remaining concealed in the recesses of politics, economy or computer science. The language of constitutions purveys a rich cultural baggage to develop new concepts and mechanisms. It represents a *lingua franca* that unifies a variety of inputs and transmits them in the wider conversation on digital rights and principles that is taking place at multiple levels in the constitutional ecosystem. These declarations are many and diverse in terms of content. However, they do not seek to declare their final word on the best constitutional solution for the digital age. Internet bills of rights aim to gradually nourish a debate, to take a cogitated and far-sighted choice on which constitutional principles should guide the virtual environment. Their legacy essentially lies in their message.

The emergence of Internet bills of rights represents an alarm sign for the whole constitutional ecosystem. Comprehensively examined, these documents can be used as a litmus test to identify the area of constitutional law that starts to show symptoms of anaemia and is consequently perceived to be in need for urgent changes. Interestingly, as Chapter 9 has illustrated, these declarations generally identify the digital environment as their scope of application but factually struggle to define its boundaries. Exemplarily, a definition of what the Internet is does not exist. In this way, one can understand that a work of conceptual definition has still to be done in order to ensure that constitutional norms addressing the challenges of the digital society will be effectively future-proof and will be able to survive the rapid development of digital technology.

The appearance of Internet bills of rights also highlights the need of the constitutional ecosystem to overtake its traditional anchoring to the state dimension. As examined in Chapter 10, these declarations appraise the global scale of contemporary society and pragmatically consider multinational technology corporations as new dominant actors that should be subject to constitutional obligations besides nation-states. In this way, Internet bills of rights highlight the presence of a gap in the constitutional ecosystem stemming from the dis-alignment between constitutional norms that are still tailored to states and the digital environment, where the guarantee of individual rights is *de facto* entrusted to private actors. A new, enlarged social contract for the digital society is claimed. Perpetuating the values of constitutionalism in the digital age implies going beyond the regulation of the binary relation citizens-state to encompass individuals, public and private dominant actors altogether, and on a global basis. A new 'we' surfaces in the constitutional dimension, and consequently more inclusive constitutional processes of deliberation are required. Openness, collaboration, participation, and multistakeholderism are proclaimed as the guiding values of future constitution-making.

Lastly, as illustrated in Chapter 11, Internet bills of rights pragmatically offer a vivid image of how the core values of contemporary constitutionalism should be articulated in the digital society. They show that digital constitutionalism should not depart from the key principles which have been elaborated over the past centuries. Values like the respect of human dignity, life, freedom, the protection of vulnerable categories of people, economic freedom, and safeguarding the environment are proclaimed unaltered. However, other principles need to be translated and further developed in order to preserve their telos in the digital society. Certain constitutional principles, such as the right to freedom of expression, freedom and secrecy of correspondence, and freedom of association and assembly, simply require to be reiterated in the context of the virtual environment. Individuals can still easily grasp their original message. Conversely, Internet bills of rights advocate for a deeper translation of the values of non-discrimination, privacy and due process. These principles are generalised and re-specified in the light of the characteristics of the digital society. In this way, these declarations establish the new principles of net-neutrality and multilingualism on the net stemming from the right to non-discrimination. The value of privacy is translated into the prohibition of mass surveillance, a right to anonymity and to encryption. The principle of due process is extended to forms of trials managed by private actors, such as in the context of online content moderation.

Moreover, as examined in Chapter 12, in the vision proposed by the Internet bills of rights, the protection of personal data definitively acquires its independence as an autonomous right, a value to protect *per se*, and not only when linked to the respect of individual privacy. E-democracy also emerges as a new fundamental principle enabling the individual to counterbalance the power of the state through the rights to open data, to e-services, and to e-participation in democratic life. The cornerstone of the constitutional ecosystem in the digital age then becomes a new right to Internet access, a vital gateway to exercising fundamental rights in the contemporary society. Such a principle would require that access be provided at affordable costs, if not for free, and in any case without discrimination and on a continuous basis without unjustifiable interruptions. The right to Internet access also implies a right to be able to make use of the Internet, thus to be educated on how to use it in order to exercise one's own personal and civic freedoms.

Internet bills of rights ultimately stress that, in the digital age, the Internet itself, intended as a digital public forum founded on determined essential values, roles, and principles of governance should be protected by constitutional guarantees. It is a right of all individuals and, at the same time, an obligation of all dominant actors to maintain it as such. Its public service value should be preserved by ensuring the continued integrity, stability, resiliency, openness, transparency, and decentralisation of its architecture. The Internet should aim for the promotion of an economically fairer world, the preservation of cultural and linguistic diversity, and the maintenance of peace. The digital forum should be based on a clear allocation of responsibilities and always be guided by the values of democracy and the rule of law. Its mechanisms of governance should be open and inclusive. No single societal sector can assume alone the responsibility to regulate the digital forum. The Internet should be governed by a multistakeholder logic, where all interested actors can participate on the basis of clear and transparent procedures, and subject to mechanisms of review.

Challenges of digital constitutionalism

In the constitutional landscape, Internet bills of rights do not represent an isolated counteraction to the challenges of the digital revolution. These declarations emerge within a constitutional conglomerate, an amalgam of constitutional layers that are elaborating a response to the complexities of contemporary society on multiple levels. Internet bills of rights do not shine at the top of the pyramid of legal sources; they do not possess that primary legal value that generally characterise constitutional norms. Yet, these texts intentionally adopt the language of constitutions to be part of the conversation reflecting which rights and principles should guide the digital society. This work has provided a comprehensive view of the contribution of these charters to such a debate. It is hoped that this will represent a basis to further advance the process of translation of our core constitutional values in the context of the digital age. Moreover, it is wished that future research will also study the extent to which the message of Internet bills of rights is permeating the rest of the porous constitutional conglomerate and, more broadly, how the other layers of the constitutional ecosystem are reacting to the advent of the digital revolution, with particular attention to national constitutions, international constitutional instruments, and non-state actors' self-regulation.

The results of such research will be quintessential to address the main challenges that digital constitutionalism currently faces. First of all, the constitutional ecosystem will have to find a suitable mix of normative instruments that will be synergistically capable to instil the core values of contemporary constitutionalism in the whole digital universe. Unfortunately, the Kelsenian pyramid of legal sources does not reflect the reality of the multilevel and composite constitutional conglomerate anymore.[7] Enshrining new principles in national constitutions is no longer enough. Digital constitutionalism will have to identify a more complex normative alchemy.

Secondly, the success of digital constitutionalism will also depend on its capability of crafting a future-proof constitutional language. The *NETmundial Multistakeholder Statement* talks of the 'agility' of the norm.[8] Constitutional counteractions should be able to survive the continuous, fast development of digital technology. They should strive to enshrine principles which are technology-neutral and refrain from addressing the specific technological issues of the *hic et nunc*. Only in this way, the danger of precocious constitutional anaemia will be forestalled. Constitutional norms certainly do not have to last forever. However, they should not aim to establish detailed rules but rather to define orienting principles.

The third, and probably the most demanding, challenge of digital constitutionalism lies within its mission of crafting a series of guiding norms for the coming decades. Contemporary society is characterised by a looming sense of anomie. It claims a set of principles that are able to orient its future development. Digital constitutionalism advocates a translation of the core values of contemporary constitutionalism. To generate guiding norms, one needs to fully understand what these values mean in the context of the digital environment. Constitutional law, indeed, is not only a mere reflection of society. The constitutional ecosystem also aims to shape the social reality according to determined values.[9] Constitutional instruments work differently from telescopes; they do not project the image of a society crystallised in the past. They devise the architecture of an ideal future and enshrine the principles that should guide societal actors to attain such a vision.[10] Lessig compares them with lighthouses, fixed reference points that help to navigate in the darkness.[11]

Constitutional changes are certainly problematical and laborious. Machiavelli wrote that:

7 On this point, see Peer Zumbansen, 'Comparative, Global and Transnational Constitutionalism: The Emergence of a Transnational Legal-Pluralist Order' (2012) 1 Global Constitutionalism 16, 50: 'the constitution is no longer a "public law" text, emanating from state authority and sitting at the pinnacle of a pyramid of legal normativity. Instead, constitutions – written or unwritten – and constitutional law must facilitate the intersection of law and politics in a radically heterarchic, modern society [...]'.

8 NETmundial (n 618).

9 See Lessig, *Code* (n 151), who distinguishes between 'codifying' and 'transformative' constitutions.

10 See Allott (n 884), who distinguishes between a 'formal', a 'material' and an 'ideal' constitution.

11 Lessig, *Code* (n 151) 4.

> There is nothing more difficult to arrange, more doubtful of success, and more dangerous to carry through than initiating change in a State's constitution. The innovator makes enemies of all those who prospered under the old order, and only lukewarm support is forthcoming from those who could prosper under the new. Their support is lukewarm partly from fear of their adversaries, who have the existing law on their side, and partly because men are generally incredulous, never really trusting new things unless they have tested them by experience.[12]

However, notwithstanding these complexities, facing the risk of an increasingly anaemic constitutional ecosystem and a disoriented society, all the stakeholders are called to give their contribution to the present constitutional moment. Empowering the constitutional framework to address the challenges of the digital revolution cannot wait anymore. It is necessary to forestall the development of a digital society devoid of the values for which our ancestors fought over the past few centuries. This is a collective duty: not only to respect our history but also for a sense of responsibility that we owe to the future. As an old adage says, we have to remember that we have not only inherited this world from our ancestors, but that, above all, we are borrowing it from our grandchildren.

12 Niccolò Machiavelli, *The Prince* (George Bull tr, Penguin Classics 1961) ch VI.

Appendix A

The dataset includes the selection of Internet bills of rights analysed in the book.

Name	Author	Year	URL
Declaration of Human Rights in Cyberspace	Robert B. Gelman	1997	http://www.be-in.com/10/rightsdec.html
Open Internet Policy Principles	Open Society Institute – Regional Internet Program Parliamentary Human Rights Foundation	1997	http://mailman.anu.edu.au/pipermail/link/1997-March/026302.html
Charter of Rights of Citizens in the Knowledge Society	Eurocities	2005	https://www.comune.modena.it/storiaretecivica/Materiale_PDF_2_marzo/Brugi_Miranda2.pdf
Principles for the Governance and Use of the Internet	Brazilian Internet Steering Committee	2009	http://www.cgi.br/principles/
Internet bill of rights, annex to Strengthening Security and Fundamental Freedoms on the Internet – an EU Policy on the Fight Against Cyber Crime	Steve Peers	2009	http://www.europarl.europa.eu/RegData/etudes/etudes/join/2009/408335/IPOL-LIBE_ET(2009)408335_EN.pdf

Name	Author	Year	URL
A Bill of Rights for the Internet	Andrew Murray	2010	http://theitlawyer.blogspot.com/2010/10/bill-of-rights-for-internet.html
Geneva Declaration on Internet Freedom	Geneva Summit for Human Rights, Tolerance and Democracy	2010	http://atlarge-lists.icann.org/pipermail/lac-discuss-es/2010/001287.html
The Charter of Human Rights and Principles for the Internet 5th ed.	Internet Rights and Principles Coalition-Internet Governance Forum	2010	http://internetrightsandprinciples.org/site/wp-content/uploads/2018/10/IRPC_english_5thedition.pdf
Declaration by the Committee of Ministers on Internet governance principles	Committee of Ministers – Council of Europe	2011	https://search.coe.int/cm/Pages/result_details.aspx?ObjectID=09000016805cc2f6
Code of ethics for the information society	UNESCO	2011	http://unesdoc.unesco.org/images/0021/002126/212696e.pdf
PEN Declaration on Digital Freedom	PEN international	2012	https://pen-international.org/app/uploads/PEN-Declaration_INTERNATIONALweb.pdf
Guiding Principles of Internet Freedom	Praxis	2012	http://www.praxis.ee/fileadmin/tarmo/Projektid/Valitsemine_ja_kodanikeühiskond/Praxis_Theses_Internet.pdf
The Digital Bill of Rights A Crowd-sourced Declaration of Rights	Free Internet Activism Sub-group – Reddit	2012	https://www.reddit.com/r/fia/comments/vuj37/digital_bill_of_rights_1st_draft/ + https://www.reddit.com/r/fia/comments/215zfk/after_seeing_tim_bernerslees_call_for_a_digital/
Code of EU Online Rights	European Commission	2012	https://ec.europa.eu/digital-single-market/sites/digital-agenda/files/Code%20EU%20online%20rights%20EN%20final%202.pdf
Digital Bill of Rights	Mashable	2013	http://mashable.com/2013/08/12/digital-bill-of-rights-crowdsource/#w5d133UGHOq5

Name	Author	Year	URL
Magna Carta for Philippine Internet Freedom	Miriam Defensor Santiago – Philippines	2013	https://www.senate.gov.ph/lisdata/1446312119!.pdf
Internet Governance Principles – NETmundial Multistakeholder Statement	NETmundial	2014	http://netmundial.br/wp-content/uploads/2014/04/NETmundial-Multistakeholder-Document.pdf
Carta internazionale dei diritti digitali	Social Innovation Society	2014	http://www.soinsociety.org/carta-internazionale-dei-diritti-digitali/
African Declaration on Internet Rights and Freedoms	African Declaration Group	2014	http://africaninternetrights.org/wp-content/uploads/2015/11/African-Declaration-English-FINAL.pdf
Marco Civil da Internet	Brazil	2014	https://www.publicknowledge.org/assets/uploads/documents/APPROVED-MARCO-CIVIL-MAY-2014.pdf
Delhi Declaration for a Just and Equitable Internet	Global meeting "Towards a Just and Equitable Internet" [Just Net Coalition]	2014	http://justnetcoalition.org/delhi-declaration
Declaration of Internet Rights	Commission – Italian Chamber of Deputies	2015	http://www.camera.it/application/xmanager/projects/leg17/commissione_internet/testo_definitivo_inglese.pdf
The Great Charter for Cambodian Internet Freedom	Mike Godwin	2015	https://www.linkedin.com/pulse/great-charter-cambodian-internet-freedom-mike-godwin
Charter of Digital Fundamental Rights of the European Union	Zeit-Stiftung	2016 (2018 revised version)	https://digitalcharta.eu/wp-content/uploads/Digital_Charter_english_2018.pdf
Digital Rights and Freedom Bill	Ujam Chukwuemeka – Nigeria	2016	http://eie.ng/wp-content/uploads/2016/06/Digital-Rights-and-Freedom-Bill-2016.pdf
Recommendation CM/Rec(2016)5 of the Committee of Ministers to member States on Internet freedom	Committee of Ministers – Council of Europe	2016	https://search.coe.int/cm/Pages/result_details.aspx?ObjectId=09000016806415fa

Bibliography

Akdeniz Y, *Internet Child Pornography and the Law: National and International Responses* (Ashgate 2008)

Alford CF, 'International Human Rights, Natural Law, and Locke' in C Fred Alford (ed), *Narrative, Nature, and the Natural Law: From Aquinas to International Human Rights* (Palgrave Macmillan US 2010)

Allott P, *Eunomia: New Order for a New World* (Oxford University Press 2001)

Alsenoy BV and Koekkoek M, 'Internet and Jurisdiction after Google Spain: The Extraterritorial Reach of the "Right to Be Delisted"' (2015) 5 International Data Privacy Law 105

Alston P, 'A Third Generation of Solidarity Rights: Progressive Development or Obfuscation of International Human Rights Law?' (1982) 29 Netherlands International Law Review 307

——— (ed), *Peoples' Rights* (Oxford University Press 2001)

Amoretti F and Gargiulo E, 'Dall'appartenenza Materiale All'appartenenza Virtuale? La Cittadinanza Elettronica Fra Processi Di Costituzionalizzazione Della Rete e Dinamiche Di Esclusione' (2010) Politica del diritto 353

Arato A, 'Conventions, Constituent Assemblies, and Round Tables: Models, Principles and Elements of Democratic Constitution-Making' (2012) 1 Global Constitutionalism 173

———, *The Adventures of the Constituent Power: Beyond Revolutions?* (Cambridge University Press 2017)

Arendt H, *The Origins of Totalitarianism* (Harcourt Brace Jovanovich 1979)

Azzariti G, 'Internet e Costituzione' (2011) Politica del diritto 367

Bani M, 'Crowdsourcing Democracy: The Case of Icelandic Social Constitutionalism' (Social Science Research Network 2012) SSRN Scholarly Paper ID 2128531 <https://papers.ssrn.com/abstract=2128531> accessed 15 August 2019

Barber NW, *The Principles of Constitutionalism* (Oxford University Press 2018)

Barberis M, 'Le futur passé de la séparation des pouvoirs' (2012) 143 Pouvoirs 5

Bassini M and Pollicino O, 'Carta Dei Diritti in Internet Verso Una Missione Culturale. Né Costituzione Né Legge.', *Verso un Internet Bill of Rights* (Aracne 2015)

Beaud O, 'L'histoire Du Concept de Constitution En France. De La Constitution Politique à La Constitution Comme Statut Juridique de l'Etat' (2009) 3 Jus Politicum 1

Bell DJ and others, *Cyberculture: The Key Concepts* (Routledge 2004)

Belli L, 'Dichiarazione Dei Diritti in Internet. Cuius Regio Eius Religio?' in Marco Bassini and Oreste Pollicino (eds), *Verso un Internet Bill of Rights* (Aracne 2015)

Belli L and Filippi PD (eds), *Net Neutrality Compendium: Human Rights, Free Competition and the Future of the Internet* (Springer International Publishing 2016)

Belli L, Francisco PAP and Zingales N, 'Law of the Land or Law of the Platform? Beware of the Privatisation of Regulation and Police', *Platform regulations: how platforms are regulated and how they regulate us* (FGV Direito Rio 2017)

Berman HJ, *Law and Revolution. The Formation of the Western Legal Tradition* (Harvard University Press 1983)

Berman P, 'Cyberspace and the State Action Debate: The Cultural Value of Applying Constitutional Norms to "Private" Regulation' (2000) 71 University of Colorado Law Review 1263

Bianchi A, *International Law Theories: An Inquiry into Different Ways of Thinking* (Oxford University Press 2016)

Blengino C, 'Non i Diritti in Internet, Ma Internet Nei Diritti' in Marco Bassini and Oreste Pollicino (eds), *Verso un Internet Bill of Rights* (Aracne 2015)

Block F, 'Karl Polanyi and the Writing of The Great Transformation' (2003) 32 Theory and Society 275

Blokker P, 'Constitutionalism and Constitutional Anomie in the New Europe' (2010) 53 Quaderni del Dipartimento di Sociologia e Ricerca Sociale <https://papers.ssrn.com/abstract=1719095> accessed 21 August 2019

———, 'Modern Constitutionalism and the Challenges of Complex Pluralism' in Gerard Delanty and Stephen P Turner (eds), *Routledge International Handbook of Contemporary Social and Political Theory* (Routledge 2011)

———, 'Grassroots Constitutional Politics in Iceland' (Social Science Research Network 2012) SSRN Scholarly Paper ID 1990463 <https://papers.ssrn.com/abstract=1990463> accessed 19 August 2019

Blume P, 'Data Protection and Privacy – Basic Concept in a Changing World' (2010) 56 Scandinavian Studies in Law 151

Bobbio N, *The Future of Democracy* (Richard Bellamy ed, Roger Griffin tr, University of Minnesota Press 1991)

———, *The Age of Rights* (Allan Cameron tr, Polity 1996)

Bogdandy A von, 'Constitutionalism in International Law: Comment on a Proposal from Germany' (2006) 47 Harvard international law journal 223

Boyle J, 'Foucault in Cyberspace: Surveillance, Sovereignty, and Hardwired Censors' (1997) 66 University of Cincinnati Law Review 177

Brems E and Gerards J, *Shaping Rights in the ECHR: The Role of the European Court of Human Rights in Determining the Scope of Human Rights* (Cambridge University Press 2013)

Brenner SW, *Cybercrime and the Law: Challenges, Issues, and Outcomes* (Northeastern University Press 2012)

Brousseau E, Marzouki M and Méadel C (eds), *Governance, Regulation and Powers on the Internet* (Cambridge University Press 2012)

Brown G (ed), *The Universal Declaration of Human Rights in the 21st Century: A Living Document in a Changing World* (Open Book Publishers 2016)

Brown GW, 'The Constitutionalization of What?' (2012) 1 Global Constitutionalism 201

Bruce G, *The Firm: The Inside Story of the Stasi* (Oxford University Press 2010)

Brysk A and Shafir G, *People out of Place: Globalization, Human Rights, and the Citizenship Gap* (Routledge 2004)

Burnette-McGrath M, 'Packingham v. North Carolina' (2019) 44 Ohio Northern University Law Review 117

Butler A, 'US Supreme Court Finds Broad Restrictions on Access to Social Media Sites Unconstitutional' (2017) 4 European Data Protection Law Review 555

Bygrave LA, *Data Privacy Law: An International Perspective* (Oxford University Press 2014)

———, *Internet Governance by Contract* (Oxford University Press 2015)

———, 'Lex Facebook', *Internet Governance by Contract* (Oxford University Press 2015)

Calabresi SG, Berghausen ME and Albertson S, 'The Rise and Fall of the Separation of Powers' (2012) 106 Northwestern University Law Review 527

Camus A, *The Myth of Sisyphus* (Justin O'Brien tr, Penguin Classics 2000)

Cannataci JA and Mifsud-Bonnici JP, 'Data Protection Comes of Age: The Data Protection Clauses in the European Constitutional Treaty' (2005) 14 Information & Communications Technology Law 5

Caravale M, 'La lettura italiana della teoria dei diritti riflessi' (2016) Rivista italiana per le scienze giuridiche 215

Carbonnier J, 'Le Code civil' in Pierre Nora (ed), *Les lieux de mémoire*, vol 2 (Gallimard 1986)

Carey JM, 'Does It Matter How a Constitution Is Created?' in Robert G Moser and Zoltan Barany (eds), *Is Democracy Exportable?* (Cambridge University Press 2009)

Casacuberta D, Senges M and Duart J-M, 'Privacy and the Need for an Internet Bill of Rights: Are There New Rights in Cyberspace?' (Social Science Research Network 2007) <https://papers.ssrn.com/abstract=2798298> accessed 3 May 2019

Casper G, 'Constitutionalism' in Leonard W Levy, Karst L Kenneth and Dennis J Mahoney (eds), *Encyclopedia of the American Constitution* (Macmillan 1986)

Cass DZ, *The Constitutionalization of the World Trade Organization: Legitimacy, Democracy, and Community in the International Trading System* (Oxford University Press 2005)

Castells M, *The Rise of the Network Society* (2nd edn, Blackwell 2000)

———, *The Power of Identity* (2nd edn, Wiley-Blackwell 2010)

Castorina E, 'Scienza, tecnica e diritto costituzionale' (2015) Rivista AIC <http://www.rivistaaic.it/la-scienza-costituzionalistica-nelle-transizioni-istituzionali-e-sociali.html>

Celeste E, 'The Scope of Application of Digital Constitutionalism. Output from an Empirical Research' (Nexa Research Papers 2017) Nexa Research Papers <https://nexa.polito.it/nexacenterfiles/E.%20Celeste%20-%20Research%20Paper.pdf>

———, 'Digital Constitutionalism: Mapping the Constitutional Response to Digital Technology's Challenges' (2018) HIIG Discussion Paper Series No 2018-02 <https://papers.ssrn.com/abstract=3219905> accessed 23 August 2018

———, 'Packingham v North Carolina: A Constitutional Right to Social Media?' (2018) 17 Cork Online Law Review 116

———, 'Terms of Service and Bills of Rights: New Mechanisms of Constitutionalisation in the Social Media Environment?' (2019) 33 International Review of Law, Computers & Technology 122

———, 'The Court of Justice and the Ban on Bulk Data Retention: Expansive Potential and Future Scenarios' (2019) 15 European Constitutional Law Review 134

———, 'Digital Constitutionalism: A New Systematic Theorisation' (2019) 33 International Review of Law, Computers & Technology 76

———, 'Digital Sovereignty in the EU: Challenges and Future Perspectives' in Federico Fabbrini, Edoardo Celeste and John Quinn (eds), *Data Protection Beyond Borders: Transatlantic Perspectives on Extraterritoriality and Sovereignty* (Hart 2021)

———, 'The Constitutionalisation of the Digital Ecosystem: Lessons from International Law' (2021) Max Planck Institute for Comparative Public Law and International Law (MPIL) Research Paper No. 2021-16 <https://papers.ssrn.com/abstract=3872818> accessed 1 July 2021

———, 'Digital Punishment: Social Media Exclusion and the Constitutionalising Role of National Courts' (2021) International Review of Law, Computers & Technology 1

Celeste E, et al., 'Digital Constitutionalism: In Search of a Content Governance Standard' in Edoardo Celeste, Amélie Heldt and Clara Iglesias Keller (eds), *Constitutionalising Social Media* (Hart 2022)

Celeste E, Heldt A and Iglesias Keller C (eds), *Constitutionalising Social Media* (Hart 2022)

Charleton JH, Ferris RG and Ryan MC (eds), *Framers of the Constitution* (National Archives and Records Administration 1986)

Cicero MT, *De Re Publica* (Clinton Walker Keys tr, William Heinemann 1928)

Citron D, 'Technological Due Process' (2008) 85 Washington University Law Review 1249

Citron DK and Pasquale F, 'The Scored Society: Due Process for Automated Predictions' (2014) 89 Washington Law Review 1

Clapham A, *Human Rights Obligations of Non-State Actors* (Oxford University Press 2006)

Cohen JE, *Configuring the Networked Self: Law, Code, and the Play of Everyday Practice* (Yale University Press 2012)

Cohendet M-A and Fleury M, 'Chronique de droit constitutionnel sur la Charte de l'environnement' (2018) 43 Revue Juridique de l'Environnement 749

Colon-Rios JI, *Weak Constitutionalism: Democratic Legitimacy and the Question of Constituent Power* (Routledge 2012)

Costanzo P, 'Il fattore tecnologico e le sue conseguenze', *Costituzionalismo e globalizzazione* (2012) <http://www.associazionedeicostituzionalisti.it/convegno-annuale-aic-costituzionalismo-e-globalizzazione-salerno-23-24-novembre-2012-relazioni.html>

Couture S and Toupin S, 'What Does the Notion of "Sovereignty" Mean When Referring to the Digital?' (2019) 21 New Media & Society 2305

Craig P, 'Constitutions, Constitutionalism, and the European Union' (2001) 7 European Law Journal 125

Dabashi H, *The Arab Spring: The End of Postcolonialism* (Zed Books 2012)

Davies T, 'Digital Rights and Freedoms: A Framework for Surveying Users and Analyzing Policies' in Luca Maria Aiello and Daniel McFarland (eds), *Social Informatics: 6th International Conference, SocInfo 2014, Barcelona, Spain, November 11–13, 2014. Proceedings* (Springer 2014)

de Goede M, *Speculative Security* (Minnesota University Press 2012)

De Gregorio G, 'The Rise of Digital Constitutionalism in the European Union' (2021) 19 International Journal of Constitutional Law 41

De Hert P and Czerniawski M, 'Expanding the European Data Protection Scope beyond Territory: Article 3 of the General Data Protection Regulation in Its Wider Context' (2016) 6 International Data Privacy Law 230

De Hert P and Kloza D, 'Internet (Access) as a New Fundamental Right. Inflating the Current Rights Framework?' (2012) 3 European Journal of Law and Technology

De Hert P and Papkonstantinou V, 'Google Spain: Addressing Critiques and Misunderstandings One Year Later Comment' (2015) 22 Maastricht Journal of European and Comparative Law 624

de La Chapelle B, 'Multistakeholder Governance - Principles and Challenges of an Innovative Political Paradigm' (2011) *MIND # 2- Internet Policy Making* <http://en.collaboratory.de/w/MIND_2_-_Internet_Policy_Making>

De Minico G, 'Towards an Internet Bill of Rights' (2015) 37 Loyola of Los Angeles International and Comparative Law Review 1

Delbrück J, 'Structural Changes in the International System and Its Legal Order: International Law in the Era of Globalization' (2001) 1 Swiss Review of International and European Law 1

DeNardis L, *The Global War for Internet Governance* (Yale University Press 2014)

DeNardis L and Hackl AM, 'Internet Governance by Social Media Platforms' (2015) 39 Telecommunications Policy 761

Deplano R, 'Fragmentation and Constitutionalisation of International Law: A Theoretical Inquiry' (2013) European journal of legal studies

Derrida J, 'Force of Law: The "Mystical Foundation of Authority"' in Drucilla Cornell, Michel Rosenfeld and David Carlson (eds), *Deconstruction and the Possibility of Justice* (Routledge 1992)

Deva S and Bilchitz D (eds), *Human Rights Obligations of Business: Beyond the Corporate Responsibility to Respect?* (Cambridge University Press 2013)

Di Federico G, *The EU Charter of Fundamental Rights: From Declaration to Binding Instrument* (Springer 2011)

Dobner P and Loughlin M (eds), *The Twilight of Constitutionalism?* (Oxford University Press 2010)

Dowdle MW and Wilkinson M (eds), *Constitutionalism beyond Liberalism* (Cambridge University Press 2016)

Dowek G, *Vivre, aimer, voter en ligne et autres chroniques numériques* (Le Pommier 2017)

Drake W, 'Multistakeholderism: Internal Limitations and External Limits' (2011) *MIND # 2- Internet Policy Making* <http://en.collaboratory.de/w/MIND_2_-_Internet_Policy_Making>

Durkheim E, *The Division of Labour in Society* (Steven Lukes ed, WD Halls tr, Palgrave Macmillan 2013)

Easterbrook FH, 'Cyberspace and the Law of the Horse' (1996) The University of Chicago Legal Forum 207

Elster J, *Ulysses Unbound: Studies in Rationality, Precommitment, and Constraints* (Cambridge University Press 2000)

———, 'Legislatures as Constituent Assemblies' in Richard W Bauman and Tsvi Kahana (eds), *The Least Examined Branch: The Role of Legislatures in the Constitutional State* (Cambridge University Press 2006)

Engle E, 'Third Party Effect of Fundamental Rights (Drittwirkung)' (2009) 5 Hanse Law Review 165

Ernst G and Heilinger J-C, *The Philosophy of Human Rights: Contemporary Controversies* (De Gruyter 2012)

Fabbrini F, 'The Constitutionalization of International Law: A Comparative Federal Perspective' (2013) 6 European journal of legal studies 7

Fabbrini F and Celeste E, 'The Right to Be Forgotten in the Digital Age: The Challenges of Data Protection Beyond Borders' (2020) 21 German Law Journal 55

Fabbrini F, Celeste E and Quinn J (eds), *Data Protection beyond Borders: Transatlantic Perspectives on Extraterritoriality and Sovereignty* (Hart 2021)

Fassbender B, 'The Meaning of International Constitutional Law' in Ronald St John Macdonald and Douglas M Johnston (eds), *Towards world constitutionalism: issues in the legal ordering of the world community* (Nijhoff 2005)

———, *The United Nations Charter as the Constitution of the International Community* (Brill Nijhoff 2009)

Finnis J, *Natural Law and Natural Rights* (Oxford University Press 2011)

———, 'Natural Law Theories' in Edward N Zalta (ed), *The Stanford Encyclopedia of Philosophy* (Winter 2016, Metaphysics Research Lab, Stanford University 2016) <https://plato.stanford.edu/archives/win2016/entries/natural-law-theories/> accessed 8 November 2018

Fischer-Lescano A, 'Redefining Sovereignty via International Constitutional Moments? The Case of Afghanistan' in Michael Bothe, Mary Hellen O'Connel and Natalino Ronzitti (eds), *Redefining Sovereignty: The Use of Force after the Cold War* (Brill-Nijhoff 2005)

———, 'Struggles for a Global Internet Constitution: Protecting Global Communication Structures against Surveillance Measures' (2016) 5 Global Constitutionalism 145

Fitzgerald B, 'Software as Discourse? A Constitutionalism for Information Society' (1999) 24 Alternative Law Journal 144

———, 'Software as Discourse? The Challenge for Information Law' (2000) 22 European Intellectual Property Review 47

Flaherty DH, *Protecting Privacy in Surveillance Societies. The Federal Republic of Germany, Sweden, France, Canada, And the United States* (The University of North Carolina Press 1989)

———, 'On the Utility of Constitutional Rights to Privacy and Data Protection' (1991) 41 Case Western Reserve Law Review 831

Flinders M, 'Constitutional Anomie: Patterns of Democracy and "The Governance of Britain"' (2009) 44 Government and Opposition 385

———, *Democratic Drift: Majoritarian Modification and Democratic Anomie in the United Kingdom* (Oxford University Press 2009)

Floridi L, *Philosophy and Computing: An Introduction* (Routledge 1999)

Flyverbom M, *The Power of Networks: Organizing the Global Politics of the Internet* (Edward Elgar 2011)

Foerstel HN, *Freedom of Information and the Right to Know – The Origins and Applications of the Freedom of Information Act* (Greenwood Press 1999)

Forsythe DP, *The Humanitarians: The International Committee of the Red Cross* (Cambridge University Press 2005)

Friedmann W, *The Changing Structure of International Law* (Columbia University Press 1964)

Frosini TE, 'The Internet Access as a Fundamental Right' (2013) 25 Federalismi.it

Fuchs C, *Internet and Society: Social Theory in the Information Age* (Routledge 2008)

——— (eds), *Internet and Surveillance: The Challenges of Web 2. 0 and Social Media* (Routledge 2011)

Garcia-Molina H, Ullman JD and Widom J, *Database Systems: The Complete Book* (2nd edn, Pearson 2008)

Georg Jellinek, *System der subjektiven öffentlichen Rechte* (Mohr 1892)
Gerber CF von, *Über öffentliche Rechte* (H Laupp 1852)
———, *Grundzüge des deutschen staatsrechts* (B Tauchnitz 1865)
Gerring J, *Social Science Methodology: A Unified Framework* (Cambridge University Press 2012)
Giacometti Z, 'Festrede Des Rektors Zaccaria Giacometti, Gehalten an Der 122. Stiftungsfeier Der Universität Zürich Am 29. April 1955: Die Freiheitsrechtskataloge Als Kodifikation Der Freiheit', *Jahresbericht 1954/55* (Art Institut Orell Füssli AG 1955) <http://bit.ly/2pXBwhn>
Gill L, Redeker D and Gasser U, 'Towards Digital Constitutionalism? Mapping Attempts to Craft an Internet Bill of Rights' (2015) Berkman Center Research Publication No 2015-15 <https://papers.ssrn.com/abstract=2687120> accessed 30 August 2018
Ginsburg T, Elkins Z and Blount J, 'Does the Process of Constitution-Making Matter?' (2009) 5 Annual Review of Law and Social Science 201
Golding W, *Lord of the Flies* (Faber & Faber 1954)
Goldsmith J and Wu T, *Who Controls the Internet? Illusions of a Borderless World* (Oxford University Press 2008)
Goldsmith JL, 'Against Cyberanarchy' (1998) 65 The University of Chicago Law Review 1199
Gomme AW, Cadoux TJ and Rhodes PJ, 'Solon', *The Oxford Companion to Classical Civilization* (Oxford University Press 2014)
Graber CB, 'Freedom and Affordances of the Net' (2018) 10 Washington University Jurisprudence Review 221
———, 'Bottom-up Constitutionalism: The Case of Net Neutrality' (2016) 7 Transnational Legal Theory 524
Grant JP and Barker JC, 'Suzerainty', *Encyclopaedic Dictionary of International Law* (Oxford University Press 2009)
Grimm D, *Sovereignty: The Origin and Future of a Political and Legal Concept* (Columbia University Press 2015)
———, *Constitutionalism: Past, Present, and Future* (Oxford University Press 2016)
Guadamuz A, 'Habeas Data: The Latin-American Response to Data Protection' (2000) 2 The Journal of Information, Law and Technology <https://warwick.ac.uk/fac/soc/law/elj/jilt/2000_2/guadamuz>
Gwyn WB, *The Meaning of the Separation of Powers: An Analysis of the Doctrine from Its Origin to the Adoption of the United States Constitution* (Tulane University 1965)
Habermas J, *The Postnational Constellation: Political Essays* (MIT Press 2001)
Hahm DE, 'The Mixed Constitution in Greek Thought' in Ryan K Balot (ed), *A Companion to Greek and Roman Political Thought* (Wiley-Blackwell 2009)
Halberstam D, 'Constitutional Heterarchy: The Centrality of Conflict in the European Union and the United States' in Jeffrey L Dunoff and Joel P Trachtman (eds), *Ruling the World?: Constitutionalism, International Law, and Global Governance* (Cambridge University Press 2009)
Hamann A and Ruiz Fabri H, 'Transnational Networks and Constitutionalism' (2008) 6 International Journal of Constitutional Law 481
Hartzog W and Richards N, 'Privacy's Constitutional Moment and the Limits of Data Protection' (2020) 61 Boston College Law Review 1687

Heldt A, 'Content Moderation by Social Media Platforms: The Importance of Judicial Review' in Edoardo Celeste, Amélie Heldt and Clara Iglesias Keller (eds), *Constitutionalising Social Media* (Hart 2022)

Henshall N, *The Myth of Absolutism: Change & Continuity in Early Modern European Monarchy* (Routledge 1992)

Hijmans H, 'Right to Have Links Removed: Evidence of Effective Data Protection' (2014) 21 Maastricht Journal of European and Comparative Law 555

Hoffmann S-L, *Human Rights in the Twentieth Century* (Cambridge University Press 2010)

Holt JC, *Magna Carta* (2nd edn, Cambridge University Press 1992)

Howard A, 'We the People Need Our Existing Bill of Rights to Apply in the Digital Domain' (*Radar*, 14 July 2012) <http://radar.oreilly.com/2012/07/digital-bill-of-rights-internet-freedom.html> accessed 7 May 2019

Im Hof U, *The Enlightenment* (Blackwell 1994)

Jakubowski A and Wierczyńska K (eds), *Fragmentation vs the Constitutionalisation of International Law: A Practical Inquiry* (Routledge 2016)

Jamart A-C, 'Internet Freedom and the Constitutionalization of Internet Governance' in Roxana Radu, Jean-Marie Chenou and Rolf H Weber (eds), *The Evolution of Global Internet Governance* (Springer Berlin Heidelberg 2014)

Jarvis J, 'A Bill of Rights in Cyberspace' (*BuzzMachine*, 27 March 2010) <https://buzzmachine.com/2010/03/27/a-bill-of-rights-in-cyberspace/> accessed 21 May 2019

Jellinek G, *The Declaration of the Rights of Man and of Citizens. A Contribution to Modern Constitutional History* (Max Farrand tr, Henry Holt 1901)

Johnson DR and Post DG, 'Law and Borders: The Rise of Law in Cyberspace' (1996) 48 Stanford Law Review

Jørgensen RF, 'An Internet Bill of Rights?' in Ian Brown (ed), *Research Handbook on Governance of the Internet* (Edward Elgar 2013)

——— (ed), *Human Rights in the Age of Platforms* (The MIT Press 2019)

Jørgensen RF and Pedersen AM, 'Online Service Providers as Human Rights Arbiters' in Mariarosaria Taddeo and Luciano Floridi (eds), *The Responsibilities of Online Service Providers* (Springer 2017)

Joseph S, 'Social Media, Political Change, and Human Rights' (2012) 35 Boston College International and Comparative Law Review 145

Kadelbach S and Kleinlein T, 'International Law - A Constitution for Mankind: An Attempt at a Re-Appraisal with an Analysis of Constitutional Principles Focus Section: Typisch Deutsch: Is There a German Approach to International Law: German Obsessions' (2007) 50 German Yearbook of International Law 303

Karavas V, 'The Force of Code: Law's Transformation under Information Technological Conditions' (2009) 10 German Law Journal 463

———, 'Governance of Virtual Worlds and the Quest for a Digital Constitution' in Christoph B Graber and Mira Burri-Nenova, *Governance of Digital Game Environments and Cultural Diversity: Transdisciplinary Enquiries* (Edward Elgar Publishing 2010)

———, 'Review Essay - Some Remarks on the Constitutionalisation of Cyberspace' (2012) 3 German Law Journal <http://www.germanlawjournal.com/index.php?pageID=11&artID=219>

Karavas V and Teubner G, 'Www.CompanyNameSucks.Com: The Horizontal Effect of Fundamental Rights on "Private Parties" within Autonomous Internet Law' (2005) 12 Constellations 262

Karppi T, *Disconnect* (University of Minnesota Press 2018)
Keane J, *Global Civil Society?* (Cambridge University Press 2003)
Keller P, 'Sovereignty and Liberty in the Internet Era' in Richard Rawlings, Peter Leyland and Alison Young (eds), *Sovereignty and the Law* (Oxford University Press 2013)
Kettemann MC, *The Normative Order of the Internet: A Theory of Rule and Regulation Online* (Oxford University Press 2020)
Klabbers J, 'Constitutionalism Lite' (2004) 1 International Organizations Law Review 31
Klabbers J, Peters A and Ulfstein G, *The Constitutionalization of International Law* (Oxford University Press 2009)
Kleinlein T, *Konstitutionalisierung Im Völkerrecht: Konstruktion Und Elemente Einer Idealistischen Völkerrechtslehre* (Springer 2012)
———, 'Between Myths and Norms: Constructivist Constitutionalism and the Potential of Constitutional Principles in International Law' (2012) 81 Nordic Journal of International Law 79
Klonick K, 'The New Governors: The People, Rules, and Processes Governing Online Speech' 131 Harvard Law Review 1598
Klonick K and Kadri T, 'How to Make Facebook's "Supreme Court" Work' *The New York Times* (18 November 2018) <https://www.nytimes.com/2018/11/17/opinion/facebook-supreme-court-speech.html> accessed 20 November 2018
Kohl U, *Jurisdiction and the Internet: Regulatory Competence over Online Activity* (Cambridge University Press 2007)
Koskenniemi M, 'Constitutionalism as Mindset: Reflections on Kantian Themes About International Law and Globalization' (2006) 8 Theoretical Inquiries in Law 9
Kuczerawy A, *Intermediary Liability and Freedom of Expression in the EU: From Concepts to Safeguards* (Intersentia 2018)
Kuhn TS, *The Structure of Scientific Revolutions* (4th edn, University of Chicago Press 2012)
Kulesza J, 'Freedom of Information in the Global Information Society: The Question of the Internet Bill of Rights' (2008) 1 University of Warmia and Mazury in Olsztyn Law Review 81
Kuner C, 'Data Protection Law and International Jurisdiction on the Internet (Part 1)' (2010) 18 International Journal of Law and Information Technology 176
———, 'Extraterritoriality and Regulation of International Data Transfers in EU Data Protection Law' (2015) 5 International Data Privacy Law 235
Kuner C, Bygrave LA and Docksey C, *Commentary on the EU General Data Protection Regulation* (Oxford University Press 2019)
Lacchè L, 'Granted Constitutions. The Theory of Octroi and Constitutional Experiments in Europe in the Aftermath of the French Revolution' (2013) 9 European Constitutional Law Review 285
Ladeur K-H, 'The evolution of the law and the possibility of a "global law" extending beyond the sphere of the state – simultaneously, a critique of the "self-constitutionalisation" thesis' (2012) Ancilla Iuris 220
Laidlaw EB, 'Private Power, Public Interest: An Examination of Search Engine Accountability' (2008) 17 International Journal of Law and Information Technology 113
———, *Regulating Speech in Cyberspace: Gatekeepers, Human Rights and Corporate Responsibility* (Cambridge University Press 2015)

Le Divellec A, 'L'articulation des pouvoirs dans les démocraties parlementaires européennes : fusion et mitigation' (2012) 143 Pouvoirs 123

Lemley MA, 'The Constitutionalization of Technology Law' (2000) 15 Berkeley Technology Law Journal 529

Lemos R, 'Internet Brasileira Precisa de Marco Regulatório Civil' *UOL* (22 May 2007) <https://tecnologia.uol.com.br/ultnot/2007/05/22/ult4213u98.jhtm> accessed 11 July 2019

Lessig L, *Code and Other Laws of Cyberspace* (Basic Books 1999)

———, 'The Law of the Horse: What Cyberlaw Might Teach' (1999) 113 Harvard Law Review 501

———, *Code: And Other Laws of Cyberspace, Version 2.0* (Basic Books 2006)

Leuf B and Cunningham W, *The Wiki Way: Quick Collaboration on the Web* (Addison-Wesley Professional 2001)

Levinson NS and Marzouki M, 'Internet Governance Institutionalization: Process and Trajectories' in Michèle Rioux and Kim Fontaine-Skronski (eds), *Global Governance Facing Structural Changes: New Institutional Trajectories for Digital and Transnational Capitalism* (Palgrave Macmillan 2015)

Lewis J, *Solon the Thinker: Political Thought in Archaic Athens* (Duckworth 2006)

Lewis JD, 'Isegoria at Athens: When Did It Begin?' (1971) 20 Historia: Zeitschrift für Alte Geschichte 129

Lijphart A, *Patterns of Democracy: Government Forms and Performance in Thirty-Six Countries* (2nd edn, Yale University Press 2012)

Lindahl H, 'Constituent Power and Reflexive Identity: Towards an Ontology of Collective Selfhood' in Martin Loughlin and Neil Walker (eds), *The Paradox of Constitutionalism: Constituent Power and Constitutional Form* (Oxford University Press 2008)

———, 'We and Cyberlaw: The Spatial Unity of Constitutional Orders' (2013) 20 Indiana Journal of Global Legal Studies 697

Lindahl HK, 'Collective Self-Legislation as an Actus Impurus: A Response to Heidegger's Critique of European Nihilism' (2008) 41 Continental Philosophy Review 323

Lintott A, 'The Theory of the Mixed Constitution at Rome' in Jonathan Barnes and Miriam Griffin (eds), *Philosophia Togata II: Plato and Aristotle at Rome* (Oxford University Press 1999)

Loughlin M, 'What Is Constitutionalisation?' in Petra Dobner and Martin Loughlin (eds), *The Twilight of Constitutionalism?* (Oxford University Press 2010)

———, 'Why Sovereignty?' in Richard Rawlings, Peter Leyland and Alison Young (eds), *Sovereignty and the Law: Domestic, European and International Perspectives* (Oxford University Press 2013)

Loughlin M and Walker N, *The Paradox of Constitutionalism: Constituent Power and Constitutional Form* (Oxford University Press 2008)

Lucas D. Introna, Helen Nissenbaum, 'Shaping the Web: Why the Politics of Search Engines Matters' (2000) 16 The Information Society 169

Luhmann N, *Law as a Social System* (Fatima Kastner and others eds, Klaus Ziegert tr, Oxford University Press 2004)

———, *Theory of Society*, vol 1 (Rhodes Barrett tr, Stanford University Press 2012)

Lynskey O, 'Deconstructing Data Protection: The "Added-Value" of a Right to Data Protection in the EU Legal Order' (2014) 63 International and Comparative Law Quarterly 569

Lyon D, *The Electronic Eye: The Rise of Surveillance Society* (Polity Press 1994)
——— (ed), *Theorizing Surveillance: The Panopticon and Beyond* (Willan 2006)
———, *Surveillance after Snowden* (Polity Press 2015)
Maboudi T and Nadi GP, 'Crowdsourcing the Egyptian Constitution: Social Media, Elites, and the Populace' (2016) 69 Political Research Quarterly 716
MacDonald R and Johnston D (eds), *Towards World Constitutionalism: Issues in the Legal Ordering of the World Community* (Brill 2005)
Machiavelli N, *The Prince* (George Bull tr, Penguin Classics 1961)
Macklem P, *The Sovereignty of Human Rights* (Oxford University Press 2015)
Maddox G, 'A Note on the Meaning of `Constitution" (1982) 76 The American Political Science Review 805
Magalhães JC, 'Critically Imagining Internet Governance: A Content Analysis of the Marco Civil Da Internet Public Consultation' (London School of Economics 2015)
Manhire T (ed), *The Arab Spring: Rebellion, Revolution and a New World Order* (Random House 2012)
Marchand S and Bourdeau M, 'Une Magna Carta pour Internet, 20 ans après' (2015) 141 Cahiers philosophiques 104
Marchart O, *Post-Foundational Political Thought: Political Difference in Nancy, Lefort, Badiou and Laclau* (Edinburgh University Press 2007)
Markham AN, *Life Online: Researching Real Experience in Virtual Space* (Rowman Altamira 1998)
Marrani D, 'The Second Anniversary of the Constitutionalisation of the French Charter for the Environment: Constitutional and Environmental Implications' (2008) 10 Environmental Law Review 9
Marsden CT, *Net Neutrality: Towards a Co-Regulatory Solution* (Bloomsbury 2010)
Marshall AM and Tompsett BC, 'Identity Theft in an Online World' (2005) 21 Computer Law & Security Review 128
Marshall TH, *Class, Citizenship, and Social Development* (Doubleday 1964)
Marzouki M, 'The "Guarantee-Rights" for Realizing the Rule of Law' in Rikke Frank Jørgensen (ed), *Human Rights in the Global Information Society* (MIT Press 2006)
Massit-Folléa F, 'Internet et Les Errances Du Multistakeholderism' (2014) 79 Politique étrangère 29
Mayer-Schönberger V and Crowley J, 'Napster's Second Life?: The Regulatory Challenges of Virtual World' (2006) 100 Northwestern University Law Review 1775
Mazeaud P, 'Le code civil et la conscience collective française' (2004) 110 Pouvoirs 152
McIlwain CH, *Constitutionalism: Ancient and Modern* (Amagi, originally published by Cornell University Press, 1947, 2007)
Medeiros FA and Bygrave LA, 'Brazil's Marco Civil Da Internet: Does It Live up to the Hype?' (2015) 31 Computer Law & Security Review 120
Merrill JH (ed), 'Constitutional Law', *American and English Encyclopaedia of Law* (Edward Thompson 1887) 670
Micklitz H-W and others (eds), *Constitutional Challenges in the Algorithmic Society* (Cambridge University Press 2022)
Milewicz K, 'Emerging Patterns of Global Constitutionalisation: Towards a Conceptual Framework' (2009) 16 Indiana Journal of Global Legal Studies 413

Miller K, 'Constitutional Law - Sex Offenses and Free Speech: Constitutionality of Ban on Sex Offenders' Use of Social Media: Impact on States with Similar Restrictions' (2018) 93 North Dakota Law Review 129

Mitsilegas V, 'Transatlantic Counterterrorism Cooperation and European Values' in Deirdre Curtin and Elaine Fahey (eds), *A Transatlantic Community of Law: Legal Perspectives on the Relationship between the EU and US Legal Orders* (Cambridge University Press 2014)

Modugno F, *Lineamenti Di Teoria Del Diritto Oggettivo* (Giappichelli 2009)

Moerel L, 'The Long Arm of EU Data Protection Law: Does the Data Protection Directive Apply to Processing of Personal Data of EU Citizens by Websites Worldwide?' (2011) 1 International Data Privacy Law 28

Mohnhaupt H and Grimm D, *Verfassung.* (2nd edn, Duncker & Humblot 2002)

Moore M, 'Cybersquatting: Prevention Better than Cure?' (2009) 17 International Journal of Law and Information Technology 220

Moorehead C, *Dunant's Dream: War, Switzerland and the History of the Red Cross* (Harper Collins 1998)

Morsink J, *The Universal Declaration of Human Rights: Origins, Drafting, and Intent* (University of Pennsylvania Press 1999)

Mueller M, *Will the Internet Fragment? Sovereignty, Globalization and Cyberspace* (Polity 2017)

———, 'Net Neutrality as Global Principle for Internet Governance' (Social Science Research Network 2007) SSRN Scholarly Paper ID 2798314 <https://papers.ssrn.com/abstract=2798314> accessed 3 December 2018

———, *Ruling the Root: Internet Governance and the Taming of Cyberspace* (MIT Press 2002)

———, *Networks and States: The Global Politics of Internet Governance* (MIT Press 2013)

Murray AD, *The Regulation of Cyberspace: Control in the Online Environment* (Routledge 2006)

Musiani F, 'The Internet Bill of Rights: A Way to Reconcile Natural Freedoms and Regulatory Needs?' (2009) 6 SCRIPTed 504

———, 'WSIS+10: The Self-Praising Feast of Multi-Stakeholderism in Internet Governance' (2013) 2 Internet Policy Review

Musiani F, Pavan E and Padovani C, 'Investigating Evolving Discourses on Human Rights in the Digital Age: Emerging Norms and Policy Challenges' (2009) 72 International Communication Gazette 359

Nemitz P, 'Constitutional Democracy and Technology in the Age of Artificial Intelligence' (2018) 376 Philosophical Transactions of the Royal Society A

Ninet AA i and Tushnet M, *The Arab Spring. An Essay on Revolution and Constitutionalism* (Edward Elgar 2015)

Oates S, 'Towards an Online Bill of Rights' in Luciano Floridi (ed), *The Onlife Manifesto: Being Human in a Hyperconnected Era* (Springer 2015)

O'Donoghue A, 'Alfred Verdross and the Contemporary Constitutionalization Debate' (2012) 32 Oxford Journal of Legal Studies 799

———, *Constitutionalism in Global Constitutionalisation* (Cambridge University Press 2014)

Oestreich G, *Geschichte der Menschenrechte und Grundfreiheiten im Umriss* (2nd edn, Duncker & Humblot 1978)

Orwell G, *Nineteen Eighty-Four* (originally published in 1949, Penguin Books 2004)

Owen D, 'On the Right to Have Nationality Rights: Statelessness, Citizenship and Human Rights' (2018) 65 Netherlands International Law Review 299

Padovani C and Santaniello M, 'Digital Constitutionalism: Fundamental Rights and Power Limitation in the Internet Eco-System' (2018) 80 International Communication Gazette 295

Pasquale F, *The Black Box Society: The Secret Algorithms That Control Money and Information* (Harvard University Press 2015)

Passaglia P, 'Internet nella Costituzione italiana' Consulta Online <http://www.giurcost.org/studi/passaglia5.pdf>

Peers S (ed), *The EU Charter of Fundamental Rights: A Commentary* (Hart Publishing 2014)

Pernice I, 'Multilevel Constitutionalism and the Treaty of Amsterdam: European Constitution-Making Revisited' (1999) 36 Common Market Law Review 703

———, 'The Treaty of Lisbon: Multilevel Constitutionalism in Action' (2009) 15 Columbia Journal of European Law 349

———, 'Die Verfassung der Internetgesellschaft: Zur Rolle von Staat und Verfassung im Zuge der digitalen Revolution' in Alexander Blankenagel (ed), *Den Verfassungsstaat nachdenken. Eine Geburtstagsgabe* (Duncker & Humblot 2014) <https://papers.ssrn.com/abstract=2964926> accessed 28 August 2018

———, 'Global Constitutionalism and the Internet. Taking People Seriously.' in Stefan Kadelbach and Rainer Hofmann (eds), *Law Beyond the State: Pasts and Futures* (Campus Verlag 2016) <http://ssrn.com/abstract=2576697.>

———, 'Vom Völkerrecht Des Netzes Zur Verfassung Des Internets: Privacy Und Digitale Sicherheit Im Zeichen Eines Schrittweisen Paradigmenwechsels' (Social Science Research Network 2017) SSRN Scholarly Paper ID 2959257 <https://papers.ssrn.com/abstract=2959257> accessed 19 October 2019

———, 'Risk Management in the Digital Constellation – A Constitutional Perspective' (2017) HIIG Discussion Paper Series No 2017-07 <https://papers.ssrn.com/abstract=3051124> accessed 18 October 2018

———, 'Risk management in the digital constellation - a constitutional perspective (part I)' (2018) IDP Revista de Internet Derecho y Política 83

———, 'Risk management in the digital constellation – a constitutional perspective (part II)' (2018) IDP Revista de Internet Derecho y Política 79

Perritt HH, 'The Internet at 20: Evolution of a Constitution for Cyberspace' (2012) 20 William and Mary Bill of Rights Journal 1115

Peters A, *Elemente einer Theorie der Verfassung Europas.* (Duncker & Humblot 2001)

———, 'Compensatory Constitutionalism: The Function and Potential of Fundamental International Norms and Structures' (2006) 19 Leiden Journal of International Law 579

———, 'The Globalization of State Constitutions' in Janne E Nijman and André Nollkaemper (eds), *New Perspectives on the Divide Between National and International Law* (Oxford University Press 2007)

———, 'Humanity as the A and Ω of Sovereignty' (2009) 20 European Journal of International Law 513

———, 'Global Constitutionalism' in Michael T Gibbons (ed), *The Encyclopedia of Political Thought* (John Wiley & Sons 2014)

Peters A and Armingeon K, 'Introduction: Global Constitutionalism from an Interdisciplinary Perspective' (2009) 16 Indiana Journal of Global Legal Studies 385

Pielemeier J, 'AI & Global Governance: The Advantages of Applying the International Human Rights Framework to Artificial Intelligence' (*Centre for Policy Research at United Nations University*) <https://cpr.unu.edu/ai-global-governance-the-advantages-of-applying-the-international-human-rights-framework-to-artificial-intelligence.html> accessed 22 May 2019

Plato, *Phaedrus and Letters VII and VIII* (Walter Hamilton tr, Penguin Classics 1973)

Podes S, 'Polybius and His Theory of "Anacyclosis". Problems of Not Just Ancient Political Theory' (1991) 12 History of Political Thought 577

Polanyi K, *The Great Transformation: The Political and Economic Origins of Our Time* (originally published in 1944, Beacon Press 2001)

Polin R, *Plato and Aristotle on Constitutionalism: An Exposition and Reference Source* (Ashgate 1998)

Pollicino O, *Judicial Protection of Fundamental Rights on the Internet: A Road towards Digital Constitutionalism?* (Hart 2021)

Pollicino O and Bassini M (eds), *Verso Un Internet Bill of Rights* (Aracne 2015)

Postman N, *Technopoly: The Surrender of Culture to Technology* (Vintage Books 1993)

Preuss UK, 'Disconnecting Constitutions from Statehood: Is Global Constitutionalism a Viable Concept?' in Petra Dobner and Martin Loughlin (eds), *The Twilight of Constitutionalism?* (Oxford University Press 2010)

Prieur M, 'La Charte de l'environnement et La Constitution Française' (2005) 35 Environmental Policy and Law 134

Radu R, *Negotiating Internet Governance* (Oxford University Press 2019)

Redeker D, Gill L and Gasser U, 'Towards Digital Constitutionalism? Mapping Attempts to Craft an Internet Bill of Rights' (2018) 80 International Communication Gazette 302

Reidenberg J, 'Lex Informatica: The Formulation of Information Policy Rules through Technology' (1998) 76 Texas Law Review 553

Reidenberg JR, 'Yahoo and Democracy on the Internet' (2002) 42 Jurimetrics 251

———, 'Technology and Internet Jurisdiction' (2005) 153 University of Pennsylvania Law Review 1951

Resta G, 'Il Diritto Alla Protezione Dei Dati Personali' in Francesco Cardarelli, Salvatore Sica and Vincenzo Zeno-Zencovich (eds), *Il codice dei dati personali. Temi e problemi* (Giuffrè 2004)

Richardson L, *A New Topographical Dictionary of Ancient Rome* (Johns Hopkins University Press 1992)

Roberts CNJ, *The Contentious History of the International Bill of Human Rights* (Cambridge University Press 2015)

Rodotà S, 'L'uomo nuovo di Internet' *La Repubblica* (28 October 2005) <https://ricerca.repubblica.it/repubblica/archivio/repubblica/2005/10/28/uomo-nuovo-di-internet.html> accessed 2 May 2019

———, 'Perché Internet Ha Bisogno Di Una Carta Dei Diritti' *La Repubblica* (14 November 2006) <http://www.repubblica.it/2006/11/sezioni/scienza_e_tecnologia/internet-30-milioni/carta-diritti-internet/carta-diritti-internet.html> accessed 2 May 2019

———, 'A Bill of Rights for the Internet Universe' (2008) 21 The Federalist Debate <http://www.federalist-debate.org/index.php/current/item/250-a-bill-of-rights-for-the-internet-universe> accessed 2 May 2019

———, 'Una Costituzione per Internet?' (2010) Politica del diritto 337

———, *Il diritto di avere diritti* (Laterza 2012)

———, *Il Mondo Nella Rete: Quali i Diritti, Quali i Vincoli* (Laterza 2014)

Rosanvallon P, *La Contre-Démocratie. La politique à l'âge de la défiance* (Le Seuil 2006)

———, *Counter-Democracy: Politics in an Age of Distrust* (Cambridge University Press 2008)

Rousseau D, 'La démocratie ou le vol de La Joconde' in Bertrand Mathieu and others (eds), *Nouvelles questions sur la démocratie* (Dalloz 2010)

Sajó A, *Limiting Government: An Introduction to Constitutionalism* (Central European University Press 1999)

Sajó A and Uitz R, *The Constitution of Freedom: An Introduction to Legal Constitutionalism* (Oxford University Press 2017)

Saldaña J, *The Coding Manual for Qualitative Researchers* (3rd edn, Sage 2016)

Sartori G, 'Constitutionalism: A Preliminary Discussion' (1962) 56 The American Political Science Review 853

Schell BH, *Online Health and Safety: From Cyberbullying to Internet Addiction* (Greenwood 2016)

Schmitt C, *Constitutional Theory* (Jeffrey Seitzer ed, (originally published in 1928), Duke University Press 2008)

Schneier B, 'Power in the Age of the Feudal Internet' (2013) MIND 16

———, *Data and Goliath: The Hidden Battles to Collect Your Data and Control Your World* (W W Norton & Company 2015)

Schultz T, 'Carving up the Internet: Jurisdiction, Legal Orders, and the Private/Public International Law Interface' (2008) European Journal of International Law 799

Schwöbel CEJ, 'Situating the Debate on Global Constitutionalism' (2010) 8 International Journal of Constitutional Law 611

Sciulli D, *Theory of Societal Constitutionalism: Foundations of a Non-Marxist Critical Theory* (Cambridge University Press 1992)

———, *Corporate Power in Civil Society* (NYU Press 2001)

Scott C, Cafaggi F and Senden L, 'The Conceptual and Constitutional Challenge of Transnational Private Regulation' (2011) 38 Journal of Law and Society 1

Scott JW, 'French Feminists and the Rights of "Man": Olympe de Gouges's Declarations' (1989) History Workshop 1

Seagrave SA, *The Foundations of Natural Morality: On the Compatibility of Natural Rights and the Natural Law* (University of Chicago Press 2014)

Senor MA, 'La Forma Della Dichiarazione Dei Diritti in Internet' in Marco Bassini and Oreste Pollicino (eds), *Verso un Intenet Bill of Rights* (Aracne 2015)

Shelton D, *Human Rights and the Environment* (Edward Elgar 2011)

Shiner RA, 'Constitutions' in Enrico Pattaro (ed), *A Treatise of Legal Philosophy and General Jurisprudence*, vol 3 'Legal Institutions and Sources of Law' (Springer 2005)

Shirey RW, 'Internet Security Glossary, Version 2' (2007) <https://tools.ietf.org/html/rfc4949#page-7> accessed 2 July 2019

Simoncini A and Longo E, 'Fundamental Rights and the Rule of Law in the Algorithmic Society' in Hans-W Micklitz and others (eds), *Constitutional Challenges in the Algorithmic Society* (Cambridge University Press 2021)

Simpson G, 'Westphalian System', *The New Oxford Companion to Law* (Oxford University Press 2008)

Slaughter A-M and Burke-White W, 'An International Constitutional Moment Focus: September 11, 2001--Legal Response to Terror' (2002) 43 Harvard International Law Journal 1
Snyder F, 'The Unfinished Constitution of the European Union: Principles, Processes and Culture' in JHH Weiler and Marlene Wind (eds), *European Constitutionalism Beyond the State* (Cambridge University Press 2003)
Solove DJ, *The Digital Person: Technology and Privacy in the Information Age* (New York University Press 2004)
Somek A, 'From the Rule of Law to the Constitutionalist Makeover: Changing European Conceptions of Public International Law' (2011) 18 Constellations 567
Spann GA, 'Constitutionalization' (2004) Saint Louis University Law Journal 709
Stokes JK, 'The Indecent Internet: Resisting Unwarranted Internet Exceptionalism Combating Revenge Porn' (2014) 29 Berkeley Technology Law Journal 929
Stolleis M, *Public Law in Germany, 1800–1914* (Berghahn Books 2001)
Suteu S, 'Constitutional Conventions in the Digital Era: Lessons from Iceland and Ireland' (2015) 38 Boston College International and Comparative Law Review 251
Suzor N, 'Digital Constitutionalism and the Role of the Rule of Law in the Governance of Virtual Communities' (phd, Queensland University of Technology 2010) <https://eprints.qut.edu.au/37636/> accessed 30 August 2018
———, 'The Role of the Rule of Law in Virtual Communities' (2010) 25 Berkeley Technology Law Journal 1817
———, 'Digital Constitutionalism: Using the Rule of Law to Evaluate the Legitimacy of Governance by Platforms' (2018) 4 Social Media + Society 1
———, *Lawless. The Secret Rules That Govern Our Digital Lives* (Cambridge University Press 2019)
Svantesson DJB, 'Extraterritoriality and Targeting in EU Data Privacy Law: The Weak Spot Undermining the Regulation' (2015) 5 International Data Privacy Law 226
Tagliabue F, Galassi L and Mariani P, 'The "Pandemic" of Disinformation in COVID-19' (2020) 2 SN Comprehensive Clinical Medicine 1287
Taylor E, 'The Privatization of Human Rights: Illusions of Consent, Automation and Neutrality' (2016) 24 Global Commission on Internet Governance Paper Series <https://www.cigionline.org/publications/privatization-human-rights-illusions-consent-automation-and-neutrality> accessed 8 July 2019
Teubner G, *Law as an Autopoietic System* (Blackwell 1993)
———, 'Global Private Regimes: Neo-Spontaneous Law and Dual Constitution of Autonomous Sectors?' in Karl-Heinz Ladeur (ed), *Public Governance in the Age of Globalization* (Routledge 2004)
———, 'Societal Constitutionalism; Alternatives to State-Centred Constitutional Theory?' in Christian Joerges, Inger-Johanne Sand and Gunther Teubner (eds), *Transnational Governance and Constitutionalism. International Studies in the Theory of Private Law* (Hart 2004)
———, 'Self-Constitutionalizing TNCs? On the Linkage of "Private" and "Public" Corporate Codes of Conduct' (2011) 18 Indiana Journal of Global Legal Studies 617
———, *Constitutional Fragments: Societal Constitutionalism and Globalization* (Oxford University Press 2012)
Teubner G and Beckers A, 'Expanding Constitutionalism' (2013) 20 Indiana Journal of Global Legal Studies 523

Teubner G and Fischer-Lescano A, 'Regime-Collisions: The Vain Search for Legal Unity in the Fragmentation of Global Law' (2004) 25 Michigan Journal of International Law 999

Thornhill C, *A Sociology of Constitutions: Constitutions and State Legitimacy in Historical-Sociological Perspective* (Cambridge University Press 2011)

Tomuschat C, 'Obligations Arising for States without or against Their Will' (1993) 241 Collected Courses of The Hague Academy of International Law 195

———, 'International Law: Ensuring the Survival of Mankind on the Eve of a New Century: General Course on Public International Law' (1999) 281 Collected Courses of The Hague Academy of International Law

Tomuschat C and Schmidt R (eds), *Der Verfassungsstaat im Geflecht der internationalen Beziehungen. Gemeinden und Kreise vor den öffentlichen Aufgaben der Gegenwart: Berichte und Diskussionen auf der Tagung der Vereinigung der Deutschen Staatsrechtslehrer in Basel vom 5. bis 8. Oktober 1977* (De Gruyter 2013)

Tribe LH, *The Constitution in Cyberspace: Law and Liberty Beyond the Electronic Frontier* (American Humanist Association 1991)

Tuckness A, 'Locke's Political Philosophy' in Edward N Zalta (ed), *The Stanford Encyclopedia of Philosophy* (Summer 2018, Metaphysics Research Lab, Stanford University 2018) <https://plato.stanford.edu/archives/sum2018/entries/locke-political/> accessed 8 November 2018

Tully S, 'A Human Right to Access the Internet? Problems and Prospects' (2014) 14 Human Rights Law Review 175

Turkle S, *Life on the Screen* (Simon and Schuster 1995)

Uerpmann R, 'Völkerrechtliche Nebenverfassungen' in Armin von Bogdandy (ed), *Europäisches Verfassungsrecht: Theoretische und dogmatische Grundzüge* (Springer Berlin Heidelberg 2003)

van Asbeck FM, *The Universal Declaration of Human Rights and Its Predecessors (1679–1948)*, vol 10 (E J Brill 1949)

Vasak K, 'A 30-Year Struggle. The Sustained Efforts to Give Force of Law to the Universal Declaration of Human Rights' (1977) XXX *UNESCO Courier* 29

Verdross A, *Die Verfassung der Völkerrechtsgemeinschaft* (Springer 1926)

Viellechner L, 'Constitutionalism as a Cipher: On the Convergence of Constitutionalist and Pluralist Approaches to the Globalization of Law' (2012) 4 Goettingen Journal of International Law 599

———, *Transnationalisierung des Rechts* (Velbrück 2013)

Vile MJC, *Constitutionalism and the Separation of Powers* (2nd edn, Liberty Fund 1967)

Villey M, *Le droit et les droits de l'homme* (Edition Quadrige 2014, Presses Universitaires de France 1983)

Walker LA, 'ICANN's Uniform Domain Name Dispute Resolution Policy' (2000) 15 Berkeley Technology Law Journal 289

Walker N, 'The Idea of Constitutional Pluralism' (2002) 65 The Modern Law Review 317

———, 'Sovereignty Frames and Sovereignty Claims' in Richard Rawlings, Peter Leyland and Alison Young (eds), *Sovereignty and the Law: Domestic, European and International Perspectives* (Oxford University Press 2013)

Walter C, 'Progress in International Organization: A Constitutionalist Reading' in Russell Miller and Rebecca Bratspies (eds), *Progress in International Law* (Brill Nijhoff 2008)

Weber M, 'Politics as a Vocation' in David S Owen and Tracy B Strong (eds), Rodney Livingstone (tr), *The Vocation Lectures* (Hackett 2004)
Weber R and Weber R, 'Social Contract for the Internet Community? Historical and Philosophical Theories as Basis for the Inclusion of Civil Society in Internet Governance?' (2009) 6 SCRIPT-ed 90
Weiler JHH, *The Constitution of Europe: 'Do the New Clothes Have An Emperor?' And Other Essays on European Integration* (Cambridge University Press 1999)
Weiler JHH and Trachtman JP, 'European Constitutionalism and Its Discontents' (1996) 17 Northwestern Journal of International Law & Business 354
Weiler JHH and Wind M (eds), *European Constitutionalism beyond the State* (Cambridge University Press 2003)
Weissbrodt D, *The Human Rights of Non-Citizens* (Oxford University Press 2008)
Wellman C, 'Solidarity, the Individual and Human Rights' (2000) 22 Human Rights Quarterly 639
Wendel M, *Permeabilität Im Europäischen Verfassungsrecht*, vol 4 (1st edn, Mohr Siebeck 2011)
Whelan DJ, *Indivisible Human Rights: A History* (University of Pennsylvania Press 2010)
White JG, 'Icann's Uniform Domain Name Dispute Resolution Policy in Action' (2001) 16 Berkeley Technology Law Journal 229
Wiener A and others, 'Global Constitutionalism: Human Rights, Democracy and the Rule of Law' (2012) 1 Global Constitutionalism 1
Wolf C, 'Impact of the CJEU's Right to Be Forgotten: Decision on Search Engines and Other Service Providers in Europe' (2014) 21 Maastricht Journal of European and Comparative Law 547
Wolfsfeld G, Segev E and Sheafer T, 'Social Media and the Arab Spring: Politics Comes First' (2013) 18 The International Journal of Press/Politics 115
Wright L, *The Looming Tower: Al-Qaeda and the Road to 9/11* (Vintage Books 2007)
Yilma KM, 'Digital Privacy and Virtues of Multilateral Digital Constitutionalism—Preliminary Thoughts' (2017) 25 International Journal of Law and Information Technology 115
———, 'Bill of Rights for the 21st Century: Some Lessons from the Internet Bill of Rights Movement' (2021) The International Journal of Human Rights 1
Zalnieriute M and Milan S, 'Internet Architecture and Human Rights: Beyond the Human Rights Gap' (2019) 11 Policy & Internet 6
Ziccardi G, *Resistance, Liberation Technology and Human Rights in the Digital Age* (Springer 2013)
Zingales N, 'Mettiamo La Dichiarazione Dei DIritti in Internet in Prospettiva' in Marco Bassini and Oreste Pollicino (eds), *Verso un Internet Bill of Rights* (Aracne 2015)
Zuboff S, *The Age of Surveillance Capitalism: The Fight for a Human Future at the New Frontier of Power* (PublicAffairs 2019)
Zumbansen P, 'Comparative, Global and Transnational Constitutionalism: The Emergence of a Transnational Legal-Pluralist Order' (2012) 1 Global Constitutionalism 16

Index